DEATH PENALTY
AND THE VICTIMS

DEATH PENALTY AND THE VICTIMS

Editor: Ivan Šimonović

Design and layout: dammsavage inc.

Cover image:
The cover features an adaptation of a photograph of a man
who is granted mercy by the victim's family, sparing him
from imminent execution. ©EPA/Arash Khamooshi

Pictures from *The Omega Suites* by Lucinda Devlin, Bochum 2000

Electronic version of this publication is available at:
www.ohchr.org/EN/NewYork/Pages/Resources.aspx

Sales no.: E.16.XIV.2
ISBN: 978-92-1-154217-2
eISBN: 978-92-1-058395-4

DEATH PENALTY
AND THE VICTIMS

New York, 2016

UNITED NATIONS
HUMAN RIGHTS
OFFICE OF THE HIGH COMMISSIONER

---

with support of

Schweizerische Eidgenossenschaft
Confédération suisse
Confederazione Svizzera
Confederaziun svizra

Federal Department of Foreign Affairs FDFA

CONTENTS

Preface – Ban Ki-moon, United Nations Secretary-General 7

Introduction – Who are the victims? Ivan Šimonović,
Assistant Secretary-General for Human Rights 9

CHAPTER 1 – MURDER VICTIMS' FAMILIES 21

1.1 Complexity of Victims' Families Position 22

• Marc Groenhuijsen, Michael O'Connell, *Arguments against
the death penalty as seen from a victimological perspective* 22

• Maiko Tagusari, *Does the death penalty serve victims?* 41

1.2 Victims' families' perspective 49

• Mickell Branham, *Listening to victims* 49

• Mireya García Ramírez, *The death penalty and the right to life* 59

1.3 Victims' Families and Closure 66

• Jody L. Madeira, *Escaping the closure trap* 66

• David Johnson, *Does capital punishment bring closure to the victims?* 75

CHAPTER 2 – THE CONVICTED AS VICTIMS? 85

2.1 Wrongful Convictions 86

• Carolyn Hoyle, *Victims of wrongful conviction in retentionist nations* 86

• Brandon Garrett, *In the shadow of the death penalty* 104

2.2 Discrimination and Mental Health Issues 111

• Ross Kleinstuber, *Discrimination and the death penalty* 111

• Sandra Babcock, *Capital punishment, mental illness, and intellectual
disability: The failure to protect individuals with mental disorders
facing execution* 128

2.3 Other cases of the death penalty against International Law 140

• Saul Lehrfreund and Roger Hood, *The inevitability of arbitrariness:
another aspect of victimisation in capital punishment laws* 140

• Salil Shetty, *Cases of the death penalty against
international law: Amnesty International's concerns* 154

• Jens Modvig, *Death penalty - torture or ill-treatment?* 164

CHAPTER 3 – THE 'HIDDEN' THIRD PARTIES AS VICTIMS 175

   3.1 Families of the Convicted 176

   • Susan F. Sharp, *Hidden victims: the families of those facing the death penalty* 176

   • Francis Ssuubi, *The impact of the Death Penalty on the children with a parent on death row or executed* 190

   • Susannah Sheffer, *Ending silence, ending shame* 206

   • Florence Seemungal, Lizzie Seal and Lynsey Black, *Impact of the imposition of the death penalty on families of the convicted in the Caribbean* 212

   • Sandra Joy, *Socio-Psychological Challenges of 'Death Row families'* 227

   3.2 Participants in death penalty proceedings and executions 249

   • Florence Seemungal, Lizzie Seal and Lynsey Black, *Death Penalty and Its Impact on the professionals involved in the execution process* 249

   • Robert Johnson, *Executioners at work: Collateral Consequences of executions for Officers Working on Death Row and in the Death House* 261

   • Ron McAndrew, *Painful then, painful now* 279

   • Susannah Sheffer, *Fighting for clients' lives: the impact of death penalty work on post-conviction capital defence attorneys* 283

   3.3 Society as the victim?

   • James R. Acker, *The death penalty: killing what we instead could be* 293

   • Walter C. Long, *The death penalty as a public health problem* 304

Afterword, Zeid Ra'ad Al Hussein, High Commissioner for Human Rights 327

Acknowledgements 333

"The right to life is the foundation of all human rights. The taking of life is irreversible, and goes against our fundamental belief in the dignity and worth of every human being. I call on all world leaders, legislators and justice officials to stop executions now. There is no place for the death penalty in the 21st century."

—*Ban Ki-moon*

PREFACE

Victims should always be at the centre of the debate on the death penalty. This book gives voice to a wide array of perspectives, including family members of crime victims, the wrongfully convicted and children of persons condemned to death, as well as judges, lawyers, prisoner staff and others whose job it is to oversee executions. Their testimonies make the brutality and trauma of the death penalty wrenchingly clear.

I have advocated forcefully and continuously for the abolition of the death penalty, and called on Member States to end executions. I have met with experts whose research shows that the death penalty does not deter crime. And I have talked with family members of crime victims who came to realize that the execution of the perpetrator did not help their families heal.

The right to life is the foundation of all human rights. The taking of life is irreversible, and goes against our fundamental belief in the dignity and worth of every human being. I call on all world leaders, legislators and justice officials to stop executions now. There is no place for the death penalty in the 21st century.

Ban Ki-moon
United Nations Secretary-General

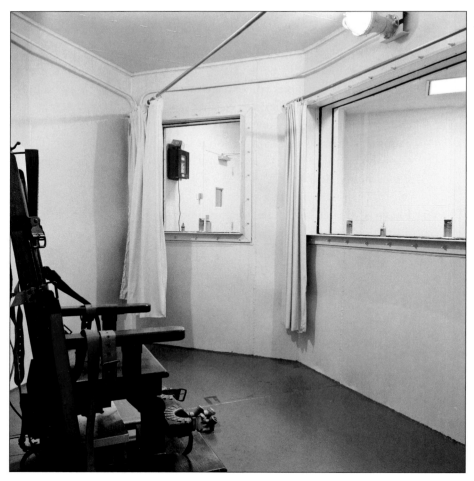

"Victim's perspectives, taken holistically, make a compelling case against the death penalty. When it comes to the death penalty, almost everyone loses."

— *Ivan Šimonović*

INTRODUCTION:
WHO ARE THE VICTIMS?

The front-page photograph is horrifying. A terrified blindfolded man is facing imminent execution. We do not see his eyes, but his face clearly reflects his fear and shock. A group of people are putting a rope around his neck…or are they?

No, they are not. In fact, they are removing the rope. By this symbolic gesture, family members of the victim are granting mercy to the convicted murderer and are halting the execution. He has not yet realized that his life has been spared at the last moment, and he is obviously in shock.

The right of victims or their families to spare the life of the crime perpetrators or influence their sentence is embedded in many cultures.[1] Therefore, it is quite obvious that when discussing the death penalty, the victims' perspective is highly relevant. From a human rights perspective, victims' views should always be at the centre. However, things become more challenging when we move to the next step and ask ourselves: who are the victims whose perspectives have to be taken into account?

There is wide consensus that the surviving family members of crime victims should also be considered as victims. They may not only suffer from crime emotionally and psychologically, but also socially and economically.[2] For practical purposes, it may be questioned how close to the victim a family member or another person needs to be in order, for example, to be entitled to compensation or to be heard by the court when the sentencing is discussed.

However, these questions are not our focus here. What we are most interested in is: what is the attitude of victims towards the death penalty,

---

1 For example, under sharia law, the principle of revenge—qisas—entitles families of the murder victim to take revenge but they also have the option to forgive the perpetrator, and receive diyat (blood money) as compensation.

2 This is also reflected in the United Nations Declaration of Basic Principles of Justice for Victims of Crime and Abuse of Power (General Assembly resolution 40/34, adopted on 29 November 1985, available herehttp://www.un.org/documents/ga/res/40/a40r034.htm).

and how does it affect them? Do victims demand the death penalty or not, and how does the imposition—or non-imposition—of the death penalty, as well as the actual execution of the crime perpetrator—or lack thereof—reflect on the victims? The fact that a large proportion of homicides are committed by family members adds pressure in making such a choice and may cause divisions among surviving family members. Does the death penalty offer closure, or does it prevent closure? How does it affect the healing process? How does it fit with retributive and restorative justice approaches? Is reconciliation with the perpetrator possible, and if so, under which conditions? Do contemporary justice systems prioritize victims' or some other interests? These and related issues are discussed in Chapter 1 of the book.

I am fully aware that expanding the concept of victims beyond the circle of persons close to the direct victims of crime may seem controversial to some. Chapter 2 raises important arguments towards considering at least some persons sentenced to death as victims themselves. In other words, not only crime victims, but also potential "victimizers" have human rights, and if they are violated, they can also be considered victims.[3]

The most obvious case are the wrongfully convicted, i.e. innocent persons who have been sentenced to capital punishment and sometimes executed for a crime they have not committed.[4] If they were given a prison sentence, after exculpatory evidence is obtained they can be released and sometimes compensated. However, if they were executed, the error cannot be undone and the harm is irreparable. They can be considered victims both of a wrongful conviction and of the irreparable character of the death penalty as a form of punishment.

There are also other grounds for the convicted to claim victim status. Extensive empirical research clearly indicates the unequal application and arbitrariness of the death penalty. Capital punishment

---

3   Clearly, this implies a wider approach, expanding the category of victims from the notion of
     victims of crime only to a notion encompassing also victims of human rights violations.

4   Wrongful convictions in death penalty cases are not that rare and can occur in all justice systems,
     including those which are sophisticated, well-resourced, and provide a series of protection layers.
     Recent research indicates that of all sentenced to death in the US from 1973 to 2004, more than
     4% were likely to be factually innocent. See Samuel R. Gross, Barbara O'Brien, Chen Hu and
     Edward H. Kennedy, Rate of False Convictions of Criminal Defendants Who are Sentenced
     to Death (2013), *Proceedings of the National Academy of Sciences, April 28, 2014, vol. 111 no. 20, pp.
     7230-7235.*

disproportionately affects members of minority and marginalized groups, be they racial, religious, national, or other minorities, migrant workers, economically poor segments of the population, or people with intellectual or mental disabilities. If someone is more likely to get the death penalty because of the colour of her skin, or because he cannot afford qualified legal representation, cannot these persons also be considered victims?

Furthermore, some of those convicted or executed are persons who for specific reasons are especially protected by international law from application of the death penalty against them. Human rights law prohibits the imposition of the death penalty against persons who were minors when committing the crime[5] and prohibits the execution of pregnant women, young mothers, and persons with mental or intellectual disabilities. For this reason, the application of the death penalty against them clearly makes them victims.

But human rights standards do not protect only certain categories of people from the death penalty. They also restrain its application to the "most severe crimes." Authoritative bodies restrict the interpretation of "the most severe crimes" exclusively to intentional murder.[6] The death penalty for any other crime, including apostasy, blasphemy, consensual adult same-sex contact, crimes against state security, terrorism, drug-related offences, or any other not including intentional murder, also makes persons convicted to death victims.[7]

And there is also an issue with the due process of law. In any criminal proceedings, respect of due process is essential to protect the rights of the accused[8]—in death penalty cases even more so, due to the irreparability of its effects. Violations of due process take various forms. The mandatory death penalty for certain categories of crimes

---

5   However, reportedly 15 states apply the death penalty for perpetrators under the age of 18.

6   Article 6(2) of the International Covenant on Civil and Political Rights (ICCPR) on right to life reduces the possibility of imposing the death penalty in retentionist states for the "most serious crimes" only. Human Rights Committee in its concluding observations on country situations consistently interprets the "most serious crimes" as intentional murder cases. It is also currently preparing a general comment on Article 6, expressing the same view (draft general comment No. 36, CCPR/C/GC/R.36). SR on extrajudicial, summary and arbitrary executions has taken the same position.

7   There are currently 33 states or territories that provide for the death penalty for drug offences unrelated to intentional killings. Amnesty International estimates that out of all executions they have recorded in 2015, 42% have been for drug-related offences alone.

8   Article 14 of ICCPR lists fair trial guarantees.

is one of them. It does not allow for individualization of guilt and adjustment of sanctions to the specifics of the case and the perpetrator, thus disregarding potential mitigating circumstances.[9] Persons who were not provided a competent defence attorney, who could not follow proceedings in a language they could understand (if necessary through interpreter), or were unable to submit relevant evidence in their favour may be all considered victims. The same applies to those who do not have the possibility to appeal the sentence or ask for clemency. Whoever has had their human rights violated during court proceedings leading to a death penalty sentence or execution can be considered a victim.

The irreparability of the execution requires more stringent safeguards than with regard to any other sentence. Therefore, many retentionist states introduce additional layers of safeguards in death-penalty cases. Additional opportunities to prepare defence, submit evidence, obtain expert opinion and appeal, or ask for clemency or pardon necessarily take time. The delay of the execution is a logical consequence. The more certain we want to be, the longer it takes.

Waiting on death row and experiencing cycles of hope and desperation in conditions of heightened security and often in solitary confinement triggers protracted psychological pressure and cyclical shocks, fear, and suffering—a "human pressure cooker", as convicts themselves have called it, that causes "death row syndrome". An increasing number of scholars consider the death penalty as a necessarily and unavoidably cruel, inhuman, or degrading punishment, and therefore against international human rights law.[10] An additional argument in the same direction comes from occurrences of botched executions, which occur "infrequently, but with regularity". There

---

9   If a death sentence is a result of a trial that has not respected article 14, in the opinion of the Human Rights Committee it represents violation of the right to life. See Human Rights Committee, General Comment No. 32 (2007), CCPR/C/GC/32, para. 59. See also Safeguards Guaranteeing Protection of Those Facing the Death Penalty, approved by Economic and Social Council resolution 1984/50 of 25 May 1984, available at:
http://www.ohchr.org/EN/ProfessionalInterest/Pages/DeathPenalty.aspx).

10   Special Rapporteur on Torture expressed the view that there is no categorical evidence that any method of execution in use today complies with the prohibition of torture and cruel, inhuman, and degrading treatment in every case. Furthermore, even if the formation of this customary norm is still under way, most conditions under which capital punishment is actually applied, renders the punishment tantamount to torture. Under less severe conditions, it still amounts to cruel, inhuman, and degrading treatment....*See* Interim Report of the Special Rapporteur on Torture and Other Cruel, Inhuman or Degrading Treatment or Punishment (A/67/279) 9 August 2012.

is no single method of execution that cannot—and sometimes did not—go wrong, causing torture and suffering of the executed.[11]

And finally, the death penalty also affects third parties. The book deals with these cases in Chapter 3. There is growing research evidence that the mental health of families, in particular children and primary care-takers of death-penalty convicts, is much more often and much strongly affected than the mental health of families of those convicted of any other sentence. Does that make them victims? I believe that it does.

Small children cannot understand why a parent has to die; teenagers cannot cope with it. Parents of convicted sons and daughters often blame themselves for what has happened to their child. Defence attorneys can also contribute to that blame in looking for mitigating circumstances of a crime in their clients' social and family settings. Social pressures on family members of crime perpetrators often force them to choose between distancing themselves from the convicted family member or face social isolation for "guilt by association". Both come at a heavy psychological toll. Some who were unfortunate enough to experience two losses of beloved ones—as a consequence of murder and as consequence of execution—point out that the horror of knowing that the date of the execution is unavoidably coming makes it even worse.[12] Others point out that it is particularly difficult to cope with grief that is socially unrecognized.

But the inner circles of the convicted are not the only ones dispro-portionately affected by the death penalty. Participants in the legal proceedings leading to the execution—be they prosecutors, defence lawyers or judges—feel the pressure related to their roles and actions and may sooner or later suffer psychological consequences. Questions such as: "have I done right?", "could I have done better?" or "who am I to decide on another person's life or death?" often continue to haunt them for the rest of their lives and sometimes completely break them down.

The psychological challenge for those who spend much time with

---

11   In a recent study, the rate of botched executions in the US was estimated to over 3%. See Austin Sarat, *Gruesome Spectacles: Botched executions and America's Death Penalty*, Stanford University Press, 2014.

12   See for example Celia McWee's statement at the press conference marking the launch of the No Silence, No Shame project in 2005.

the convicted before their executions, such as wardens, medical doctors or religious counsellors, can be even worse, especially if they also witness or participate in the execution. Even when they do not want to be there, they may feel that they owe it to the person whom they have dealt with and in whose tragic destiny they have played a role. Being there may be a form of empathy, as well as of self-punishment.

We cannot but conclude that the death penalty in one way or another produces a long line of victims. Of course, they are not victims of the same act, but they are still victims of the related crime and punishment cycle, which includes capital punishment.

The victims' family members are victims of a criminal act.

The convicted persons may be considered victims if the criminal response of the justice system violated their human rights, either through wrongful convictions, unequal and discriminatory implementation of justice, or violating international law by not respecting due process, imposing the death penalty for crimes that do not meet the "most serious crimes" threshold, or being among the categories of perpetrators that should be protected from the death penalty (minors, persons with mental or intellectual disabilities, pregnant women and young mothers).

Third parties are the "hidden victims" of the death penalty as a justice response to the committed crime. They do not become victims because of factual or legal mistakes; the death penalty as a form of punishment disproportionally affects the mental health and well-being of family members of the convicted person (especially children and primary caretakers), as well as third persons included in criminal proceedings or executions.

The above-mentioned victims are obviously different in many respects. Why address them together? Because only such a holistic approach enables us to reflect on the effects of the criminal justice response involving capital punishment and its overall consequences. In acknowledging the differences between various groups of victims, it becomes clear that their various perspectives have to be taken into account when deciding whether to keep the death penalty or not.

And now the final challenge. The death penalty is not only a criminal policy or a human rights matter but also an issue of fundamental political importance. It reflects the core relationship between the individual and the state, defining the character of the "social contract". The existence of the death penalty is consistent with the cult of the state, its sovereign power and its broad prerogatives, including the right to take away the lives of its citizens. The citizen's right to life is confronted with the state's right to kill. Which one is more powerful, and which one will prevail?

The prevalence of a state's entitlement to execute is both a cause and a consequence of the broader social and political setting, and it opens up many dilemmas. Is it not likely that a state with a license to kill when and where it considers necessary would also be more prone to send its citizens to wars that go beyond self-defence or to use excessive force or torture under the pretext of a threat to national security? Is a state entitled to kill a dangerous state? Can we go so far as to say that citizens of retentionist states may be in a way considered victims of the death penalty, because it is an important element of a broader social and political context that negatively reflects on their human rights?[13]

Balancing the weight of their crime and the punishment, perpetrators of some horrific crimes may deserve to die. But are we entitled to kill them? In my view, any killing is wrong: state-sanctioned killing is also wrong, and potentially very dangerous.[14] State-sponsored killings are always cold, calculated and premeditated. A barbaric reaction to a barbaric act is continuing the cycle of violence and contributes to the perpetuation of a culture of violence. The state's contempt for life negatively reflects on its citizens. If a state is allowed to kill, then it sends a message that killing is not always wrong—it is just a question of distribution of power and interests in the society: who, when and for what reason is entitled to kill. In my view, the focus of state reaction should not primarily be to provide for revenge but to break the cycle of violence by condemning barbarism and reforming

---

13 Moral objection to the death penalty led a number of companies to prevent prison authorities from purchasing their drugs for lethal injections. Hopefully, it may be a sign of taking the United Nations Guiding Principles on Business and Human Rights seriously and a form of social self-defence against the death penalty.

14 As Pope Francis put it at the 6th World Congress Against the Death Penalty: "'*Though shalt not kill*' has absolute value and applies to the innocent and the guilty."

the perpetrator. The perpetrator may deserve to die, but we should not kill him, because we are better than that. The fact that he is a murderer should not make us murderers as well. The punishment should be life-affirming and not life-ending.

So, what to replace the death penalty with? Although life without parole spares the life of the perpetrator and to a high degree serves the purpose of special prevention (he or she will never be able to kill again), and retribution (he or she will never walk free again), it kills hope. Not only the hope of the perpetrator, but the hope of society that everyone—if mentally sane—can be reformed and deserves a second chance to be fully integrated into society. In a way, life without parole represents a "death penalty in disguise" and can also be considered cruel.[15] By not reacting to the cruelty of a crime through another form of cruelty, society also acknowledges its imperfections and the potentially negative impact that social conditions—such as a life of victimization, hardship, deprivation, or discrimination—may have had on the individual, thus contributing to the commission of crime.

Victims' perspectives, taken holistically, make a compelling case against the death penalty. When it comes to the death penalty, almost everyone loses.

Victims' family members mostly end up frustrated. If they are against the death penalty and the death penalty is imposed on the perpetrator, the cycle of violence is continuing instead of being broken. If they want revenge, just a few can get it, and often, only after many years. Meanwhile, the expectation of the execution prevents closure. In most retentionist states, a number of those convicted do not get capital punishment or, after being sentenced, are never executed, thereby tormenting families who seek revenge. Family members ask themselves over and over again: Why is my child's loss of life less worthy of capital punishment then someone else's? Should I have insisted to witness or witnessed better? Would it have been different if the court did not feel that my wife does not support the death penalty? Even in cases when the court imposes the capital punishment, the actual execution may be far away, if it ever comes. In the United

---

15 Along the same line of reasoning, the European Court for Human Rights has qualified a sentence of life without a parole as a violation of European Convention on Human Rights.

States, for example, the current duration of stay on a death row prior to execution is 16 years. Just like convicted persons on death row and their families, victims seeking revenge are affected by cycles of hope and frustration if the execution is postponed. While the one side is hoping for life, the other side is hoping for death. For many victims seeking revenge, the retention of the possibility of the death penalty is like passing to a thirsty man a glass of salty water.

Convicted persons are too often victims of various forms of human rights violations. There is no justice system immune from factual mistakes, inequality of treatment, and discrimination. Rather to the contrary, many convicted suffer additional human rights violations, with the lack of respect for due process of law often being one of them. The more powerless and more marginalised they are, the more likely it is that they will be adversely affected. They are sometimes defended by legal representatives who are intoxicated, sleep during hearings, or forget about important deadlines for appeals. They are executed for being drug mules while their bosses stay out of reach of the justice system.

Third parties, be they the family of the convicted or participants in judicial proceedings or the execution, are disproportionately more affected by the death penalty than other forms of punishment. It is not a matter of perception: much research clearly demonstrates the disproportionate negative effects of the death penalty on their mental health and well-being.

A judge from the only retentionist country in South America told me that after he had sentenced a man to death for the first time, he could not wait to run to his chambers to throw up. As you will read in the book, a man who participated in executions has middle-of-the-night bedside visits of the executed who stare at him.

Who is then gaining by retaining the death penalty? Usually public opinion is in favour of the death penalty—the less informed about it, the more so. Therefore, for politicians, it is conveniently opportunistic not to go against the stream. It may be too harsh to say that it means "killing for votes," but it clearly reflects lack of leadership in moving the human rights agenda forward. It also suits the ones who want to be seen as tough on crime. It is much easier to be tough on crime by retaining the death penalty than by fixing the justice system and making it more efficient (which, unlike the death penalty, definitely deters crime).

On a more abstract level, the death penalty is a part of a certain world view that favours a strong state, limiting the human rights of its citizens. The death penalty is a power symbol, and executions historically demonstrated the right of the sovereign and the inviolability of government authority.[16] The death penalty is a close relative of other human rights violations, such as excessive use of force; torture and other forms of cruel, inhuman, or degrading treatment; and discrimination. Therefore, I strongly believe that the fight against the death penalty is one of the great civil rights struggles of our time. I am convinced that there is a strong correlation between states that execute and states that resort to excessive use of force, torture, and inhuman and degrading treatment. But it is not only states: individuals who support the death penalty are much more likely to be more lenient towards excessive use of force, torture, inhuman and degrading treatment, and some other human rights violations. But this may be the theme for another book.

I am fully aware that the approach to the perspectives of the victims on the death penalty as reflected in this book will provoke tough discussions. This may be a welcome challenge. Continued serious discussions on the death penalty from different perspectives may be exactly what we need. There is a strong and empirically proven positive correlation between the evidence-based discussion on the death penalty and moving away from it.

So let us discuss!

Ivan Šimonović
Assistant Secretary-General for Human Rights

---

16   See Michel Foucault, *Discipline and Punish: The Birth of the Prison*, New York, Vintage Books, 1979.

View from the Witness Room, The Omega Suites
© Lucinda Devlin

"When one realizes the diversity
of victims and the great pain each
victim suffers, one would doubt that
the death penalty serves victims."

— *Maiko Tagusari*

CHAPTER 1
MURDER VICTIMS' FAMILIES

1.1
COMPLEXITY OF VICTIMS' FAMILIES POSITION

1.2
VICTIMS' FAMILIES' PERSPECTIVE

1.3
VICTIMS' FAMILIES AND CLOSURE

1.1 Complexity of Victims' Families Position

ARGUMENTS AGAINST THE DEATH PENALTY AS SEEN FROM A VICTIMOLOGICAL PERSPECTIVE

Marc Groenhuijsen[1]and Michael O'Connell[2]

The death penalty is a controversial topic for debate. Whereas some feel it to be an integral part of their culture, dictating that the most severe crime shall be punished by the ultimate sanction, others are convinced that no matter the circumstances, a state can never be justified in deliberately taking the life of one of its citizens. For simplicity's sake, we limit this exposition to situations where murder has been committed. That is the archetypical act which could lend itself to the imposition of the death penalty. The basic principle underlying this reflex is the *ius talionis*, in present day language equated with "an eye for an eye." A few examples suffice to convince us that things are not that simple. Murder can be committed in various ways and forms, which can bring us both very distant to the idea of the death penalty and rather close to it.

Allow us to begin with the ultimate extreme represented by the Holocaust. Imagine Adolf Hitler did not commit suicide, but was caught by the allied forces. Would he have been tried in a court of law and be given the death penalty? We doubt it. It is much more likely that he would have been shot on sight. Today we refer to this practice as "summary execution."[3] Or, alternatively, consider the plot, in 1944, when several officers within the army conspired to kill Hitler. Obviously, had they succeeded many thousands of lives would have been saved. With hindsight, they would have been

---

1   Professor in criminal law and victimology at Tilburg University in The Netherlands. President of the World Society of Victimology.

2   Commissioner for Victims' Rights, South Australia. Secretary-General of the World Society of Victimology.

3   Lippman, M. 1989. "Government sponsored summary and arbitrary executions." *Florida International Law Journal*. p. 401 ff (see Westlaw). *See also*, Alston, Philip. 2006. *Report by the Special Rapporteur on civil and political rights, including the question of disappearances and summary executions*. E/CN.4/2006/53 (UN).

hailed as heroes. But back then: should or would they have been tried and on conviction sentenced to death?

Back to more mundane proportions. Thomas Lawrence (widely known as Lawrence of Arabia) wrote that when on a military expedition in World War I, he witnessed an enraged Hamed the Moor murder Salem, a member of another tribe. Lawrence, being aware of the Arab custom of the "blood feud," realised that to prevent a "tribal bloodbath," Hamed should be killed, and that is what he did. Should he, given his admission and his explanation, have been found guilty of murder and executed albeit that he prevented endless violence?

Susan Falls, an Australian woman, killed her husband but claimed she did so after suffering over two decades of violent abuse. Assuming this is not a case of justifiable self-defense, there are probably very few people in their right minds who would argue she would deserve the death penalty.

Undoubtedly, some of these cases are easier to address than others. Yet all challenge the fundamental principle "Thou shalt not kill," which calls for the question as to the limits of a punitive response to these kinds of incidents. The application of that principle in some circumstances might seem clear but in others vague. Mindful of such, evaluating the death penalty from a victimological perspective (as proposed by this chapter) without identification and analysis of arguments for and against is unwise. To do otherwise, one might easily stumble then fall victim to rhetoric rather than traverse truths intelligently.

Debate on the death penalty is tethered to many ethical and religious tenets. There are many throughout the world who support the death penalty while many others oppose it staunchly. Suppose since childhood you were taught that it is right to avenge harm done to you or your loved ones, even by taking the perpetrator's life. Conversely, assume you were socially conditioned that it is wrong to seek retribution, at least to the extent of killing the perpetrator. One standard allows for the death penalty, while the other does not. They cannot both be correct. What is to be decided between them? And, who is to decide which right is right?

Members of the World Society of Victimology (WSV) have encountered such struggle on several important occasions. For the past decade, the WSV's Executive Committee (WSV EC) has confronted the question on whether to support campaigns for the elimination of the death penalty. The question came to prominence most recently when other international criminal justice organisations invited the WSV to partner on an international campaign to abolish the death penalty. In 2010, the WSV EC tasked several members to prepare a discussion paper on the arguments for and against the death penalty from a victimological perspective. In 2013, these members presented a summary of their findings rather than a publishable paper.[4] The WSV EC's vote on the invitation carried by a majority (with no-one voting against) in favour of the WSV adopting a policy opposed to the death penalty and to joining the campaign.

The WSV EC held that killing people supposedly to gain justice for victims of crime violates the human right to life and does not affirm the sanctity of life. It too often results in injustice, so in a cruel irony it victimises. On top of that, it turns out to be an affront to many victims (including those bereaved by murder) and rather than alleviate pain and anguish, it can cause more pain and anguish. This is a principled view, backed up by empirical evidence and by experience from service providers. Nevertheless, it is uncertain to what extent the membership of the WSV supports this position. There has been no ballot among the membership. And neither has there been a poll among so-called victim advocates. Hence the implications of this principled position are unclear. The WSV just might lose some of its members. Or it could be embraced by new ones applauding this stance. Have individual members in those countries where the death penalty is practiced been looked upon as contemptuous of their governments? The answer is unclear to many.

So: how did the WSV EC reach its decision? What were the arguments put and views considered by the WSV EC? This chapter does not allow for a comprehensive exploration of the arguments for and against the death penalty. Instead, it points to the more widely known arguments from a focused victimological-perspective.

---

4   Garkawe, S. & O'Connell, M. 2013. *The death penalty: Report of the Standards and Norms Committee.* World Society of Victimology (unpublished).

First, however, some preliminary remarks on the question: what is victimology? In one of the earliest textbooks to contain a chapter on victimology, Stephen Schafer[5] wrote, "early criminologists have not shed any clear light upon the nature of [the importance of the victim's relationship to the crime, or the] interplay [so] they did not evolve the dynamic possibilities of victimology." In the 1940s two criminologists did, however, query the extent to which the victim contributed to or was culpably involved in his or her demise. Although others took up such matter, the plight of the victim of crime did not attain prominence until the mid-1960s, and victimology did not start to emerge as a "science parallel" to criminology until a decade later.[6]

The WSV defines victimology as "the scientific study of the extent, nature and causes of criminal victimisation, its consequences for the persons involved and the reactions thereto by society, in particular the police and the criminal justice system as well as voluntary workers and professional helpers."[7] Others define victimology more widely. Some incorporate victims of natural phenomena, such as natural disasters, and victims of human rights abuses, such as abuse of power that might not be criminal in the place the victimisation happened.[8] Some include auto- or self-victimisation, such as suicide. Common to all, however, is the concept that the victim should be at the centre of scientific endeavour.[9] Debate on the death penalty can be tackled from both the narrow penal scope of victimology as well as the more global human rights scope of victimology; and, arguably on rare occasions the concept of auto-victimisation might be helpful.

No matter the point of view, all are challenged as to what responses are appropriate in a civilised society to the problem of unlawful killing of human beings. All agree there should be a better solution

---

5   Schafer, S. 1976. *Introduction to criminology*. Reston, VA: Prentice Hall. p.143.

6   Mendelsohn, 1937, 1956; see also von Hentig 1940, 1941.

7   van Dijk, J. 1997. "Victimology." In J.J.M. van Dijk, R.G.H. van Kaam & J. Wemmers, eds., *Caring for Crime Victims: Selected Proceedings of the Ninth International Symposium on Victimology -- Amsterdam, August 25-29*. Monsey, NY: Criminal Justice Press. p. 4. *See also*, O'Connell, M. 2008. "Victimology: A study in social science in waiting." *International Review of Victimology* 15(2): pp. 91-104.

8   For methodological implications *see* Groenhuijsen, Marc. 2009. "Does victimology have a theoretical leg to stand on? Victimology as an academic discipline in its own right?" In Frans Willem Winkel, Paul Friday, Gerd Kirchhoff & Rianne Letschert, eds., *Victimization in a multi-disciplinary key: recent advances in victimology*. Nijmegen: Wolf Legal Publishers.

9   O'Connell, M. 2008. "Victimology: A study in social science in waiting." *International Review of Victimology* 15(2): pp. 91-104.

than state-sanctioned killing as punishment. The death penalty, given pointers outlined later in this chapter, for any crime is against the better judgment of victimology, albeit that some in the "victims' movement" take a contrary view. Against this background, it has to be noted that during the past decades, increasing attention has been paid to instances of mass victimization, including atrocities committed in international conflicts or by national governments suppressing (parts of) their own populations. Victimologists have become aware that these particular types of crimes or abuses of power can easily lead to new calls for inflicting the death penalty. Yet it is significant that the UN, when establishing the International Criminal Court in order to deal with these types of situations, deliberately did not include the death penalty in the Statute of Rome and its related governing legal documents. Instead, it found different ways to address legitimate victims' interest in the very worst instances of victimization.[10]

The WSV holds that all victims, as human beings, have a fundamental right to be treated with respect, which is a personal attribute, and to dignity, which is an interpersonal attitude.[11] In accordance with international law, including the United Nations Declaration of Basic Principles of Justice for Victims of Crime and Abuse of Power (1985), victims have other fundamental rights, including access to information and to participate in the making of key decisions that impact them and access to medical, psychological, financial, and practical assistance. The WSV acknowledges that when crime happens, there are other human beings involved who, although referred to as suspects, defendants, and offenders, are also human beings who have fundamental rights, including the right to a fair trial and the right not to be subject of cruel and unusual punishment. It is important to reflect for a moment on the meaning of the preceding observation. The WSV has consistently promoted the "emancipation" of the victim in society in general, and in criminal justice systems in particular. However, the WSV, while thus being supportive of legitimate victims' rights, has never adopted an anti-offender attitude. That is because the views of

10 Groenhuijsen, Marc & Pemberton, Antony. 2011. "Genocide, Crimes against Humanity and War Crimes. A Victimological Perspective on International Criminal Justice." In Rianne Letschert, Roelof Haveman, Anne-Marie de Brouwer & Antony Pemberton, eds., *Victimological Approaches to International Crimes: Africa, Intersentia*. Cambridge/Antwerp/Portland.
11 Dubber, M.D. 2002. *Victims in the war on crime: The use and abuse of victims' rights*. New York: New York University Press. p. 156.

the WSV stem from the conviction that reform of criminal justice is not a zero-sum-game.[12] Adding useful victims' rights does not necessarily restrict offenders' rights. In other words: victims' rights can never compromise the offender's right to a fair trial or to be immune from cruel or unusual punishment.

The state plays a central role in both upholding the rights of victims and the rights of victimisers. The criminal law (including underlying tenets such as the rule of law) helps the state discharge this role. The law is supposed to function as, among other things, a deterrent to potential victimisers. It also empowers the state to threaten, impose, and inflict punishment. Furthermore, as Dubber[13] explains in the context of proven criminal victimisation, victims have a right to measures to vindicate the violation of, for instance, the security of their person. Conversely, strange as it may look at first sight, the victimiser has a right to be held accountable, for instance, to be punished. Through criminal law and procedures, the state provides a process to settle clashes of rights but also protecting of rights. In too many nations, however, the law and procedures are neither a guarantee of victims' rights nor victimisers' rights. In such nations, criminal justice systems can amount to a "degradation ceremony"[14] or "shameful ritual."[15] The imposition of the death penalty is a prime example of that degradation and shame.

More than a decade ago three writers—Howard Zehr, Diane Robertson, and Rachel King[16] —laid out the arguments for and against the death penalty from the perspectives of those bereaved by murder in the United States. Zehr used words and portraits of victim-survivors of violent crime, including murder, to lay open the painful and ongoing

---

12   Groenhuijsen, Marc. 2009. "Does victimology have a theoretical leg to stand on? Victimology as an academic discipline in its own right?" In Frans Willem Winkel, Paul Friday, Gerd Kirchhoff & Rianne Letschert, eds., *Victimization in a multi-disciplinary key: recent advances in victimology*. Nijmegen: Wolf Legal Publishers. *See also*, Groenhuijsen, Marc. 2014. "The development of international policy in relation to victims of crime." *International Review of Victimology* 20(1):p. 31-48.

13   Dubber, M.D. 2002. *Victims in the war on crime: The use and abuse of victims' rights*. New York: New York University Press. p. 156.

14   Garkinkel, H. 1956. "Conditions of successful degradation ceremonies." *American Journal of Sociology*, p. 420.

15   Dubber, M.D. 2002. *Victims in the war on crime: The use and abuse of victims' rights*. New York: New York University Press. p. 157.

16   Zehr. H. 2001. *Transcending: Reflections of crime victims*. Intercourse, PA: Good Books. *See also*, Robertson, D. 2002. *Tears from heaven; voices from hell—The pros and cons of the death penalty as seen through the eyes of the victims of violent crime and death row inmates throughout America*. San Jose: Writers Club Press, and King, R. 2003. *Don't kill in our names: Families of murder victims speak out against the death penalty*. New Jersey: Rutgers University Press.

journey towards healing, not closure. He concluded that victim-survivors want a "restoration of equity," which entails denunciation of the wrongdoing, absolution of the victim, and attribution of responsibility. In his view, these elements of justice for victims are inherent in restorative justice but not in retributive justice. Robertson[17] asserted that to tackle violent crime there should be severe punishment, but she also proffered that there should be a "more effective solution" than "lock 'em away and throw away the key" or "fry 'em." King[18] surmises that the many voices of those who have faced the "ugliness of violence firsthand" then chosen to "forgive" rather than add to "the violence with execution" have set themselves free and "brought a small measure of peace to our troubled world." The arguments canvassed by these writers (who interviewed several dozen victims) serve as a backdrop for the structure of the rest of this chapter.

In the 1960s, the drafters of the International Covenant on Civil and Political Rights began moves for the abolition of the death penalty in international law.[19] Since then, international law has evolved so in general it forbids the death penalty and its use is preserved for the most heinous crimes[20]. International law also provides for the right to fair trial and due process. An unfair trial or failure to adhere to due process could result in the wrongful conviction of an innocent person. If such results in execution of the death penalty, the error is grave and, tragically, cannot be undone.[21] Despite the legal safeguards, the World Society of Victimology notes the observation of the United Nations High Commissioner for Human Rights, Zeid Ra'ad Al Hussein, that "*No judiciary, anywhere in the world, is so robust that it can guarantee that innocent life will not be taken, and there is an alarming body of evidence to indicate that even well-functioning legal systems have sentenced to death men and women who were subsequently proven innocent.*" There are too many reported cases of prosecutorial and judicial errors to militate against

---

17 Robertson, D. 2002. *Tears from heaven; voices from hell—The pros and cons of the death penalty as seen through the eyes of the victims of violent crime and death row inmates throughout America.* San Jose: Writers Club Press. p. xi.

18 King, R. 2003. *Don't kill in our names: Families of murder victims speak out against the death penalty.* New Jersey: Rutgers University Press. p. 5.

19 *See* the International Covenant on Civil and Political Rights, Article 6.

20 *See* United Nations General Assembly Resolutions 2007, 2008, 2010 and 2012 on a moratorium on the use of the death penalty.

21 Death Penalty Project. 2014. *The inevitability of error.* London: The Death Penalty Project. Available from http://www.deathpenaltyproject.org/wp-content/uploads/2014/07/The-inevitabili-ty-of-error-English.pdf. (accessed 25 August 2016).

the risk that innocent lives can be lost. From a theoretical point of view, it can even be maintained that in imposing the death penalty, there is an *inevitability* of caprice and mistake.[22]

Arguably, those who assert that deterrence justifies the death penalty bear the burden of proving that it is a deterrent. Some advocates for the death penalty point to its preventive nature. That the threat and, in some cases, actual execution, may deter one murder per year is put as adequate reason to warrant the continuation of the death penalty as a legitimate punishment for the most serious crimes. However, there is another side to this argument. Indeed, logic and empirical evidence seem to also point in the very opposite direction. Threatening potential perpetrators with capital punishment means that they have nothing more to lose. They can and will do anything they can in order to prevent being arrested, even if that means committing additional serious crime. In that sense, the ultimate sanction can be counterproductive—we will return to this issue later on. Further, the carrying out of the death penalty is seen as fitting retribution for murder—but is it? Retribution is, after all, only one of the objectives of punishment. Punishment as a remedy for crime should also be future-looking in terms of rehabilitation, public safety and, if practical, restoration. That the death penalty is deserved, even if in the eyes of the majority of people, is not enough to justify it. It must do some good or, asserts Hospers,[23] prevent *"some evil."*

The death penalty is also said to bring finality, some say, but does it? Certainly the executed murderer cannot kill again. The deliberate taking of a person's life rests however on a flawed premise that if the murderer is killed then there is a cancelling out of his or her crime. Some victims who believed the death penalty would give them satisfaction have discovered this is not the case. Over time, many victims feel uncomfortable that the offender is dead.[24] They are denied, for instance, the opportunity to get answers to key

---

22 Black, Charles. 1974. *Capital Punishment: the Inevitability of Caprice and Mistake.* New York: W.W. Norton & Company Inc.

23 Hospers, J. 1961. *Human conduct: An introduction to the problems of ethics.* New York: Harcourt, Brace & World. p. 451.

24 Zehr. H. 2001. *Transcending: Reflections of crime victims.* Intercourse, PA: Good Books. *See* also Robertson, D. 2002. *Tears from heaven; voices from hell—The pros and cons of the death penalty as seen through the eyes of the victims of violent crime and death row inmates throughout America.* San Jose: Writers Club Press, and King, R. 2003. *Don't kill in our names: Families of murder victims speak out against the death penalty.* New Jersey: Rutgers University Press.

questions they have about the deceased, the circumstances of his or her death, or an explanation.

Although throughout history, victimisers have been subjected to cruel and unusual punishments, it is evident that claims such punishment deters potential victimisers is inconclusive. Similarly, the assertion that the death penalty (either threatened or executed) reduces homicide or other violent crime is just not supported by reliable research. As indicated above, the exact opposite might very well be the case.

Criminological and psychological studies confirm that most victimisers do not act rationally, so few prospective murderers consider the threat of the death penalty.[25] As the aforementioned Susan Falls' case shows, some who kill act impulsively, perhaps in anger or under tremendous emotional stress. Others kill in moments of passion. Some do not have the mental competence to weigh the possibility of execution. Even if the threat of the death penalty is being considered, others do not expect to be apprehended.[26]

There is no strong evidence that would-be murderers fear the death penalty more than they fear the threat of life imprisonment, with or without a chance at parole. Studies over decades reveal that the death penalty is no greater deterrent than life imprisonment.[27] Notably in the USA, states that do not execute murderers generally have *lower* rates of murder than those states that execute murderers.[28] The same can be said internationally when comparisons are done between countries that do not employ the death penalty with those that do. For example, almost three decades after abolishing the death penalty, there was a 44% *decline* in murders in Canada.[29] In addition, there is some evidence that the death penalty instead of deterring would-be

---

25   Radelet, M.L. & Lacock, T.L. 2009. "Do executions lower homicide rates? The views of leading criminologists." *Journal of Criminal Law & Criminology* 99(2):489-508. *See* alsoRadelet, M. & Akers R. 1996. "Deterrence and the death penalty: the views of the experts." *Journal of Criminal Law & Criminology* 87(1):1-16.

26   Radelet, M.L. & Lacock, T.L. 2009. "Do executions lower homicide rates? The views of leading criminologists." *Journal of Criminal Law & Criminology* 99(2):489-508.

27   Radelet, M.L. & Lacock, T.L. 2009. "Do executions lower homicide rates? The views of leading criminologists." *Journal of Criminal Law & Criminology* 99(2):489-508. *See* also, Lamperti, J. *Does Capital Punishment Deter Murder? A brief look at the evidence.*

28   Robertson 2008, p. 11

29   Amnesty International (Australia). 2016. *Death penalty.* Amnesty International. Available from https://www.amnesty.org/en/what-we-do/death-penalty/. (accessed 25 August 2016).

murderers may even incite criminal violence.[30] We already mentioned the driving factor of avoiding detection. Here we can add that capital punishment can even effectively create a class of outlaws who have nothing more to lose and hence nothing more to fear. Similarly, as the father of a murder victim stated, "teaching people to respond to violence with violence will, again, only breed more violence." Hence, the World Society of Victimology holds that killing people who kill sends an incoherent message to the public at large. Further, rather than prevent victimisation, the death penalty might exacerbate the risk of becoming a victim.

Some claim valuing the murderer's life devalues the victim's life. This is misleading. In fact it is morally wrong to pitch debate on the death penalty as valuing the life of the murderer over that of his or her victim. All life should be valued. All human beings have a right to life. The value of life cannot be taught by killing a killer. Both victims and murderers are people who have a measure of dignity (a personal attribute), respect (an interpersonal attitude) and desert (an interpersonal claim).[31]

The death penalty process and the execution of the murderer, should it happen, is not about the personhood of the victim and his or her rights. Murder disturbs the balance of justice in a society. However, succumbing to violence by 'legalised murder' neither restores the balance for that society, nor does it restore the victim's family to the status that preceded the murder. Moreover as Coretta King pronounced, "Justice is never advanced in the taking of human life." Taking the life of a murderer is unjust punishment, especially in light of the fact that, for instance, the United States of America executes only a small percentage of those convicted of murder. These unfortunate perpetrators are typically not the worst offenders but merely the ones with the fewest resources to defend themselves.[32]

With respect to race, studies in the United States have repeatedly shown that a death sentence is far more likely where a white person

---

30   Rosenberg, P.H. 2002. "The Death Penalty Increases the Violent Crime Rate." In M. E Williams, ed., *Opposing Viewpoints: The Death Penalty*. San Diego: Greenhaven Press.

31   Dubber, M.D. 2002. *Victims in the war on crime: The use and abuse of victims' rights*. New York: New York University Press. p. 156.

32   *See, for example*, Death Penalty Information Centre. 2013. *The 2% death penalty: How a Minority of Counties Produce Most Death Cases at Enormous Costs to All*. USA: Death Penalty Information Centre. Available from http://www.deathpenaltyinfo.org/twopercent. (accessed 25 August 2016).

is murdered than where a black person is murdered. The death penalty is racially divisive because it appears to count white lives as more valuable than black lives.[33] Conscious and unconscious discrimination pervades criminal justice systems. This results in patterns of racial disparities that is a significant barrier to victims' families attaining truth, which is important for victims and the public.[34] Some offenders have mental (personality) disorders. It is unjust to punish them with the death penalty; instead, they should be detained then given psychological treatment. Such discrimination disturbs some victims' families.

International and domestic laws, as well as criminal justice systems, should be grounded on the rule of law and principles that demonstrate a respect for life, including the life of a murderer. Laws and systems should not formalise feudal notions such as "payback" or foster desire for revenge. To paraphrase Martin Luther King, behaviour can be regulated by law; such law might not change the heart, but it should regulate the heartless. The father of a person killed in the Oklahoma City bombing in the United States in 1995 said the death penalty "is simply vengeance; and it was vengeance that killed [my daughter] ....Vengeance is a strong and natural emotion. But it has no place in our justice system."[35] Therefore rather than support punishment by death, the World Society of Victimology notes that many victims' families denounce the use of the death penalty. Executing the murderer of their loved ones is quite often an affront to them and only causes more pain.

Interviews of victims' families confirms that the legal procedure leading up to the death penalty can be a traumatising experience, often requiring them to relive the pain and suffering of the death of their loved one for many years.[36] Judge Manck in sentencing a murderer observed that death penalty trials and appeals can last many years "with multiple painful rehashings of the crime." He said, "It is an outrageous

---

33 Black, Charles. 1974. *Capital Punishment: the Inevitability of Caprice and Mistake.* New York: W.W. Norton & Company Inc.

34 Zehr. H. 2001. *Transcending: Reflections of crime victims.* Intercourse, PA: Good Books: Intercourse.

35 Zehr. H. 2001. *Transcending: Reflections of crime victims.* Intercourse, PA: Good Books: Intercourse. p. 62.

36 King, R. 2003. *Don't kill in our names: Families of murder victims speak out against the death penalty.* New Jersey: Rutgers University Press. *See also* Zehr. H. 2001. *Transcending: Reflections of crime victims.* Intercourse, PA: Good Books.

way to penalize victims."[37] The prolonged litigation battle and resultant outrageousness can prevail across generations. As the parents of a murder victim who oppose the death penalty aptly told a conference audience, "We hope our two remaining children do not have to grow up with the lingering, painful reminder of what the defendant took from them, which years of appeals would undoubtedly bring."[38]

The litigation can also impact those convicted murderers awaiting a decision on whether they will be executed or not. The uncertainty, prison environment and conditions, and lack of rehabilitative programmes can produce severe mental health issues and physical suffering for those on death row. This is not desirable. Criminal punishment itself involves the deliberate restriction on an offender's liberty. This should occur "in order to produce good consequences (which … includes the prevention of bad ones)."[39] According to Miles Kemp, the parent of a murder victim, "People shouldn't go to prison so they can suffer."[40] The welfare of the prisoner, even a murderer, is an integral factor in every debate on structural victimisation in prisons.

It is evident that the pain and anguish of victims' families cannot be healed through the execution of those whose crime have thrust them into such a state of emotional and psychological torment. The promise of healing fosters false hope. Some members of victims' families are even outright offended that others would promote execution on their behalf, for the benefit of their healing or their revenge.[41] Ron Carlson, an abolitionist, continued his advocacy for elimination of the death penalty with greater intensity after his sister, Karla, was murdered. Contrary to respect and dignity for such moral courage, some victims' families who publicly advocate for abolition of the death penalty encounter ridicule and abuse from other murder victims' families. Such is a third source of victimisation after the offender and the criminal justice system: others bereaved

---

37   McCaffrey, R., "Inmate Given Life Without Parole In 2006 Slaying of Roxbury Guard," *Washington Post*, January 29 2008.

38   Flatow, N. 2015. *Why These Victims' Parents Don't Want The Death Penalty For The Boston Bomber.* Think Progress, April 17. Available from http://thinkprogress.org/justice/2015/04/17/3648237/victims-parents-dont-want-death-penalty-boston-bomber/ (accessed 25 August 2016).

39   Hospers, J. 1961. *Human conduct: An introduction to the problems of ethics.* New York: Harcourt, Brace & World. p. 454.

40   Zehr. H. 2001. *Transcending: Reflections of crime victims.* Intercourse, PA: Good Books. p. 89.

41   Murder Victims' Families for Reconciliation. 2016. Available from http://www.mvfr.org/. (accessed 25 August 2016).

by murder. This third source of victimisation can be disrespectful, demoralising, and dehumanising.

Kristin Froelich, whose brother was murdered in the United States of America, suffered depression and confronted other mental health issues.[42] As she grappled with "surviving" the various sources of victimisation, she discovered restorative justice, which prioritised offender accountability and victim healing. Restorative justice programmes have the potential to offer victims, including those bereaved by murder, a facilitated encounter with the offender. Rather than focus on the law breaking, the encounter focuses on the actual harm.[43] Instead of the state doing justice to the offender, restorative justice means the victims, the offender, and others affected (for example, the community) engage to the extent reasonably practical in determining a just outcome.

The World Society of Victimology has joined others in various discourses on restorative justice. Its position is that restorative justice is enshrined in a draft convention on victims' rights. Article 9, headed "Restorative justice," reads,

(1) State Parties shall endeavour, where appropriate, to establish or enhance systems of restorative justice, that seek to represent victims' interests as a priority. State shall emphasize the need for acceptance by the offender of his or her responsibility for the offence and the acknowledgement of the adverse consequences of the offence for the victim in the form of a sincere apology.

(2) State Parties shall ensure that victims shall have the opportunity to choose or to not choose restorative justice forums under domestic laws, and if they do decide to choose such forums, these mechanisms must accord with victims' dignity, compassion and similar rights and services to those described in [the draft] Convention.

---

42 Froehlich, K, "Honest debate needed on the death penalty," *The Middletown Press*, 2010. Available from http://www.middletownpress.com/article/MI/20100430/NEWS/304309988. (accessed 1 September 2016). See also, Froehlich, K. *Senate Bill 40 to Repeal Delaware's Death Penalty.* Testimony, 25 March 2015. Available from https://www.aclu-de.org/wp-content/uploads/2015/04/Kristin-Froehlich-.pdf. (accessed 1 September 2016).

43 *See, for example*, Death Penalty Focus. 2016. *Death Penalty Can Prolong Suffering for Victims' Families.* San Diego: Death Penalty Focus. Available from www.deathpenalty.org. (accessed 25 August 2016).

Frankly speaking, this set of conditions for successful restorative justice forums will in actual practice exclude many, if not a large majority of, murder cases. And even if some form of mediation is endeavoured, it will usually take place in a prison setting, long after the crime was committed. But even so, when careful consideration of the bereaved family is observed, it can be a useful mechanism to amend the traditional approach taken by the criminal justice system.

There are said to be other viable alternatives, such as life without parole.[44] Although the World Society of Victimology Executive Committee did not discuss that option, Garkawe and O'Connell pointed out that proponents for life without parole argue it delivers punishment without the re-opening of emotional and psychological hurt endured while a murderer seeks to save him or herself from the death penalty by making appeal after appeal, after appeal.[45]

In truth any remedy in case of murder is unsatisfactory. The thing victims' families want (which would give real satisfaction) is to bring back to life the deceased, their loved one.[46] Capital punishment cannot resurrect the dead. On the contrary, it causes family members more pain than other sentences.[47] The death penalty rests on the tragic illusion that taking the murderer's life defends the victim's life and life in general.[48]

Death penalty cases in some United States' states can last for two decades. Making a prisoner wait for years to be executed is cruel for him or her as well as his or her family who are often overlooked. Family and friends of the murderer are indirectly punished for the crime of their loved ones. Sharp highlights the challenges faced by

---

44   *See, for example*, Maryland Commission on Capital Punishment. 2008. Available from http://www.mdcase.org/node/114. (accessed 25 August 2016).

45   Garkawe, S. & O'Connell, M. 2013. *The death penalty: Report of the Standards and Norms Committee.* World Society of Victimology (unpublished).

46   *See, for example*, Brucker in Zehr. H. 2001. *Transcending: Reflections of crime victims.* Intercourse, PA: Good Books. p. 77.

47   Dieter, R.C. 1993. *Sentencing for Life: Americans Embrace Alternatives to the Death Penalty.* Death Penalty Information Center. Available from http://www.deathpenaltyinfo.org/sentencing-life-americans-embrace-alternatives-death-penalty. (accessed 25 August 2016).

48   Flatow, N. 2015. *Why These Victims' Parents Don't Want The Death Penalty For The Boston Bomber.* Think Progress, April 17. Available from http://thinkprogress.org/justice/2015/04/17/3648237/victims-parents-dont-want-death-penalty-boston-bomber/. (accessed 25 August 2016).

these people.[49] She points to the neglect, stigmatisation, shaming, and social isolation. She contrasts that assistance provided to victims' families with that provided to families of those accused of murder, and reveals a lack of assistance for the latter. Sharp also draws on some similarity about the effects of the appeal process on murderers' families[50] and victims' families. Further, murderers' families have to deal with people who clamour for the execution of the person they love as well as knowing some victims' families and members of the public at large watch the execution killing of their loved one at the appointed time.

Likewise, experience in the United States of America shows it is an illusion to think that inflicting the death penalty is cheaper for society than alternative punishments. The death penalty is an expensive legal remedy.[51]

Appeals processes allowing death penalty cases to traverse back and forth between state and federal courts are costly. Such cost can be greater than supporting a death row prisoner for the rest of his or her life in custody.[52] For example, Brambilla reported that the cost of sentencing 408 people to death in a US state was an estimated $816 million higher than the cost of life without parole.[53] Should the death penalty be repealed and alternative punishments employed, the expected savings could be reallocated to victim assistance such as grief counselling for those bereaved by murder. As Victoria Coward whose son was murdered in 2007 aptly said,

> If we are serious about helping surviving victims — all of
> us — we need to see the bigger picture. The bigger picture
> is that the death penalty is given in fewer than 1% of cases,
> yet it sucks up millions and millions of dollars that could
> be put toward crime prevention or victims' services. What
> I wouldn't give for a tiny slice of those millions to give my

---

49 Sharp, S. 2005. *Hidden Victims: The Effects of the Death Penalty on Families of the Accused*. New Brunswick, NJ: Rutgers University Press.

50 Ibid.

51 Lamperti, J. *Does Capital Punishment Deter Murder? A brief look at the evidence*. See also, Costanzo, M. & White, L. 1994. "An overview of the death penalty and capital trials: history, current status, legal procedures, and cost." *Journal of Social Issues* 50(2):1–18.

52 Rankin, B., "Georgia executions rise, while death sentences plummet," *Atlanta Journal-Constitution*, June 18, 2016.

53 Brambila, N, "Executing justice: Pennsylvania's death penalty system costs $816 million," *The Reading Eagle*, June 17, 2016.

grieving daughters some professional help to process the death of their brother.[54]

The World Society of Victimology in addition acknowledges that imprisoning a murderer for life without parole, so he or she will effectively die in prison, can also be cruel. Like the death penalty, it deprives the murderer the opportunity:

- To take responsibility for having killed somebody
- To walk in the shoes of each of his or her victim's family
- To know what goes through minds of each member of the victim's family
- To acknowledge that he or she destroyed a family
- To show true feelings of remorse and demonstrate he or she knows the harm he or she has done
- To live with the repercussions of his or her crime

Hence, we caution against taking a sentence of life without parole lightly. Recently, no-one less than Pope Francis spoke out in no uncertain words against this sanction. He recounted that a short time ago the life sentence was taken out of the Vatican's Criminal Code. And he added: "A life sentence is just a death penalty in disguise."[55] In the same vain, the European Court for Human Rights has condemned a sentence of life without parole as a violation of the European Convention on Human Rights (1950). In a series of landmark decisions, the Court held that every prisoner is entitled to have his sentence at some point in time reviewed by a competent court, with a realistic prospect of an eventual release from prison.

These above-mentioned pointers match many victims' needs and expectations.[56] A few victim-survivors even suggest that the prosecution's focus on the death penalty or other harsh penalty fosters a

---

54   Equal Justice USA. 2016. *A Failure for Victims' Families: In their own words: Stories of a broken system.* Equal Justice USA. Available from http://ejusa.org/learn/victims-voices/(accessed 25 August 2016).

55   WSV et.al. 2014, NO 2014 version only 2015, p.22

56   *See, for example,* Mokricky, Silvosky, and Welch in Zehr. H. 2001. *Transcending: Reflections of crime victims.* Intercourse, PA: Good Books.

desire to avenge and undoes a desire for mercy.[57] Some victims worry that those punished for murder might be innocent. If so, an executed death penalty cannot be repaired. It is irrevocable. The pursuit of violent punishment becomes an element of the circle of violence associated with the death penalty.[58]

Murder victims' families are not alone in challenging the death penalty. It seems that many people in most countries do not condone the death penalty. Consistent with such sentiment, most United Nations member-states have abolished the death penalty and many have abolished it in in practice but not necessarily in domestic law. Several states continue to use this ultimate sanction frequently: China, Iran, Iraq, Saudi Arabia, and the United States. Thus, in 2012 the United Nations General Assembly reiterated its requests "upon all States to establish a moratorium on executions with a view to abolishing the death penalty."[59] It also called upon "States that have abolished the death penalty not to reintroduce it, and encourages them to share their experience in this regard."[60]

In addition, there is concern that in some countries that there are racial and cultural divisions over the appropriateness of the death penalty. One United States' study for instance showed that in a southern state, about two thirds of African Americans oppose the death penalty, whereas about two thirds of white people support it.[61] A much earlier national study showed that about 44% of Americans support life without parole, while 41% supported the death penalty and about 15% were undecided.[62] Across the globe, public opinion is clearly a complex and constantly evolving assortment of views. Variations in survey results can be attributed to the methodology

57   Associated Press, "Slain Colorado prison guard's dad fights to testify," *The Denver Post*, February 12, 2014. Available from http://www.denverpost.com/2014/02/12/slain-colo-prison-guards-dad-fights-to-testify/ (accessed 25 August 2016).

58   Vaughn, C. 2006. *Living with the death penalty: The Aftermath of Killing and Execution in the United States*. USA: Xlibris Corporation.

59   cfr. United Nations General Assembly 2007, 2008, 2010.

60   United Nations General Assembly. 2012. *Moratorium on the use of the death penalty*. Resolution A/RES/67/176. Available from http://www.un.org/en/ga/search/view_doc.asp?symbol=A/RES/67/176. (accessed 25 August 2016).

61   Cope, C., "Most South Carolinian blacks say Dylann Roof should get life without parole," *The Herald*, June 12, 2016.

62   Dieter, R.C. 1993. *Sentencing for Life: Americans Embrace Alternatives to the Death Penalty*. Death Penalty Information Center. Available from http://www.deathpenaltyinfo.org/sentencing-life-americans-embrace-alternatives-death-penalty. (accessed 25 August 2016).

and the instrument as well as the prevailing circumstances when conducted. Some surveys reveal shortcomings in people's knowledge on the death penalty as punishment, as administered, and so on. Over-time comparisons of results that suggest views shifting towards less favour for the death penalty within a particular country also show the influence of political and religious leadership. The United Nations report Move Away from the Death Penalty: Lessons in South-East Asia, for example, cites shifting attitudes towards the elimination of the death penalty in the Philippines and Mongolia to illustrate the importance of political leadership.[63] The report also points to the critical influence that reform in these countries had in the Asia region.

A delegation for the World Society of Victimology witnessed necessary religious leadership when in 2014 Pope Francis repealed the death penalty as punishment under canon law.[64] In doing so, he went a major step further than his predecessors (St John Paul II condemned the death penalty in Encyclical Letter *Evangelium Vitae*, n. 56, as does the *Catechism of the Catholic Church*, n. 2267). No matter how serious the crime, he told his audience, to kill a person is an offence to the "inviolability of life." He has repeated his condemnation of the death penalty many times, including in 2016 telling the 6th World Congress against the Death Penalty that "it does not render justice to victims, but instead fosters vengeance. The commandment 'Thou shalt not kill' has absolute value and applies to the innocent and the guilty." He has also cast the death penalty as contrary to "the dignity of the human person" and urged all to seek instead God's "merciful justice". His exhortation is not unique as several of the world's great religions share convictions that prescribe a duty not to kill. As a result, many people oppose to the death penalty because it clashes with their beliefs. Mindful of that commonality in beliefs, the World Society of Victimology holds that "All people have an obligation to preserve the body and life of other people."[65]

---

63   OHCHR. 2014. *Move away from the death penalty: Lessons learned in south-east Asia*. Canberra: Office of the High Commissioner for Human Rights, Regional Office for South-east Asia. Online.

64   WSV et al. 2015. *For a real human justice*. Pope Francis & Association Internationale de Droit Pénal, Société Internationale de Criminologie, Société Internationale de la Défense Sociale, International Penal and Penitentiary Foundation, World Society of Victimology, Asociación latinoamericana de Dcho. Penal y criminología.

65   As Psalm 82:4.

We now come to our conclusions. The death penalty has always been a very controversial issue. Like societies across the globe, the World Society of Victimology has struggled with the question of the death penalty since it was founded in 1979. The issue, however, came to prominence in the past decade. The WSV's executive committee has concluded that the death penalty is imperfect, cruel, and inhumane punishment that is arbitrarily, even unfairly, inflicted on too often the vulnerable.

The death penalty violates human rights. It is a cruel and arguably barbaric punishment against a human being. To some of the world it is one of the worst acts of human nature. It defies doctrines and theologies of the world's great religions.

A death penalty might perhaps have been slightly justifiable if it were able to prevent future crimes on a massive scale, but this has not been the case. It is more likely that the exact opposite is the case. Homicide crime statistics from those countries that invoke the death penalty do not prove at all that exacting justice by death has the effect of deterrence or decreases the incidence of crime. This article has also debunked the notion that executing people rather than imprisoning them is cheaper. It is not.

As this article has revealed, there are many reasons for victimologists and victims themselves to oppose the death penalty. It is evident ultimately that the question on whether to employ the death penalty is a moral one. Mindful of this, we conclude there is no excuse in indulging in it. Importantly, such support for the abolition of the death penalty does not imply tolerance for murder or indeed any violent crime. We oppose the death penalty not just for what it does to those guilty of heinous crimes, but for what it does and does not do for those impacted by such crimes as well as for what it does to all across the societies of the world we share.

DOES THE DEATH PENALTY SERVE VICTIMS?

Maiko Tagusari[1]

Just like in many other countries, in Japan it is quite often said and widely believed, that the death penalty should be retained *for victims*— more precisely, surviving family of murder victims. For example, in November 2014, Japan's Cabinet Office conducted an opinion survey on the legal system including the death penalty,[2] and its showed that more than half (53.4%) of respondents who approved of retention of the death penalty said that if the penalty were abolished, victims' relatives would be left without a feeling of closure.

A prerequisite for such an assertion is that the death penalty serves victims in some way or other. But when one realizes the diversity of victims and the great pain each victim suffers, one would doubt that the death penalty serves victims.

When people talk about the death penalty and victims, victims are often portrayed in a stereotypical way: the bereaved have deep hatred toward offenders and want death for them. In reality, however, there are various victims. Each of them is unique. Describing victims in a uniform manner is wrong, just as treating all capital offenders "as members of a faceless, undifferentiated mass to be subjected to the blind infliction of the penalty of death"[3] is wrong.

Infrequent Imposition of the Death Penalty

Many people believe murderers deserve death, but offenders are not given the penalty of death in vast majority of murder cases. The

---

1   Secretary-General, Center for Prisoners' Rights, Japan. The author is grateful to Professor David. T. Johnson for his helpful comments.
2   As an overall analysis of the survey, see Mai Sato & Paul Bacon, *The Public Opinion Myth: Why Japan retains the death penalty,* available from: http://www.deathpenaltyproject.org/wp-content/uploads/2015/08/The-Public-Opinion-Myth1.pdf#search='death+penalty+focus+myth+public+opinion+Japan. (accessed 24 August 2016).
3   *Woodson v. North Carolina*, 428 U.S. 280.

Penal Code of Japan provides that "a person who kills another shall be punished by the death penalty or imprisonment with work for life or for a definite term of not less than five years."[4] Thus, in case of murder conviction, sentencers in Japan have wide range of options other than death. Every year, just a handful of defendants accused of murder are sentenced to death—ranging from two to 14 between 2005 and 2014—while hundreds of others receive sentences of imprisonment, whether life or definite terms ranging from five to 30 years.[5] Similarly in the United States, only 2% of murder and non-negligent manslaughter[6] convictions result in a death sentence.[7]

Such infrequent imposition of the death penalty moves some survivors to seek the death penalty. Fumiko Isogai collected as many as 330,000 signatures on a petition calling for death for all three offenders who had brutally murdered her daughter for pecuniary gain. In response to the campaign, public prosecutors demanded that all of the three should be sentenced to death, and the district court sentenced two of them to death. It is quite rare that two or more defendants get the sentence of death when the number of the murder victim was one. However, Isogai, who had struggled so hard to send the all offenders to gallows, was disappointed with the outcome. She was further disturbed when one of the two death-sentenced defendants appealed against the sentence and consequently got it reduced at the High Court[8] to life imprisonment (the other abandoned his right of appeal and accepted the death).[9]

For a person whose loved one was brutally killed, the act of murder is obviously a crime of the utmost gravity. However, when the

---

4   Penal Code of Japan, art.199.

5   Annual Report of Judicial Statistics.

6   In Japan, a crime classified as 'non-negligent manslaughter', i.e., "intentionally and without legal justification causing the death of another when acting under extreme provocation", constitutes 'murder'.

7   Sean Rosenmerkel, Matthew Durose and Donald Farole, Jr., Ph.D, U.S. Department of Justice. 2009 (rev. 2010). "Felony Sentences in State Courts, 2006-Statistical Tables." *Bureau of Justice Statistics*. Available from http://www.bjs.gov/content/pub/pdf/fssc06st.pdf. (accessed 13 May 2016).

8   The sentence of life imprisonment for the defendant, Yoshitomo Hori, was upheld by the Supreme Court. However, three years after finalization of the sentence, Hori was accused of separate murders and sentenced to death. He appealed to the High Court and the case is still pending.

9   In Japan, despite repeated recommendations by UN Human Rights Committee and Committee against Torture, appeal against the sentence of death is not mandatory.

criminal is sentenced to lesser punishment than death, it implies that the act does not deserve the ultimate punishment.[10] This is simply unacceptable for many family members. If we are to respect the feelings of each of such people, we have to bring back an old system under which the death penalty was almost automatically meted out to every defendant convicted of murder.

For many years, quite a few retentionist states have reduced the number of death-eligible crimes, typically by breaking down murder into several subcategories and making only certain types of murder punishable by death. In order to avoid convicting the innocent and to impose the ultimate punishment only on "those who deserve it," to take a cautious approach to the sentence of death is inevitable. In fact, retentionists often rely on this point when they try to justify retention of the death penalty.[11] To expand the scope of the penalty is not only unjust but also unrealistic in Japan or the United States.

In sum, despite the public's belief that the death penalty serves victims' families as alleviator of their grief, the penalty is rarely applied and therefore does not play any role for overwhelming majority of victims. Rather, there are bereaved members who are frustrated by inactive use of the existing penalty.

---

10   With regard to this point, Scott Turow wrote that "once we make the well-being of victims our central concern and assume that execution will bring them the greatest solace, we have no principled way to grant one family this relief and deny it to another. From each victim's perspective, his loss, her anger, and the comfort each victim may draw from seeing the killer die are the same whether her loved one perished at the hands of the Beltway Sniper or died in an impulsive shooting in the course of a liquor-store holdup. The victims-first approach allows us no meaningful basis to distinguish among murders." Scott Turow, *Ultimate Punishment: A lawyer's Reflections on Dealing with the Death Penalty* (2003), at 54.

11   For example, the government of Japan insists that "Judgment on selecting the death penalty is made extremely strictly and carefully, based on the criteria shown in the judgment of the Supreme Court on July 8, 1983. As a result, the death penalty is imposed only on a person who has committed a heinous crime carrying great criminal responsibility that involves an act of killing victims intentionally." (Comments by the Government of Japan on the Concluding Observations of the Human Rights Committee [CCPRIC/JPN/CO/6], 27 July 2015). On top of such argument, taking into account recent judicial adjudications which try to limit sentencing discretion in lay judge trial, it is very unlikely that the scope of the death penalty will be drastically expanded in Japan. From 2013 to 2014, three death sentences rendered by lay judge trial courts were reversed by the Tokyo High Court and replaced with life imprisonment. All the three High Court decisions were upheld by the Supreme Court in February 2015.

Victims Who are Family Members of both Victims and Offenders

We should also note that there are many people who are undoubtedly victims but often omitted from a category of victims.

Murders often take place among family. Statistics from Japan's White Paper on Crime show that in about a half of murder cases, offenders are family members of victims. In 2014, 48.3% of murder victims were relatives of their assailants and the rate was as high as 53.5% in 2013.[12] I admit these rates are characteristically high when compared to other countries, such as the United States and Canada, but even in these two countries, homicides committed by family member amount to a considerable number.[13] In such cases, the surviving members are simply not recognized as victims.

In 2011, Japan's Ministry of Justice issued a report on serious offences among family, and the report says that the rate of family members who show leniency toward offenders overwhelms that of those who demand severe punishment. As for murder cases, 66.6% said they would forgive offenders, while those who demanded severe punishment for offenders were 25%.[14] Although family members' attitudes vary depending on relationships between victims and offenders or impact of crimes on their lives, it is true that there are a considerable number of people who are relatives of both victims and offenders and therefore do not necessarily want the death penalty for offenders.

Even an offender who committed murder among his or her family could face a sentence of death.[15] Among them is a case of Kiyotaka

---

12 White Paper on Crime, 2015.

13 According to *Homicide Trends in the United States, 1980-2008*, among homicides for which the victim/offender relationships were known, 22% of victims were killed by a spouse or other family member, available from http://www.bjs.gov/content/pub/pdf/htus8008.pdf. (accessed 12 May 2016). As for Canada, 34.9% of all solved homicides committed between 2000 and 2009 were committed by family members. See *Family Violence in Canada: A Statistical Profile*, available from http://www.statcan.gc.ca/pub/85-224-x/85-224-x2010000-eng.htm. (accessed 12 May 2016).

14 *A Report of Research Section of Research and Training Institute*, vol. 45, March 2011. The research team analyzed 72 family murder cases that were tried at Tokyo District Court during the periods 1975-1978, 1989-1992, and 2005-2008.

15 Especially as for children whose parents were sentenced to death for murdering another parents, the Quaker United Nations Office has issued excellent reports, including *Lightening the Load of the Parental Death Sentence on Children*, available from http://www.quno.org/resource/2013/6/lightening-load-parental-death-sentence-children. (accessed 24 August 2016).

Oyama, father of Hiroto Oyama. Kiyotaka killed his wife—Hiroto's mother—as well as his foster father. Hiroto says he was discriminated against as a son of a criminal while he had to endure suffering as a victim's family member. His hatred toward Kiyotaka was so strong that he felt like killing the father himself. However, after Kiyotaka was sentenced to death, Hiroto visited him at the detention centre, and through meetings and correspondence, changed his mind. In the High Court hearing, he took the stand for his father and testified that he wanted him to continue to live and atone for his sins. Nevertheless, the death sentence was upheld by the High Court and then by the Supreme Court. Currently, Kiyotaka awaits his execution at the detention centre. Hiroto stresses that he wants the public to know that there are family members of victims who do not want death for assailants.[16]

Thus, we must also bear in mind that when someone argues retention of the death penalty for the sake of victims, victims who are also family of offenders are ignored.[17] Although they seldom speak out about their painful experiences, they are victims, who were seriously hurt by offences but are given little attention to their inexpressible sufferings.

Changes in Victims' Feelings

As seen in Hiroto's case, victims' feelings are changeable. And it is true that, even among victims who are not relatives of offenders, there are people who experience changes in their minds and do not want their offenders to be hanged.

In 1983, Masaharu Harada's younger brother Akio was killed in a murder for life-insurance money disguised as traffic accident. The culprits were three men including Akio's employer, Toshihiko Hasegawa, who had committed another two murders. Harada testified against Hasegawa, demanding ultimate punishment for him.[18] Hasegawa, together with one of his accomplices, was sentenced to death.

---

16 Daisuke Sato, "Son wants killer dad to atone, not hang," *The Japan Times*, February 21, 2013.

17 Furthermore, it could be said that they are often legally discriminated against. As an example in Japan, Act on Payment of Crime Victim Benefit provides that family members might not benefit when a crime was committed among the family members (Article 6, item 1).

18 Japan uses a unitary trial system, and victims and their family members are not prohibited from expressing their opinions about possible sentences for defendants.

Prior to his conviction, Hasegawa had started to write letters to Harada, expressing his apologies and remorse, but Harada simply trashed most of them without reading. But almost 10 years after the murder, Harada decided to visit Hasegawa at the detention centre and ask him why he had chosen his brother as a victim of his crime. It was the first time that Harada directly heard the words of apologies from Hasegawa. Harada says he felt the apologies were sincere and the meeting with Hasegawa brought some sort of healing to him. One day, Harada blamed Hasegawa for being responsible for death of his son, who had committed suicide after the father's arrest. For Harada, Hasegawa was the only one at whom he could express anger and rage.[19]

However, several months after Hasegawa's death sentence had been upheld by the Supreme Court, the authorities prohibited Harada from visiting Hasegawa. With the time of execution approaching, Harada finally submitted a petition to then Justice Minister Masahiko Koumura, requesting that Hasegawa not be executed. The minister did not give any attention to the petition. On 27 December, 2001, Hasegawa was hanged.

Harada unequivocally says he never forgave Hasegawa. Like many other victims, his daily life was completely damaged by the crime. He says that the crime "pushed him over a cliff," but the execution of Hasegawa did not rescue him from the bottom of the cliff. His feelings were not eased by the hanging. He describes the death penalty as a system which pushes offenders over the cliff alike, without any meaningful aid for victims.[20] Several years later, Harada established an organization named Ocean,[21] which aims to promote victim-offender meetings and casts questions on the system of the death penalty that eliminates possibilities of meetings between surviving family and offenders.

---

19 Exactly as Mickell Branham and Richard Burr wrote, "victims have questions only the offender can answer. Victims want to be heard not only by the community at large, but specifically by the offender and his or her representatives. The offender is the one the victims want to tell about their pain." Branham, Mickell and Burr, Richard. 2008. "Understanding Defense-Initiated Victim Outreach and Why It Is Essential in Defending a Capital Client." *Hofstra Law Review* 36(3), Article 14, available from http://scholarlycommons.law.hofstra.edu/hlr/vol36/iss3/14. (accessed 24 August 2016).

20 Kentaro Isomura, "Tsugunai towa Nani ka" ["What is atonement?"], *Asahi Shimbun*, July 9, 2015.

21 Ocean is an affiliate organization of Murder Victims Families for Human Rights (MVFHR).

Although Harada's case is often mentioned as "exceptional," I also recall the words of another family member who had continued a struggle to see an offender sentenced to death for nearly 13 years. Hiroshi Motomura's wife and baby daughter were murdered by an 18-year-old boy.[22] He had been originally sentenced to life imprisonment, but the Supreme Court reversed it and remanded the case for further hearing. He was resentenced to death. When the Supreme Court finally upheld the ultimate punishment, Motomura said, "the death sentence was what I had demanded and therefore is satisfactory. But I don't feel glad. I just solemnly accept the outcome."[23] Then he added that he had felt uneasy to be regarded as an advocate of the death penalty. "Time is the best consultant. I became able to see the incident dispassionately." He said that for the deprivation of the lives of his wife, his daughter, and the offender to not end in vain, "I hope, with this case as a start, people would think what we should do to realize a society without incidents which would result in death sentences."[24] He also revealed that he had got remarried, saying that "I am weak but I could meet a wonderful woman who supports me. I think it is also important to live a forward-looking life, with a smile on my face."

On the one hand, each victim is unique; on the other hand, victims share common experiences. As victims who lost their loved ones to violent acts, they are severely hurt, and their daily lives are completely broken. Nevertheless, they need to live on. They have to live their own lives. In order that they could recover from oppressive sorrows and damages, they desperately need someone's support.

Fumiko Isogai delivered a speech before an audience of 300, six months after the execution of Tsukasa Kanda, who had been sentenced to death for the murder of her daughter. While she repeated her dissatisfaction at sentencing decisions, she talked about how she had been hurt by people's careless remarks or attitudes, and she stressed the necessity of supports for victim's families from right after the crime.[25] No doubt, she had also been pushed over the cliff and

---

22 In Japan, persons under 20 years of age are treated as juvenile.

23 Minoru Matsutani, "Double-killer as minor will face gallows," *The Japan Times*, February 21, 2012.

24 *Mainichi Shimbun* (local news for Okayama Prefecture), February 20, 2010.

25 *Mainichi Shimbun*, November 29, 2015.

left there without sufficient supports. Throughout the criminal justice procedure for the case, she devoted herself to a campaign seeking the death penalty. Media had vigorously reported her devotion to the petition campaign and the public's attention was also focused on punishment. The public simply did not imagine how desperately the mother was in need of support.

Demands for capital punishment obscure the victim's desperate needs for support, and accordingly recovery of the bereaved tends to be left behind.

Coming back to the cases of Harada and Motomura, it could be said that both of them successfully stepped forward, although it took many years, to rebuild their respective lives. But consequently, they faced criticism instead of applause: Harada's open expression of his concerns with the death penalty triggered the argument that he is not "a real victim," and Motomura was vilified for his remarriage.

In short, an approach that places a great emphasis on the punishment pushes aside, and in some cases even denies, the importance of recovery of victims and their need for support.

As discussed above, the large majority of victims are not stakeholders in the process of capital sentencing. Many victims are marginalized and never speak of their experiences publicly. In the course of efforts to retrieve their peaceful lives, such silent victims may experience some changes of mind. None of them takes exactly the same path as others.

What is certain is that if we want to truly respect *each* victim, we cannot cite victims as justification for retaining the death penalty, at the very least without detail or clarification.

Thus I conclude that one cannot assert "the death penalty serves victims."

1.2 Victims' families' perspective

LISTENING TO VICTIMS

Mickell Branham[1]

"An evil deed is not redeemed by an evil deed of retaliation. Justice is never advanced in the taking of a human life. Morality is never upheld by a legalized murder." Coretta Scott King[2]

The exorbitant financial cost of the death penalty in America is well-documented, and there is plenty of evidence to support the abolition of capital punishment on the basis of fiscal responsibility alone.[3] These resources could be directed instead toward efforts to reduce, prevent, and solve crimes of violence as well as to provide reparations and restitution to victims. But as impressive as the figures are, there is a much greater cost to societies that cling to the death penalty, one that is much more difficult to measure: the loss of integrity not only by perpetuating violence but by increasing it exponentially.

A society that respects life does not deliberately kill human beings. An execution is a violent spectacle of official homicide, and one that endorses killing to solve social problems—the worst possible example to set for the citizenry, and especially children. Governments worldwide have often attempted to justify their lethal fury by extolling the purported benefits that such killing would bring to the rest of society. The benefits of capital punishment are illusory, but the bloodshed and the resulting destruction of community decency are real.[4]

For the past two decades, defense teams in capital cases have begun to open dialogues with surviving family members of murder victims, and the community has learned some extraordinary lessons. While a

---

1   Mickell Branham is an attorney who specializes in mitigation and restorative processes. She lives in Washington, D.C.

2   Coretta Scott King's speech to the National Coalition to Abolish the Death Penalty, Washington, D.C., 26 Sept., 1981.

3   Death Penalty Information Center, updated May 12, 2016. Available from www.dpic.org. (accessed 24 August 2016).

4   https://www.aclu.org/case-against-death-penalty. (accessed 24 August 2016), p. 5, 1 June, 2016.

few capital defense teams in the United States had regularly reached out to victims and survivors in their cases, the vast majority traditionally did not. That began to change following the Oklahoma City bombing in 1995, which prompted the community's introduction to principles of restorative justice and an evolution in criminal defense practice that was long overdue.[5]

Listening to and learning from victims[6] since that time, our community has become better informed and has broadened its understanding of how victims' needs might better be met within the judicial process. Victims are forced into a very public forum during a profound grieving process. Losing a loved one to severe violence tremendously complicates the struggle individuals face to regain balance and meaning in their lives.

Dan Levey, who lost his brother to homicide in 1996, described it powerfully:

> Murder breaks all the sacred rules, knows no fairness, and can never be compensated for or undone. It provokes fear and rage and tempts us to battle it on its terms instead of our own. Murder drives even the most loving and compassionate people to the edge of that fine line that separates our respect for life from our violent potentials. The aftermath of murder takes us straight through hell, where we stand eye to eye with the evil that hides behind human faces, and what we do in the face of the evil defines us for what lies ahead. The aftermath of murder is nothing less than a full-blown emotional and spiritual struggle.[7]

That struggle is often complicated by insensitive and intrusive media coverage, along with pressure placed on surviving families to either support or oppose capital punishment. Again, as Mr. Levey described, "When the death penalty spotlight shines on survivors, they risk getting

---

5   Mickell Branham & Richard Burr. 2008. "Understanding Defense-Initiated Victim Outreach and Why It Is Essential in Defending a Capital Client." *Hofstra Law Review*.

6   The term "victim" is used in this article to include surviving family members of homicide victims, who often consider and refer to themselves as victims as well.

7   Levey, Dan. 2006. "Feelings from the Heart." In *Wounds That Do Not Bind: Victim-Based Perspectives on the Death Penalty*. Durham, NC: Carolina Academic Press. p. 36.

ridiculed by either anti-death-penalty advocates or pro-death-penalty advocates. For survivors, it is a no-win situation."[8]

Without question, victims should be treated with sensitivity, respect, and fairness by all who work with them regardless of how they feel about the death penalty. The political pressure brought to bear by a capital prosecution exacerbates the potential for re-victimization in the courtroom and can further complicate the grieving process. "It takes victims out of their own journey and places them in the trial game …. One result is that the victim is transformed from an out-sider searching for a variety of answers (spiritual, emotional, financial and legal) to an integral part of an adversarial process…. Healing and understanding take a back seat to winning."[9] As anyone familiar with the legal system can attest, "If one set out by design to devise a system for provoking post-traumatic symptoms, one could not do better than a court of law."[10]

Victims' experiences and needs can vary greatly, but common among these needs are those of safety, information, validation, vindication, and the need to be heard. When we deeply listen to victims, we have a greater understanding of the imperative to create systems and methods for effective and meaningful resolution of the harms caused by violent crime. Many victims and survivors have needs that have nothing to do with achieving a sentence of death and would be undermined by imposition of the death penalty.

Clifford O'Sullivan Jr. was only 4 years old when his mother, Kellie O'Sullivan, was murdered in 1993. At the tender age of 6, he was placed on the witness stand by a California prosecutor to testify in support of the death penalty for the man responsible for her death. "All I think is that what the bad man did to my mom should happen to him. It's really sad for my family 'cause she was one of the greatest mothers I've met." In the years that followed, others around Clifford celebrated the death verdict and told him this was

---

8   Ibid., p. 46.

9   Loge, Peter. 2006. "The Process of Healing and the Trial as Product: Incompatibility, Courts, and Murder Victim Family Members." In *Wounds That Do Not Bind: Victim-Based Perspective on the Death Penalty*. Durham, NC: Carolina Academic Press. p. 421.

10 Herman, Judith. 1992. *Trauma and Recovery: The Aftermath of Violence—from domestic abuse to political terror*. New York: Harper Collins. p. 72.

his victory. But Clifford learned otherwise. "You don't heal."[11] In January 2014, he explained in *The Contributor* in Nashville, Tennessee, "I retract the blessing I gave to those who once seemed so eager to cast stones in my name. Having been scarred by personal experience, and having witnessed the wounding of others, sometimes as a result of my own actions, my faith now resides in the law of love alone." Clifford eventually determined that his journey needed to include a face-to-face meeting with the man responsible for his mother's death.

Victim requests for dialogue with defendants are increasing. Individual journeys toward recognizing this need can take many forms. Clifford began volunteering with Tennessee's death row inmates long before meeting his mother's murderer on California's death row. Linda White, whose daughter Cathy was killed in Texas in 1986, began teaching in two Texas prisons, and her life, as she describes, it, has never been the same. She eventually participated in a victim-offender dialogue with one of the men responsible for her daughter's murder, calling it "a profoundly liberating experience."

It is truly hard to come to grips with the last moments of your loved one's life and how he or she died—for me this has always been the most challenging issue. Meeting with him gave me some degree of peace with that aspect of it, almost as if she gave us a message in those last moments, a legacy of who she was and what she wanted to leave behind. And it made me realize that my work over the last nineteen years was exactly the memorial that she deserved.[12]

Linda began to realize from her research and her own experience that prisoners often see themselves as just as worthless as the public does and that efforts to see them and treat them as human beings can have a tremendous impact.

Almost all states in the US have victim-offender dialogue or mediation programs. However, victim access to these programs in cases of serious violence has been limited, and non-existent in federal cases,

---

11   "At age 6, he pushed for mom's killer to die. Now he's not so sure," *The Tennessean*, May 15, 2015.
12   White, Linda. 2006, "A Tiger by the Tail." In *Wounds That Do Not Bind*. Durham, NC: Carolina Academic Press. p. 67.

in spite of the growing number of victim requests. Meetings between defendants and family members of victims in cases of severe violence require careful planning and preparation and should be facilitated only by trained professionals, but the benefits of dialogue and mediation to victims are measurable, and avenues to making these programs more widely available need to be explored.[13]

The victims' rights movement has grown rapidly in the US since the 1970s, prompting federal and state legislation broadening the rights of victims and survivors to participate in trials of those accused of crimes against them. But in one area of victims' rights, recognition and respect remains elusive in most cases absent unusual circumstances. When victims articulate needs inconsistent with or opposed to that of prosecutors on the case, victims can feel shut out of the judicial process.

In the case of *Colorado v. Edward Montour*, concerning the killing of a corrections officer in 2002, the parents of the victim, Eric Autobee, opposed the prosecutor's decision to again seek the death penalty after Montour's original sentence was overturned. When the prosecutor chose to ignore the family's decision, Bob Autobee continued to press the prosecutor to drop the death penalty and even picketed outside the courthouse as potential jurors lined up to enter. The prosecutor's response was to remove the victim's family members from his list of witnesses to be called during sentencing. While many victims in similar circumstances quietly defer to prosecution decisions, this experience spurred Bob Autobee to activism. Defense counsel asked the court for permission to allow the Autobees to testify at sentencing as defense witnesses, prompting prosecution objections.

The Autobee family's reasoning was beautifully articulated in a court filing that stated, in part:

Despite the inhumanity he saw around him, Eric would not speak disdainfully of inmates, but, instead, recognized their human dignity. The crime affected the Autobees not just because of their beloved son's loss, but also because of who they became after this loss. After Eric's death, their warm feelings of love that Eric always nurtured turned

---

13 Rossi, Rachel. 2008. "Meet Me on Death Row: Post-Sentence Victim-Offender Mediation in Capital Cases." *Pepperdine Dispute Resolution Law Journal* 9(1):185-210.

into cold feelings of vengeance and violence. Originally, the Autobees fervently supported the prosecution's efforts to seek absolute retribution. Over time, however, and with reflection, they realized that Eric would not have wanted this for himself or for them; Eric would not have wanted someone killed in his name, nor would he have wanted his family to live in the darkness of hatred. The Autobees know this because they know how Eric lived: by loving life, saving lives, and extending mercy to the merciless.[14]

Although victims are not allowed to testify on their views of punishment either for or against the death penalty, victims who are opposed to capital punishment should not be prohibited from participating in the judicial process. A striking example of empowering these victims occurred during the sentencing phase of the trial of Zacarias Moussaoui in 2006, where family members who lost loved ones on September 11, 2001, testified on behalf of the defense. Federal prosecutors strenuously objected to any victim family members being allowed to testify during the defense presentation.

Described in the press as "noble and generous," 9/11 family members took the stand one by one to tell stories about their loved ones and stories of compassion, tolerance, and peace-building to educate the jurors and the community of their values. Donald Bane, whose son Michael was killed in the north tower of the World Trade Center, testified, "I thought what was needed were bridges of understanding with the people who would do this kind of thing." In his community, he began organizing meetings between Christians and Muslims. Marilyn Rosenthal, whose son Josh was killed, wanted to testify out of a sense of patriotic duty. "Everybody … wants something good and positive to come out of what happened. For me that meant finding out everything." Anthony Aversano told the jury of his struggle to deal with his anger of September 11 after losing his father that day. "I saw if I went down the path of wanting retaliation … I would give my life over to them. If I was to succumb to fear, to succumb to the terror … I give up my life. I can't possibly have an open heart and still be afraid or angry or vengeful."[15]

14 Cohen, Andrew. 2014. "When Victims Speak Up in Court—In Defense of the Criminals," Available from http://www.theatlantic.com/national/archive/2014/01/when-victims-speak-up-in-court-in-defense-of-the-criminals/283345/ (accessed 24 August 2016).

15 "Families of 9/11 Victims Testify for Moussaoui Defense," *Reuters*, April 19, 2006.

In other cases, family members who disagreed with the prosecution's pursuit of the death penalty have taken their case to the press. Upon a conviction in federal district court arising from the Boston Marathon bombings, surviving family members Bill and Denise Richards published in the *Boston Globe* their plea for prosecutors to drop the death penalty.

> We understand all too well the heinousness and brutality of the crimes committed. We were there. We lived it. The defendant murdered our 8-year-old son and maimed our 7-year-old daughter, and stole part of our soul. We know that the government has its reasons for seeking the death penalty, but the continued pursuit of that punishment could bring years of appeals and prolong reliving the most painful day of our lives. We hope our two remaining children do not have to grow up with the lingering, painful reminder of what the defendant took from them, which years of appeals would undoubtedly bring.[16]

In spite of their plea, the United States Attorney proceeded to obtain a death verdict.

Last year in Charleston, South Carolina, family members of parishioners slain during their Bible study appeared at the initial hearing to speak directly to the young man who killed their loved ones. Felicia Sanders said to him, "We welcomed you Wednesday night in our Bible study with welcome arms. You have killed some of the most beautiful people that I know. Every fiber in my body hurts and I'll, I'll never be the same. Tywanza Sanders was my son. But Tywanza Sanders was my hero. Tywanza was my hero .... May God have mercy on you." Wanda Simmons told him, "Although my grandfather and the other victims died at the hands of hate, this is proof, everyone's plea for your soul, is proof that they lived in love and their legacies will live in love. So hate won't win. And I just want to thank the court for making sure that hate doesn't win."[17]

---

16 "To End the Anguish, Drop the Death Penalty," *The Boston Globe,* April 16, 2015.

17 "The Powerful Words of Forgiveness Delivered to Dylan Roof by Victims' Relatives," *The Washington Post,* June 19, 2015.

President Obama during his eulogy for the Reverend Clementa C. Pinckney called on the nation to emulate the grace that the reverend displayed in his work and that the people of South Carolina demonstrated after the massacre of the nine worshippers at their church. In the spring of 2015, the US Department of Justice announced its intention to seek the death penalty in the case, prompting Ta-Nehisi Coates to write, "The hammer of criminal justice is the preferred tool of a society that has run out of ideas. In this sense, Roof is little more than a human sacrifice to The Gods of Doing Nothing."[18]

Seeking vengeance is commonly accepted as the norm for "justice" in our culture even as the evidence grows that it may have a negative impact on both victims and the community.[19] A report from the New Jersey Death Penalty Study Commission found that "the non-finality of death penalty appeals hurts victims, drains resources, and creates a false sense of justice. Replacing the death penalty with life without parole would be certain punishment, not subject to the lengthy delays of capital cases; it would incapacitate the offenders; and it would provide finality for victims' families."[20]

So many victims, even following such extraordinary loss and pain, refuse to dismiss the inherent potential worth of the life of the individual who took everything away from them. This is not weakness but something that in itself stands as a firm rejection and condemnation of the insidious action of murder perpetrated against them. This is ancient wisdom, that we are all interconnected. In our web of relationships, crime represents a tear in the web, a sign of imbalance. It calls to us to put things right. Because we are all interconnected, this can be accomplished only by engaging *all* of those impacted by the crime: the victims, those who harmed them, and the community—addressing the community and offender obligations along with the needs of everyone.[21]

Crime does not occur in a vacuum. Those who inflict harm on others are often prior victims of violence themselves. When trauma is

---

18   Ta-Nehisi Coates. 2016. "Killing Dylan Roof." *The Atlantic* available from http://www.theatlantic.com/politics/archive/2016/05/dylann-roof-death-penalty/484274/. (accessed 24 August 2016).

19   *See* Marilyn Armour & Mark Unbreit. 2012. "Assessing the Impact of the Ultimate Penal Sanction on Homicide Survivors: A Two State Comparison." *Marquette Law Review* 96(1):1-123.

20   *See* New Jersey Death Penalty Commission. 2007. *Death Penalty Study Commission Report.* p. 61.

21   For an in-depth discussion of this, *see* Howard Zehr. 1990. *Changing Lenses: A New Focus for Crime and Justice.* Scottdale PA: Herald Press.

unhealed, its impact has a ripple effect as those who have suffered harm may evolve into aggressors themselves.[22] When this is exacerbated by common societal problems of racism, poverty, institutional failure, addiction, abuse, negligence, mental illness, or intellectual disability, it can produce a perfect storm for a violent crime that could likely have been prevented and never should have occurred.

Bud Welch, whose 23-year-old daughter, Julie, was killed in the Oklahoma City bombing, described this painful realization:

> At first I was in absolute pain. All I wanted was to see those people fried. I was smoking three packs of cigarettes a day and drinking heavily. I was physically and mentally sick. I was stuck on April 19, 1995. Looking back, I call that the temporary insanity period.

> I went down to the bomb site and stood right underneath the survivor tree. A statement that Julie made got to echoing in my mind. We were driving across Iowa and heard a radio story about an execution in Texas. Julie's reaction was, "Dad, all they're doing is teaching hate to their children." I didn't really think a hell of a lot about it at the time, but then, after she was dead, I got to thinking about it.

> I knew that the death penalty wasn't going to bring her back, and I realized that it was about revenge and hate. And the reason Julie and 167 others were dead was because of the very same thing: revenge and hate. It was McVeigh and Nichols' hate against the federal government. They would never have performed that act if they hadn't felt justified that they were doing the right thing for their cause, just like we think we're doing the right thing for our cause when we execute prisoners.[23]

Systems that impose the death penalty on citizens ignore the very human stories of the individuals charged with these crimes and

---

22 *See, generally* Yoder, Carolyn. 2005. *The Little Book of Trauma Healing: When Violence Strikes and Community Security is Threatened.* Intercourse, PA: Good Books.

23 Welch, Bud. 2001. "I Was Stuck on April 19, 1995." In *Transcending: Reflections of Crime Victims, Portraits and Interviews* by Howard Zehr. Intercourse PA: GoodBooks. p. 60.

often ignore the voices of victims themselves. Victims and defendants have complex, powerful stories that teach us how much we have in common. In their stories, in our common ground, we find the information relevant to effectively address violence. The adversarial nature of our criminal justice system does not lend itself to a deep understanding of these complex dynamics, but effective, long-term solutions to the problem of violent crime require just that. We are living in a time of extraordinary uncivil discourse. Fear and anxiety contribute to a climate of division and dehumanization of "the other." It will require courageous and positive leadership to bring us back to remembering our common humanity. These victims can show us the way forward.

THE DEATH PENALTY AND THE RIGHT TO LIFE

Mireya García Ramírez[1]

I am the sister of Vicente Israel García Ramírez, detained and disappeared since 1977, when he was a young man of 19. I am a member and leader of the Association of Families of the Detained and Disappeared, which at the start Chile's military dictatorship, with immeasurable support and protection from the Christian churches, launched a crusade for truth and justice that is today active, legitimized and respected by society.

The ongoing and systematic violation of the right to life and the integrity of people; the banning of political, social, cultural and community institutions and organizations; the permissiveness and acceptance of the judiciary and the media; the creation of criminal groupings financed by the state such as the National Intelligence Directorate (DINA) and the National Information Centre (CNI); the use of hundreds of public and private locations as centers for detention, torture, death and disappearance throughout the country—these are some of the many factors supporting a state using a national security doctrine and the existence of a "home-grown enemy" as a pretext for exterminating political dissidents.

Chile became a vast prison, and society was exposed to a new and traumatizing repressive policy that harmed the institutions, the national soul, and thousands of families that still place their hopes in justice despite the fact that penalties have been imposed on human rights violators in less than 10% of the cases.

The family trauma caused by the repression, the ignorance of the final destination of the bodies of the detained and disappeared, and the lack of justice are three factors making the forced disappearance of persons an ongoing torture, which, 43 years after the coup

---

1   Former Vice-chair of the Chilean Association of Relatives of Detained and Disappeared Persons in Chile.

d'état, has now reached and hurt a second and a third generation of victims' relatives.

In this context of political repression, the death penalty was applied in Chile to political dissidents by invoking, for instance, the Law of Flight, the Curfew, the State of Internal Warfare and the summary proceedings in military courts or simply by the use and abuse of power against the defenseless civilian population.

We have used the term "death penalty" to describe the sentences of military tribunals. However, political prisoners were murdered or executed in various locations and circumstances: during prisoner transfers; during curfews in the case of people not carrying identity papers; in villages during large-scale raids or on a city bridge. We were able to identify at least 2,298 people killed. Their families were given death certificates describing the cause of death, which was usually internal hemorrhaging due to gunshot wounds. About 1,250 detained and disappeared persons were also put to death, executed by various brutal methods.

One of these methods was lethal torture, making this brutal practice an agonizing death penalty. In such cases, there was no need for sentencing or shooting: it was sufficient to cause indescribable suffering in order to administer the most extreme, irreversible, and irreparable punishment.

In the case of nine pregnant women, the torture also took the lives of their unborn children. The death penalty is the most extreme form of torture and torture is the most extreme form of death penalty. Both have the same goal and combine to produce suffering and death.

Corpses were thrown into deep tunnels, into the sea, into abandoned mines; corpses were buried in the desert, in unmarked graves in cemeteries, or in an urban wasteland.

Without democratic institutions to which we could appeal and despite the complicity of the judiciary with the dictatorship, we insisted that they must adopt an attitude commensurate with their mandate and principal function: to investigate, to produce the detained and disappeared persons alive and to punish the crimes against the life and integrity of the political prisoners.

About 12,000 appeals were submitted to the courts. With the exception of a few fruitless investigations and one action for *amparo* granted, more than three decades elapsed until a few magistrates admitted that they should investigate, determine criminal responsibility, and punish the perpetrators. And so the Legislative Decree on Amnesty, in existence since 1976, ceased to apply and sentences began to be enforced in special prisons. The legal arguments focused and still focus on state responsibility, respect for international humanitarian law, and the particularly serious nature of the large-scale crimes against humanity.

One of our demands was that the human rights violators should be given sentences commensurate with the crimes committed and that the sentences should be served in full, since crimes against humanity are not subject to amnesty or to the statute of limitations.

It is our view that imprisonment is one way of preventing a repetition of these contemptible deeds and that it provides fair and necessary redress for the harm caused. All the rights of our families were violated with extreme cruelty; the death penalty could have been an option in view of the irreparable harm sustained over many years by the families and society. However, this was never an option for the organizations defending human rights. Basically, our struggle for the right to life and integrity of persons was and is incompatible with taking lives, even those of cruel criminals such as the agents of repression. Perhaps because of the feeling of greater connection that argues against the use of the death penalty, we were unable to advocate the same sentence as was previously applied to our executed, detained and disappeared relatives.

For champions of human rights, the death penalty is unacceptable even in those cases in which we might emotionally be inclined to consider that it would be a fair punishment or when our first instinct is to think that a murderer deserves the same punishment. Our attitude of diametrical opposition is based on values and is our contribution to humanism and to the right and correct use of the law and of legislation.

For those participating in global struggles for respect for life and those building a pro-life culture, two ways of understanding and administering justice cannot coexist.

In 2001, in the middle of the transition to democracy, the Chilean Government enacted the law abolishing the death penalty, which had been applicable for 126 years, for nonpolitical offences, replacing it by life imprisonment for at least 40 years. The event was announced at a public ceremony, which we attended in order to demonstrate our full commitment to the lives of all persons. That was undoubtedly a historic day, on which the pro-life option defeated the pro-death option.

The right to life and to its protection is a fundamental right of human beings. Without life, there is no existence and therefore no exercise of all the human rights inherent in people. In his encyclical *Evangelium Vitae*, John Paul II stated that abolition of the death penalty must be viewed in the context of a system of penal justice ever more in line with human dignity. We share this view.

A society so disrespectful of the right to life as was Chilean society during the dictatorship had the moral obligation to reverse a law which in itself does not help to solve the problems of criminality that affect societies every day. This is where an effort must be made to gradually reduce as far as possible the social, psychological, and economic externalities causing shameful actions and to enhance security, prevention, timely justice and punishment that fits the crime.

Most countries have abolished the death penalty. But, when human rights are violated and the result is death, the practice of capital punishment is being perpetuated. This is no small matter if we consider that extrajudicial killings are a reality today that has exactly the same irreversible and irreparable effects as the death penalty still legally in force in some nations.

Countless reports are being received, especially by Amnesty International, about people detained and subjected to cruel, inhuman, and degrading treatment who after confessing under torture are condemned to death. In such cases, the violation of human rights is total and inhuman for the condemned person and for his or her family.

Although there are differences of opinion on the subject, the continued existence of the death penalty in countries with a military justice system, including Chile, is a dangerous source of concern when one considers that, in an emergency situation, it would suffice to declare a state of internal warfare in order to legitimize the death penalty.

I wish to refer to the murder and disappearance of the military recruit Michael Nash because he refused to fire on a group of political prisoners in Iquique who were falsely accused under the Law of Flight. He was arrested, taken to the Pisagua concentration camp in the north of the country and from there was made to disappear. In this case, which is not unique, a young man performing compulsory military service was murdered for refusing to kill. This was paradoxical, cruel, and a clear example of how states of emergency permit and legitimize unfair and abusive behavior.

Although the death penalty is a serious violation of the fundamental principle of the Universal Declaration of Human rights, which states in Article 3 that "Everyone has the right to life, liberty and security of person," and of Article 6 of the International Covenant on Civil and Political Rights, which states that "Every human being has the inherent right to life," it is still applied—not in most countries but with increasing impunity.

Fortunately, the growing awareness of the inviolability of the right to life, the contribution of instant mass media posting condemnations on social networks, the role of the press, and the interconnectivity of regions and countries mean that these facts are widely known and condemned.

If globalization has one positive effect, it is precisely the possibility of accessing and disseminating information and of reacting at the level of governments, international bodies, and civil society.

The abolition of the death penalty all over the world and ratification of the international instruments establishing a moratorium are part of the state policy of Chile concerning human rights and, of course, the wish of organizations and relatives of victims of the dictatorship. We have charted a course of fighting for the life, security, and integrity of all human beings.

Precisely because our struggle is also forward-looking, it seeks to prevent a repetition of human rights violation resulting in death or having serious physical, psychological, or social after-effects. For the champions of human rights, the global, effective and vigilant abolition of the death penalty is a goal of life protection and compliance with and observance of the Convention on Forced Disappearance of Persons. Mankind has not succeeded in abolishing the death penalty, which is still applied in various parts of the world.

Application of the death penalty on criminal, political, religious or other grounds makes no distinction as to effect or cruelty. Different methods may be used but, regardless of the degree of violence exercised by states or power groups when killing someone, this is not an act consonant with the right to life, without which all other rights are unattainable. It illustrates power and mastery over the life of another that achieves no positive effect, either deterrent or corrective. In addition, there is an aggravating factor that should be an important argument in favour of its total abolition: the definite possibility of error and the impossibility of restoring to life someone who has been deprived of it.

One example is the case of Kirk Bloodsworth, who at the age of 23 was arrested and accused of the rape and murder of a 9-year-old girl in Maryland. He was sentenced to die in the gas chamber. Eight years later, he was exonerated by DNA testing.

In hundreds of cases of political killings committed under the dictatorship, the accusations were absurd fallacies concocted in order to kill, to snuff out the existence of those who were described as home-grown enemies under the National Security Doctrine, a topic studied in the School of the Americas of sad reputation.

The death penalty is a human rights violation, regardless of whether or not it is supported by public opinion. History is replete with human rights violations that were supported but that are now viewed with horror.

The death penalty is a violation of a fundamental human right—the right to life. And it is the ultimate example of cruel, inhuman, and irreparable punishment, regardless of the method used to apply it.

Abolition of the death penalty is the task before us today, requiring the commitment and the conviction of the democratic states of the world, together with the organizations that champion human rights and with civil society. Abolition of the death penalty and executions will help to enhance the value of life as a unique and irreplaceable gift.

1.3 Victims' Families and Closure

ESCAPING THE CLOSURE TRAP

Jody L. Madeira[1]

Over the past 30 years, victims have had a complex, contested, and controversial relationship with capital punishment. Often, difficulties arise because of so-called "closure" claims—the idea that executions are therapeutic for family members and help them to heal from the trauma of their loved one's murder. In 1991, the already-potent victim's rights movement gained a powerful victory following the United States Supreme Court's ruling in *Payne vs. Tennessee* that family members of murder victims deserved a place and, more importantly, a voice in criminal courtrooms through the provision of victim impact testimony. This opportunity allowed victims' families to describe exactly how a loved one's murder had changed their lives, which critics contended could encourage a sympathetic jury to award a death sentence.

On the other hand, death penalty proponents argued that this would help victims' families attain closure. Thereafter, the popularization and politicization of "closure" claims beginning in the 1990s gave family members' impact testimony and implicit or explicit pleas for a death sentence additional gravitas. Yet, these "closure" claims conflict with other family members' strong protests that closure is a myth, that executions do not restore murdered loved ones to life, and that states should not be permitted to execute offenders in victims' or survivors' names.

Still other family members contend that closure is a process whereby one learns to move forward in the aftermath of a loved one's murder, necessitating that one learn to both work through internal trauma and negotiate institutional proceedings such as criminal trials. If one frequent criticism of the death penalty is that incarceration on death row and execution undermine inmates' dignity, it is also true that the politicization of "closure" claims sacrifices victims' families in perpetuation of the death penalty, undermining their dignity and leading to

---

1   Professor of Law and Louis F. Niezer Faculty Fellow at Indiana University Maurer School of Law, Indiana, United States.

further traumatization.

In many death penalty states, such as Texas, Oklahoma, and Ohio, victims' families are also allowed to witness the executions of their loved ones' murderers. Execution chambers often have one or more rooms where government officials, reporters, and the victims' family members (and perhaps those of the inmate as well) watch inmates take their last breaths. State attorneys general may employ "victim advocates" who update victims' families on legal developments and prepare them to witness an execution. Less frequently, states facilitate witnessing by closed circuit broadcast.

Today, victims and "closure" claims continue to be bound together in American mainstream media, politics, culture and society in a way that adds to the apparent legitimacy of "closure" claims. These institutions often cover, discuss, and historicize murders in ways that magnify family members' trauma, thereby strengthening their asserted need for closure, and, by association, justifying the execution of their loved one's killers. Prosecutors, news stations, and others allege that family members await the executions of their loved one's murderers to recognize the victims' worth, obtain accountability, and "close that chapter" in their lives. Popular conceptions of what closure should provide thus comes to define the expected role for victims' family members—to advocate for their offender's execution as a therapeutic intervention.

But these promises most often prove elusive; even though family members can now give impact testimony, criminal trials are focused upon a suspect's guilt or innocence and not the murder victim or her surviving family members, who may regard these specialized legal proceedings as cold and unfeeling. Moreover, procedural aspects of death sentences also undermine asserted links between executions and closure, in particular a lengthy appeals process that often postpones executions for a decade or more, the high likelihood that a death sentence will be overturned on appeal, and a lethal injection death that many view as anticlimactic because it can appear quick, painless, and peaceful. Nationwide, two-thirds of death sentences are overturned on appeal; of these, more than 80% receive a sentence less than death, a ratio of one execution for every

326 murders.[2] Those offenders who kill white victims or who come from a handful of counties in certain states are disproportionately likely to be executed.[3] Far from proving therapeutic, then, the politicization of closure claims when set against capital punishment's procedural realities likely create further distress and even trauma for family members.

Understanding and reforming victims' role in capital punishment therefore necessitates decoupling it from closure claims so as to critically examine whether and how these individuals actually experience this concept. To these ends, a case study of a particular event, such as the Oklahoma City bombing, can provide a useful context in which to assess how family members negotiate closure expectations. Indeed, the Oklahoma City bombing effectively illustrates both how social institutions can exacerbate the very need for closure that a state proposes to alleviate through execution and how "closure" concepts break down in practice. Moreover, "closure" claims leave out another category of victims' families that capital punishment creates: family members of the condemned inmates, who must also endure years of appeals and potentially an execution that will take the life of their loved one.

I spent the sweltering month of July 2004 in Oklahoma interviewing family members and survivors of the Oklahoma City bombing about how Timothy McVeigh's capital trial and execution impacted their lives.[4] On April 19, 1995, McVeigh lit the fuse on a truck bomb that he had designed and built with conspirator Terry Nichols; the bomb decimated the Alfred P. Murrah Federal Building in Oklahoma City, Oklahoma, killing 168 individuals and injuring more than 680 others. The blast also damaged 324 buildings in a 16-block radius and was responsible for an estimated $652 million in damages. While McVeigh was sentenced to death in his federal trial in 1997, Nichols was sentenced to life in prison without possibility of parole in both federal and state trials. McVeigh was executed on June 11, 2001, in Terre Haute, Indiana. His execution was witnessed by 242 individuals, 10 of whom viewed the proceedings live in Indiana

---

2   Richard C. Dieter. 2011. *Struck by Lightning: The Continuing Arbitrariness of the Death Penalty Thirty-Five Years After Its Re-instatement in 1976.* Death Penalty Information Center, Washington D.C.

3   Ibid.

4   J. Madeira. 2012. *Killing McVeigh: The Death Penalty and the Myth of Closure.* New York: New York University Press.

and 232 who watched the execution via closed circuit broadcast in Oklahoma City.

I always thought it ironic that my dissertation research on this hot issue, conducted during the most oppressive months of the year, generated the coolest advice I ever received: "Forgiveness is a gift you give yourself." That pragmatic statement came from family member Bud Welch, whose young daughter Julie was murdered in the bombing. I sat in Bud's living room, captivated, as he spoke of the first days and weeks following the bombing, when he frankly admitted wanting to physically attack McVeigh with anything that came to hand. And yet, Bud noted, there came a point when he realized just how much of his energy he had been wasting on thoughts of McVeigh, just how many physical, mental, and emotional resources he had been devoting to his hatred of this perpetrator. Bud realized that his own well-being depended upon his ability to sever himself from McVeigh, to regain control over his life and emotions and reconnect with his previous values. This resolution not only placed him on the path to meeting McVeigh's father and sister years later, it contributed greatly to his decision to memorialize his daughter Julie through becoming an internationally known anti-death-penalty advocate.

Bud Welch's perspective on the importance of forgiveness was merely one among many reactions to McVeigh's visibility and the question of how he should be held accountable. Most family members and survivors wanted McVeigh to be executed, but for a variety of reasons. Some felt that this execution was important because the death penalty was the harshest available sentence, and what type of crime would merit such a punishment if not this bombing, which had claimed 168 lives? Still others felt that McVeigh had to be executed to complete the process of accountability. In a phenomenon unique to cases that receive extraordinary levels of media coverage, many felt that McVeigh had to die to terminate the extraordinary and discomfiting visibility he had enjoyed in the years leading up to his execution. Family members and survivors perceived this visibility was particularly noxious in the months prior to his death, which witnessed the airing of McVeigh's *60 Minutes* interview with Ed Bradley from death row; the publication of his authorized biography, *An American Terrorist;* and expanded media coverage following Attorney General John Ashcroft's decision to allow Oklahoma City witnesses to view the execution via a closed circuit broadcast from the chamber in Terre Haute, Indiana. In contrast, a minority who opposed the death penalty did not want McVeigh to be executed at all.

But despite desiring McVeigh's execution for whatever reason, the vast majority of individuals I interviewed had one important thing in common: voluntarily or involuntarily, they had stepped back into the "new normal" of their lives fairly soon after the bombing. They had come home from the hospital, returned to work, begun to fulfil family obligations, and even joined bombing-related groups, such as the effort to build a national memorial commemorating those lost and injured. For all of these individuals, closure, if it existed at all, was to be found somewhere other than McVeigh's execution chamber. Very few were singularly focused on McVeigh's death, most often because they had returned to their lives, which were necessarily altered, but busy nonetheless, and other matters such as healing, families, and careers received the lion's share of their attention.

I found it surprising that so few individuals were preoccupied with McVeigh's execution, simply because legal proceedings and media coverage encouraged such obsessive attentions. Round-the-clock cable news, McVeigh's own predilection for seeking media attention, and lengthy trials culminating in days of victim impact testimony all facilitated a fixation on McVeigh and his crimes. Thus, the vast majority of family members and survivors who did not become preoccupied with McVeigh's execution had to consciously choose not to award McVeigh and his actions such a profound investment of their attention and other personal resources. This decision to look away did not always involve forgiveness, and certainly never entailed forgetting about either McVeigh or his murderous acts. Rather, it meant heeding a survival instinct that warned them such an obsession would jeopardize their well-being and that of their family members and friends.

It was fortunate that the vast majority of witnesses did not regard the execution as the font from which their healing would spring. On the morning of McVeigh's execution on June 11, 2001, 242 witnesses—10 live, and 232 in Oklahoma City—watched McVeigh's last breaths. The vast majority of witnesses felt that his death was anticlimactic because it was too easy, too quick, or too painless. Few anticipated that the execution would give them closure—an expectation that likely would have made McVeigh's death very distressing, even traumatizing.

Now, years later, I often think back to those hours I spent in the living rooms and kitchens of family members and survivors, listening to them speak about how they decided whether or not to become involved in bombing-related groups, to attend or participate in trials, to attend the execution. It must have been agonizing for them to negotiate McVeigh's visibility in the legal proceedings and the mass media, to turn away from the false promises of closure. Closure is such a seductive concept; if executions actually provided closure to victims' families, it seems heartless to deny them opportunities to advocate for its imposition or to witness an offender's last moments. But victim's families routinely reject the popular notion of closure; those who were interested enough to witness McVeigh's execution expressly did so for other reasons, such as seeing the accountability process through to completion. Thus, the attraction of executions must stem from other reasoning, such as the banal factors that lead states to retain capital punishment is the harshest available sentence.

In 2013, Marilyn Peterson Armour and Mark Umbreit published the first "systematic inquiry directly with survivors about whether obtaining the ultimate punishment affects their healing."[5] Their findings suggest that the mere fact that capital punishment is possible might be the strongest explanation for its popularity among family members.[6] Comparing victims' family members in Texas, an ardent death penalty state, and Minnesota, a state offering only life without the possibility of parole, Armour and Umbreit found that Minnesota family members whose offenders received life without parole exhibited better physical, psychological, and behavioral health. They further found that family members were satisfied with life without parole because it was the most severe punishment and even those who preferred the death penalty felt that they received the best available sentence.

---

5   M. Armour and M. S. Umbreit. 2012. "Impact of the ultimate penal sanction on the healing of
     family survivors of homicide victims: A two state comparison." *Marquette Law Review* 96(1):1-123.
6   Ibid.

Moreover, Armour and Umbreit highlight another reason why family members and survivors might experience greater well-being in states with life without parole and not the death penalty: the promise of "closure" being tied to a lengthy appeals process that often postpones executions for a decade or longer. Over half of the family members in Texas were "mildly to exceedingly worried" about the appeals process and feared that the offender's sentence might be overturned after findings of mental retardation, innocence, or a technicality. They also resented the length of the process and the limited communications they received about legal proceedings. Tellingly, while 30% of Minnesota family members had no "actual or mental relationship" with the murderer—conscious decisions not to think about the murderer, not referring to the murderer by name, or statements that the murderer was irrelevant—this was true for only 5% of Texas family members.

In the Oklahoma City bombing context, McVeigh chose to terminate his appeals and was executed a scant four years after his trial—a very short period compared to the usual delays on the state level between trial and execution. But these years still took a toll upon family members and survivors, particularly because McVeigh's visibility was so intense during this period. In McVeigh's case, a sentence of life without parole would not only have truncated available appeal opportunities, but likely would have drastically reduced McVeigh's newsworthiness and thus his visibility. McVeigh's co-defendant, Terry Nichols, received multiple life without parole sentences in federal court and in Oklahoma state court. He is currently incarcerated in ADX Florence, a federal supermax prison in Florence, Colorado, and has all but disappeared from public view. After Nichols' federal trial for the deaths of eight federal employees did not result in a death sentence, several family members and survivors advocated that Nichols be tried again in Oklahoma state court. In those subsequent trials, Nichols again received life without parole sentences, leaving family members and survivors with no recourse but to adjust, which they did in due course. The outcome of Nichols' trials suggests that, had McVeigh received life without parole instead of the death penalty, even those who were disappointed would have had little choice but to accept this eventuality—that is, work toward their own version of closure, as all need to do regardless of what sentence a perpetrator receives.

Admittedly, the Oklahoma City bombing is a unique crime in many respects, including the number of victims and the fact that few perpetrators receive as much attention as Timothy McVeigh, much of which was of his own making. Yet, this incident illustrates why expectations perpetuated by "closure" claims fail and how family members can be traumatized by what happens in the aftermath of a horrific crime as well from the crime itself. If family members and survivors felt that McVeigh was an involuntary presence in their lives for four years, then how do other victims' families endure being tied to an offender through appeals and media coverage for over a decade? And if "closure" is best attained through participation in the trial process and then the execution, what happens when a crime remains unsolved and a perpetrator is never found?

Fortunately, and tellingly, some family members have realized these possibilities might come to pass and requested life without parole sentences to avoid the high potential for secondary victimization and further traumatization that accompanies capital punishment. The parents of Matthew Shepard, a young man who was horrifically beaten and left to die on a fence in Laramie, Wyoming in 1998, asked that the two men who had carried out these crimes receive life without parole sentences instead of the death penalty so that they need not be tied to these offenders throughout the appellate process. Further combating popular ideas about what will lead to closure, other family members have begun to fight back against institutional policies that retraumatize victims. No Notoriety, an organization founded by Tom and Caren Teves after their son, Alex, was murdered by James Holmes in the Aurora theater shooting on July 20, 2012, is pushing to reduce mass killings by ending media practices that give shooters infamy and notoriety, such as eliminating the "gratuitous use" of killers' names and photographs in favour of a focus on victims, survivors, and rescue workers. Publications such as *People* magazine, professional associations such as the Florida chapter of the Society of Professional Journalists, and individual journalists have adopted these policies. Such efforts might in fact represent the new forefront of the victims' rights movement, where family members, having won their battles to be considered relevant to issues of criminal accountability, to voice their needs and concerns, and to participate in criminal proceedings, now try to reform these institutions and their practices to align with how closure is actually achieved. Such reforms, if successful, will likely decrease the potential for secondary victimization or retraumatization.

Moving forward, it is essential to defuse the politicization of closure by decoupling victims' families from expectations perpetuated by "closure" claims so as to avoid giving them false hopes that watching their loved one's killer die will provide a therapeutic release. The most dangerous consequence of politicizing closure is not perpetuating the myth that closure exists, but in reinforcing and prolonging the consequences that popular "closure" claims have when family members begin to believe in them, expect closure to happen in a certain way, and take steps in a misguided quest to pursue it that likely false version of "closure." If these steps include advocating for an offender's execution, then this quest can become more than misguided; it can turn deadly. The reasons that family members give for preferring executions, whether following more infamous events such as the Oklahoma City bombing or other murders that do not receive as much public attention—attaining accountability, seeking the harshest available punishment, and removing the offender from public view—can all be more expeditiously accomplished by imposing other sentences such as life without parole. These sentences end the accountability process more swiftly because they do not trigger the lengthy capital habeas appeals process, more promptly attain completion since these sentences are less likely to be reversed on appeal, and quickly decrease offenders' visibility without the likely final bump in publicity that accompanies the offender's execution.

DOES CAPITAL PUNISHMENT BRING CLOSURE TO THE VICTIMS?

David T. Johnson[1]

"Let us call [capital punishment] by the name which, for lack of any other nobility, will at least give the nobility of truth, and let us recognize it for what it is essentially: a revenge."
Albert Camus, *Reflections on the Guillotine*.[2]

"Justice is not a form of therapy, meaning that what is helpful to a particular victim…is not necessarily just and what is just may not be therapeutic."
Wendy Kaminer, *It's All the Rage*.[3]

The Rise of "Closure" and the Return of Revenge

Why do about 40 countries retain capital punishment and continue to carry out executions on a regular basis? Answers to this question vary by country and culture, but in recent years many societies have started to offer some version of the reply that victims need it and want it—and that states should satisfy their preferences. As US President Bill Clinton remarked in 1996, "When someone is a victim, he or she should be at the center of the criminal justice process, not on the outside looking in."[4] The view that victims should occupy center stage of the capital process rests on at least two premises: that law has failed whenever a person is murdered, and that law should serve the interests of victims when it responds to this uniquely horrible occurrence. Many states that retain capital punishment root its use in

---

1   Professor of Sociology, University of Hawaii.
2   Camus, Albert. 1960. *Resistance, Rebellion, and Death: Essays*. New York: Vintage International. p. 197.
3   Kaminer, Wendy. 1995. *It's All the Rage: Crime and Culture*. New York: Perseus Books. p. 84.
4   Quoted in Madeira, Jody Lynee. 2012. *Killing McVeigh: The Death Penalty and the Myth of Closure*. New York and London: New York University Press. p. 138.

retribution, and retribution by the state has been called "the victim's vengeance in disguise."[5]

The hunger of victims for revenge may well be "the least discussed and most pervasive force in the desire to punish."[6] But support for revenge varies over time and space. Some societies believe that "revenge is a kind of wild justice, which the more man's nature runs to it, the more ought law to weed it out."[7] This kind of view prevailed in the US Supreme Court's *Furman v. Georgia* decision of 1972, which held 5-4 that capital punishment as then practiced was unconstitutional, and which produced separate opinions by each of the nine Justices, most of which "denounced retribution as a bad reason to punish."[8] But other societies proceed from the premise that payback on behalf of victims is a legitimate purpose of capital punishment, even when cultural conventions make it unacceptable to acknowledge the victim's desire for vengeance as motivation.[9] On this view, "the law has no choice but to satisfy the craving" for revenge if survivors would otherwise gratify their passion for vengeance outside the law.[10] On this view, critics of revenge are "apocalyptically underinformed" about how the impulse for vengeance has served the cause of justice in human history.[11] And on this view, societies sacrifice a great deal when they renounce "the age-old project of seeking the precise correction of commensurate wrongs."[12]

If the US Supreme Court's efforts to distance the death penalty from vengeance culminated in the *Furman* decision of 1972, the "return of revenge" to American capital punishment occurred in the late 1980s,[13] when the Court held that capital sentencing must be a "reasoned moral choice" which embodies individualized treatment,

5   Holmes, Oliver Wendell. 1909. *The Common Law*. Boston: Little, Brown.
6   Connolly, William E. 1995. *The Ethos of Pluralization*. Minneapolis, MN: University of Minnesota Press. p. 42.
7   Bacon, Francis. 1625. "Of Revenge." In Francis Bacon, *Essays, Civil and Moral*. Whitefish, MT: Kessinger Publishing, LLC (reprinted in 2010). pp. 1-10.
8   Blecker, Robert. 2013. *The Death of Punishment: Searching for Justice Among the Worst of the Worst*. New York: Palgrave Macmillan. p. 15.
9   Jacoby, Susan. 1983. *Wild Justice: The Evolution of Revenge*. New York: Harper & Row. p. 2.
10 Holmes, Oliver Wendell. 1909. *The Common Law*. Boston: Little, Brown. p. 45.
11 Miller, William Ian. 2006. *Eye for an Eye*. New York: Cambridge University Press. p. 206.
12 West, Robin. 2006. "Advance Praise for *Eye for an Eye*." In William Ian Miller, *Eye for an Eye*. New York: Cambridge University Press. back cover.
13 Sarat, Austin. 2001. *When the State Kills: Capital Punishment and the American Condition*. Princeton and Oxford: Princeton University Press. p. 33.

reliability, and "the retributive element of personal culpability."[14] The word "closure" first appeared in American media reports in the same year.[15] Prior to 1989, this term had not been used in death penalty stories in the American print media. By 2001 it had appeared more than 500 times, and hundreds of times more on television. Subsequently, the concept of closure, which has no official place in American legislation or legal proceedings, has become one of the leading memes in unofficial discussions of capital punishment. The frequent invocation of "closure" in discussions of American capital punishment and other death penalty systems reflects that fact that murder survivors routinely hear about the killer as long as the killer is alive. This motivates many survivors to speak about the need to end the capital process by carrying out an execution so that they can come to final terms with their grief.[16]

The Myth of Closure

But in many ways closure is a myth.[17] It is not what contemporary cultures of capital punishment say it is—absolute finality—because survivors of homicide are never "over and done with" their loss. It is not the sense that something bad has finally come to an end, because the suffering of survivors does not end. It is not a state of being at all. Rather, closure is best conceived as a process of "memory work" by which survivors construct meaningful narratives about a killing and

---

14   *Penry v. Lynaugh*, 1989, as explained in Bowers, William J., Benjamin D. Fleury-Steiner, and Michael E. Antonio. 2003. "The Capital Sentencing Decision: Guided Discretion, Reasoned Moral Judgment, or Legal Fiction." In James R. Acker, Robert M. Bohm, and Charles S. Lanier, eds., *America's Experiment with Capital Punishment: Reflections on the Past, Present, and Future of the Ultimate Penal Sanction*. Durham, NC: Carolina Academic Press. pp. 413-467, p. 415.

15   Zimring, Franklin E. 2003. *The Contradictions of American Capital Punishment*. New York: Oxford University Press, p. 60.

16   The rise of "closure" and the return of revenge in capital punishment systems in the United States, Asia, the Middle East, and elsewhere can also be seen in the evolution of Roger Hood's (1989) report to the United Nations Committee on Crime Prevention and Control, which was first published in 1989 as *The Death Penalty: A Worldwide Perspective*. New York: Oxford University Press. The original edition of this fine book did not include an index entry for "victims", nor did the subsequent two editions, which were published in 1996 and 2002. But editions four and five, which were co-authored by Carolyn Hoyle and published in 2008 and 2015, contain numerous entries under "victims" (18 lines under "victims" in the 2008 index and 26 lines in the 2015 index). *See* also, Turow, Scott. 2003. *Ultimate Punishment: A Lawyer's Reflections on Dealing with the Death Penalty*. New York: Farrar, Straus and Giroux. p. 51.

17   Madeira, Jody Lynee. 2012. *Killing McVeigh: The Death Penalty and the Myth of Closure*. New York and London: New York University Press.

how they have dealt with it, adjusted, and healed.[18] In this sense, the quest for closure is a process that continues for as long as the survivor is alive, and the myth of closure is a warning that survivors must not surround themselves with walls of "false comfort" about a finality that is illusory.[19] As Julian Barnes has observed:[20]

> And you do come out if it, that's true. After a year, after five. But you don't come out of it like a train coming out of a tunnel, bursting through the downs into sunshine and that swift, rattling descent to the Channel; you come out of it as a gull comes out of an oil-slick. You are tarred and feathered for life.

The ascendance of "closure" in different cultures of capital punishment illustrates the influence that changes in language can have on public attitudes toward the death penalty. When the death penalty is treated as a victim-service program, three effects frequently follow.[21] First, closure provides the inherently horrifying process of executing a person with a positive patina that citizens can endorse, for it is easier for most citizens to say "I support victims" than to say "I want vengeance." Second, when closure is a main aim of capital punishment, citizens do not need to worry about whether executions are an excessive use of power by and for the government, because the closure frame de-governmentalizes the death penalty by rendering the state a servant of society rather than its master. Third, in some societies the language of "closure" connects capital punishment to a history of community control of punishment. In the United States, closure has been linked to the bloody traditions of lynching and vigilantism.[22] In Japan, the language of closure can be linked to rhetorics of repentance and atonement that have been salient for centuries.[23] And in the People's Republic of China, the need to serve

---

18   Madeira, Jody Lynee. 2012. *Killing McVeigh: The Death Penalty and the Myth of Closure*. New York and London: New York University Press. p.xxv.

19   Madeira, Jody Lynee. 2012. *Killing McVeigh: The Death Penalty and the Myth of Closure*. New York and London: New York University Press. p. 274.

20   Barnes, Julian. 1990 (reissue). *Flaubert's Parrot*. New York: Vintage. p. 161.

21   Zimring, Franklin E. 2003. *The Contradictions of American Capital Punishment*. New York: Oxford University Press. p. 62.

22   Zimring, Franklin E. 2003. *The Contradictions of American Capital Punishment*. New York: Oxford University Press. p. 89.

23   Botsman, Daniel V. 2005. *Punishment and Power in the Making of Modern Japan*. Princeton and Oxford: Princeton University Press.

victims is a "standing requirement" in the capital process that helped drive a steep rise in death sentences and executions that started in the 1980s.[24] In these countries and others, closure and cognate terms assert the importance of serving victims, soften perceptions of capital punishment, and reinforce support for an institution whose other justifications (deterrence, retribution, moral proportion, and so on) have been debunked, discredited, debilitated, or disabled. In short, closure is a myth that performs important political functions in this age of abolition.[25] What David Garland observed about the death penalty in the United States has relevance in other societies as well:

> Capital penalties are made to operate as "tokens of esteem," allocating an enhanced status to selected constituents. And though victims' relatives sometimes resist the suggestion that they are honored by having the wrongdoer killed – just as they sometimes dispute the glib notion that a death sentence provides them with "closure"—these ideas have become elements of political common sense and now function as rationales for capital punishment.[26]

How "Serving Victims" Does a Disservice to Victims

Many critics of capital punishment see the impulse to use executions to "serve victims" as rooted in sentiments of retribution and revenge, but this may be "subtly off the mark."[27] As Scott Turow observes in an account of his own conversion from death penalty retentionist to agnostic to abolitionist, the justice that survivors of homicide seek is more like the justice embedded in the concept of restitution, for both rest on the premise that an offender ought not end up better off than his victim. To survivors of homicide it is "unconscionable

---

24   Fu, Hualing. 2016. "Between Deference and Defiance: Courts and Penal Populism in Chinese Capital Cases." In Bin Liang and Hong Lu, eds., *The Death Penalty in China: Policy, Practice, and Reform.* New York: Columbia University Press. pp. 274-299, p. 283.

25   Zimring, Franklin E. 2003. *The Contradictions of American Capital Punishment.* New York: Oxford University Press. p. 61.

26   Garland, David. 2010. *Peculiar Institution: America's Death Penalty in an Age of Abolition.* Cambridge, MA: The Belknap Press of Harvard University Press. p. 293.

27   Turow, Scott. 2003. *Ultimate Punishment: A Lawyer's Reflections on Dealing with the Death Penalty.* New York: Farrar, Straus and Giroux. p. 53.

and infuriating that after all the misery the murderer has wrought," he still gets to experience many of the small joys of life, making his life better than the survivor's.[28] But if the moral power of this desire for something like restitution cannot be denied, its implementation is problematic in three ways.

First, some proponents of capital punishment "hide behind victims" by identifying with their wrath, for this is a more comfortable expression of their own retributive feelings.[29] In countries such as the United States and Japan, this kind of hiding is especially striking among prosecutors, who claim they want to serve survivors when the latter's preferences align with their own but who ignore survivors' preferences when they point in a different direction. Prosecutors also fail to serve victims by neglecting to inform them that the jurisprudential requirements for capital cases will result in prolonged litigation before an execution can occur. Where "super due process" is required (as in the United States), or where the appellate process is slow (as in Japan), any sense of finality is forestalled for years or even decades.[30] This is how it should be, for in the administration of capital punishment, the quick is the enemy of the careful.

Second, decisions about the death penalty are too important to be made mainly by or for survivors. As Turow observes, "In a democracy, no minority, even those whose tragedies scour our hearts, should be empowered to speak for us all."[31] Enabling survivors to control the capital process makes no more sense than empowering the survivors of Pearl Harbor or Hiroshima to decide what memorials should be erected on the sites that were bombed. It is difficult to answer questions about "the proper role for citizens' preferences in structuring the governance of punishment in democratic systems."[32] While the preferences of citizens who are also victims and survivors are often relevant and sometimes important, they must not be allowed to trump other legitimate practical and jurisprudential considerations.

---

28 Ibid.
29 Turow, Scott., 2003. *Ultimate Punishment: A Lawyer's Reflections on Dealing with the Death Penalty.* New York: Farrar, Straus and Giroux. p. 55.
30 Ibid.
31 Turow, Scott., 2003. *Ultimate Punishment: A Lawyer's Reflections on Dealing with the Death Penalty.* New York: Farrar, Straus and Giroux. p. 56.
32 Zimring, Franklin E., Gordon Hawkins, and Sam Kamin., 2001. *Punishment and Democracy: Three Strikes and You're Out in California.* New York: Oxford University Press.

Third and most important, the desire to "serve victims" through capital punishment actually does a disservice to many victims, for the existence of capital punishment creates resentment among the many victims and survivors whose cases are *not* deemed capital. In the United States and Japan—the two developed democracies that retain capital punishment and continue to carry out executions on a regular basis—prosecutors seek a sentence of death in only a small fraction of all murder cases: in recent years, about one death sentence sought for every 100 to 200 homicides.[33] For many survivors and citizen-onlookers, the severity of a sentence is treated as a measure of how much the deceased victim is valued. In this context, a death sentence is taken as a "token of esteem" for the deceased.[34] But administering capital punishment carefully means there will be few executions, and the non-pursuit of capital sanctions in potentially capital cases fosters the perception that many homicide victims are under-esteemed. To prevent this perception, prosecutors would need to start seeking capital sentences at rates not seen since the Salem Witch Trials or Tokugawa Japan. Even the most ardent supporters of capital punishment do not want to go back to those futures.

The Future

When the death penalty is framed as a matter of serving victims and helping them achieve closure—as is often the case today—one effect is to legitimate a sanction that has become increasingly difficult to justify on other grounds. It is no coincidence that the rise of "serving victims" rhetoric in the United States and Japan corresponded with death penalty increases in both societies—in Japan after 2000,[35] and in the United States a decade earlier.[36] Framing capital punishment as a matter of meeting victims' needs also privatizes an inherently public act and thereby insulates it from scrutiny and criticism that it

---

33 Johnson, David T. 2011. "American Capital Punishment in Comparative Perspective" (a review essay on David Garland's *Peculiar Institution: America's Death Penalty in an Age of Abolition*). *Law & Social Inquiry* 36(4):1033–1061. p. 1052.

34 Simon, Jonathan, and Christina Spaulding. 1999. "Tokens of Our Esteem: Aggravating Factors in the Era of Deregulated Death Penalties." In Austin Sarat, ed., *The Killing State: Capital Punishment in Law, Politics, and Culture*. New York: Oxford University Press. pp. 81–113.

35 Johnson, David T., and Franklin E. Zimring. 2009. *The Next Frontier: National Development, Political Change, and the Death Penalty in Asia*. New York: Oxford University Press. p. 69.

36 Zimring, Franklin E. 2003. *The Contradictions of American Capital Punishment*. New York: Oxford University Press. p. 51.

would otherwise receive. The death penalty must be recognized for what it essentially is: a revenge.[37] And whatever else it is, vengeance is a violent emotion that insists on its own righteousness, not a principled justification.[38] It is therefore a dangerous emotion, not least to the person who feeds it. As Confucius is said to have cautioned 25 centuries ago, "Before you embark on a journey of revenge, dig two graves."

Since the late 1980s, the number of countries to abolish capital punishment has increased remarkably.[39] The main explanation for this surge in abolition is the emergence of a new "human rights dynamic" that "recognizes capital punishment as a denial of the universal human rights to life and to freedom from tortuous, cruel, and inhuman punishment".[40] Closure and its cousin "victim-service" are complementary ways of framing capital punishment that had little salience in postwar Europe while that continent was abolishing its death penalties.[41] The fate of capital punishment in those parts of the world that still retain it today will be shaped by the ongoing battle between two competing frames. Is the death penalty mainly a victim service program? Or is it fundamentally a matter of human rights?

37 Camus, Albert. 1960. *Resistance, Rebellion, and Death: Essays*. New York: Vintage International. p. 197.

38 Aladjem, Terry K. 2008. *The Culture of Vengeance and the Fate of American Justice*. New York: Cambridge University Press.

39 Hood, Roger, and Carolyn Hoyle. 2015. *The Death Penalty: A Worldwide Perspective* (5th ed.). New York: Oxford University Press.

40 Hood, Roger, and Carolyn Hoyle. 2009. "Abolishing the Death Penalty Worldwide: The Impact of a 'New Dynamic'." In Michael Tonry, ed., *Crime and Justice*. Chicago: University of Chicago Press, Vol. 38, No. 1, pp. 1-63. Available from https://www.upf.edu/mastercriminologia/_pdf/13_14/Lectura_30_octubre_-_Hood_and_Hoyle_2009.pdf. (accessed 24 August 2016).

41 Hammel, Andrew. 2010. *Ending the Death Penalty: The European Experience in Global Perspective*. New York: Palgrave Macmillan.

Gas Chamber, The Omega Suites
©Lucinda Devlin

"The majority of the world's countries are now abolitionist for all crimes. Most of those that retain the death penalty do not actually use it, and the minority of states that still execute people frequently do so in violation of prohibitions and restrictions set out under international law."

— *Salil Shetty*

CHAPTER 2
THE CONVICTED AS VICTIMS?

2.1
WRONGFUL CONVICTIONS

2.2
DISCRIMINATION AND MENTAL
HEALTH ISSUES

2.3
OTHER CASES OF DEATH PENALTY
AGAINST INTERNATIONAL LAW

2.1 Wrongful Convictions

VICTIMS OF WRONGFUL CONVICTION IN RETENTIONIST NATIONS

Carolyn Hoyle[1]

Introduction

Over three decades ago, in 1985, the UN published its influential Declaration of Basic Principles of Justice for Victims of Crime and Abuse of Power. Wrongful convictions caused by the deliberate or inadvertent perversion of the criminal process, should fit squarely within the declaration's terms, for many such cases arise directly from the abuse of state power. However the declaration was silent on this population of victims. Indeed, throughout, victims of wrongful convictions have struggled to find a collective voice and have not, in the main, found representation among politicians and policy makers. Regardless of jurisdiction, they have received little official support and have not been subject to the same rigorous academic scrutiny as crime victims. While this is unfortunate for all of those who are wrongfully convicted, it is particularly tragic for people who are imprisoned under sentence of death and for those who are subsequently executed following a wrongful conviction.

Lack of interest and the failure of states to take responsibility for the harms caused by wrongful convictions cannot be understood by reference to an absence of injury. While physical injuries to crime victims are readily apparent, research on victims of wrongful conviction has conclusively demonstrated that they suffer similar forms and levels of psychological harm as crime victims, and, of course, this is aggravated in respect to those under sentence of death. The wrongly

---

1   Director of the Centre for Criminology, University of Oxford, United Kingdom. Part of this article draws on material presented in Roger Hood and Carolyn Hoyle. 2015. *The Death Penalty: A Worldwide Perspective*, Oxford: Oxford University Press. I gratefully acknowledge my co-author, Roger Hood.

convicted "often must deal with long-term personality change, post-traumatic stress and other psychiatric disorders, and the difficulties of coping with stigma, grief and loss."[2] Indeed, the experiences of the wrongfully convicted have been likened to those of victims of torture.[3] Imprisonment can create dependence on institutional structures. To cope with it, some prisoners turn to aggression, while others become isolated, withdrawn, and depressed. "Wrongful incarceration compounds these typical effects of imprisonment in ways that are only beginning to be understood,"[4] with violence playing a "part of daily existence inside ... to ensure their survival in the hostile prison environment" and most contemplating suicide during their incarceration.[5]

While effects such as PTSD are similar to the experiences of victims of serious crime, those who have been wrongfully convicted have been harmed by the state. It is the state that has failed them and so the state should have an obligation not only to make amends, which states so often fail to do, but also to try to prevent these harms in the first place. This article will explore the protections in place to guard against wrongful conviction in countries that retain the death penalty. It will present evidence that in all countries that administer capital punishment—even those with well-resourced criminal justice systems—these protections can, and do, fail, and innocent men and women are wrongfully convicted.

International Protections against wrongful conviction

Acquittal or later exoneration of the innocent is the main test of the effectiveness of procedural safeguards. While criminal justice agents and witnesses will err, and some self-interested people will

---

2   R. J. Norris. 2012. "Assessing compensation statutes for the wrongly convicted." *Criminal Justice Policy Review* 23:352-374:p. 355.

3   H. Weigand. 2009. "Building a life: The wrongfully convicted and exonerated." *Public Interest Law Journal* 18:427; Westervelt, S. D. & Cook, K. J. 2009. "Framing innocents: The wrongly convicted as victims of state harm." *Crime, Law, and Social Change* 53:259–275.

4   M. C. Delaney, K. A. Findley and S. Sullivan. 2010. "Exonerees' hardships after Freedom." *Wisconsin Lawyer* 83:18.

5   K. Campbell and M. Denov. 2004. "The burden of innocence: Coping with a wrongful imprisonment." *Canadian Journal of Criminology and Criminal Justice* 46:139-164:pp. 145-49.

lie, a fair and safe criminal justice system should have in place robust procedural safeguards to protect suspects and defendants from human fallibility, from deception, and from systemic faults in the criminal justice process.

Most academic studies of wrongful conviction have drawn data from the US, but there is good reason to believe that their findings have applicability beyond that jurisdiction. They identify the same set of likely sources: eyewitness misidentification, false confessions, perjured testimony, forensic error, tunnel vision, prosecutorial misconduct, and ineffective defence.[6] Research suggests that capital exonerations are more likely in cases where investigations are hurried, where police officers presume the suspect had "criminal proclivities" and in sensational cases.[7] Errors are more likely to occur in the investigative phases and these errors snowball, making it less likely that they will be reversed. Of course, the main protection against police and prosecution malpractice or against fallible forensic evidence is a good legal defence. However, even in the US, this is far from guaranteed in capital cases, with one study suggesting that ineffective defence was the "biggest contributing factor" to wrongful conviction in capital cases over a 23-year period.[8]

An innovative study by Jon Gould and his colleagues of 460 cases where the defendant had been indicted for a violent felony between 1980 and 2012, 260 of which had been exonerated at or after conviction and 200 ("near misses") who had been acquitted or had charges dismissed before conviction on the basis of factual innocence, found that 10 factors help explain why an innocent defendant, once indicted, ends up erroneously convicted rather than released:[9]

> ... the age and criminal history of the defendant, the punitiveness of the state, *Brady* violations [where the prosecution

---

6   *See, for example,* J. B. Gould and R. A. Leo. 2011. "One hundred years later: Wrongful convictions after a century of research." *Journal of Criminal Law and Criminology* 100(3):825-868:p. 838.

7   Ibid. p. 861.

8   J. S., Liebman, J. Fagan, V. West, & J. Lloyd. 2000. "Capital attrition: Error rates in capital cases, 1973-1995." *Texas Law Review* 78:1839-1865.

9   Jon. B. Gould, Julia Carrano, Richard Leo, and Joseph Young. December 2012. *Predicting Erroneous Convictions: A Social Science Approach to Miscarriages of Justice.* Report submitted to US Department of Justice. Available from https://www.ncjrs.gov/pdffiles1/nij/grants/241389.pdf. (accessed 24 August 2016).

withheld exculpatory evidence], forensic error, a weak defense and prosecution case, a family defence witness, an inadvertent misidentification, and lying by a non-eyewitness.

These factors were exacerbated by "tunnel vision," which prevented the system from correcting the error. [10]

Clearly, from the initial crime report to the final appeal against conviction, rigorous and robust safeguards need to be in place so that only the guilty are convicted, and only those deserving of the highest penalty get it. If due process safeguards—both pre and post-trial—work as they should, innocent men and women should not be wrongly convicted and sentenced to death, and if they are, they should not be executed. It is important, therefore, to consider what protections *should* be in place, under international law, in those countries that retain the death penalty, and whether they are effective.

Article 14 of the International Covenant on Civil and Political Rights (ICCPR 1966), which came into force in 1976, and has been ratified by member states with only a few exceptions, mandates that criminal sanctions can only be imposed against an individual who has been subject to due process of law which guarantees a presumption of innocence, a fair opportunity to answer the charges brought against him or her before a duly constituted court, and the assistance of a well-qualified defence counsel. In the context of capital punishment, because execution is irrevocable, due process protections are even more significant, as without them, use of the death penalty contravenes Article 6(1) of the ICCPR, which states that "No one shall be arbitrarily deprived of his life."

In order to make clear what international standards specifically entailed as far as those facing the death penalty were concerned, the Economic and Social Council (ECOSOC) in 1984 promulgated safeguards guaranteeing their rights. Under human rights law, all states that retain the death penalty are required to put these safeguards into practice.

Safeguard No. 4 is aimed at avoiding any danger that an innocent person could be sentenced to death by providing that: "Capital

---

10   Ibid at iii.

punishment may be imposed only when the guilt of the person charged is based on clear and convincing evidence *leaving no room for an alternative explanation* of the facts" (my emphasis). Safeguard No. 5, which mentions the "final judgment", makes it clear that the safety of the conviction must be questioned throughout the process right up to appeal and clemency proceedings and that anyone suspected or charged with a crime for which capital punishment may be imposed should have adequate legal assistance at all stages of the proceedings. In 1989 ECOSOC, strengthened this safeguard by emphasising that special protection should be provided "by allowing time and facilities for the preparation of their defence, including the adequate assistance of counsel at every stage of the proceedings, above and beyond the protection afforded in non-capital cases" [my emphasis]. Furthermore, the safeguards were strengthened in 1996 when retentionist countries were reminded that they should bear in mind various basic principles and standard minimum rules aimed at reinforcing the safeguards[11] to ensure that all fair trial guarantees contained in Article 14 of the ICCPR were put into practice.

Since then UN documents have reiterated these messages, and similar statements have been made by the European Court of Human Rights (e.g., Öcalan v Turkey[12] and the Inter-American Court of Human Rights (e.g., *Ramirez v Guatemala).*[13] And in 2007, the Human Rights Committee adopted its general comment No. 32 on Article 14 which made clear that the imposition of a death penalty following a trial in which the provisions of Article 14 have not been respected con-stitutes a violation of the right to life. Hence, where, for whatever reason, jurisdictions cannot ensure respect for fair trials they should impose a moratorium on executions.

Not surprisingly, when retentionist countries have been asked peri-odically through the United Nations Quinquennial Surveys whether they abide by the fourth and fifth safeguards nearly all have said that they do comply, for no country would blatantly admit that it executed

---

11   "Basic Principles on the Independence of the Judiciary"; "Basic Principles on the Role of
     Lawyers"; "Guidelines on the Role of Prosecutors"; "Body of Principles for the Protection of All
     Persons under Any Form of Detention or Imprisonment"; and "Standard Minimum Rules for the
     Treatment of Prisoners" (Resolution 1996/15[3] and [4]).
12   ECHR 2005 IV, 166.
13   June 20 2005, 79.

persons who could have been innocent. However, as the conclusion to the UN Secretary-General's Eighth Quinquennial report in 2010 made clear: "It appears to be beyond dispute that innocent people are still sentenced to death."[14]

Indeed, the assurances of retentionist jurisdictions cannot be taken at face value in some countries, for there may be a wide gap between the aspirations of procedural law and the actual practices of a criminal justice system, as is evident in most Asian countries, according to various authoritative reports from human rights groups such as Amnesty International and Penal Reform International, as well as the UN. Of course, this is even more likely to be the case in those countries which have never responded to the United Nations' requests for information and for whom the administration of the death penalty is a state secret, such as North Korea or Vietnam.

One of the most persuasive arguments against the death penalty among those unsympathetic to principled objections is that no safeguards can be devised that can absolutely rule out the incidence of wrongful conviction and execution. Annual Reports from Amnesty International provide proof. The 2015 report recorded 112 exonerations of death row prisoners in nine countries in 2014: Bangladesh (4), China (2), Jordan (1), Nigeria (32), Sudan (4), Tanzania (59), USA (7), Viet Nam (2) and Zimbabwe (1). Of course these are but a proportion of those who may be wrongfully convicted but who find no post-conviction relief, of which a majority are likely to be found on the death rows of countries with poor human rights standards. The release of prisoners from death row on the grounds of innocence generated debates about the fallibility of criminal justice and the risks of executing innocent people "in several countries, including countries where support for capital punishment has traditionally been strong, such as China, Japan, Vietnam and the USA."[15]

While some in the West might not be surprised by miscarriages of justice in Vietnam, for example, there is, understandably, concern that America cannot protect its citizens from wrongful convictions

---

14   United Nations Economic and Social Council (ECOSOC). *Capital punishment and implementation of the safeguards guaranteeing protection of the rights of those facing the death penalty.* Report of the Secretary General, E2010/10.

15   Amnesty International. 2015. *Death Sentences and Executions 2014.* ACT 50/001/2015. pp. 6-7.

in cases that might result in capital punishment. The US has developed a death penalty jurisprudence that recognizes that "death is different" and therefore worthy of "super due-process."[16] From the decision to prosecute right through to the right to appeal and the opportunities for clemency or pardon, capital defendants have different experiences to those facing life imprisonment or other lesser sentences. Despite these enhanced protections within the most advanced retentionist democracy in the world, things can – and do - go wrong. America's super due process does not prevent innocent persons being sentenced to death or executed. The prospects therefore must be poor for suspects and defendants in developed countries like Japan, which do not provide such procedural safeguards, or in countries with poor human rights records such as North Korea. Before considering such countries, we turn to the evidence of wrongful convictions in America.

Wrongful convictions in America

Brandon Garrett, an expert in wrongful convictions in the US, recently wrote: "If a majority of the Supreme Court justices eventually strike down the death penalty as unconstitutional, Henry Lee McCollum may be an important reason why."[17] McCollum is one of a growing number of people to have been released from the death rows of retentionist states in America after DNA testing of evidence that remained hidden for decades finally exonerated them. More than 1,600 wrongfully convicted persons have been released in the US in the past 25 years, with over 156 of those having been released from a death sentence.[18] McCollum, like others before him, was a vulnerable man—being both young and mentally disabled— and he had confessed to a serious crime that he had not committed. Procedural hurdles should have halted his conviction, but they did not. Such exonerations reveal a failure of criminal procedure, with

---

16 This jurisprudence began with Furman v. Georgia, 408, US 238 (1972) and has since been developed. *See further*, J. Abramson. 2004. "Death-is-Different Jurisprudence and the Role of the Capital Jury." *Ohio State Journal of Criminal Law* 2:117: at note 1.

17 Brandon Garrett. *Coerced confessions and jailhouse snitches: why the death penalty is so flawed.* Available from *http://theconversation.com/coerced-confessions-and-jailhouse-snitches-why-the-death-penalty-is-so-flawed-43147.* (accessed 20 August 2015).

18 *See* Death Penalty Information Center Database on Exonerations. Available from http://www.deathpenaltyinfo.org/innocence-and-death-penalty. (accessed 24 August 2016).

police, prosecutors, expert witnesses, judges, and juries at times bearing some responsibility.[19]

Of course, this is nothing new. In 2009, two brothers, Thomas and Meeks Griffin, were pardoned by the state of South Carolina nearly 100 years after they were executed for murder.[20] And in December 2015 a judge vacated the conviction of George Stinney Jr., a 14-year old African American, executed in 1944 in South Carolina, after a trial characterized by various errors, racism, and a lack of an adequate defence. As in most cases, Stinney Jr. was not the only victim of this wrongful conviction. His family, located deep in the Jim Crow South, fled their home for fear of repercussions following his conviction and execution.[21] As in many such cases, the vicarious trauma of wrongful conviction creates further "victims."

Until recently, exonerations of wrongfully convicted defendants were regarded as aberrations, and the fact that they had been discovered was taken as reassurance that the system was able to correct its errors. What has changed is that "these once-rare events have become disturbingly commonplace."[22] The full scale of "serious reversible error" found in death penalty convictions in the United States was first revealed in 2000 by Professor James Liebman and colleagues. Their study, of every capital conviction and appeal between 1973 and 1995, found that in 68% of cases that had reached the final third stage of state and federal appeal during this period (a process that on average took nine years), an error had been found sufficient to overturn the original capital conviction. The most common causes of these errors, accounting for 76% of the cases, were found to be: "egregiously incompetent defence lawyers," police and prosecutorial misconduct, and faulty instructions to jurors. Furthermore, 82% of those who had their

---

19 S. Bright. 2004. "Why the United States will join the rest of the world in abandoning capital punishment." In H. Bedau and P. Cassell, eds. *Debating the Death Penalty*. New York: Oxford University Press. p. 153.

20 http://www.nbcnews.com/id/33310170/ns/us_news-crime_and_courts/t/sc-men-executed-get-state-pardon/#.Uzvk461dXtE. (accessed 24 August 2016).

21 Lindsey Beaver, *The Washington Post*, December 18, 2014.

22 Samuel R. Gross, Kristen Jacoby, Daniel J. Matheson, Nicholas Montgomery, and Sujata Patil. 2005. "Exonerations in the United States 1989 through 2003." *Journal of Criminal Law and Criminology* 95:523–560:p. 523. Much of the evidence of wrongful convictions in the US has come from the work of innocence projects, available from http://www.innocenceproject.org/. (accessed 24 August 2016).

death sentences overturned were not subsequently sentenced to death on a retrial, and 7% were found to be innocent of the capital crime. Thus, only 11% of those originally sentenced to death were judged to deserve such a sentence when the errors of the original trial were corrected.[23] These data alone provide sufficient evidence that the checks and balances discussed above failed in the majority of cases in the US during this time. Professor Gross and colleagues found, from a study of all 340 exonerations in the United States from 1989 to 2003, that exonerations from death row are more than 25 times more frequent than exonerations of other prisoners convicted of murder, and more than 100 times more frequent than for all imprisoned felons.[24]

The conservative response to all this evidence has been perhaps predictable, namely that it merely proves how thorough the American appeal process is in ensuring that innocent persons are not executed.[25] It has been claimed that many whose convictions are reversed are only "legally" or "technically" innocent, rather than factually innocent; and that the miniscule risk of executing an innocent is far outweighed by the utilitarian benefits of the death penalty, namely retribution and deterrence.[26] However, a recent study by Gross and colleagues of all 7,482 defendants sentenced to death in the US between January 1973 and December 2004 suggests that about 4.1% were factually innocent: "With an error rate at trial of over 4% it is all but certain that several of the 1,320 defendants executed since 1977 were innocent."[27]

The fact of the matter is that many of the cases where certain innocence has been established have come to light not through the thoroughness of the state's review processes, but through the vagaries of luck, through confessions of other criminals, by the

---

23 James S. Liebman, Jeffrey Fagan, Valerie West, and Jonathan Lloyd. 2000. "Capital Attrition: Error Rates in Capital Cases, 1973–1995." *Texas Law Review* 78:1771–1803.

24 Samuel R. Gross, Kristen Jacoby, Daniel J. Matheson, Nicholas Montgomery, and Sujata Patil. 2005. "Exonerations in the United States 1989 through 2003." *Journal of Criminal Law and Criminology* 95: 523–560: pp. 524, 527–529, and 552.

25 Paul Cassell. 2000. Cited in Gross et al, ibid. at pp. 1.

26 Margaret Griffey and Laurence E. Rothenberg. 2006. "The Death Penalty in the United States." In *The Death Penalty in the OSCE Area, Background Paper.* Warsaw, Poland: OSCE. pp. 41–42.

27 Samuel R. Gross, Barbara O'Brien, Chen Hu and Edward H. Kennedy. 2014. "Rate of false conviction of criminal defendants who are sentenced to death." *PNAS* 111 (20):7230-7235. Available from http://www.pnas.org/content/111/20/7230.full.pdf. (accessed 24 August 2016).

hard effort of campaigners outside the official criminal justice system,[28] and by the now widespread availability of genetic fingerprint DNA testing.[29]

A comprehensive study by Brandon Garrett of all 200 persons who had by early 2007 been exonerated in the US through the use of DNA evidence, which included 14 persons who had been sentenced to death, showed conclusively "the inability of appeal courts to effectively review claims relating to the central unreliable and false evidence supporting these convictions". In the 14 capital cases the evidence had been "surprisingly weak."[30] One of the most remarkable cases of false confession was that of Earl Washington, who had come within nine days of execution before DNA cleared him of any involvement in the murder. But because he had confessed it was not until seven years later that he was released from prison when the DNA was shown to match another person.[31] As Liebman has put it, "Suddenly and starkly, DNA reveals us and our institutions to be what they strive to escape notice for being: inherently but often unknowably—and thus—incurably—flawed, unreliable and untrustworthy."[32]

Over the past decade, various states—including California, Florida, Illinois, Louisiana, Oklahoma, Pennsylvania, and Texas, among others—have established Criminal Justice Reform Commissions to investigate the causes and remedies of wrongful convictions. In most states, they have led to reforms relating to eyewitness and forensic evidence and to reducing the prevalence of false confessions (the 30-member North Carolina Actual Innocence Commission is considered to be a national model for effectiveness and reform).[33] Nevertheless, recent reports by the American Bar Association provide evidence that the death penalty in states such as Texas, Kentucky and

28 M. Radelet and H. A. Bedau. 1998. "The Execution of the Innocent." *Law and Contemporary Problems* 61:105–217:p. 118. Also, S. Gross. 1998. "Lost Lives: Miscarriages of Justice in Capital Cases." *Law and Contemporary Problems* 61:125–152.

29 Robert Weisberg. 2005. 'The Death Penalty Meets Social Science: Deterrence and Jury Behavior under New Scrutiny." *Annual Review of Law and Social Science* 1:151–170:p. 170.

30 Brandon L. Garrett. 2011. *Convicting the Innocent: Where Criminal Prosecutions Go Wrong.* Boston: Harvard University Press.; See also Jeffrey L. Kirchmeier. 2006. "Dead Innocent: The Death Penalty Abolitionist Search for a Wrongful Execution." *Tulsa Law Review* 42:403–435.

31 Personal communication from Professor Brandon Garrett.

32 James S. Liebman. 2002. "The New Death Penalty Debate: What's DNA got to do with it?" *Columbia Human Rights Law Review* 33:527–552:p. 547.

33 http://www.innocenceproject.org/Content/Criminal_Justice_Reform_Commissions_Case_Studies.php. (accessed 24 August 2016).

Missouri still lacks adequate protections to prevent innocent persons from being sentenced to death and executed.[34] It may seem strange that in a country such as America, with its lengthy and multi-layered appeals process, innocent people could still be executed, especially as the decision of the Supreme Court in *Herrera v Collins*[35] in effect confirmed that the execution of an innocent person would be unconstitutional. However, the "daunting standard of proof" is such that review is "extraordinarily rare."[36]

The dramatic decline in death sentences and executions in 2015 suggests that the US could move away from capital punishment in the next few years, eliminating the risk of innocent people being executed, though not sentenced to life without the prospect of parole. However, there is little prospect of abolition in Iran, Saudi Arabia, North Korea and other frequent-executing states, and it is in such countries that due process protections are most inadequate.

Evidence of wrongful convictions around the retentionist world

The last decade has provided evidence of wrongful convictions from various countries around the world, including Belize, China, Japan, Malawi, Malaysia, Pakistan, Papua New Guinea, the Philippines, and Trinidad and Tobago. One of the most famous cases was that of Iwao Hakamada who, in March 2014, became only the fifth man to be freed from death row in Japan after spending 47 years on death row, in solitary confinement, for the murders of two children and their parents. Hakamada had provided a confession after 20 days of interrogation, with no lawyer present, during which he was tortured. Decades later, following the discovery of new DNA evidence and proof that prosecutors had fabricated the case against him, Hakamada, an old and ailing man, was released with no apology or official

---

34 American Bar Association. *The Texas Death Penalty Assessment Reports.* Available from http://www. americanbar.org/groups/committees/death_penalty_representation/resources/dp-policy.html. (accessed 24 August 2016).

35 *Herrera v Collins*, 506 US 390 (1993).

36 Carol Steiker and Jordan Steiker. 2009. "Report to the ALI Concerning Capital Punishment." Annex to *Report of the Council to the Membership of The American Law Institute On the Matter of the Death Penalty.* New York: American Law Institute. p. 17.

state acknowledgement of accountability.[37] A recent report by the London-based Death Penalty Project describes the exoneration of the other four Japanese men who served between 28 and 33 years in solitary confinement. Like Hakamada, and many other wrongfully convicted persons around the world, Menda, Saitagawa, Matsuyama, and Shimada were all convicted following long and brutal interrogations that produced false confessions.[38]

In a dramatic gesture, President Ma Ying-jeou of Taiwan apologised in 2011 to the mother of Chiang Kuo-ching, a soldier who had been wrongly executed in 1997 for the rape and murder of a 5-year-old girl. The president pardoned Chiang and offered his mother reparation after another man had confessed to the crime. Other death row exonerations, after trials that relied on false confessions following torture, have resulted in the Taiwanese government paying compensation to wrongfully convicted people and campaigners calling for abolition.[39] Despite this, there have been more than 30 executions in Taiwan since these cases came to light in 2011.

Evidence is likely to be the most dubious where the prosecution relies on forced confessions obtained through torture. Over the past few years, there have been reports of this happening in Afghanistan, Algeria, Bahrain, Belarus, China, Iran, Iraq, North Korea, the Palestinian Authority, Saudi Arabia, Taiwan, and Yemen.[40] Amnesty International cites 90 cases of death row inmates who had been convicted of terrorism or other crimes on the basis of "forced confessions"; at least 14 were executed during 2013.[41]

Some of the more notorious wrongful convictions in China have followed pre-trial treatment described by defendants as torture. Nie

---

37 Terence McCoy, "Japan frees world's longest serving death row inmate after more than 45 years," *Washington Post Morning Mix,* March 27, 2014.

38 The Death Penalty Project. 2014. *The Inevitability of Error: The administration of justice in death penalty cases.* p. 8.

39 "Execution error raises new question about death penalty," *The China Post* , September 2, 2011; Dennis Engbarth, "Wrongful execution reopens death penalty debate", available from http://www.ipsnews.net/2011/02/taiwan-wrongful-execution-reopens-death-penalty-debate/ (accessed 24 August 2016); "Taiwan compensates trio after 11 years on death row," *Channel News Asia, Global Post.*

40 Amnesty International. 2015. p. 7. *See further* Hood and Hoyle. *The Death Penalty: A worldwide perspective,* Oxford: Oxford University Press. ch. 7.

41 Amnesty International. 2014. *Death Sentences and Executions in 2013.* pp. 32-36; Amnesty International. 2013. *Death Sentences and Executions in 2012.* p. 25.

Shubin was wrongfully executed in 1995 for the rape and murder of a local woman; a crime that another man later confessed to. Similarly, She Xianglin and Teng Xingshan, convicted for murdering their wives, were shown to be innocent when their wives reappeared several years later; too late for Teng Xingshan who had already executed.[42] Zhao Zuohai was tortured and forced to confess to the murder of a fellow peasant farmer. His death sentence was commuted to a 29-year prison sentence but after serving 11 years his "victim" returned to the village alive and well. Unfortunately for Zuohai, his wife had left him, married another man and given up his two children for adoption. He claims that while in prison he confessed to this "crime" nine times following severe beatings.[43]

In China, "diverse forms of torture and inhumane treatment, to extract information from the accused" create "a high risk that innocent people will be convicted on the basis of false confessions extracted by torture."[44] Pressures on police departments to solve crimes in a timely fashion and quotas for the resolution of crimes, along with a belief among police "that torture is the most efficient method to get a confession"[45] further reinforce the police's widespread use of torture.[46] This is exacerbated by the widespread use of incompetent counsel in a country with a very limited number of qualified lawyers, widespread misuse of evidence when police circumvent recent reforms introducing procedural safeguards, and the inclusion of illegally obtained evidence at trial. The Supreme People's Court review of death sentences remains rudimentary and lacking in transparency, increasing the difficulty of discovering and correcting misjudged cases. Indeed, the vice president of the Supreme People's Court of China recently alluded to the failure to test for DNA evidence and the use of illegally obtained evidence in cases.[47]

---

42   Amnesty International Asia Pacific Office. 2006. *China: The Death Penalty, A Failure of Justice.*

43   Clifford Coonan, "Zhao Zuohai: Beaten, Framed and Jailed for a Murder that Never Happened," *The Independent*, May 14, 2010. Available from http://www.independent.co.uk/news/world/asia/zhao-zuohai-beaten-framed-and-jailed-for-a-murder-that-never-happened-1973042.html. (accessed 24 August 2016).

44   Na Jiang. 2013. "A comparison of wrongful convictions in death penalty cases between China and the United States." *International Journal of Law, Crime and Justice* 41:144-166:p.145.

45   Wu Xiaofeng. 2011. "An analysis of wrongful convictions in China." *Oklahoma City University Law Review* 36(2):451-469:p. 455.

46   Na Jiang, (n 44) 146.

47   *See* Børge Bakken. 2013. "Capital Punishment Reform, Public Opinion, and Penal Elitism in the People's Republic of China." In Hood and Deva, eds. *Confronting Capital Punishment in Asia: Human Rights, Politics and Public Opinion*. Oxford: Oxford University Press. pp. 189-190, 199.

A report to the Human Rights Council in 2013 recorded breaches of fair trial guarantees in the administration of the death penalty in relation to Cuba, Japan, Iraq, Saudi Arabia, Afghanistan, Bangladesh, Gambia, Saint Kitts and Nevis, and North Korea.[48] The 2015 report of the Secretary-General provided evidence of due process breaches in Cuba, Ethiopia, Iran, Iraq, Japan, Uganda, and the United States.[49] Amnesty International found that in the *majority of countries* where people were sentenced to death or executed in 2014 the death penalty was imposed after proceedings that failed to meet international fair trial standards, raising particular concerns in relation to court proceedings in Afghanistan, Bahrain, Bangladesh, China, Egypt, Iran, Iraq, North Korea, Pakistan, Saudi Arabia and Sri Lanka, adding that:

> In several countries … sentences were based on "confessions" that may have been extracted through torture or other ill-treatment. In Iran some of these "confessions" were broadcast on television before the trial took place, further breaching the defendants' right to presumption of innocence.[50]

There is also concern that in some countries where there is civil conflict death sentences have been imposed following trials "in absentia" without adequate legal safeguards under Articles 6 and 14 of the ICCPR. This was the case in 2014 in Algeria, Jordan, Lebanon, Libya, and the Palestinian Authority. Of equal concern is the sentencing of large groups of individuals in mass trials, as has been seen recently in Egypt. These cases are characterised by lack of timely access to legal representation and lack of respect for the presumption of innocence, with many such trials held in absentia.

In Vietnam, where—like China—the death penalty remains a state secret, Amnesty International reports that trials fall short of international standards of fairness, with considerable risk of wrongful convictions and executions. For example, in 2014 the Supreme Court declared Nguyen Thanh Chan innocent of a 2004 murder to which

---

48   UN Human Rights Council (HRC). July 2013. *The Question of the Death Penalty: Report of the Secretary-General.* A/HRC/24/18. pp. 10–11.

49   UN Economic and Social Council. "Capital punishment and implementation of the safeguards guaranteeing protection of the rights of those facing the death penalty." Report of the Secretary-General, E/2015/49.

50   Amnesty International. 2015. *Death Sentences and Executions 2014.* ACT 50/001/2015.

another man had confessed in October 2013 and authorized the stay of execution of Ho Duy Hai one day before it was due to go ahead because of doubts surrounding his conviction.[51]

In some countries, the presumption of innocence is clearly not held in high regard. The International Federation for Human Rights (FIDH) has reported that in many courts in Iran "the judge plays the role of the interrogator, prosecutor and judge all at the same time…. In the overwhelming majority of criminal and political cases, judges do not presume that defendants are innocent until proven guilty. The guiding principle seems to be the other way round."[52] Indeed, in May 2013, Iran passed its new Islamic Penal Code which specifically rejects the principle of presumption of innocence in regard to *moharebeh* (corruption on earth), theft, and accusation of fornication or sodomy *(Art. 121)*.[53] Elsewhere, the UN Human Rights Committee has concluded that the appearance of defendants handcuffed and in steel cages in Belarus and the use of the term "criminal" by state officials before a finding of guilt was a clear breach of the right to a fair trial.[54]

Fair trials require that defendants and their representatives have sufficient time and facilities for the preparation of their defences. Contrary to this, some countries, such as Pakistan and Bangladesh, have enacted, sometimes by decree or under military law, legislation aimed at speeding up the trial process and expediting all processes of post-trial review, making it difficult to prepare an adequate defence. In 2013 a Bangladesh court sentenced 152 people to death for offences committed during the 2009 uprising following a mass trial involving 846 defendants during which the accused had little or no access to lawyers.[55]

The importance of the absolute right to effective counsel with adequate legal aid has been stressed repeatedly by the UN Human Rights Counsel, yet various reports from human rights bodies demonstrate the lack of effective counsel in Afghanistan, Iran, Japan, Nigeria, Saudi

---

51 Amnesty International. 2015. p. 40.

52 FIDH. 2009. *Iran/Death Penalty: A state Terror Policy.* p. 26.

53 FIDH. June 2013. *Iran/Death Penalty: A State Terror Policy*, special edition for the 5th World Congress against the death penalty. p. 3.

54 See, *Vladislav Kovalev et al v Belarus*, Communication No. 2120/2011 (14 December 2012). UN doc CCPR/C/106?D/2120/20120.

55 "Dhaka sends 152 soldiers to the gallows for 2009 mutiny," *The Pioneer*, November 6, 2013.

Arabia, and South Sudan. But the situation can be equally dire in India, despite it being a reasonably wealthy democracy. Recent research by the National Law University Delhi, based on 400 interviews with people on death rows across India, shows that most death-sentenced prisoners are from "low" castes, dalits and minorities. They are illiterate and poor, and they have little or no access to knowledge about rights or remedies, and no real access to lawyers. Most were convicted on the basis of recoveries arising out of confessions in a police station and over 80% of them stated that they were tortured.[56]

Miscarriages of justice are more likely when there are "crackdowns" on crime, especially terrorist offences. Overzealous police may be more inclined to misinterpret or even fabricate evidence or to extract confessions by torture or other illegitimate methods when the world is waiting for a result. This will be exacerbated by poor legal defence and by an over-readiness of courts to convict. Thus, in China during the "strike hard campaigns" of 1997 and 1998 there were several reports of wrongful convictions, resulting from the "swift and severe punishment" that is the leitmotif of the Yanda policy.[57] It is therefore of concern that 2014 saw the death penalty being used in response to real or perceived threats to state security in various countries, not least Egypt. Pakistan ended a six-year moratorium on capital punishment after the terrorist attack on a school in Peshawar and executed more than 300 in the 12 months following. China instigated another "strike hard" campaign in response to terrorism in the Xinjiang Uighur Autonomous Region. In the short period between June and August 2014, 21 people were executed in this region in relation to terrorist attacks.[58]

Exonerations from death row in the US occur during the lengthy appeals process, but appeal to a higher court is not guaranteed in all retentionist jurisdictions. In Iran, where annual official executions have been rising considerably over the past decade, approximately half of the executions are for drug-related crimes, yet under Article 32 of the Anti-Narcotics Law, those sentenced to death for drug-related

---

56 Discussions with Project Team in December 2015 at NLU Delhi, *see also* http://www.deathpenaltyindia.com/media/most-death-row-convicts-are-poor/. (accesssed 24 August 2016).

57 Susan Trevaskes. 2012. *The Death Penalty in Contemporary China.* New York: Palgrave Macmillan. p. 18.

58 Amnesty International. 2015. p. 11.

offences do not have the right to appeal. And Iran's Revolutionary Courts appear not to follow any recognizable due process. Defendants need sufficient time and other resources for appeals, and yet in Equatorial Guinea, four political opponents of the president were sentenced to death by a military court in April 2010 and then executed in secret within one hour. And in April 2014 the UN reported that a man had been executed by firing squad for killing an elder in Somalia just nine days after the crime had been committed. Clearly, there may have been innocents among these, but they were unable to secure any post-conviction relief.

This review of the evidence provided by human rights groups and academics suggests that no retentionist country fully abides by the safeguards established by the United Nations and the ICCPR. Rather than occasional aberrations in otherwise rigorous criminal justice systems, wrongful convictions are an inevitable part of the justice landscape, even in countries that try hard to meet international standards, and as such demonstrate how easy it is for abuses of human rights to occur when capital punishment is on the statute book and put into effect.

Conclusion

The exoneration of innocent people who have spent time on the death rows of retentionist nations provides succour to the worldwide abolitionist movement. Nothing disturbs the public's sense of injustice and recognition of the frailties and human mistakes endemic in death penalty administration more than unequivocal proof of innocence. In the United States, the recognition that innocent people have been, and continue to be, sentenced to death and executed has done more to bolster the abolitionist movement than anything else in the past decade. Hence, many see it as the only effective route to abolition.

However, while innocence has undoubtedly driven the American abolitionist cause for the past decade and continues to have some currency, it obviously cannot be dissociated from the human rights argument that the death penalty inevitably, and however administered, violates universally accepted human rights. Given that what is at stake is the arbitrary deprivation of life, we should no longer underestimate the impact of the stigmatising of retentionist countries by the abolitionist world. In the closing decades of the twentieth century, abolitionists felt the need to justify their position; now countries that make regular use of the death penalty are on the defensive, needing to establish rationales for retention in spite of wrongful convictions. They do so by reference to public opinion or the purported deterrent effect of capital punishment, arguments that do not stand up to empirical evidence.[59]

All must be done, where and while capital punishment persists, to make sure that the realities of criminal procedure match up to the international standards for the protection of those facing the sentence of death. Further, much more should be done by states to repair the harms caused by wrongful convictions: to compensate the exonerated or their families, to provide emotional and practical support to the wrongfully convicted to allow them to rebuild their shattered lives, and to hold to account those who are responsible for miscarriages of justice. However, it needs to be recognised that many problems arise by virtue of the very existence of the death penalty and the emotions it arouses. The complete avoidance of wrongful conviction and execution of the innocent remains an aspiration that has no hope of being reached. Procedural reform—pre- and post-conviction—as well as state reparation schemes will simply never be sufficient to meet the human rights objections to capital punishment.

One year on from Hakamada Iwao's release from death row in Tokyo, he provides testimony to the harmful effects of wrongful conviction. The 79-year-old man typically has a blank expression. After more than half his life confined in solitary detention in a five-square-meter cell, he is mentally ill, at times withdrawn, at times overcome by raging anger. But when he was released, in a moment of clear eloquence, he spoke out not against the death penalty for innocent people, but against it for anyone: "It is absolutely unacceptable for a nation state to kill its people."[60] He was right.

---

59 C Hoyle and R Hood. 2014. "Deterrence and Public Opinion." In United Nations Human Rights, ed., *Moving Away from the Death Penalty: Arguments, Trends and Perspectives*. New York: UNHR.

60 Hiroka Shoji. 2015. *One year since Hakamada's release, how much has really changed for Japan's death row inmates?* Amnesty International. Avaiable from https://www.amnesty.org/en/latest/campaigns/2015/03/one-year-since-hakamadas-release/. (accessed 24 August 2016).

IN THE SHADOW OF THE DEATH PENALTY

Brandon L. Garrett[1]

The American death penalty today produces the fewest death sentences that it has in three decades. Just over 50 defendants were sentenced to death in 2015, while several hundred were sentenced to death each year in the 1990s, during the modern height of American death sentencing. Although death sentences have declined, and most states have abolished the practice in recent years, 31 states retain the death penalty.[2] In those states, the presence of the death penalty still casts a powerful shadow, even if no death sentences result. Defendants may plead guilty fearing the death penalty, including defendants that are innocent, poorly represented, vulnerable, and undeserving of harsh sentences.

"This was the worst experience of my professional life. It still haunts me," recalled the former first assistant district attorney for McLennan County, Texas. He was recalling the case of Calvin Washington, tried for capital murder in Waco, Texas, in 1987. The prosecutor said the "only part" of the "terrible" trial that he does "not still regret," was the fact that the jury was divided in Washington's case, resulting in a life sentence for him and a co-defendant. "Imagine how much worse this tragedy could have been" if they had been "sentenced to death or, God forbid, put to death before their innocence could be proven."[3] Washington was exonerated by DNA tests after serving 14 years in prison. While he was not sentenced to death, one wonders what role the death penalty played in the rush to judgment that occurred at this "terrible" trial.

Douglas Warney was the first person to be charged under New York's new death penalty statute in 1996, and he later recalled that

---

1   Justice Thurgood Marshall Distinguished Professor of Law, University of Virginia School of Law, United States.

2   Portions of this piece are adapted from excerpts of a forthcoming book examining the decline of the death penalty in America. Brandon L. Garrett. *The Triumph of Mercy: How the Demise of the Death Penalty can Revive Criminal Justice.* In contract, Cambridge, MA:Harvard University Press.

3   Letter to Senate and House Conferees, Prosecutor Opposes Death Penalty Provision in Patriot Reauthorization Act, Nov. 8, 2005, available from https://www.hrw.org/news/2005/11/08/prosecutor-opposes-death-penalty-provisions-patriot-reauthorization-act. (accessed 24 August 2016).

he was "lucky," in one way, since he avoided the death penalty and instead received 25 years to life. Warney served six years in prison before DNA testing exonerated him for a murder he did not commit. He was mentally ill and had falsely confessed, like so many of the exonerees in murder cases, and the entire case revolved around his supposedly detailed confession. As in the other cases, the detective as emphatic that he did not "suggest any answers" to Warner, like the murder weapon, what the victim was wearing, and what the victim was cooking for dinner, and the prosecutor insisted, "who could possibly know these things if you hadn't been inside that house, inside the kitchen?"

Untold numbers of innocent people, facing the death penalty, did not get sentenced to death, but still served long sentences for murders that they did not commit. We know of quite a few people who like Warney received harsh results in the shadow of the death penalty. In addition to the 20 DNA exonerees who were sentenced to death, another 16 were charged with the death penalty but received some other sentence at trial.

I have found that at least 12 more DNA exonerees pleaded guilty rather than face the death penalty at a trial. Like the death row exonerees, the exonerees who escaped the death penalty had mostly falsely confessed. Sixteen of the entire group of 28 exonerees who faced the death penalty but did not receive it had falsely confessed. Sixteen had informants testify in their cases. Many came within a hair of a death sentence. Exoneree Larry Ruffin, for example, had a hung jury at trial, which is the only reason he was not sentenced to death for a murder he did not commit (along with two other innocent people who were also convicted). His exoneration came too late. When DNA tests cleared him 30 years later, he had already died in prison eight years before.[4]

We may never know how many more innocent people were informally threatened with the death penalty and pressured into false confessions or guilty pleas. For example, some people, like DNA exoneree Chris Ochoa, falsely confessed because detectives threatened

---

4   Innocence Project. Larry Ruffin, available from http://www.innocenceproject.org/cases-false-imprisonment/larry-ruffin. (accessed 24 August 2016).

them with the death penalty during the interrogation. Ochoa was interrogated for 12 hours, and told that he had a choice between death by lethal injection and falsely confessing and implicating his best friend. The detectives showed him photos of death row. They showed him where on his arm the needle with the execution drugs would be inserted. They told him that he would be "fresh meat" for the other prisoners. They also started and stopped the tape recorder, so that they could tell Ochoa details about the crime with the recording off. Ochoa's friend, Richard Danziger, was also wrongly convicted, and was beaten in prison and suffered brain damage. All the while, the culprit remained at large; eventually he wrote letters to Texas officials, including then-Governor George W. Bush, saying that two innocent men were in prison for a murder he committed. Only after 12 years were the DNA tests finally conducted, and Ochoa and Danziger cleared.[5] In other cases, defendants pleaded guilty because their lawyers convinced them not to risk the death penalty at trial.

Studies have documented how much more likely, in general, murder defendants are to plead guilty when facing the death penalty. This occurred, for example, in New York State after it reintroduced the death penalty in 1995.[6] A recent study of murder cases in Georgia found that the threat of the death penalty increased the probability of a plea agreement by 20–25 percent.[7] The severity of the resulting sentence, of course, will also be affected by the ability to seek the death penalty. To be sure, effective defense lawyers can use plea bargaining as a way to save their client's lives.[8] Some prosecutors may also be reluctant to propose bargains in cases where they desire the death penalty. That is clearly changing, since death sentences have become quite rare in the United States. Still, for decades, the US Supreme Court has said that the fact that a defendant might plead guilty to avoid the death penalty does not make a plea involuntary. Indeed, even if the defendant maintains innocence, said the court in

---

5 Center of Wrongful Convictions, Christopher Ochoa, available from http://www.law.northwest-ern.edu/legalclinic/wrongfulconvictions/exonerations/tx/christopher-ochoa.html. (accessed 24 August 2016).

6 Ilyana Kuziemko. 2006. "Does the Threat of the Death Penalty *Affect* Plea Bargaining *in Murder Cases? Evidence from New York's 1995 Reinstatement of Capital Punishment.*" *American Law and Economics Review* 8(1):116–142.

7 Sherod Thaxton. 2013. "Leveraging Death." *J. Crim. L. & Criminology* 103(2):475.

8 Welsh S. White. 2006. *Litigating in the Shadow of Death.* Ann Arbor: University of Michigan Press. pp. 145–171.

its 1970 ruling in *North Carolina v. Alford*, a plea to avoid the death penalty may be voluntary if "competent counsel" gave advice that it was "to the defendant's advantage."[9]

Twenty individuals have been exonerated from death row based on DNA evidence in the United States, and many more have been exonerated from death row based on other new evidence of their innocence. We know that there is a "uniquely high rate of exoneration" in death penalty cases, and as professors Sam Gross and Barbara O'Brien have estimated that there is a 4.1% rate of exoneration in all death penalty cases.[10] As I have described, the shadow the death penalty cases is far wider than just those innocent individuals who were exonerated having been sentenced to death. There are those cases of individuals who were charged with the death penalty but were innocent and were still convicted of lesser sentences.

Still other innocent people narrowly avoided the death penalty because the crimes occurred when the death penalty was not the law in a given state. For example, Paul Terry and Michael Evans were sentenced to hundreds of years in prison for rape and murder in Illinois, but since the murder occurred in 1976 and not 1977 when Illinois brought back the death penalty, they could not receive it; they were exonerated years later by DNA tests. Former Governor Mario Cuomo urged New Yorkers to rethink the death penalty in light of the DNA exonerations of three men, John Kogut, Dennis Halstead, and John Restivo, after serving 18 years in prison for a murder they did not commit: "If New York had the death penalty in the 1980s," each of them "would most likely have been executed before DNA evidence in their case proved their innocence."[11] In addition to those DNA exoneration cases, still more individuals exonerated by non-DNA evidence pleaded guilty to avoid the death penalty.[12]

---

9   *North Carolina v. Alford*, 400 U.S. 25, 31 (1970); see also *Brady v. United States*, 397 U.S. 742, 758 (1970).

10 Samuel R. Gross et al. 2013. "Rate of False Conviction of Criminal Defendants Who are Sentenced to Death." *PNAS* 11:7230. Available from http://www.pnas.org/content/111/20/7230. abstract. (accessed 24 August 2016).

11 Frank R. Baumgartner et al. 2008. *The Decline of the Death Penalty and the Discovery of Innocence.* Cambridge: Cambridge University Press. p. 80.

12 Samuel R. Gross et al. 2005. "Exonerations in the United States 1989 Through 2003." *J. Crim. L. & Criminology* 95(2):523-53:pp.544-46.

More people were sentenced to death under statutes declared unconstitutional by the U.S. Supreme Court. Currently many of those on Florida's death row await relief having been sentenced to death under a scheme that unconstitutionally permitted the judge and not the jury to sentence them.[13] Countless thousands of individuals have been executed in the past but who would no longer be eligible for the death penalty today. For example, before the 1970s, much of the death penalty was directed towards non-murders such as rape, and prior to the court outlawing the practice, juveniles and the intellectually disabled could be executed.

U.S. Supreme Court Justice John Paul Stevens announced his opposition to the death penalty in 2008, citing evidence from DNA exonerations: "Whether or not any innocent defendants have actually been executed, abundant evidence accumulated in recent years has resulted in the exoneration of an unacceptable number of defendants found guilty of capital offenses."[14] More recently, in the case of *Glossip v. Gross* in 2015, Justice Stephen Breyer dissented, joined by Justice Ruth Bader Ginsburg, calling the current practice of the death penalty is categorically unconstitutional.[15] Justice Breyer singled out the case of Henry McCollum, and noted that although there are endemic delays in death penalty cases, it took 20 years after the Supreme Court denied relief to McCollum for new DNA evidence to surface and to prove his innocence.[16] Justice Breyer noted that murder cases can be "accompanied by intense community pressure on police, prosecutors, and jurors to secure a conviction" which may create "a greater likelihood of convicting the wrong person."[17]

These data presented illustrate how the innocence problem with the death penalty goes far beyond exonerations and extends to the entire criminal process in which the death penalty is used. One set of reforms to address these problems seeks to improve the accuracy of evidence in all criminal cases, not just death penalty cases, so that flawed forensic evidence, suggestive eyewitness identification

---

13   *Hurst v. Florida*, 136 S.Ct. 616 (2016).

14   *Baze v. Rees*, 553 U.S. 35, 85–86 (2008) (Stevens, J. dissenting).

15   *Glossip v. Gross*, 135 S.Ct. 2726, 2771-2776 (2015) (Breyer, J. dissenting).

16   Ibid. at 2557 (Breyer, J. dissenting).

17   Ibid.

procedures, coercive interrogation techniques, and false informant testimony is not used in criminal cases. Far more effort in the scientific community and in the legal community has been directed towards accuracy-related reforms. For just one recent example, in 2014, the National Academy of Sciences published an important report, "Identifying the Culprit: Assessing Eyewitness Identification."[18] I was a member of the committee that produced the report, and it recommends sweeping changes to improve the regulation of eyewitness identification testimony.

A second set of reforms has to do with sentencing. The death penalty highlights larger problems with excessive and inflexible punishment. The role that the death penalty plays in trials that do not result in the death penalty and plea bargaining suggests a broader concern that excessive punishments give prosecutors far too powerful weapons in negotiating criminal cases. For defense lawyers, as one put it, "If they offer you anything less than death and you don't take it, imagine if you guessed wrong." For prosecutors, as one put it, "I'm not a rabid proponent of the death penalty [but] if it has an upside, it's that we've resolved some cases with pleas of life without parole where that was the appropriate sentence."[19] That advantage comes with a cost, in at least some states, since in death penalty cases, defendants may receive far more experienced and better-resourced lawyers.[20] As another prosecutor noted, using the death penalty as leverage is not a cost or time saver, where: "You know, capital cases aren't cheap, so you're spending a lot of money because most of these cases don't resolve themselves until shortly before the trial."[21] The net result may be wasteful and unjust, and it may overproduce life sentences in an era in which the death penalty is inexorably in decline in the United States. Indeed, the populations of individuals serving life without parole have skyrocketed, even as death sentences are waning. In the United States today, over 50,000 prisoners are serving life without parole, while only about 3,000 people remain on death rows. Over 160,000 prisoners, are

---

18   National Research Council Report. 2014. *Identifying the Culprit: Assessing Eyewitness Identification.*
19   Susan Ehrhard. 2008. "Plea Bargaining *and the* Death Penalty: An Exploratory Study." *Just. Sys. J.* 29:pp. 313, 316, 320.
20   Brandon L. Garrett. 2017. "The Decline of the Virginia (and American) Death Penalty." *Georgetown Law Journal* 105.
21   Susan Ehrhard-Dietzel. 2012. "The Use of Life and Death as Tools in Plea Bargaining." *Crim. Just.* 37:pp. 89, 99.

serving life sentences with a possibility of parole, but often not a great likelihood of parole.[22]

Thus, the problem of overly harsh sentencing, in a system with poor quality of evidence gathering, inadequate defense resources, and overbearing prosecutorial power, is a problem not just in death penalty cases, although they so vividly illustrate it, but more broadly in criminal justice systems worldwide. As the shadow of the death penalty fades, we will have to confront those larger sources of error and injustice.

22　*The Sentencing Project, Life Goes On.* 2012. Available from http://sentencingproject.org/doc/publi-cations/inc_Life%20Goes%20On%202013.pdf. (accessed 24 August 2016).

2.2 Discrimination and Mental Health Issues

DISCRIMINATION AND THE DEATH PENALTY

Ross Kleinstuber[1]

Introduction

In the G8 group of countries, only the United States and Japan still use the death penalty, and of these two, the US sentences far more people to death and carries out far more executions.[2] This is especially troubling given the fact that empirical research indicates that the death penalty in the United States is still being implemented in a racially biased manner despite nearly half a century of efforts by the US Supreme Court to fashion death-sentencing procedures that limit discretion and reduce biases. This chapter will explore the efforts by the US Supreme Court to reduce racial disparities in the administration of the death penalty, provide a brief overview of the scholarly evidence that suggests that such efforts have been largely unsuccessful, and discuss some of the social, structural, and historical realities that continue to plague efforts to administer the American death penalty in a fair and neutral manner and continue to ensure that it remains infected with bias.

THE US SUPREME COURT AND THE "MODERN" ERA OF DEATH SENTENCING

Prior to 1972, American states were free to administer the death penalty however they wanted for pretty much any crime they wanted without any federal oversight. As described in greater detail below, this reality led to a scenario in which the death penalty was utilized in a racially discriminatory way. It was more likely to be used by the former slave states (i.e., the southern states that made up the

---

1   Assistant Professor, University of Pittsburgh Johnstown, United States.
2   Amnesty International. 2016. *Death Sentences and Executions 2015*. London: Amnesty International.

Confederacy during the US Civil War), it was implemented for a wide range of offenses committed by blacks, and it was used far more often against blacks but rarely used against whites.[3] In response to the racially disproportionate manner in which the death penalty was being implemented, in 1972 the US Supreme Court declared all existing death penalty statutes unconstitutional.[4] The court did not abolish the death penalty *per se*; it simply said that the way the penalty was being implemented was discriminatory. In response, most American states cobbled together new death-sentencing laws. Some of these (like mandatory death sentences) were rejected by the court,[5] but in 1976, the court upheld the use of what became known as "guided discretion" statutes.[6] Guided discretion statutes were designed to split the guilt and punishment decisions into two separate phases of trial and to give jurors direction and guidance on how to determine an appropriate sentence. Most of these statutes required jurors to consider aggravating and mitigating factors. Aggravating circumstances are things that make the crime worse and the defendant more worthy of a death sentence. They include things like torturing the victim prior to death, killing multiple people, or killing a police officer. Mitigating circumstances are the opposite; they are things like a history of abuse, low intelligence, or diminished culpability that make the defendant less deserving of a death sentence. The goal of these statutes was to force judges and jurors to consider objective legally relevant factors and therefore reduce racial bias in sentencing outcomes. Unfortunately, as the next section demonstrates, these efforts have failed to eradicate discrimination in the administration of the American death penalty.

---

3   Banner, S. 2002. *The Death Penalty: An American History.* Cambridge, MA: Harvard University Press. *See* also, Grosso, C. M., O'Brien, B., Taylor, A., & Woodworth, G. 2014. "Race Discrimination and the Death Penalty: An Empirical and Legal Overview." In J. R. Acker, & C. S. Lanier, *America's Experiment with Capital Punishment: Reflections on the Past, Present, and Future of the Ultimate Penal Sanction.* (3rd ed.). Durham, NC: Carolina Academic Press. pp. 525–576.

4   *Furman v. Georgia*, 408 US 238 (Supreme Court 1972).

5   *Woodson v. North Carolina*, 428 US 280 (Supreme Court 1976).

6   *Gregg v. Georgia*, 428 US 153 (Supreme Court 1976).

EMPIRICAL RESEARCH ON DEATH PENALTY DISCRIMINATION

Who Gets Sentenced to Die?

It should be noted that the evidence indicates that since 1972, there has been a reduction in the degree of racial bias in the implementation of the death penalty, especially in the South, but racial bias is far from being eliminated.[7] Fifteen years after the US Supreme Court invalidated existing capital statutes for being implemented in a racially discriminatory manner, the court's commitment to racial equality was put to the test in the case of *McCleskey v. Kemp* (1987). In this case, Warren McCleskey presented statistical evidence from more than 2,000 murder cases in Georgia (the state in which he was convicted) that showed that 21% of black defendant–white victim cases resulted in a death sentence but only 8% of white defendant–white victim, 3% of white defendant–black victim, and 1% of black defendant–black victim cases resulted in a death sentence. They also showed that the races of the victim and perpetrator influenced the decision of prosecutors to seek a death sentence. Prosecutors sought the death penalty 70% of the time when the offender was black and the victim was white, 32% of the time when both were white, 19% of the time when the offender was white and the victim was black, and 15% of the time when both were black. After subjecting the data to statistical controls for legally relevant non-racial variables, the researchers concluded that those who killed whites were 4.3 times more likely to be sentenced to death than those who killed blacks and that blacks who killed whites were the most likely to be sentenced to death.[8] The Supreme Court accepted the validity of the statistical evidence presented by McCleskey, but they refused to overturn his death sentence because he was unable to "prove that the decision makers in *his* case acted with discriminatory purpose."[9] In other words, statistical evidence of discriminatory application was no longer considered

7   Grosso, C. M., O'Brien, B., Taylor, A., & Woodworth, G. 2014. "Race Discrimination and the Death Penalty: An Empirical and Legal Overview." In J. R. Acker, & C. S. Lanier, *America's Experiment with Capital Punishment: Reflections on the Past, Present, and Future of the Ultimate Penal Sanction* (3rd ed.). Durham, NC: Carolina Academic Press, pp. 525–576.
8   Baldus, D. C., Woodworth, G., & Pulaski, C. A. 1990. *Equal Justice and the Death Penalty: A Legal and Empirical Analysis.* Boston, MA: Northeastern University Press.
9   *McCleskey v. Kemp*, 481 US 279 (Supreme Court 1987).

sufficient to invalidate the death penalty; rather a defendant challenging his or her sentence would need to demonstrate discriminatory intent on the part of some person involved in his or her specific case.[10] This ruling, in effect, makes it impossible to challenge the death penalty on grounds of racial discrimination.[11]

Nonetheless, researchers have continued to document the racial breakdown of death sentences and executions in the United States, and the evidence indicates that the discriminatory application of the death penalty is not an isolated phenomenon that is unique to Georgia or to an earlier period in US history. It infects the death-sentencing process nationwide up to the present day. In 1990, the US General Accounting Office (GAO) analyzed the 28 existing post-1972 empirical studies on racial discrimination in the administration of the death penalty and concluded that "those who murdered whites were found to be more likely to be sentenced to death than those who murdered blacks."[12] The GAO concluded that "race-of-victim— influence was found at all stages of the criminal justice process" although it "was stronger for the earlier stages of the judicial process (e.g. prosecutorial decision to charge defendants with a capital offense, decision to proceed to trial rather than plea bargain) than in later stages" and that the finding "was remarkably consistent," being found in 82% of the studies analyzed.[13] On the other hand, the GAO determined that the evidence of race-of-defendant discrimination was equivocal.[14] More than half the studies did find a race-of-defendant effect, but of those nearly a quarter found that white defendants were more likely to be sentenced to death while the remaining three-quarters concluded that black defendants were more likely to be sentenced to death.[15]

Since 1990, statistical techniques have advanced greatly, data have become more accessible, and society has changed. Therefore, Grosso,

---

10   Ibid.

11   Alexander, M. 2012. *The New Jim Crow: Mass Incarceration in the Age of Colorblindness.* New York: New Press.

12   US General Accounting Office. February 1990. *Death Penalty Sentencing: Research Indicates Pattern of Racial Disparities.* p. 5. Available from http://www.gao.gov/assets/220/212180.pdf. (accessed 9 May 2016).

13   Ibid.

14   US General Accounting Office. February 1990. *Death Penalty Sentencing: Research Indicates Pattern of Racial Disparities.* Available from http://www.gao.gov/assets/220/212180.pdf. (accessed 9 May 2016).

15   Ibid., p. 6.

et al. reviewed more than three dozen empirical studies of death penalty discrimination performed in more than two dozen jurisdictions throughout the US (including the federal and the US military death penalties) since 1990.[16] They concluded that—in line with the GAO's conclusions 24 years earlier—there is strong evidence that those convicted of killing white victims are significantly more likely to be sentenced to death than those convicted of killing blacks or Hispanics and that there is limited evidence to suggest that black defendants may be more likely to be sentenced to death than white defendants. This reality is compounded in cases with a black defendant and a white victim: blacks who are convicted of killing white victims are the most likely to be sent to death row. This bias is present in the (unreviewable) prosecutor's decision to seek a death sentence and in the jury's (or judge's) decision to impose a death sentence, and it has been found throughout the United States.[17] Not all studies reach these same conclusions, but a large majority of the published research over the last quarter-century does.[18]

Who Supports the Death Penalty?

In addition to the evidence on the discriminatory application of the death penalty, there is empirical evidence that support for the death penalty is conditioned by racism. For more than 50 years, polls have consistently shown that white Americans are far more supportive of the death penalty than black Americans,[19] and scholarly research has repeatedly found that one of the most important predictors of whites'

16 Grosso, C. M., O'Brien, B., Taylor, A., & Woodworth, G. 2014. "Race Discrimination and the Death Penalty: An Empirical and Legal Overview." In J. R. Acker, & C. S. Lanier, *America's Experiment with Capital Punishment: Reflections on the Past, Present, and Future of the Ultimate Penal Sanction* (3rd ed.). Durham, NC: Carolina Academic Press, pp. 525–576.

17 Ibid.

18 Ibid.

19 Cochran, J. K., & Chamlin, M. B. 2006. "The Enduring Racial Divide in Death Penalty Support." *Journal of Criminal Justice* 34:85–99. *See* also, Dugan, A. 2015. *Solid Majority Continue to Support Death Penalty.* Available from http://www.gallup.com/poll/186218/solid-majority-continue-support-death-penalty.aspx-?g_source=position2&g_medium=related&g_campaign=tiles. (accessed 10 May 2016), and Pew Research Center. 2015. *Less Support for Death Penalty, Especially Among Democrats.* Available from http://www.people-press.org/2015/04/16/less-support-for-death-penalty-especial-ly-among-democrats/. (accessed 10 May 2016).

attitudes toward the death penalty is racial prejudice.[20] In fact, a recent experiment by Peffley and Hurwitz found that when whites are presented with evidence that the death penalty discriminates, they are *more* likely to support the death penalty.[21]

INSTITUTIONAL COMPONENTS OF THE AMERICAN DEATH PENALTY

Supporters of the death penalty often dismiss the evidence of racial discrimination by suggesting that this does not make the penalty *per se* problematic; rather, the penalty remains just, it simply needs to be implemented in a more neutral manner.[22] However, eliminating these biases is not a straightforward task because there are numerous institutional and historical aspects to American society that contribute to the discriminatory manner in which the death penalty operates and that suggest that it is not possible to eliminate bias from the American death penalty because it is inherently racist.

Present Institutional Arrangements

First, due to the high degree of racial residential segregation in American society,[23] black and white Americans are likely to experience the world in vastly different ways. Black Americans are far more likely to be burdened with crime-producing social forces while the white Americans who are likely to sit in judgment over black capital defendants are unlikely to have any direct experience with these social forces and thus are unlikely to be able to empathize with

---

20 Barkan, S. E., & Cohn, S. F. 1994. "Racial Prejudice and Support for the Death Penalty by Whites." *Journal of Research in Crime and Delinquency* 31:202-209. See also, Bobo, L. D., & Johnson, D. 2004. "A Taste for Punishment: Black and White Americans' Views on the Death Penalty and the War on Drugs." *Du Bois Review* 1(1):151-180; Soss, J., Langbein, L., & Metelko, A. R. 2003. "Why Do White Americans Support the Death Penalty?" *Journal of Politics* 65(2):397-421, and Unnever, J. D., & Cullen, F. T. 2007. "The Racial Divide in Support for the Death Penalty: Does White Racism Matter?" *Social Forces* 85(3):1281-1301.

21 Peffley, M., & Hurwitz, J. 2007. "Persuasion and Resistance: Race and the Death Penalty in America." *American Journal of Political Science* 51(4):996-1012.

22 Van den Haag, E. 1986. "The Ultimate Punishment: A Defense." *Harvard Law Review* 99(7):1662-1669.

23 Jargowsky, P. A. 2015. *The Architecture of Segregation: Civil Unrest, The Concentration of Poverty, and Public Policy.* Available from http://www.tcf.org/assets/downloads/Jargowsky_Architectureof Segregation.pdf. (accessed 25 September 2015). *See also* Rothstein, R. 2015. "The Racial Achievement Gap, Segregated Schools, and Segregated Neighborhoods: A Constitutional Insult." *Race and Social Problems* 7:21-30.

the plight of the typical black capital defendant or to understand why such social forces are relevant. As Craig Haney has explained, black defendants are more likely than white defendants to experience mitigating circumstances that are "structured into their social histories by the nature of the society into which they have been born."[24] These factors include a greater likelihood of growing up poor, being more likely to live in high-poverty and high-crime neighborhoods with failing schools, and having less social mobility than white Americans.[25] These factors are also race-specific as poor whites are more likely to be integrated into middle-class neighborhoods,[26] and poor white neighborhoods are less violent, less likely to be disrupted by publics works projects, more stable, and more likely to offer employment opportunities.[27] Experiencing these social factors that are more likely to be present in the lives of black Americans early in life is conduvice to crime and violence later in life,[28] and thus, due to social structures that trap black Americans at the bottom of American society, deny them legitimate opportunities, and keep them confined to the poorest and most violent neighborhoods, black Americans are more likely to engage in lethal violence in the first place.

Compounding the problem, because white Americans—even poor whites—are especially unlikely to experience anything remotely

---

24 Haney, C. 2005. *Death by Design: Capital Punishment as a Social Psychological System*. New York: Oxford University Press. p. 1558.

25 Alexander, K., Entwisle, D., & Olson, L. 2014. *The Long Shadow: Family Background, Disadvantaged Urban Youth, and the Transition to Adulthood*. New York: Russel Sage Foundation. *See also* Jargowsky, P. A. August 9, 2015. *The Architecture of Segregation: Civil Unrest, The Concentration of Poverty, and Public Policy*. Available from http://www.tcf.org/assets/downloads/Jargowsky_ArchitectureofSegregation.pdf. (accessed 25 September 2015); Pew Charitable Trusts. 2012. *Pursuing the American Dream: Economic Mobility Across Generations*. Available from http://www.pewtrusts.org/~/media/legacy/uploadedfiles/pcs_assets/2012/pursuingamericandreampdf.pdf. (accessed 19 May 2015), and Rothstein, R. 2015. "The Racial Achievement Gap, Segregated Schools, and Segregated Neighborhoods: A Constitutional Insult." *Race and Social Problems* 7:21-30.

26 Jargowsky, P. A. 2015. *The Architecture of Segregation: Civil Unrest, The Concentration of Poverty, and Public Policy*. Available from http://www.tcf.org/assets/downloads/Jargowsky_ArchitectureofSegregation.pdf. (accessed 25 September 2015).

27 Alexander, K., Entwisle, D., & Olson, L. 2014. *The Long Shadow: Family Background, Disadvantaged Urban Youth, and the Transition to Adulthood*. New York: Russel Sage Foundation.

28 Haney, C. 2003. "Mitigation and the Study of Lives: On the Roots of Violent Criminality and the Nature of Capital Justice." In J. R. Acker, R. M. Bohm, & C. S. Lanier, eds., *America's Experiment with Capital Punishment: Reflections on the Past, Present, and Future of the Ultimate Penal Sanction*. Durham, NC: Carolina Academic Press. pp. 469-500. *See also* Loeber, R., & Farrington, D. P., eds. 2001. *Child Delinquents: Development, Intervention, and Service Needs*. Thousand Oaks, CA: Sage, and Wasserman, G. A., Keenan, K., Tremblay, R. E., Cole, J. D., Herrenkohl, T. I., Loeber, R., & Petechuk, D. 2003. *Risk and Protective Factors of Child Delinquency*. Washington, DC: US Department of Justice. Available from https://www.ncjrs.gov/pdffiles1/ojjdp/193409.pdf. (accessed 3 February 2011).

similar to what poor black Americans experience, they have difficulty empathizing with black capital defendants or comprehending the relevance of the most powerful mitigating evidence these defendants have to offer.[29] This means that when white Americans become jurors in capital cases, they are likely to discredit much of the mitigating evidence presented by non-white defendants and thus unwittingly disadvantage those defendants, especially when black defendants are accused of murdering white victims. Studies of capital juror decision-making have found that, in general, they tend to be dismissive of mitigation drawn from a defendant's background and life history.[30]

This tendency is compounded when the defendant is black, because jurors view the same evidence as less mitigating when the defendant is black than when the defendant is white[31] and white capital jurors are less willing than their black counterparts to consider mitigating life history evidence when the defendant is black.[32] White jurors are also more likely to see black defendants as "dangerous" than white defendants.[33] These realities are especially true in cross-racial cases involving black defendants and white victims, where white jurors are less receptive to mitigating evidence of all kinds and are more likely to support a death sentence than black jurors are.[34] All of these factors combine to create a scenario where the likelihood of a death sentence increases dramatically when there are at least five white male jurors and decreases substantially when there is at least one black male juror,[35]

---

29 Fleury-Steiner, B. 2004. *Jurors' Stories of Death: How America's Death Penalty Invests in Inequality.* Ann Arbor, MI: University of Michigan Press. *See* also, Haney, C. 2004. "Condemning the Other in Death Penalty Trials: Biographical Racism, Structural Mitigation, and the Empathetic Divide." *DePaul Law Review* 53:1557-1589.

30 Kleinstuber, R. 2013. "We're All Born with Equal Opportunities: Hegemonic Individualism and Contextual Mitigation Among Delaware Capital Jurors." *Journal of Qualitative Criminal Justice and Criminology* 1:152-180.

31 Lynch, M., & Haney, C. 2000. Discrimination and Instructional Comprehension: Guided Discretion, Racial Bias, and the Death Penalty. *Law and Human Behavior* 24:337-356.

32 Lynch, M. 2006. "Stereotypes, Prejudice, and Life-and-Death Decision Making: Lessons from Laypersons in an Experimental Setting." In C. J. Ogletree, & A. Sarat, eds., *From Lynch Mobs to the Killing State: Race and the Death Penalty in America.* New York: NYU Press. pp. 182-219.

33 Bowers, W. J., Steiner, B. D., & Sandys, M. 2001. "Death Sentencing in Black and White: An Empirical Analysis of the Role of Jurors' Race and Jury Racial Composition." *University of Pennsylvania Journal of Constitutional Law* 3:171-274.

34 Bowers, W. J., Sandys, M., & Brewer, T. W. 2004. "Crossing Racial Boundaries: A Closer Look at the Roots of Racial Bias When the Defendant is Black and the Victim is White." *DePaul Law Review* 53:1497-1538. *See* also, Bowers, W. J., Steiner, B. D., & Sandys, M. 2001. "Death Sentencing in Black and White: An Empirical Analysis of the Role of Jurors' Race and Jury Racial Composition." *University of Pennsylvania Journal of Constitutional Law* 3:171-274.

35 Bowers, W. J., Steiner, B. D., & Sandys, M. 2001. "Death Sentencing in Black and White: An Empirical Analysis of the Role of Jurors' Race and Jury Racial Composition." *University of Pennsylvania Journal of Constitutional Law* 3:171-274.

but this does not mean that jurors are being consciously or deliberately racist. As sociologist Thomas W. Brewer has concluded, the research findings suggest that this "racial variation in capital sentencing may not be dominated by such nefarious forces such as overt prejudice. Subconscious attributions of behavior and a fundamental misunderstanding of … the lives led by many capital defendants may play a greater role than previously thought."[36]

Second, cultural imagery has the tendency to construct black Americans as dangerous and threatening "outsiders" who are less than fully human. US society has a long history of creating stereotypes of black Americans as dangerous, lustful "beasts" that have been used to justify slavery, Jim Crow segregation, and even lynching.[37] These stereotypes are often passed down across generations and get reinforced by existing social institutions. For example, both the news media and fictional dramas in American society give disproportionate attention to crime, especially serious violent crime. However, this attention is racially skewed.[38]

The media tend to give greater attention to street crimes (which are disproportionately committed by poor minorities) than white collar crimes and to focus on crimes committed by black strangers and with white female victims (even though most street crimes are committed by white Americans and even though black males are disproportionately victimized).[39] Children's television shows also have a tendency to reinforce racial stereotypes, particularly stereotypes about crime and violence.[40] Because the typical American is unlikely to have any direct experience with crime, the images they get in the media are likely to have a strong influence on their views of crime, which means that the media's racialized coverage

36 Brewer, T. W. 2004. "Race and Jurors' Receptivity to Mitigation in Capital Cases: The Effect of Jurors', Defendants', and Victims' Race in Combination." *Law and Human Behavior* 28:529-545: p. 543.

37 Alexander, M. 2012. *The New Jim Crow: Mass Incarceration in the Age of Colorblindness.* New York: New Press.

38 Beckett, K., & Sasson, T. 2004. *The Politics of Injustice: Crime and Punishment in America* (2nd ed.). Thousand Oaks, CA: Sage. *See also*, Glassner, B. 1999. *The Culture of Fear: Why Americans Are Afraid of the Wrong Things.* New York: Basic.

39 Glassner, B. 1999. *The Culture of Fear: Why Americans Are Afraid of the Wrong Things.* New York: Basic.

40 Giroux, H. A., & Pollock, G. 2010. *The Mouse that Roared: Disney and the End of Innocence.* Lanham, MD: Rowman & Littlefield.

of crime is likely to generate an image of young, black males as dangerous and threatening in the minds of most Americans.[41]

This imagery is not necessarily conscious, but when actors are given wide discretion—such as in the decision to seek or impose a death sentence—subconscious stereotypes can have a powerful influence on how we perceive and respond to others. As Fleury-Steiner has noted, "The contemporary criminal justice system's well-documented differential treatment of poor blacks cannot typically be understood as the result of overt discrimination, as in other historical periods, but rather as the function of the dominant group's normative expectations of poor blacks as dangerous, lawless, or immoral."[42] For example, in a recent experimental study, white participants were likely to over-perceive threat in black male faces and to over-perceive friendliness in white male faces.[43] In this study, white participants were shown either two white or two black faces. The first face was either angry, neutral, or smiling; the second face was always neutral. When first presented with an angry (threatening) face, the subjects tended to carry the threat over to the second (neutral) face when they were presented with two black faces but not when presented with two white faces. The opposite was true when first presented with a smiling (friendly) face. Subjects tended to carry the friendliness over to the second (neutral) face when the faces were white but not when they were black.[44] This result is likely the result of negative stereotypes in American society that portray black males as threatening and that form the subconscious lens through which they are perceived.[45]

Third, because police officers are human, they are also likely to be influenced by these cultural messages and to use their authority against non-whites more often than against whites—often without even

---

41 Alexander, M. 2012. *The New Jim Crow: Mass Incarceration in the Age of Colorblindness.* New York: New Press. *See* also, Beckett, K., & Sasson, T. 2004. *The Politics of Injustice: Crime and Punishment in America* (2nd ed.). Thousand Oaks, CA: Sage, and Glassner, B. 1999. *The Culture of Fear: Why Americans Are Afraid of the Wrong Things.* New York: Basic.

42 Fleury-Steiner, B. 2004. *Jurors' Stories of Death: How America's Death Penalty Invests in Inequality.* Ann Arbor, MI: University of Michigan Press, p. 4.

43 Shapiro, J., Ackerman, J. M., Neuberg, S. L., Maner, J. K., Becker, D.V., & Kenrick, D.T. 2009. "Following in the Wake of Anger: When Not Discriminating is Discriminating." *Personality and Social Psychology Bulletin* 35(10):1356-1367.

44 Ibid.

45 Ibid.

realizing it. They are more likely to focus their patrol efforts in poor, minority communities, and they are more likely to stop and search non-white pedestrians and motorists with substantially less suspicion or probable cause.[46] This creates a scenario where more innocent blacks and fewer guilty whites get arrested, a fact that has profound downstream consequences as it means that non-white Americans (especially black Americans) are more likely to accumulate legally relevant aggravating factors (like a criminal record) than white Americans even when their behaviors are the same. This form of institutional discrimination is actually hidden from statistical studies of death penalty discrimination because they control for legally relevant variables that are actually the result of racialized forces in US society.

Finally, the very structure of death penalty trials works to the disadvantage of non-white defendants. As Haney has shown, there are numerous mechanisms built into the structure of capital trials that encourage death verdicts.[47] By allowing the prosecution to go first, the structure of a capital trial causes the jury to be bombarded with evidence of the gory details of the defendant's murderous conduct absent any opportunity to humanize or explain the defendant's behavior. This encourages jurors to see the defendant solely as an agent of violence for an extended period of time before being given an opportunity to connect his or violence to prior life events. Additionally, capital trials create a sense of social distance between jurors and the defendant that make it more difficult to empathize with the defendant, and capital trials tend to focus on the idea of "future dangerousness," which causes jurors to resort to a form of vicarious self-defense in which killing the defendant is acceptable in order to protect others from his or her future violence.[48] Although these mechanisms are present no matter what the defendant's and victim's races are, they tend to have a greater influence when the defendant is not white and when the victim is white.

---

46 Alexander, M. 2012. *The New Jim Crow: Mass Incarceration in the Age of Colorblindness.* New York: New Press. *See* also, Harris, D. 2002. *Profiles in Injustice: Why Racial Profiling Cannot Work.* New York: New Press, and New York Civil Liberties Union. 2014. *Stop & Frisk During the Bloomberg Administration: 2002-2013.* Available from http://www.nyclu.org/files/publications/stopand-frisk_briefer_2002-2013_final.pdf. (accessed 29 September 2014).

47 Haney, C. 2005. *Death by Design: Capital Punishment as a Social Psychological System.* New York: Oxford University Press.

48 Ibid.

To serve on a capital jury, potential jurors must go through a process known as death qualification. Basically, jurors are asked about their opinions on the death penalty and are excluded from a capital jury if they are opposed to the death penalty or if they are not able to render the legally appropriate sentence because of their strong opposition to or support for the death penalty. This process ends up excluding certain groups of people more than others, and those who end up getting seated on capital juries are more likely to be white, male, conservative, punitive, pro-prosecution, conviction prone, and supportive of the death penalty than are those who are rejected.[49] What this means is that those very individuals who are least likely to be able to empathize with the hardships endured by the typical non-white capital defendant and the least likely to comprehend the relevance of structural mitigation—conservative white males—are the very individuals most likely to be selected to serve on a capital jury. Therefore, when capital defendants are not white, the morally disengaging structure of and the social distance created by a capital trial are compounded by the actual social distance between jurors and defendants, and the focus on future dangerousness is amplified by the engrained social stereotypes of black males as threatening that many whites subconsciously possess. This is especially true when the victim is white because the jurors are more likely to find those crimes personally threatening. Research has found that jurors are more likely to support a death sentence when they are the same race as the victim[50] and when they are able to empathize with the victim.[51] As such, the death qualification process is likely to place non-white defendants and those accused of killing white victims at a disadvantage relative to other defendants.

---

49 Fleury-Steiner, B. 2004. *Jurors' Stories of Death: How America's Death Penalty Invests in Inequality.* Ann Arbor, MI: University of Michigan Press. *See* also, Young, R. L. 2004. "Guilty Until Proven Innocent: Conviction Orientation, Racial Attitudes, and Support for Capital Punishment." *Deviant Behavior* 25:151-167.

50 Bowers, W. J., Steiner, B. D., & Sandys, M. 2001. "Death Sentencing in Black and White: An Empirical Analysis of the Role of Jurors' Race and Jury Racial Composition." *University of Pennsylvania Journal of Constitutional Law* 3:171-274.

51 Sundby, S. E. 2003. "The Capital Jury and Empathy: The Problem of Worthy and Unworthy Victims." *Cornell Law Review* 88:343-381.

Historical Context of the American Death Penalty

In addition to the present institutional arrangements that maintain the American death penalty, one must understand that "Slavery, criminal justice, lynchings, and capital punishment are historically closely intertwined in the United States."[52] In other words, the legal execution of convicted killers (and rapists) in the United States cannot be divorced from America's history of race-based slavery or the extra-judicial lynchings of black Americans (and other racial minorities) that characterized the post-slavery era. While this statement may seem radical, a brief examination of the rise and fall of lynching as a tool of social control in the American South lends support to this viewpoint. Following the abolition of slavery in the United States, whites in the South increasingly resorted to lynching blacks for any number of real or perceived transgressions as a method of creating fear and thus re-establishing white supremacy and white control over recently freed slaves. There is little question that this recourse to vigilantism was a method of racial control, designed to maintain white supremacy by terrorizing subordinate racial groups who posed a potential threat to white dominance. As Tolnay and Beck have noted, a lynching was most likely to occur when southern whites felt economically threatened, and the intensity of violence against subordinate groups increased as the perceived threat they posed to the dominant group increased.[53] Not coincidentally, the use of extra-judicial lynching was accompanied by the use of the legal system to formally assert white domination over black Americans through black codes, convict leasing (a form of slavery in which blacks who were convicted of violating the racist laws of the time period were leased to landowners to work on a plantation in much the same way that slaves had been worked prior to abolition), and Jim Crow segregation.[54]

By the 1930s, criticism of lynching had increased, and the negative publicity it received caused southern states to reduce and eventually

---

52 Marquart, J. W., Ekland-Olson, S., & Sorensen, J. R. 1994. *The Rope, the Chair, and the Needle: Capital Punishment in Texas, 1923-1990.* Austin: University of Texas Press.

53 Tolnay and Beck, 1995.

54 Alexander, M. 2012. *The New Jim Crow: Mass Incarceration in the Age of Colorblindness.* New York: New Press. *See also,* Oshinsky, D. M. 1996. *"Worse Than Slavery": Parchman Farm and the Ordeal of Jim Crow Justice.* New York: Free Press.

eliminate their reliance on these extra-judicial killings.[55] However, as the use of lynch mobs declined in the twentieth century, the use of the death penalty increased: "The hundred-a-year lynchings of the 1890s were matched by similar numbers of legal executions in the 1930s," which caused many critics to coin the term "legal lynching."[56] Unsurprisingly, in the early part of the twentieth century, the death penalty was used far more often against blacks and for a wider variety of offenses than against whites. The connection between lynching and the death penalty can be most clearly seen in the executions of convicted rapists, a practice the US Supreme Court did not abolish until 1977. The prototypical lynching scenario in the post-Civil War period involved a black man being killed for allegedly raping a white woman. When legal executions began to replace lynching, this pattern remained. The death penalty was used for rape almost exclusively in the South,[57] and it was reserved almost exclusively for blacks accused of raping white women.[58]

In Texas, for example, African Americans who raped white women were 35 times more likely to be sentenced to death than to prison, and Hispanics who raped white women were twice as likely to be sent to death row than to prison, but all other racial combinations were more likely to result in a prison sentence.[59] Overall, 701 of the 771 people executed for rape between 1870 and 1950 whose race is known were black,[60] and no white man in the American South was ever executed for raping a black woman.[61] However, the discriminatory application of the death penalty was not limited to rape cases: "Throughout the South, for all crimes, black defendants were

55 Marquart, J. W., Ekland-Olson, S., & Sorensen, J. R. 1994. *The Rope, the Chair, and the Needle: Capital Punishment in Texas, 1923-1990.* Austin: University of Texas Press.

56 McFeely, W. S. 1997. *A Legacy of Slavery and Lynching: The Death Penalty as a Tool of Social Control.* Available from http://www.nacdl.org/CHAMPION/ARTICLES/97nov03.htm. (accessed 24 August 2016).

57 Banner, S. 2002. *The Death Penalty: An American History.* Cambridge, MA: Harvard University Press. p. 228.

58 Foerster, B. J. 2012. *Race, Rape, and Injustice: Documenting and Challenging Death Penalty Cases in the Civil Rights Era.* (M. Meltsner, ed.) Knoxville: University of Tennessee Press.

59 Marquart, J. W., Ekland-Olson, S., & Sorensen, J. R. 1994. *The Rope, the Chair, and the Needle: Capital Punishment in Texas, 1923-1990.* Austin: University of Texas Press.

60 Banner, S. 2002. *The Death Penalty: An American History.* Cambridge, MA: Harvard University Press. p. 230.

61 McGuire, D. L. 2010. *At the Dark End of the Street: Black Women, Rape, and Resistance--a New History of the Civil Rights Movement from Rosa Parks to the Rise of Black Power.* New York: Alfred A. Knopf.

executed in numbers far out of proportion to their population."[62]
Even for the crime of murder, blacks were disproportionately rep-
resented in the death chamber, especially in the American South.[63]
In other words, "The death penalty was a means of racial control."[64]

The legacy of slavery and lynching is still evident today. First, the
modern death penalty is more likely to be employed against those
who kill women—especially white women[65]—and it has been discovered that the harsher treatment given to those who kill white
women can be explained mostly by the sexualized nature of some
white female-victim killings.[66] If the death sentence truly is a
modern, legalized form of lynching, it is sensible that offenses against
white women—especially sexual crimes—would be the most likely
to provoke a death sentence. Second, Southerners are more likely to
support the death penalty,[67] and the overwhelming majority of American executions in the modern era have taken place in the states of the
former Confederacy.[68] Three-quarters of the executions carried out
in 2015 occurred in the former Confederacy, and the remaining ones
occurred in the border states of Missouri and Oklahoma.[69] Lastly,
social scientists have found that the more a state used lynching during

62 Banner, S. 2002. *The Death Penalty: An American History.* Cambridge, MA: Harvard University Press. p. 230.
63 Banner, S. 2002. *The Death Penalty: An American History.* Cambridge, MA: Harvard Universi-ty Press. p. 230. *See* also, Grosso, C. M., O'Brien, B., Taylor, A., & Woodworth, G. 2014. "Race Discrimination and the Death Penalty: An Empirical and Legal Overview." In J. R. Acker, & C. S. Lanier, *America's Experiment with Capital Punishment: Reflections on the Past, Present, and Future of the Ultimate Penal Sanction* (3rd ed.). Durham, NC: Carolina Academic Press. pp. 525–576.
64 Banner, S. 2002. *The Death Penalty: An American History.* Cambridge, MA: Harvard University Press. p. 230.
65 Holcomb, J. E., Williams, M. R., & Demuth, S. 2004. "White Female Victims and Death Penalty Disparity Research." *Justice Quarterly* 21(4):877–902. *See* also, Williams, M. R., & Holcomb, J. E. 2001. "Racial Disparity and Death Sentences in Ohio." *Journal of Criminal Justice* 29(3):207–218.
66 Williams, M. R., Demuth, S., & Holcomb, J. E. 2007. "Understanding the Influence of Victim Gender in Death Penalty Cases: The Importance of Victim Race, Sex-Related Victimization, and Jury Decision Making." *Criminology* 45(4):865–891.
67 Saad, L. 2013. *US Death Penalty Support Stable at 63%.* Available from http://www.gallup.com/poll/159770/death-penalty-support-stable.aspx. (accessed 10 May 2016).
68 Chokshi, N. 2014. *See Where Every Execution Has Taken Place Since 1977, in One Map.* Available from https://www.washingtonpost.com/blogs/govbeat/wp/2014/03/28/see-where-ev-ery-execution-has-taken-place-since-1977-in-one-map/. (accessed 10 May 2016). *See* also, Garland, D. 2010. *Five Myths About the Death Penalty.* Available from http://www.washington-post.com/wp-dyn/content/article/2010/07/16/AR2010071602717.html. (accessed 5 May 2016); Marquart, J. W., Ekland-Olson, S., & Sorensen, J. R. 1994. *The Rope, the Chair, and the Needle: Capital Punishment in Texas, 1923-1990.* Austin: University of Texas Press, and Vandiv-er, M. 2006. *Lethal Punishment: Lynchings and Legal Executions in the South.* New Brunswick, NJ: Rutgers University Press.
69 Death Penalty Information Center. 2015. *The Death Penalty in 2015: Year End Report.* Available from http://deathpenaltyinfo.org/documents/2015YrEnd.pdf. (accessed 16 December 2015).

Reconstruction, the greater its propensity to use the death penalty in the modern era.[70] Furthermore, Jacobs, et al. found that a state's propensity to use the death penalty increased as the percentage of residents who are black increased.[71]

The historical connection between lynching and slavery and the death penalty is also evident at the local level. Only 20% of American counties have sentenced anyone to death and only 15% of American counties have had a case result in an execution since the death penalty was re-instated in 1976.[72] A mere 2% of US counties account for the majority of death sentences and executions carried out in the modern era[73]; these counties also accounted for nearly two-thirds of the death sentences imposed in 2015.[74] What distinguishes these counties from the rest of the US? Well, the county that uses the death penalty the most in the US is Harris County, located in eastern Texas,[75] and, as it turns out, eastern Texas is the region of Texas with the strongest heritage of slavery.[76] A recent study of Maricopa County, Arizona, another county that makes frequent use of the death penalty, discovered that the death penalty "operates in a field of violently contested racial boundaries" where racial boundaries are fortified through "historical white terrorism" and "zones of racial exclusion."[77]

CONCLUSION

The evidence reviewed in this chapter is quite disheartening. Despite efforts by the US Supreme Court to limit discrimination in the

---

70 Jacobs, D., Carmichael, J. T., & Kent, S. L. 2005. "Vigilantism, Current Racial Threat, and Death Sentences." *American Sociological Review* 70:656-677.

71 Jacobs, D., Carmichael, J. T., & Kent, S. L. 2005. "Vigilantism, Current Racial Threat, and Death Sentences." *American Sociological Review* 70:656-677.

72 Dieter, R. C. 2013. *The 2% Death Penalty: How a Minority of Counties Produce Most Death Cases At Enormous Cost to All.* Available from http://www.deathpenaltyinfo.org/documents/TwoPercentReport.pdf. (accessed 3 February 3, 2016).

73 Ibid.

74 Death Penalty Information Center. 2015. *The Death Penalty in 2015: Year End Report.* Available from http://deathpenaltyinfo.org/documents/2015YrEnd.pdf. (accessed 16 December 2015).

75 Phillips, S. 2009. "Legal Disparities in the Capital of Capital Punishment." *Journal of Criminal Law & Criminology* 99(3):717-756. *See* also, Price, M. J. 2015. *At the Cross: Race, Religion, & Citizenship in the Politics of the Death Penalty.* New York: Oxford University Press.

76 Marquart, J. W., Ekland-Olson, S., & Sorensen, J. R. 1994. *The Rope, the Chair, and the Needle: Capital Punishment in Texas, 1923-1990.* Austin, TX: University of Texas Press.

77 Fleury-Steiner, B., Kaplan, P., & Longazel, J. 2015. "Racist Localisms and the Enduring Cultural Life of America's Death Penalty: Lessons from Maricopa County, Arizona." *Studies in Law, Politics, and Society* 66:63-85.

application of the American death penalty, dozens of studies from all across the US have concluded that it continues to be used in a racially biased manner, more often when the victim is white, especially when the accused killer is black.[78] There are numerous structural, institutional, and historical aspects to American society that help to maintain the discriminatory application of the death penalty and which are likely to impede *any* effort to apply the punishment in a fair and neutral manner. More disquieting, the historical connections between slavery, lynching, and the modern death penalty suggest that the modern death penalty is really just a modern, legalized form of lynching that is used to control a "threatening" black population.[79] Considering lynching was clearly directed at controlling blacks and maintaining white supremacy, the correlation between lynching and the death penalty implies that the death penalty is actually a form of racial control more so than a form of social control. In fact, black opposition to the death penalty is often rooted in a sense that it is a practice—like lynching—that is designed to devalue black lives and to maintain control over blacks through the constant threat of violence.[80] Combining the historical connections between the death penalty and more overt systems of racial control, the greater support for the death penalty among whites, the finding that racial prejudice is a strong predictor of death penalty support among whites, and the institutional impediments to the fair and neutral administration of the death penalty, leads to the conclusion that the American death penalty may be an inherently racist institution that can *never* be applied in fairly.

---

78 Grosso, C. M., O'Brien, B., Taylor, A., & Woodworth, G. 2014. "Race Discrimination and the Death Penalty: An Empirical and Legal Overview." In J. R. Acker, & C. S. Lanier, *America's Experiment with Capital Punishment: Reflections on the Past, Present, and Future of the Ultimate Penal Sanction* (3rd ed.). Durham, NC: Carolina Academic Press. pp. 525-576.

79 Jacobs, D., Carmichael, J. T., & Kent, S. L. 2005. "Vigilantism, Current Racial Threat, and Death Sentences." *American Sociological Review* 70:656-677.

80 Price, M. J. 2015. *At the Cross: Race, Religion, & Citizenship in the Politics of the Death Penalty.* New York: Oxford University Press.

CAPITAL PUNISHMENT, MENTAL ILLNESS, AND INTELLECTUAL DISABILITY: THE FAILURE TO PROTECT INDIVIDUALS WITH MENTAL DISORDERS FACING EXECUTION

Sandra Babcock[1]

Introduction

On September 25, 1992, just days after his family tried to have him committed to a psychiatric hospital, Kelsey Patterson shot two people, removed all of his clothing except for a pair of socks, then waited in the street for the police to arrest him.[2] Prosecutors charged him with capital murder. During his trial, Mr. Patterson frequently spoke of "remote control devices" and "implants" that controlled his behavior.[3] The prosecution conceded that he was severely mentally ill. Nevertheless, he was convicted and condemned to death.

The courts found him "competent" to be executed. On May 18, 2004, after he was escorted to the room where he was put to death, the warden asked him if he had a final statement. Reporters described Kelsey Patterson's response as follows:

> Statement to what? Statement to what? ... They're doing this to steal my money. My truth will always be my truth. No kin to you ... undertaker ... murderer. Go to hell. Get my money. Give me my rights. Give me my rights. Give me my life back.

---

1   Clinical Professor, Cornell Law School, New York, United States and Director of Death Penalty Worldwide, www.deathpenaltyworldwide.org. The author is grateful to Delphine Lourtau, the Research Director of Death Penalty Worldwide, for her comparative research on legislation relating to mentally ill and intellectually disabled offenders.

2   Janet Elliott, "Parole Panelists Who Urged Mercy Defer to Perry," *Houston Chronicle, May 20, 2004.*

3   Mike Tolson, "Plea Rejected, Mentally Ill Man Executed," *Houston Chronicle*, May 19, 2004.

He continued to mumble until the flow of lethal chemicals stopped his speech.[4]

The case of Kelsey Patterson illustrates all too well the gap between international norms and state practice regarding mentally disabled offenders facing the death penalty. At a formal level, there is little dispute that severely mentally ill or intellectually disabled offenders should be exempt from the application of the death penalty. The UN Safeguards Guaranteeing Protection of the Rights of Those Facing the Death Penalty ("Safeguards"),[5] adopted in 1984, provide that the death penalty shall not be carried out "on persons who have become insane." In subsequent resolutions, the Economic and Social Council, Human Rights Commission, and General Assembly have called on states to eliminate the death penalty for persons suffering from mental or intellectual disabilities.[6] Human rights treaty bodies and regional commissions have likewise found that states have an obligation not to execute individuals with intellectual disabilities or serious mental illnesses.[7] Commentators have argued that the prohibition on the execution of the insane is so well-established that it has attained the status of customary international law.[8]

States rarely proclaim their right to execute those who suffer from mental disorders.[9] Nevertheless, executions of mentally ill offenders have recently been documented in China, Pakistan, Brazil, and the United States—and there is every reason to believe that thousands

4   Texas Execution Information Center, Execution Report: Kelsey Patterson. 2004. Available from http://www.txexecutions.org/reports/322-Kelsey-Patterson.htm?page=2. (accessed 24 August 2016). An excellent summary of Mr. Patterson's case is provided in Amnesty International, *Another Texas Injustice: The Case of Kelsey Patterson, Mentally Ill Man Facing Execution*, March 18, 2004. Available from https://www.amnesty.org/en/documents/AMR51/047/2004/en/. (accessed 24 August 2016).
5   ECOSOC. 25 May 1984. *Safeguards Guaranteeing Protection of the Rights of Those Facing the Death Penalty*. Res 1984/50 [hereinafter "ECOSOC Safeguards"].
6   ECOSOC. *Implementation of the Safeguards Guaranteeing Protection of the Rights of Those Facing the Death Penalty*. Res 1989/64 (24 May 1989); UNCHR Res 67 (2003) UN Doc E/CN.4/RES/2003/67; UNGA, *Moratorium on the Use of the Death Penalty*. Res. 69/186 (18 Dec. 2014).
7   See, e.g., *Francis v. Jamaica*, Communication No. 606/1994, U.N. Doc. CCPR/C/54/D/606/1994, Aug. 3, 1995; *Sahadath v. Trinidad and Tobago*, Communication No. 684/1996, CCPR/C/74/D/684/1996, Apr. 15, 2002; *Tamayo Arias v. United States, para. 165, Case 12.873, Report No. 44/14, Inter-American Commission on Human Rights, Jul. 17, 2014.*
8   William Schabas. 1993. "International Norms on Execution of the Insane and the Mentally Retarded." *Criminal Law Forum* 4(1):95-117:pp. 114.
9   In this essay, I use the terms "mental disorders" and "mental disabilities" to encompass individuals with mental illnesses as well as those with intellectual disabilities or cognitive disorders caused by brain injury.

of individuals with mental disorders remain on death row around the world.[10] Researchers in the United States have estimated that anywhere from 15% to 50% of individuals in US prisons are mentally ill.[11] In the United Kingdom, a recent study found that 25% of women and 15% of men in prison reported symptoms indicative of psychosis.[12] Little research has been conducted on the topic in the Global South, but available studies indicate large numbers of mentally ill offenders. For example, authors of a recent study of the prison population in nine Latin American countries concluded:

> The prevalence of psychiatric conditions among prisoners in Latin America is greatly underestimated, and because of the lack of awareness about mental illness among service providers in Latin American prisons, oftentimes these conditions go unrecognized or are not treated properly.[13]

The lack of data regarding prisoners with intellectual disabilities is even more striking. Little research has been conducted on the prevalence of intellectual disabilities among the prison population in the Global South. In many retentionist states, trained psychiatrists are scarce: Sierra Leone, for example, has only one psychiatrist to address the needs of a population traumatized by violent conflict.[14] The Privy Council for the Commonwealth Caribbean has repeatedly decried the shortage of qualified forensic psychiatrists to conduct

---

10   In 2005, the UN Secretary General noted that "even though most responding countries state that the insane and the mentally retarded are shielded from the infliction of the death penalty and especially from execution, reports of mentally ill and retarded persons facing the death penalty have continued to emerge during the five years covered by the seventh survey." ECOSOC Report of the Secretary-General, *Capital punishment and implementation of the safeguards guaranteeing protection of the rights of those facing the death penalty*, (2005) UN Doc E/2005/3.

11   See *Treatment Advocacy Center. How Many Individuals with Serious Mental Illness are in Jails and Prisons?, Available from* http://www.treatmentadvocacycenter.org/problem/consequences-of-non-treatment/2580 (accessed 24 August 2016); Olga Khazan, "Most Prisoners Are Mentally Ill," *The Atlantic*, April 7, 2015, available from http://www.theatlantic.com/health/archive/2015/04/more-than-half-of-prisoners-are-mentally-ill/389682/. (accessed 24 August 2016).

12   See *Prison Reform Trust, Mental Health Care in Prisons, available from* http://www.prisonreformtrust.org.uk/projectsresearch/mentalhealth (accessed 19 May 2016).

13   Santiago Almanzar, Craig L. Katz, and Bruce Harry. 2015. "Treatment of Mentally Ill Offenders in Nine Developing Latin American Countries." *J. American Academy of Psychiatry and the Law* 43:340–49.

14   Emmanuel Akyeampong, Allan G. Hill, and Arthur Kleinman, eds. 2015. *The Culture of Mental ILlness and Psychiatric Practice in Africa. Bloominton: Indiana University Press.* Mental health providers are scarce in other Sub-Saharan African countries, as well. *See Atalay Alem, Lars Jacobsson, and Charlotte Hanlon. 2008. "Community-based mental health care in Africa: mental health workers' views." World Psychiatry 7(1):54-57. Available from www.ncbi.nlm.nih.gov/pmc/articles/PMC2327237/. (accessed 16 February 2015).*

mental health assessments.[15] The identification and assessment of such prisoners is made more complicated by the lack of suitable test instruments normed on the local population. In Malawi, for example, researchers have yet to develop a test to assess intellectual functioning in the adult population. Of the more than 200 persons sentenced to death there in the past 20 years, not a single one was assessed prior to trial to determine if he was intellectually disabled. There is every reason to believe that such practices are the norm, rather than the exception, in other retentionist states.

Amnesty International estimates that there are currently 20,292 persons on death rows around the world.[16] Even if only 15% were mentally ill or intellectually disabled—an extraordinarily conservative estimate—that would amount to over 3,000 individuals who, according to international standards, should not be subjected to the death penalty.[17] Yet these prisoners remain largely undetected and ignored by both national criminal justice systems and the international community.

Definitions

Perhaps because it is a taboo subject in many countries, most lawyers, judges and juries have a poor understanding of mental health and how it relates to capital prosecutions. While individuals who are actively psychotic or profoundly intellectually disabled may be easily identifiable, most mentally disabled prisoners do not meet these criteria. The symptoms of mental illness change over time, and an individual who is seriously mentally ill may have periods when he or she functions quite normally. Similarly, most prisoners with intellectual disabilities cannot be identified through casual conversation. They may be able to work, marry, read and write, and keep abreast of current events. Moreover, many mentally ill and intellectually disabled persons have learned coping strategies to prevent others from detecting their impairments. These factors make it very difficult for

---

15   Report of the Secretary-General. 2005. *Capital punishment and implementation of the safeguards guaranteeing protection of the rights of those facing the death penalty. UN Doc E/2005/3.*

16   Amnesty International. 2016. *Death Sentences and Executions 2015.* p. 7.

17   By all indications, the prevalence of mental illness among the death row population is even higher than among the prison population.

the layperson to successfully identify offenders with mental disorders that may be relevant to their culpability as well as their eligibility for capital punishment.

At the outset, it is important to understand the distinction between mental illness and intellectual disability. Intellectual disability is also known as mental retardation or learning disability. In more antiquated penal codes, it may be known as "idiocy." The World Health Organization defines intellectual disability as follows:

> A condition of arrested or incomplete development of the mind...especially characterized by impairment of skills manifested during the developmental period, skills which contribute to the overall level of intelligence, i.e. cognitive, language, motor, and social abilities.[18]

By contrast, mental illness is a medical condition that disrupts a person's thinking, feeling, mood, ability to relate to others and daily functioning. Serious mental illnesses include major depression, schizophrenia, bipolar disorder, obsessive-compulsive disorder, post-traumatic stress disorder and borderline personality disorder.

The Relevance of Mental Health in Death Penalty Cases

Mental health has a direct bearing on four separate—but related—questions that should be posed in every capital proceeding. The first relates to an offender's *sanity. The central tenet of this doctrine is that* an individual may not be held criminally liable if she or he could not appreciate the nature or wrongfulness of their actions at the time of the offense. For example, the Criminal Code of Ghana excludes from criminal responsibility individuals whose "idiocy, imbecility, or any mental derangement or disease affecting the mind" prevents them from understanding the nature or consequences of their actions.[19] Although states have adopted varying definitions of the state of mind necessary to exempt an individual from criminal liability, an

---

18   World Health Organization. 1996. *I CD-10 Guide for Mental Retardation. p. 1.*
19   Ghana Criminal Code of 1960, art. 27, amended by Act No. 646 of 2003.

overwhelming majority embrace this concept. Research conducted by Death Penalty Worldwide indicates that only one country—North Korea—has failed to recognize this principle.

The second question relates to an offender's *fitness to stand trial*. A prisoner who cannot understand the character or consequences of his legal proceedings is not "fit" or "competent" to stand trial. Under the Nigerian penal code, for example, a person found to be of "unsound mind" who is not "capable of making his defence" may be sent to a psychiatric hospital, and the trial will be postponed until the person regains "sound mind."[20] This is a fairly standard response to offenders who are deemed to mentally ill to participate in their own defense.

The third question asks whether an offender has a mental or intellectual disability that exempts him or her from capital punishment altogether. This is the inquiry mandated by the UN Safeguards and resolutions described above. Significantly, this question should be asked *before* any death sentence is imposed, as well as *after* an offender is sentenced to death and before the execution is carried out. The fourth and final question asks whether the offender suffers from any mental impairment that *mitigates* responsibility for the offense, even where it does not operate as a categorical bar to execution. In many states that retain the death penalty, these last two questions are simply ignored, usually because criminal justice stakeholders are not adequately trained in concepts of mental health and their relevance to capital litigation.

A casual observer may wonder why a state cannot fulfill its international obligations by applying the time-honored legal definitions of "sanity" and "fitness" to stand trial described above. After all, don't these concepts identify the most mentally ill offenders? Moreover, if a prisoner is found to be insane, she or he cannot be convicted of any crime, let alone a capital crime—and a person who is unfit to stand trial is similarly protected so long as mental illness prevents them from participating in their defense. Clearly, these provisions protect a certain subset of floridly mentally ill persons.

---

20   Nigeria Criminal Procedure Act, arts. 222-224, Laws of the Federation of Nigeria Ed. 2000 Ch. 80, June 1, 1945, as updated to Dec. 31, 2000.

In practice, however, many mentally ill and intellectually disabled offenders fail to meet the criteria set forth in the definitions of "sanity" and "fitness." As an initial matter, the definitions of "insanity" in most penal codes do not encompass individuals with mild intellectual disabilities. Individuals with intellectual disabilities are not psychotic; they do not have delusional belief systems or experience hallucinations as a result of their disability. Individuals with intellectual disability may have trouble processing information, responding to social cues, and exercising good judgment—particularly under stress. But they can often understand the wrongfulness of their actions, and for this reason they may not meet the legal definition of "insanity." As Justice Stevens explained in the seminal case of *Atkins v. Virginia*:

> Mentally retarded persons frequently know the difference between right and wrong and are competent to stand trial. Because of their impairments, however, by definition they have diminished capacities to understand and process information, to communicate, to abstract from mistakes and learn from experience, to engage in logical reasoning, to control impulses, and to understand the reactions of others. ... Their deficiencies do not warrant an exemption from criminal sanctions, but they do diminish their personal culpability.[21]

In other words, someone who is intellectually disabled (and who does not also suffer from a mental illness) does not commit a crime in the grips of a delusion that she is slaying a demon. Rather, she may overreact in a situation that calls for a more moderated response. Or she may commit a crime at the suggestion of a more dominant (and intelligent) co-defendant. Definitions of "insanity," however, are not typically focused on such nuances.[22] In most countries, the definition of insanity is either limited to individuals with serious mental illnesses or is so vague that its application to individuals with intellectual disabilities is unclear.

---

21 *Atkins (n 32) (citations omitted).*

22 There are notable exceptions: Jamaica's penal code provides that a person suffering from "abnormality of mind" due to "a condition of arrested or retarded development or any inherent cause induced by disease or injury" so as to "substantially impair his mental responsibility" cannot be convicted of murder. Jamaica Offences Against the Person Act, art. 5(1), 2005. This provision is sometimes called a "diminished capacity" defense.

Moreover, the definitions of "insanity" and "fitness" are limited in other ways. First, they are fixed to specific points in time. Definitions of "fitness to stand trial" focus exclusively on a prisoner's mental competency at the time of trial—and once a prisoner's mental health is restored, he or she may be prosecuted and condemned to death. Definitions of "insanity" do not exempt from punishment *all* persons who are mentally ill, but only those were unable to control their actions or understand the wrongfulness of their actions at the time of the offense. Yet, as noted above, the symptoms of mental illness wax and wane over time, and someone who appears "normal" two weeks after the commission of a crime may have been severely mentally ill at the time of the offense. For this reason, mentally ill individuals may fall through the cracks of the system unless they are evaluated by competent mental health professionals—who, as noted above, are in short supply in many countries.

China's legislation on this point is illustrative: it provides that no criminal responsibility attaches to a "mental patient" if he or she "causes harmful consequences at a time when he or she is unable to recognize or control his or her own conduct." However, a mental patient "whose mental illness is of an intermittent nature shall bear criminal responsibility if he commits a crime when he is in a normal mental state."[23] But what about persons who develop mental illnesses *after they are convicted and sentenced to death?* Prison conditions, combined with the enormous stress of living under a death sentence, often exacerbate pre-existing mental illnesses or cause previously healthy prisoners to develop mental disorders.[24] Yet research conducted by Death Penalty Worldwide indicates that only a handful of retentionist states have adopted legislative provisions designed to prevent the execution of prisoners who have become mentally ill while awaiting execution.[25]

---

23 Criminal Law of the People's Republic of China (as amended to 25 February 2011) art. 18.
24 UNSG Report 2009 (n 41), para. 91 ("It is not uncommon for a person to become insane subsequent to conviction and sentence of death, and in such cases execution is forbidden by the third safeguard.").
25 These countries include Algeria, Antigua and Barbuda, Cuba, Ethiopia, Guatemala, Japan, Jordan, Syria, Tajikistan, and Thailand. This review was conducted by searching the database maintained by Cornell Law School's *Death Penalty Worldwide*, which tracks legislation in 88 retentionist states and territories, including legislation regarding the application of the death penalty to individuals with mental or intellectual disabilities. See *Death Penalty Worldwide*, available from www.deathpenalty-worldwide.org. (accessed 24 August 2016).

Some offenders suffer from less serious mental impairments and may not be fully exempt from capital punishment. For this group, the fourth question noted above—namely, whether the offender suffers from any mental impairment that *mitigates* responsibility for the offense—must be explored prior to sentencing. A person with a brain injury, for example, may be emotionally volatile and less able to exercise impulse control. A person with very low intelligence may have difficulty processing information and responding appropriately in times of stress, even though he or she does not meet the definition of intellectual disability. A person who has experienced great loss or the stress associated with privation, abuse, or community violence, may experience heightened impulsivity and greater susceptibility to drug and alcohol addiction. In these examples, the affected person may be more inclined to commit a crime because of a mental disorder, even when that disorder is not completely debilitating. Mental health as mitigation does not seek to excuse criminal behavior, but to explain it—and by doing so, justify the imposition of a lesser sentence.

In countries with a mandatory death penalty, judges are prohibited from considering mental health as mitigating in the way I have just described. But even in countries where judges could, in theory, take such evidence into account, it is rarely presented—with a few notable exceptions. In the United States, legal defense teams frequently consult multiple mental health experts in preparing for the sentencing phase of trial. Experts in brain injury, intellectual disability, trauma, mental illness, fetal alcohol spectrum disorder, and other mental disorders evaluate prisoners, prepare detailed reports, and testify at trial. And in the Commonwealth Caribbean, courts have found that the defendant has the right to a mental health evaluation in all death penalty cases.[26] In many other countries, issues of mental health (apart from sanity and fitness) are almost never explored. This is attributable, in part, to a lack of resources and suitable experts. It is also the consequence of a lack of awareness and training regarding the relevance of mental health as a mitigating factor.

Addressing these challenges is no easy task. The first hurdle is reaching consensus on which mentally disabled prisoners should be completely

---

26 *Pipersburgh v. The Queen* UKPC 11 (2008); Inter-American Court of Human Rights, *Dacosta Cadogan v. Barbados*, 128 (10), Sep. 24, 2009, available from http://www.corteidh.or.cr/docs/casos/articulos/seriec_204_ing.pdf. (accessed 24 August 2016).

exempt from capital punishment. A decade ago, the UN Secretary-General recommended "clarifying the safeguards to be applied to the mentally ill as opposed to the insane or the mentally retarded," after noting that the application of these prohibitions was clouded by competing interpretations.[27] And in his 2009 report on the implementation of the third Safeguard, the Secretary General observed:

> The real difficulty with the safeguard lies not in its formal recognition but in its implementation. Whereas with juvenile offenders or pregnant women, the determination that a person belongs to the protected category is relatively straightforward, there is an enormous degree of subjectivity involved when assessing such concepts as insanity, limited mental competence and "any form of mental disorder". The expression "any form of mental disorder" probably applies to a large number of people sentenced to death.[28]

Nevertheless, the international community has done little to advance a dialogue about mental illness and intellectual disability. A useful starting point for this dialogue would be the recently revised United Nations Standard Minimum Rules for the Treatment of Prisoners ("Mandela Rules"). Rule 39.3 provides:

> Before imposing disciplinary sanctions, prison administrations shall consider whether and how a prisoner's mental illness or developmental disability may have contributed to his or her conduct and the commission of the offence or act underlying the disciplinary charge. Prison administrations shall not sanction any conduct of a prisoner that is considered to be the direct result of his or her mental illness or intellectual disability.

Rule 39 recognizes that mental disorders must be considered as a mitigating factor ("how a prisoner's mental illness or developmental disability may have *contributed* to his or her conduct") and as a justification for imposing no penalty at all ("*Prison administrations shall*

---

27   UNSG Report 2005, *supra*.
28   ECOSOC. 2009. *Report of the Secretary-General: Capital punishment and implementation of the safeguards guaranteeing protection of the rights of those facing the death penalty.* UN Doc E/2010/10.

not sanction any conduct ... that is considered to be the direct result of his or her mental illness or intellectual disability"). And in order to make this assessment, prison administrations must be informed by the opinion of competent experts in the field.

Another challenge is resource constraints and lack of human capacity. But even in states with limited resources and few qualified psychiatrists, there are ways to enhance the protection of persons with mental disabilities. In Malawi, for example, where (to the author's knowledge) there are currently no qualified psychiatrists, a team of lawyers and mental health workers have created a questionnaire to screen the death row population for intellectual disabilities, brain damage and mental illness. The questionnaire is administered by volunteers, students, and paralegals, some of whom have received basic training on mental health. If the prisoner's responses indicate a possible mental disorder, the team alerts a mental health worker, who then interviews the prisoner. To assess intellectual functioning, mental health workers have begun to administer the Raven's Progressive Matrices, a nonverbal intelligence test that can be used with illiterate prisoners in a variety of cultural settings. Although the Raven's has not been normed on the Malawian population, it is nonetheless useful as a screening tool to identify prisoners who may be intellectually disabled.

Malawian paralegals have been trained to interview family members, friends, and neighbors of prisoners to identify risk factors for intellectual disability (such as a mother's use of alcohol while pregnant) and symptoms of delayed development as well as mental illness. This information is then provided to mental health workers, who can develop a more complete picture of the prisoner's mental health. In a number of recent death penalty cases, Malawian courts have considered mental disorders as mitigating factors justifying a lesser sentence.[29] For example, in the case of a mother convicted of poisoning her two children and trying (but failing) to kill herself, the High Court observed that the "homicide was committed in circumstances that strongly suggest that the convict was mentally imbalanced." The court noted that "[e]vidence of 'mental or emotional disturbance',

---

29   See, e.g., *R. v. Makolija, No. 12 of 2015 (Nyirenda, J), Mar. 4, 2015; R. v. N'dala, No. 42 of 2015 (Nyirenda, J), Aug. 8, 2015.*

even if it falls short of meeting the definition of insanity, may none-theless make an offender less culpable on a murder charge and this should be considered in mitigation of sentence."[30]

The Malawi model could prove instructive for states facing similar resource constraints. At an international level, diplomats, scholars and jurists should devote greater attention and resources to the challenges of implementing international protections for persons with mental disabilities. At a minimum, states should be urged to adopt legislation or administrative regulations that mandate competent mental health evaluations of prisoners facing the death penalty, both before and after trial. International experts in the field of mental health should develop partnerships with their colleagues in the Global South to build capacity to conduct such evaluations. Through these efforts, we can build awareness of the prevalence of mental disabilities in the prison population, and reduce the risk that mentally disabled prison-ers will be subjected to capital punishment.

---

30 *R. v. Makolija*, No. 12 of 2015 (Nyirenda, J), Mar. 4, 2015, p. 10.

2.3 Other cases of the Death Penalty against International Law

THE INEVITABILITY OF ARBITRARINESS: ANOTHER ASPECT OF VICTIMISATION IN CAPITAL PUNISHMENT LAWS

Saul Lehrfreund[1] and Roger Hood[2]

INTRODUCTION

As capital punishment becomes ever more restricted in its scope, those countries that retain it have been made more and more aware of a fatal flaw: the inevitability of arbitrariness, and inequity in the infliction of the penalty that amounts to victimization through violation of international human right norms which protect the right to life. This is the case whether the death penalty is the mandatory punishment for a capital offence or whether discretion to inflict it resides with the courts.

To be justified in accordance with developing international standards and constitutional requirements, capital punishment would have to be administered impartially, equitably, under legal procedures that protect the rights of the accused and the convicted from unfair trial and choice of penalty, and in a way that not only avoids mistaken judgment but also discrimination and arbitrariness in its infliction.

As far as the mandatory death penalty is concerned, a body of case law from around the world has reflected a growing consensus that its imposition is cruel and inhuman and amounts to an arbitrary deprivation of life. As Justice Stewart stated in *Woodson v. The State of North*

---

1   Saul Lehrfreund, MBE, LL.D (Hon), is co-executive director of The Death Penalty Project and Visiting Professor at the School of Law, University of Reading, United Kingdom.

2   Roger Hood, CBE, QC (Hon), DCL, is Professor Emeritus of Criminology and Emeritus Fellow of All Souls College, University of Oxford, United Kingdom.

Carolina (1976),[3] this is because a mandatory death sentence "… treats all persons convicted of a designated offence not as uniquely individual human beings, but as members of a faceless, undifferentiated mass subjected to the blind infliction of the death penalty"— the court having been deprived of its discretion to determine the appropriate punishment in a capital case.

While this is a decisive reason for abolishing the mandatory death penalty, evidence has also been mounting to prove that the problem of arbitrariness cannot be avoided by substituting a discretionary death penalty and restricting it by law or sentencing guidelines to certain categories and circumstances of the "most serious" murders and to persons whose motivations and propensities to committing further grave crimes and their incapacity to "reform" are believed to make them the only ones that are "death worthy." This is because there is an inevitable element of subjectivity involved in making such crucial judgments, either by legislators when attempting to distinguish in law and define in statute the types or circumstances of murder or any other capital crime that solely merit death; or by the prosecution authorities in deciding for which of such cases they should seek the death penalty; or by judges (and in some jurisdictions juries) who have to decide whether or not the facts before them make the imposition of the death penalty "inevitable."

Attempts to restrict in various ways the imposition of capital punishment by providing the right to seek pardon or commutation from the executive is not an acceptable substitute (even though it is a necessity until the death sentence is abolished altogether), because this involves the determination of a matter of life or death through a political, not a judicial, system, which is also prone to arbitrariness and discrimination.

In the space available, this article cannot cover all this ground in detail. It will therefore concentrate on showing that not only has support for the mandatory death penalty been undermined by a combination of constitutional judgments and legislative reforms, it has in most countries where it is maintained in law not been enforced by executions; either at all, or on anything like the scale required by law. Furthermore, evidence has emerged that, even in countries where,

---

3   428 US 280 (1976).

according to opinion polls, the support of the public for capital punishment in abstract is very high, most respondents to such polls do not favour its *mandatory* infliction when confronted with examples of capital cases, thus depriving the mandatory death penalty of any popular legitimacy. Finally, recent critiques of even the most constrained determinate capital punishment systems have shown that even they have not been able to overcome the fatal flaw of arbitrariness.

The mandatory death penalty in retentionist countries

Among the steadily dwindling number of nations that retain the death penalty in law—now amounting to 88—only 39 are known to have judicially executed any persons within the past 10 years. Only 14 (or maybe 16) of these "active executioners" maintain the mandatory death penalty. All but three of these countries apply it under sharia law for murder and usually some other crimes.[4] Under sharia law, the mandatory sentence may not be enforced because the principle of qisas allows for the families of victims of murder to forgive the perpetrator or to accept payment (diya) in compensation for the death. This mechanism, which is in effect like a private system of clemency, may be applied arbitrarily depending on the characteristics of the case and the sympathies of the parties concerned.

Thus, only three active retentionist countries with a secular legal system now retain the mandatory death penalty: Malaysia (for murder, drug trafficking and certain firearms offences); Nigeria (for murder and in states applying sharia law for a wider range of crimes); and Singapore (for intentional murder, drug trafficking and some firearms offences). However, in Malaysia the mandatory death penalty is under review; in Singapore it has recently been restricted in scope;[5] and in Nigeria it is susceptible to constitutional challenge of the kind that has been successful in other Commonwealth countries. Furthermore,

---

4   The active retentionist countries that apply the mandatory death penalty under sharia law are: Afghanistan, Iran, Kuwait, Libya, Nigeria, Pakistan, Palestine Authority, Saudi Arabia, Sudan Yemen, and United Arab Emirates, The website www.deathpenaltyworldwide.org (accessed 24 August 2016) notes that Somalia and South Sudan may also have a mandatory death penalty for murder, but it is "unsure".

5   *See* Wing-Cheong Chan. 2016. "The Death Penalty in Singapore: in Decline but Still Too Soon for Optimism." *Asian Journal of Criminology,* forthcoming.

even where the death penalty is mandatory, this does not mean that it will be regularly enforced by executions. For example, the deputy prime minister of Malaysia announced at the end of March 2016 that 829 persons had been sentenced to death between 2010 and March 2016 but only 12 executions had taken place in this period.[6]

In addition, another 13 countries currently retain the mandatory death penalty but are regarded by the United Nations as "abolitionist de facto", having not executed anyone for at least 10 years.[7] It is important to recognise that in these countries the imposition of the mandatory death penalty still has many negative consequences for those on whom it is imposed, in particular their confinement in separate and inferior penal conditions, uncertain as to the future policy of government regarding their fate.[8]

Challenges to the mandatory death penalty: domestic and international litigation

The United States Supreme Court, the Indian Supreme Court, the Judicial Committee of the Privy Council, the Supreme Court of Bangladesh and the Supreme Courts of Uganda and Malawi, as well as the Inter-American Court of Human Rights, the Inter-American Commission on Human Rights and the United Nations Human Rights Committee have all reached the same conclusion: the death penalty cannot be imposed without judicial discretion to consider the gravity of the offence and any mitigating circumstances relating to the circumstances of its commission and the characteristics of the convicted person. Therefore, the prohibition of the mandatory imposition of the death penalty is becoming ever closer to attaining the status of a *jus cogens* norm of international human rights law. What follows is a brief review of these decisions.

---

6   Reported in Hands Off Cain *eNewsletter*, 15, 61, March 31, 2016.

7   These countries are: Barbados, Brunei (sharia), Guinea, Qatar (sharia), Myanmar, Ghana, Kenya (upheld for armed robbery), Maldives, Niger, Sri Lanka, Tanzania, Kenya, and Trinidad and Tobago.

8   In Kenya, there have been two recent conflicting decisions of the Court of Appeal on the mandatory death penalty (*Mutiso v. Republic* [2011] 1 E.A.L.R; and *Mwaura v R*, Crim. App. 5/2008 [October 2008, 2013]). In March 2016, the Supreme Court of Kenya heard arguments on the constitutionality of the mandatory death penalty in *Muruatetu and Mwangi v. Republic* (Petitions Nos. 15 and 16 of 2015) and this case will resolve the conflict/split among the different Court of Appeal panels. The outcome will have implications for more than 2,500 condemned prisoners who were all subjected to the mandatory death penalty and have exhausted their appeals.

In 1976, the United States Supreme Court in *Woodson v North Carolina*[9] and *Roberts v Louisiana*[10] invalidated the mandatory death sentence for murder contained in revised statutes which were intended to avoid arbitrariness by restricting capital punishment only to the most egregious kinds of murder, for whom the punishment should be made certain. It did so on the grounds of humanity:

In capital cases the fundamental respect for humanity underlying the Eighth Amendment…requires consideration of the character and record of the individual offender and the circumstances of the articular offence as a constitutionally indispensable part of the process of inflicting the penalty of death.

A similar approach was adopted by the Indian judiciary. In *Bachan Singh v. State of Punjab* (1980), the Indian Supreme Court had held that the death penalty (which had already been restricted by requiring "special reasons" to be recorded when imposing it) must be reserved for the "rarest of rare" cases.[11] Three years later in *Mithu v State of Punjab* (1983)[12] the Court found the mandatory death penalty to be disproportionate and unconstitutional:

A provision of law which deprives the Court of the use of its wise and beneficent discretion in a matter of life and death, without regard to the circumstances in which the offence was committed and, therefore, without regard to the gravity of the offence, cannot but be regarded as harsh, unjust and unfair.

International tribunals, including the UN Human Rights Committee, have consistently found that the mandatory death penalty violates Article 6(1) of the International Covenant on Civil and Political Rights (ICCPR), the American Convention on Human Rights and the American Declaration of the Rights and Duties of Man as it has been deemed to be both an arbitrary deprivation of life and a cruel, inhuman, or degrading form of punishment. Examples of judgments of the Human Rights Committee are *Thompson v. Saint Vincent and*

---

9   See Note 3 above.
10   431 US 633 (1976).
11   *Bachan Singh v. State of Punjab* 2SCJ 474 (1980).
12   2 SCR 690 (1983).

the Grenadines[13] and most recently the case of *Johnson v. Ghana*,[14] the first decision of the Committee in a complaint brought against Ghana under the Optional Protocol to the ICCPR. In June 2002, when the Inter-American Court of Human Rights addressed the mandatory death penalty for the first time in the case of *Hilaire, Constantine and Benjamin et al v. Trinidad and Tobago*, it also held that the mandatory imposition of the death penalty for all offences of murder violated article 4(1) of the American Convention on Human Rights which enshrines the right to life in very similar terms to Article 6(1) of the Covenant. In 2007, this decision was followed by the court in the case of *Boyce et al v. Barbados*[15] and in September 2009, in the case of *Cadogan v. Barbados*.[16]

This body of persuasive nonbinding jurisprudence, created at an international level in recent years, has increasingly been made available to national constitutional courts who have in many cases adopted international human rights norms in domestic constitutional jurisprudence. This has been particularly evident in the legal challenges to the mandatory nature of the death penalty in the Caribbean, Africa, and most recently, Bangladesh, with domestic laws being invalidated where they have been found to violate international human rights norms on the death penalty. As a result, criminal justice regimes are in many cases operating in closer conformity with international human rights norms—a process that has been described as "the harmonization of death penalty regimes across borders."[17]

In their seminal judgment in *Reyes v. Queen*,[18] the Judicial Committee of the Privy Council held that the imposition of a mandatory death

---

13 (Communication No. 806/1998), U.N. Doc. CCPR/C/70/D/806/1998, at para.8.2. Also *Kennedy v. Trinidad and Tobago*, (Communication No. 845/1998), U.N. Doc. CCPR/C/74/D/845/1998; *Carpo v. The Philippines*, (Communication No. 1077/2002), U.N. Doc. CCPR/C/77/D/1077/2002; *Lubuto v. Zambia*, (Communication No. 390/1990), U.N. Doc. CCPR/C/55/D/390/1990/Rev.1; *Chisanga v. Zambia*, (Communication No. 1132/2002), U.N. Doc. CCPR/C/85/D/1132/2002; *Mwamba v. Zambia*, (Communication No. 1520/2006), U.N. Doc. CCPR/C/98/D/1520/2006.

14 *Johnson v. Ghana* (Communication no 2177/2012), U.N. Doc. CCPR/C/110/D/2177/2012 (March 27, 2014).

15 Inter-American Court of Human Rights, Judgment of 20 November 2007.

16 Inter-American Court of Human Rights, Judgment of 24 September 2009. Following these decisions, the government of Barbados has committed itself to abolishing the mandatory death penalty.

17 *See* Andrew Novak. 2014. *The Global Decline of the Mandatory Death Penalty: Constitutional Jurisprudence and Legislative Reform in Africa, Asia and the Caribbean*. Ashgate Publishing.

18 2 AC 235 (2002). See also *R v. Hughes* 2 AC 259 (2002); *Fox v. R* 2 AC 284 (2002); and *Bowe and Davis v. The Queen* 1 WLR 1623 (2006).

sentence on all those convicted of murder was "disproportionate" and "inappropriate" and thus inhuman and degrading. In so doing, it construed the domestic law so as to conform closely with international human rights norms. As Lord Bingham observed:

> To deny the offender the opportunity, before sentence has been passed, to seek to persuade the court that in all the circumstances to condemn him to death would be disproportionate and inappropriate is to treat him as no human being should be treated and thus to deny his basic humanity.[19]

In recent years, the highest courts in three African jurisdictions have likewise concluded that imposing the death penalty with no discretion to impose a lesser sentence in appropriate cases violates the constitutional prohibition of inhuman or degrading treatment or punishment. This conclusion was reached by the Constitutional Court of Uganda, in *Kigula & 416 Others v. Attorney-General (2005)*[20] later affirmed by the Supreme Court of Uganda,[21] and by the Court of Appeal of Malawi in *Twoboy Jacob v. The Republic*.[22]

The same conclusion was reached in 2010, in the case of *Bangladesh Legal Aid and Services Trust v. Bangladesh (Shukur Ali)*,[23] where the High Court of Bangladesh declared unconstitutional Section 6(2) of the Women and Children Repression Prevention (Special) Act which provided for the mandatory death sentence for those convicted of killing a woman or child after rape. The decision was affirmed by the Supreme Court of Bangladesh in 2014, which emphasised that: "Determination of appropriate measures of punishment is judicial and not executive functions."[24]

The constitutional courts described above have, in recent years, therefore adopted an interventionist approach to the application of the death penalty, and in so doing have removed the mandatory death penalty

---

19 2 AC 235 (2002) at para. 43.
20 Constitutional Petition No. 6 of 2003, Judgment of 10 June 2005.
21 *Attorney-General v. Kigula* UGSC 15 (2008).
22 Criminal Appeal Case No. 18 of 2006, Judgment of 19 July 2007.
23 30 B.L.D. 194 (2010) (High Ct. Div. of Bangladesh Sup. Ct.).
24 *Bangladesh Legal Aid and Services Trust and others v. The State* (Appellate Division, Supreme Court of Bangladesh) (5 May 2015).

and introduced judicial discretion. By contrast, the courts in Singapore[25] and Ghana[26] have rejected this approach.[27] The Singapore Court of Appeal and the Supreme Court of Ghana have emphasised that the reform of death penalty laws is a matter exclusively for parliament and not the courts and as such have been guided by a spirit of judicial restraint and deference to the legislature. Notwithstanding the fact that the Singapore parliament has modified its mandatory death penalty provisions and the Government of Ghana has maintained a moratorium on executions and indicated that it is committed to abolition,[28] this is simply an outdated view of the role of the judiciary. It has been stigmatised as an abdication of judicial responsibility. If judges are the ones vested with the authority to interpret the constitution, then it is for judges to state what is or is not inhuman treatment.[29]

A political issue: Does the public demand the mandatory death penalty?

Countries that continue to resist the call to abolish the mandatory death penalty (and indeed capital punishment in general) frequently claim that to do so without the support of public opinion would undermine respect for the law and the authority of the state and its criminal justice institutions. Such countries do not accept that the issue can be determined solely by theoretical principles of jurisprudence and human rights but contend that it should reflect the will and tolerance of the governed populace, as well as those who administer the legal system.[30]

---

25 See *Yong Vui Kong v. Public Prosecutor* 2 S.L.R. 491 (2010).

26 See *Johnson v. Republic* S.C.G.L.R 601 (Ghana) (2011).

27 As regards Trinidad and Tobago, the Judicial Committee of the Privy Council in *Matthew v. State of Trinidad and Tobago* 1 AC 433 (2005), held that, although the mandatory death penalty did amount to cruel and inhuman punishment by virtue of the "savings clause" in the Constitution of Trinidad and Tobago, only Parliament could repeal the law. On the same day the JCPC came to the same conclusion as regards the Constitution of Barbados in the case of *Boyce and Joseph v. The Queen* 1 AC 400 (2005).

28 According to the recent study of public opinion in Ghana it appears that among a sample of residents of Accra, the capital, well over half would support abolition for all three crimes currently subject to the death penalty. *See* Justice Tankebe, K.E Boakye and A.P. Atupare. 2015. *Public Opinion and the Death Penalty in Ghana,* Accra: Centre for Criminology and Criminal Justice.

29 *See* Andrew Novak. 2015. "The Abolition of the Mandatory Death Penalty in India and Bangladesh: A Comparative Commonwealth Perspective." *Global Business & Development Law Journal* 28.

30 *See* Roger Hood and Carolyn Hoyle. 2015. *The Death Penalty. A Worldwide Perspective* (5th ed.). Oxford: Oxford University Press. Chapter 10: "A Question of Opinion or a Question of Principle"; and Mai Sato. 2014. *The Death Penalty in Japan. Will the Public Tolerate Abolition?* Weisbaden: Springer V.S.

Until recently, empirical evidence of public and professional opinion on the mandatory death penalty has been absent, and countries that maintain it have relied instead on opinion polls that reflect their perception of general support for capital punishment. In two such countries, Trinidad and Tobago and Malaysia, opinion polls have been published within the last five years that have shown that, while around 90% of respondents said that they favoured the death penalty, only a minority supported the mandatory infliction of capital punishment on conviction for murder in Trinidad[31] and for murder, drug trafficking and certain firearms offences in Malaysia.[32] A further survey of judges, prosecutors and counsel in Trinidad also showed a very low level of support for retaining the inflexible mandatory penalty of death.[33]

The findings of the public opinion polls were remarkably consistent. To begin with, the surveys of the general population (1,000 in Trinidad and 1,535 in Malaysia) showed that only a minority of citizens felt that they were very well informed about the law and use of the death penalty in their countries. Indeed, in Malaysia only 4 out of 10 knew that the death penalty was the only sentence that a judge could impose for murder and drug trafficking. After being informed of the meaning of a mandatory sentence, respondents were asked simply whether they were in favour of death being the punishment for everyone or whether the judge should be allowed to decide whether or not to choose the death penalty according to the circumstances, and, if in favour, whether they were very strongly in favour or simply preferred it rather than giving the judge discretion.

In Trinidad, only 26% favoured the mandatory penalty, but most of them "strongly". In Malaysia the proportion was higher: 56% said they favoured the mandatory penalty for murder; between 25% and 44% were in favour of it for drug trafficking, depending on the type of drug concerned; and 45% for firearms offences, even when nobody had been killed. For all three crimes the majority who said

---

31 Roger Hood and Florence Seemungal, 2011. *Public Opinion on the Mandatory Death Penalty in Trinidad,* London: The Death Penalty Project.

32 Roger Hood. 2013. *The Death Penalty in Malaysia. Public opinion on the mandatory death penalty for drug trafficking, murder and firearms offences,* London: The Death Penalty Project.

33 Roger Hood and Florence Seemungal. 2009. *A Penalty Without Legitimacy: The Mandatory Death Penalty in Trinidad and Tobago.* London: The Death Penalty Project.

they favoured the mandatory death penalty said they were "strongly in favour."

In order to test whether those who said that they favoured the mandatory penalty in "abstract," sub-samples of the respondents were each presented with scenarios of typical cases, some with aggravating factors and others with mitigating circumstances, that might appear before the courts in these countries. If those who said they supported the mandatory death penalty consistently practiced what they said they supported, they would be expected to choose death as the appropriate sentence in all of the cases that they were asked to judge.

The results were very revealing. In Trinidad, only a minority (39%) of the 26% who said they favoured the mandatory death penalty for murder actually "sentenced" to death *all* three cases they were asked to judge. This amounted to only about 1 in 10 of the whole sample of 1,000 persons. Taking into account the total sample, including those who favoured a discretionary death penalty, only 20% thought that death was the appropriate sentence for all three cases of murder they were asked to judge. In Malaysia, only 14% of the 56% who said they favoured the mandatory death penalty for murder actually chose death as the appropriate penalty for all the scenario cases of murder they judged and this amounted to only 8% of the total number of respondents who judged the murder scenarios. Similarly, in judging cases of drug trafficking, only 8% chose death as the punishment for all the scenario cases. Indeed, only 1.2 persons in 100 judged death to be the appropriate punishment in all the examples of murder, drug trafficking, and firearms offences (12 cases in all) that were judged. This was decisive evidence that there was virtually no support for the mandatory deterrent system for such a wide range of crimes in Malaysia.

The only study known to us of the views of criminal justice professionals as regards the mandatory death penalty was carried out in Trinidad and Tobago. A total of 51 such persons, including 16 judges of the high court, 22 experienced prosecutors, and 13 members of the Criminal Bar, were asked whether they were in favour of the status quo. Only one judge, one member of the bar and two prosecutors (just 8% of the total) were content with law as it stood, and almost two-thirds favoured a discretionary system for all cases of murder with guidelines provided for its application or complete abolition.

The evidence from these countries shows that a large majority of those citizens who continue to support capital punishment believe that it must be administered with discretion after consideration of all the relevant facts—situational, circumstantial, and personal—that might ensure that death is not an excessive, disproportionate, and unmerited punishment. There was certainly no evidence to suggest that public opinion would be a barrier to a political decision to abandon the mandatory penalty of death.

The persistence of arbitrary deprivation of the right to life: The Indian experience

As the litany of cases from international tribunals and the constitutional courts summarised above make clear, judicial sentencing discretion in capital cases is a constitutional requirement as long as the death penalty is an available sanction. The abolition of the mandatory death penalty, by requiring that the appropriate sentence for each person convicted of a capital case must be individualised when reaching a judgment of whether the circumstances conform to the purposes of capital punishment, has drastically reduced, in most countries, the number of death sentences imposed. This has of course cut death row populations and limited (but not eliminated) the reliance on executive decisions whether or not to grant clemency in cases where the mandatory sentence is clearly excessive or inappropriate. It is a step in the right direction towards the UN policy of restricting the use of the death penalty, but it is a fallacy to suppose that simply changing the law to permit discretionary use of capital punishment can eliminate arbitrariness. It has been convincingly shown that no system for administering a discretionary death penalty can be devised, however restrictive the guidelines might be, that would be able to eliminate arbitrary judgments of who among the convicted should be selected as death worthy. Moreover, those who are sentenced to death and executed are much more likely to be among the least powerful of all who are convicted of capital crimes. There is a large literature and judicial experience to support this conclusion.[34] In this short contribution, we draw attention to the experience of India, which led the Law Commission of India, in its Report on the Death Penalty in 2015, to conclude that its discretionary system for restricting the infliction of the death penalty—originally seen as major progressive reform—was so flawed in practice that it should be abolished for all ordinary crimes.[35]

In relation to the number of murders recorded and the number of convictions for murder, the number of death sentences imposed in India is very small—97 persons were sentenced to death in 2012, a year when over 34,000 murders were recorded and over 7,000 persons convicted of murder. There is a probability of only 0.3% that a murder will lead to a death sentence being imposed. Enforcement of the death penalty is exceptionally rare: only one execution for an *ordinary* (non-terrorist inspired) murder has been carried out since 1995—an execution in 2004 for the rape and murder of a juvenile. This is a rate of one execution for murder in 20 years among a population in excess of 1 billion people.[36] Yet in India, death sentences continue to be imposed, subjecting at least 477 prisoners at present to the inhumanity and psychological stress of being condemned to death. The problem identified by the Law Commission is that while the sentencing guidelines set out by the Supreme Court in *Bachan Singh* and subsequent judgments, in an attempt to restrict the application of capital punishment solely to the "rarest of the rare" cases, had reduced the proportion of persons convicted of murder sentenced to death, it had failed to avoid arbitrariness in the selection of those prisoners whose crimes were judged to fall into the category of the "rarest of the rare" as compared to many other cases of murder whose perpetrators escaped the death penalty. The system has thus been described as a "lethal lottery."

The Law Commission of India expressed its grave concern that capital punishment has been "arbitrarily and freakishly imposed." Indeed,

---

34 For a review of the literature *see* Roger Hood and Carolyn Hoyle n. 27 above, Chapter 8 "Deciding who should die: problems of inequity, arbitrariness and racial discrimination," and the contributions in United Nations. 2015. *Moving Away from the Death Penalty: Arguments, Trends and Perspectives*. Chapter 3, "Discrimination."

35 The Law Commission of India, *"The Death Penalty,"* Report No 262, August 2015.

36 Three executions have taken place in India since 2004, all for terrorist-related offences: Ajmal Kasab in 2012; Afzal Guru in 2013 and Yakub Memon in 2015.

the Supreme Court had on numerous occasions expressed concern about arbitrary sentencing in death penalty cases and acknowledged that the threshold of the "rarest of the rare" cases has been subjectively, variedly, and inconsistently applied. The application of this doctrine had not followed a discernible pattern and there had been notable inconsistencies with death sentences often being imposed according to the personal predilections of the judges rather than being based on agreed and sound sentencing principles. The Law Commission noted that different courts, including panels of the Supreme Court, had reached diametrically opposite results in cases which had similar facts and circumstances, creating a lack of consistency and want of uniformity.[37] In recommending the abolition of the death penalty for ordinary crimes in India, the Law Commission concluded that:

There exists no principled method to remove such arbitrariness from capital sentencing. A rigid standardization or categorization of offences which does not take into account the difference between cases is arbitrary in that it treats different cases on the same footing. Anything less categorical, like the *Bachan Singh* framework itself, has demonstrably and admittedly failed.

It should be noted that many of the guideline principles adopted in India have been applied in the Caribbean and African countries, which have adopted a similar model post the abolition of the mandatory death penalty.

Concluding Remarks

Whether the death penalty is mandatory or discretionary, ultimately there is no known way for it to be administered without an element of arbitrariness. A discretionary system is certainly preferable to a mandatory scheme, as echoed by constitutional courts and international human rights tribunals who have virtually eliminated the mandatory death penalty globally, but, as the experience of India has shown, even a selective discretionary system creates victims of human rights violations.

---

37 *See* Surya Deva. 2013. "Death Penalty in the 'Rarest of Rare' Cases: A Critique of Judicial Choice-making." In Roger Hood and Surya Deva, eds., *Confronting Capital Punishment in Asia: Human Rights, Politics and Public Opinion*. Oxford: Oxford University Press. pp. 238-286.

Countries which still retain the death penalty—whether mandatory or discretionary—are being faced with convincing evidence of the abuses, discrimination, unfairness, error and inhumanity which inevitably accompany it in practice. The abolition of the mandatory death penalty should thus be seen as a step in the right direction. But the death penalty, however administered and imposed, will always breach the right to life and the prohibition on cruel, inhuman, and degrading punishment. The majority of the world's nations now recognize that the only solution is the total abolition of the death penalty.

CASES OF THE DEATH PENALTY AGAINST INTERNATIONAL LAW: AMNESTY INTERNATIONAL'S CONCERNS

Salil Shetty[1]

In 2015 we passed a crucial milestone—after four additional countries fully abolished the death penalty, the majority of the world's countries are now abolitionist for all crimes. Most of those that retain the death penalty do not actually use it, and the minority of states that still execute people frequently do so in violation of prohibitions and restrictions set out under international law.[2]

One of Amnesty International's main concerns is the continued use of the death penalty for crimes that do not meet the threshold of "most serious crimes" to which the imposition of this punishment must be restricted under international law, and which has been interpreted to refer to intentional killing.[3] This violation of international law is predominantly associated with drug-related offences, and a significant proportion of those who were victims of the death penalty in 2015 had been convicted of such crimes.

This article therefore examines in particular the use of the death penalty and the associated violations of international law that Amnesty International has documented in several drug-related cases. It further highlights how people from disadvantaged socio-economic backgrounds, as well as foreign nationals, are at greater risk of having their rights violated when facing the death penalty. It also considers contradictions found in state policies on this matter that could result in the imposition of the death penalty.

---

1   Secretary-General of Amnesty International.

2   For more information on the global use of the death penalty in 2015, *see* Amnesty International. 2016. *Death Sentences and Executions 2015*. (ACT 50/3487/2016). Available from https://www. amnesty.org/en/documents/act50/3487/2016/en/. (accessed 24 August 2016).

3   *Report of the Special Rapporteur on extrajudicial, summary or arbitrary executions*, UN doc. A/67/275, 9 August 2012.

The death penalty for drug-related offences

Ali Agirdas, a Turkish man convicted of drug trafficking after an unfair trial, was executed on 20 November 2014 in Saudi Arabia. He had been convicted and sentenced to death by a general court in Riyadh in 2008, and his conviction and sentence were later upheld by a court of appeal and the supreme court before being ratified by the Saudi king.

Ali Agirdas had no interpreter or lawyer during his interrogation and trial. He was only assisted by a lawyer during his appeal and was convicted on the basis of a written statement he had signed during his interrogation. The statement was in Arabic, a language he spoke a little but could not read, and incriminated him in the trafficking of drugs, even though he had maintained he was innocent of the crime. During his trial, Ali Agirdas told the court he did not know what was in the document when he signed it.

The impact of the death penalty in his case, however, was not limited to him nor did it end with his execution. His family were not told he was about to be executed, and it appears from his last phone call to them on 19 November, a day before his execution, that neither was he. The family only learned about his death in the afternoon of 20 November, when their relatives and neighbours told them that his execution had been reported on the official Saudi Press Agency website. For almost two years now, Ali Agirdas' family has asked the authorities to return his body to them, without success. To date, they have not even been told where it is buried.[4]

Ali Agirdas' case is, unfortunately, far from the only one Amnesty International has documented in relation to the use of the death penalty for drug-related offences in recent years. In 2015, 685 of the 1,634 executions that Amnesty International recorded globally (excluding China)[5] were for drug-related offences. This means a staggering 42%

---

4   Amnesty International. 2014. *Saudi Arabia: Urgent Action, Further information: executed, body not returned to family.* (MDE 23/034/2014). Available from https://www.amnesty.org/en/documents/mde23/034/2014/en/. (accessed 24 August 2016).

5   Amnesty International's global figures on the use of the death penalty have excluded China since 2009 because of the challenges in obtaining reliable data. China considers the death penalty a state secret. Monitoring is hampered by China's lack of transparency and the limitations placed on civil society activity.

of all known executions were carried out for offences that should not even be punished by death under international law and standards.

The International Covenant on Civil and Political Rights (ICCPR) unequivocally restricted the use of the death penalty to the "most serious crimes," while setting abolition as the ultimate goal. The UN General Assembly reiterated this safeguard when it endorsed, without a vote, the Safeguards Guaranteeing Protection of the Rights of Those Facing the Death Penalty,[6] which clearly state that, "In countries which have not abolished the death penalty, capital punishment may be imposed only for the most serious crimes, it being understood that their scope should not go beyond intentional crimes, *with lethal or other extremely grave consequences*" (emphasis added).

The UN Human Rights Committee, the body tasked with the interpretation of the ICCPR, has on numerous occasions found that drug-related offences do not meet the criterion of "most serious crimes,"[7] a finding reiterated on repeated occasions by other UN independent experts.[8] This interpretation was most recently upheld by the UN Special Rapporteur on extrajudicial, summary or arbitrary executions who, in his 2012 report, stated that, "Domestic law should provide that death sentences may never be mandatory and may be imposed only for those crimes that involve intentional killing. The death penalty may not be imposed for drug-related offences unless they meet this requirement."[9]

Yet drug-related offences, which can include different charges of drug trafficking or drug possession, are currently punished or punishable by death in 33 countries.[10] Only one third of these countries, on

---

6   UNGA resolution 39/118 of 14 December 1984, which endorsed the UN Economic and Social Council resolution 1984/50 of 25 May 1984.

7   UN Human Rights Committee. 2005. *Concluding observations: Thailand.* (CCPR/CO/84/THA). para. 14; UN Human Rights Committee. 2007. *Concluding observations: Sudan.* (CCPR/C/SDN/CO/3). para. 19.

8   Philip Alston. 2007. *Report of the Special Rapporteur on extrajudicial, summary or arbitrary executions.* UN Doc. (A/HRC/4/20). para. 53; 2009. *Report of the Special Rapporteur on torture and other cruel, inhuman or degrading treatment or punishment.* (A/HRC/10/44). para.66.

9   *Report of the Special Rapporteur on extrajudicial, summary or arbitrary executions.* (A/67/275). para.122.

10 Bahrain, Bangladesh, Brunei Darussalam, China, Cuba, Democratic People's Republic of Korea, Democratic Republic of the Congo, Egypt, India, Indonesia, Iran, Iraq, Jordan, Kuwait, Laos, Libya, Malaysia, Myanmar, Oman, Pakistan, Qatar, Republic of Korea, Saudi Arabia, Singapore, South Sudan, Sri Lanka, Sudan, Syria, Thailand, United Arab Emirates, United States of America, Viet Nam and Yemen. This list includes different definitions and circumstances of the offence, including drug trafficking resulting into death, drug trafficking not resulting into death or drug trafficking by agents of the state.

average, have imposed death sentences or carried out executions for such crimes in recent years, but this is not a satisfactory answer to the requirements of international law.[11]

Additional violations of international law: unfair trials, use of death penalty on juvenile offenders and mandatory death sentences

In addition to violating the restriction on the crimes for which the death penalty may be used, countries that use the death penalty for drug-related offences often do so in violation of most basic guarantees of due process. Under international human rights law and standards, people charged with crimes punishable by death are entitled to the strictest observance of all fair trial guarantees and to certain additional safeguards.[12] The authorities of countries that still retain the death penalty have frequently claimed that they apply this punishment in line with restrictions set out in international law and standards. However, Amnesty International has documented numerous instances in which established international safeguards have been flouted, including in cases of people convicted of, and sentenced to death for, drug-related offences. Often this is because the laws regulating the administration of justice and the death penalty do not comply with international instruments, or because officials responsible for law enforcement and the administration of justice violate the rights of defendants and prisoners.

In the great majority of cases that Amnesty International has been able to document, those facing the death penalty for drug-related offences have been individuals from disadvantaged or marginalized socio-economic backgrounds, with no or little means to pay for legal assistance.[13] This has not only exposed them to an increased risk of

---

11 In 2015, China, Indonesia, Iran, Kuwait, Laos, Malaysia, Saudi Arabia, Singapore, Sri Lanka, Thailand, United Arab Emirates and Viet Nam.

12 Among others, UN Economic and Social Council resolution 1984/50 of 25 May 1984.

13 *See, for example,* Amnesty International. 2015. *Flawed justice—Unfair trials and the death penalty in Indonesia.* (ASA 21/2334/2015). Available from https://www.amnesty.org/en/documents/asa21/2434/2015/en/. (accessed 24 August 2016); Amnesty International. 2015. *Killing in the name of justice - The death penalty in Saudi Arabia.* (MDE 23/2092/2015). Available from https://www.amnesty.org/en/documents/mde23/2092/2015/en/. (accessed 24 August 2016); and Amnesty International. 2016. *Growing up on death row—The death penalty and juvenile offenders in Iran.* (MDE 13/3112/2016).

torture or other ill-treatment to extract "confessions" during investigations conducted without the presence of a lawyer, but also resulted, in many cases, in defendants not benefitting from adequate legal representation, being unable to appeal against their death sentences, and being executed following grossly unfair trials. In cases in which the proceedings do not adhere to the highest standards of fair trial, the imposition of the death penalty constitutes an arbitrary deprivation of life, a clear violation of international human rights law.

Both international human rights law and customary international law are clear on the prohibition of the use of the death penalty against individuals who were under 18 years of age when the crime was committed. Despite this, juvenile offenders continue to be under sentence of death in at least eight countries—Bangladesh, Indonesia, Iran, Maldives, Nigeria, Pakistan, Papua New Guinea and Saudi Arabia.[14]

In Iran, individuals convicted of drug-related offences that occurred when the person was under 18 years old have been sentenced to death and executed. Janat Mir, who was 14 or 15 years old at the time of the crime, was executed for drug-related offences in 2014. Mohammad Ali Zehi, whom Amnesty International also believes was a juvenile offender, was sentenced to death for drug-related offences and was on death row between 2008 and 2015. The supreme court quashed his death sentence in November 2015 and ordered a retrial. At the time of writing, the retrial had not begun, but as based on proceedings in other cases, we fear his juvenility at the time of the crime may not be recognized by the court and he will once again be sentenced to death.[15]

In several countries including Iran, Malaysia and Singapore,[16] drug-related offences continue to be mandatorily punished by death despite the fact that mandatory death sentences, even for the most serious

---

14 Amnesty International. 2016. *Death sentences and executions in 2015.* (ACT 50/3487/2016), Available from https://www.amnesty.org/en/documents/act50/3487/2016/en/. (accessed 24 August 2016).

15 Amnesty International. 2016. *Growing up on death row —The death penalty and juvenile offenders in Iran.* (MDE 13/3112/2016). p.57. Available from https://www.amnesty.org/en/documents/mde13/3112/2016/en/. (accessed 24 August 2016).

16 While some sentencing discretion was introduced in Singapore under the Misuse of Drugs Act in 2012, defendants can still be mandatorily sentenced to death.

crimes, are contrary to international law.[17] This, coupled with the automatic presumption of trafficking for those found in possession of certain amounts of prohibited substances, has resulted in the violation of the presumption of innocence and fair trial rights, as well as in the imposition of the death penalty on people like Shahrul Izani bin Suparaman.

Shahrul Izani bin Suparaman was 19 years old when the Malaysian police found him with 622 grams of cannabis in September 2003. Because of the quantity, he was presumed to be trafficking drugs and charged with his first criminal offence. After spending more than six years in detention awaiting trial, he was convicted of drug trafficking and given a mandatory death sentence in December 2009. The court of appeal heard and dismissed his appeal on the same day on 12 October 2011. On 26 June 2012 the Federal Court heard and dismissed his appeal. While he still has the possibility of being spared execution if the Malaysian authorities grant his clemency plea, his case is one of many Amnesty International has recorded where the state has made a young person sentenced for possession of drugs pay with his or her life.

At further disadvantage: foreign nationals

Another striking fact associated with the use of the death penalty for drug-related offences is that foreign nationals constitute a significant proportion of those sentenced to death and executed for these crimes globally, often after being arrested and convicted as low-level "couriers". Foreign nationals are often at a greater disadvantage before criminal justice systems particularly when they cannot afford adequate legal assistance or do not speak or read the language used by the courts.[18] International law affords foreign nationals charged with criminal offences the additional protections of consular and language assistance. For those far away from home and without the support of

---

17 Human Rights Committee. 2004. *Pagdayawon Rolando v. Philippines*. Communication No. 1110/2002, UN doc. (CCPR/C/82/D/1110/2002). para. 5.2.

18 *See, for example,* Amnesty International. *Flawed justice-Unfair trials and the death penalty in Indonesia.* (ASA 21/2334/2015). pp.40-45; Amnesty International. *"Killing in the name of justice—The death penalty in Saudi Arabia.* (MDE 23/2092/2015). pp.24-27. *See also* Christof Heyns. 2015. *Report of the Special Rapporteur on extrajudicial, summary or arbitrary executions, to the 70th Session of the General Assembly.* UN doc. (A/70/304).

their families and social networks, consular assistance can be critical throughout the process, including in gathering evidence that could enable them to support their defence or to present mitigating factors at sentencing or when appealing for clemency. However, these safeguards are not always implemented in practice.

Amnesty International has documented numerous cases where the authorities have failed to notify relevant consular officials of the arrest of their nationals or to provide the accused with translation and interpretation throughout the proceedings from the time of arrest. Discriminatory laws and practices have also resulted in foreign nationals not being able to make use of all avenues of appeal available to the country's own nationals. In Indonesia, for example, Law No. 24/2003 on the Constitutional Court stipulates that only Indonesian nationals can apply for a constitutional review of any legal provision. The Constitutional Court has refused to hear applications brought forward by foreign nationals, including on the constitutionality of the death penalty for drug-related offences. Yet, as a state party to the ICCPR, Indonesia has the obligation to ensure an effective remedy, equality before the law, and equal protection of the law without discrimination, including on the basis of nationality.[19]

Foreign nationals can also find themselves at a disadvantage depending on whether or not their country of nationality actually provides consular assistance and on the effectiveness of any such assistance. Factors that influence whether effective consular assistance is provided to an individual are varied and include the status of the death penalty in their country of nationality as well as the resources available to the relevant consulate. A succession of governments in Canada, for example, has resulted in notable changes in the way Canada intervenes on behalf of its nationals facing the death penalty in other countries. In 2009, the administration introduced guidelines requiring Canadians on death row abroad to apply formally for a discretionary clemency intervention by the Canadian government. This followed a decision by the Canadian authorities to revoke the policy of providing assistance automatically in all cases. However, soon after its election on 19 October 2015, the new government reaffirmed its total opposition

---

19   See, for example, Amnesty International. *Flawed justice-Unfair trials and the death penalty in Indonesia.* (ASA 21/2334/2015). pp. 45-46.

to the death penalty in all cases and announced the end of Canada's selective clemency and intervention policy.[20]

The additional challenges facing foreign nationals accused of criminal offences and the failures and limitations of consular and language assistance can undermine individuals' ability to defend themselves. This in turn heightens the risk of an execution being arbitrary.[21]

Contradictions and collective responsibilities

The issue of consular assistance to foreign nationals in drug-related cases is one where responsibility for the outcome of death penalty cases partly rests with a state other than the one in which the death penalty is imposed and implemented. It can draw attention to contradictions in states' positions when it comes to the death penalty and how they can indirectly contribute to the imposition of this punishment.

In recent years, some countries have taken robust action to prevent the execution of their nationals abroad while continuing to execute foreigners and their own nationals at home. For example, the Ministry of Foreign Affairs of Indonesia has worked closely with other government agencies, including the National Narcotics Agency, to intervene in support of Indonesian nationals on death row overseas. In 2011, then-President Susilo Bambang Yudhoyono established a task force to provide legal and consular assistance to Indonesians on death row abroad. Between 2011 and 2014, 240 Indonesians who were facing executions abroad had their death sentences commuted.[22] At the same time, at home, the country's highest authorities ordered the resumption of executions specifically for drug-related offences. In 2015, President Joko Widodo stated publicly that the government will deny any application for clemency made by people

---

20   Global Affairs Canada. 2016. *Canada reaffirms commitment to human rights.* Available from http://www.international.gc.ca/media/aff/news-communiques/2016/02/15a.aspx?lang=eng&_ga=1.43 006053.1390101966.1465782695. (accessed 24 August 2016).

21   *See* footnote 16 for selected publications by Amnesty International on this topic. See also *Report of the Special Rapporteur on Extrajudicial, summary or arbitrary executions*, UN doc. (A/70/304). 7 August 2015, pp.16-19.

22   Antara. 2014. *Government saves 190 Indonesians from death sentence: Yudhoyono.* Available at: http://www.antaranews.com/en/news/95328/government-saves-190-indonesians-from-deathsentence-yudhoyono. (accessed 24 August 2016). *See also* Amnesty International. 2015. *Death sentences and executions in 2014.* (Index: ACT 50/0001/2015). p.31.

sentenced to death for drug-related crimes saying that, "This crime warrants no forgiveness."[23]

The use of the death penalty for drug-related offences has also shown that abolitionist countries and intergovernmental organizations need to do more to ensure that their actions do not result in the imposition of the death penalty. Cooperation over law enforcement programmes, the provision of technical assistance, and extradition of defendants without seeking assurances that the death penalty would not be imposed can lead to some abolitionist countries and inter-governmental organizations inadvertently supporting and bearing partial responsibility for the imposition of the death penalty in other countries.[24] For example, UNODC-led training projects for count-er-narcotics forces, aiding sniffer dog programmes and other initiatives resulted in an increase in drug seizures in Iran — a country where in recent years Amnesty International has recorded an increase in the number of executions carried out, including for drug-related offenc-es.[25] It is therefore critical that governments and intergovernmental organizations exercise due diligence to ensure that all programmes and policies are carried out in full compliance with international law and other standards, including on the use of the death penalty, while continuing advocating for its worldwide abolition.

Finally, Amnesty International has too often seen governments invok-ing the death penalty as an "effective" public safety measure against crime, or even as a legitimate measure to control drug use and addic-tion. While protecting people from crime and tackling drug abuse and its impact on our health are legitimate goals for governments to pursue, how they choose to do so matters. The death penalty is never the solution — and there is no evidence that the death penalty acts as any greater deterrent to crime, including drug-related crimes,

---

23   President Joko Widodo's speech during the opening of the national coordination meeting on tackling drugs in Jakarta, 4 February 2015, available from http://www.setneg.go.id/index.php?op-tion=com_content&task=view&id=8712&Itemid=26 (accessed 24 August 2016); Antara. 2014. *No mercy for drug dealers: President.* Available from: http://www.antaranews.com/en/news/96848/no-mercy-for-drug-dealers-president%20/. (accessed 24 August 2016).

24   *See, for example, Report of the Special Rapporteur on extrajudicial, summary or arbitrary executions.* UN doc. (A/70/304), 7 August 2015; and *Report of the Secretary-General to the Human Rights Council.* UN doc. (A/HRC/21/29), 2 July 2012.

25   Amnesty International. 2011. *Addicted to death-Executions for drugs offences in Iran.* (MDE 13/090/2011). Available from https://www.amnesty.org/en/documents/mde13/090/2011/en/, (accessed 24 August 2016).

than other forms of punishment.[26] When it comes to preventing the abuse of drugs and reducing its associated health harms, policies based primarily on a law enforcement approach and the imposition of harsh punishments, of which the death penalty is the extreme, not only have not been shown to be effective,[27] but have, on the contrary, contributed to widespread human rights violations and abuses.[28]

The use of capital punishment for drug-related offences is illustrative of the alarming state practice of imposing and implementing death sentences in violation of the most basic safeguards guaranteeing the protection of the rights of those facing the death penalty, put in place to protect against the arbitrary deprivation of life for any crime. It is often those from disadvantaged socio-economic backgrounds who are at greater disadvantage in the criminal justice system. Pending full abolition of the death penalty, governments have a critical role to play to ensure the rights of the prisoners and their families are protected; and that their own policies do not contribute to the use of the death penalty elsewhere. All of us, in turn, must keep on documenting these violations and advocating for the use of the death penalty in any circumstances finally to be brought to an end.

26   Amnesty International. 2013. *Not making us safer: Crime, public safety and the death penalty*. (ACT 51/002/2013). Available from https://www.amnesty.org/en/documents/act51/002/2013/en/. (accessed 24 August 2016).

27   *Report of the Special Rapporteur on the right of everyone to the enjoyment of the highest attainable standard of physical and mental health*. UN doc. (A/65/255), 6 August 2010, pp.16-22; Degenhardt L, Chiu W-T, Sampson N, Kessler RC, Anthony JC, et al. 2008. "Toward a global view of alcohol, tobacco, cannabis, and cocaine use: Findings from the WHO World Mental Health Surveys." *PLoS Med* 5(7). Available from http://journals.plos.org/plosmedicine/article?id=10.1371%2Fjournal. pmed.0050141. (accessed 24 August 2016); *see also* Global Commission on Drug Policy. 2011. *War on Drugs-Report of the Global Commission on Drug Policy*. Available from http://www.globalcom-missionondrugs.org/wp-content/themes/gcdp_v1/pdf/Global_Commission_Report_English. pdf. (accessed 24 August 2016).

28   *Study on the impact of the world drug problem on the enjoyment of human rights - Report of the United Nations High Commissioner for Human Rights to the Human Rights Council*. 4 September 2015. UN doc. (A/HRC/30/65).

DEATH PENALTY — TORTURE OR ILL-TREATMENT?

Jens Modvig[1]

Introduction

During 2015, death sentences took place in 61 countries, and at least 1,998 persons were sentenced to death. The estimated total number of prisoners with death sentences was more than 20,000 at the end of 2015, and a minimum of 1,634 persons were executed in 2015 by means of beheading, hanging, lethal injection or shooting.[2] Still, there are indications that the death penalty is a diminishing phenomenon since the number of countries who have abolished death penalty grew from 48 to 103 between 1991 and 2015.

When considering whether death-sentenced prisoners are subjected to torture or ill treatment, it may be useful to consider separately (1) the circumstances surrounding the death sentence (2) the time waiting for the execution, and (3) the execution itself and the circumstances surrounding it.

The concept of torture is defined in Article 1 of the UN Convention against Torture and other Cruel, Inhuman or Degrading Treatment or Punishment. Here, in Article 1, torture is defined as:

Any act by which severe pain or suffering, whether physical or mental, is intentionally inflicted on a person for such purposes as obtaining from him or a third person information or a confession, punishing him for an act he or a third person has committed or is suspected of having committed, or intimidating or coercing him or a third person, or for any reason based on discrimination of any kind, when such pain or suffering is inflicted by or at the instigation of or with the consent or acquiescence of a public official or other person acting in

---

1   Director, Chief Medical Officer at DIGNITY - Danish Institute Against Torture and Chair of the United Nations Committee Against Torture.

2   Amnesty International. 2016. *Death sentences and executions 2015.* Available from https://www. amnesty.org/en/documents/act50/3487/2016/en/, (accessed on 9 June 2016).

an official capacity. It does not include pain or suffering arising only from, inherent in or incidental to lawful sanctions.

Other cruel, inhuman or degrading treatment or punishment (in short, ill-treatment) is, however, not well-defined. Torture and ill-treatment may be distinguished by the presence or absence of a purpose,[3] and possibly also by the severity of the suffering. This means that ill-treatment may be considered as the infliction of severe pain or suffering, physical or mental, by a public authority, although not intentional and not serving a specific purpose.

The death penalty is imposed and executed in both developed and developing countries. Very different circumstances apply, e.g. in terms of execution methods and procedures, waiting time between sentence and execution, judicial procedures, and reviews leading to a death sentence. Further, there are great differences in terms of the information available about the conditions under which prisoners sentenced to death are held while waiting for the execution, the number of sentenced prisoners, the number of executions, and the characteristics of the sentenced prisoners. In some countries, most of such information is publically available, while in others this information is considered a state secret. On many occasions, different UN bodies have urged states to establish transparency regarding such information.[4]

The question to be addressed in this chapter, thus, is whether persons sentenced to death are at risk of being inflicted severe pain or suffering—in connection with their sentence, while waiting for the execution, or during the execution process.

Torture or ill-treatment in connection with the death sentence

In the majority of the countries where the death penalty is applied, there are reports of torture.[5] Torture is often used to extract confessions

---

3   N.S. Rodley. 2002. "The definition(s) of torture in international law." *Current Legal Problems* 55:467-93. Available from www.corteidh.or.cr/tablas/r08113.pdf (accessed on 9 June 2016).

4   *For example*, UN Economic and Social Council in its Resolution 1989/64 24 May 1989.

5   Amnesty International. *Annual Report 2015/2016*. Available from https://www.amnesty.org/en/latest/research/2016/02/annual-report-201516/. (accessed on 10 June 2016); Human Rights Watch. *World Report 2016*. Available from https://www.hrw.org/world-report/2016. (accessed on 10 June 2016).

during interrogations by the police. This implies that in a substantial number of cases, prisoners sentenced to death have been tortured in order to confess the crime that they are now sentenced for.

Torture victims typically suffer severe physical and mental health consequences in terms of post-traumatic stress disorder, depression and anxiety, sleep disorders, poor concentration, and chronic pain.[6] The psychological symptoms of torture are likely to worsen considerably when a victim is confined in death row due to the conditions that apply. In particular, victims of torture showing classical symptoms will suffer from poor access to medical and psychological treatment or even symptom relief; they also will suffer from abnormal conditions for human interaction, including severe overcrowding or solitary confinement. Such cases are likely to amount to ill-treatment or, if access to treatment is intentionally denied, even to torture.

WAITING FOR THE EXECUTION

Mentally ill prisoners on death row

A mental illness is a condition that impacts a person's thinking, feeling or mood and may affect his or her ability to relate to others and function on a daily basis.[7] This includes conditions such as attention deficit hyperactivity disorder, anxiety disorders, autism, bipolar disorder, borderline personality disorder, depression, dissociative disorders, eating disorder, obsessive-compulsive disorders, post-traumatic stress disorder, schizoaffective disorder, and schizophrenia.

People with *severe* mental illness may be defined as adults who currently or during the past year have a diagnosable mental, behavioral, or emotional disorder of sufficient duration to meet criteria specified within the Diagnostic and Statistical Manual of Mental Disorders that

6   Zachary Steel; Tien Chey; Derrick Silove; et al. 2009. "Association of Torture and Other Potentially Traumatic Events With Mental Health Outcomes Among Populations Exposed to Mass Conflict and Displacement: A Systematic Review and Meta-analysis." *JAMA* 302(5):537-549. Available from http://jama.jamanetwork.com/article.aspx?articleid=184348. (accessed on 10 June 2016).

7   National Alliance on Mental Illness. *Mental health conditions.* Available from https://www.nami.org/Learn-More/Mental-Health-Conditions. (accessed on 11 June 2016).

has resulted in functional impairment which substantially interferes with or limits one or more major life activity.[8]

International law prohibits the execution of persons with severe mental illness.[9] While many countries have legislation that relieves mentally ill persons of criminal liability, persons who may have developed or have been diagnosed with severe mental health illness after the sentence are not necessarily protected against capital punishment.[10] And even if relief from criminal liability applies, there are no assurances that all suspected offenders with a severe mental illness are actually identified and not sentenced. In the United States, it has been estimated that 5–10% of those on death row have severe mental illness.[11]

The actual number of death row prisoner and executed prisoners with severe mental health illnesses is not known, although many case stories exist.[12]

The need for mental health facilities including on death row is reflected in a court case (*Coleman v. Brown*), where the court ruled that prison officials under the California Department of Corrections and Rehabilitation (CDCR) violated the cruel and unusual punishment clause of the US Constitution because they did not provide adequate mental health care. The court identified six areas where the CDCR needs to make improvements: screening, treatment programs, staffing, accurate and complete records, medication distribution, and suicide prevention. Also, the court found that prison officials violated the law by depriving prisoners of involuntary medication. Finally, the court found that prison officials violated the Constitution by punishing prisoners for misconduct, placing them in administrative

8   Federal Register, Vol. 58 No. 96, published Thursday May 20, 1993, pp. 29422-29425, here from National Institute on Mental Health. *Director's Blog: Getting Serious About Mental Illnesses*. Available from http://www.nimh.nih.gov/about/director/2013/getting-serious-about-mental-illnesses. shtml. (accessed on 13 June 2016).

9   E.g., *Safeguards guaranteeing protection of the rights of those facing the death penalty*. UN Economic and Social Council Resolution 1984/50 of 25 May 1984. Available from http://www.ohchr.org/EN/ ProfessionalInterest/Pages/DeathPenalty.aspx. (accessed on 10 June 2016).

10 Death Penalty Worldwide. *Mental Illness*. Available from https://www.deathpenaltyworldwide.org/ mental-illness.cfm. (accessed on 11 June 2016).

11 Mental Health America. *Position Statement 54: Death Penalty and People with Mental Illnesses*. Available from http://www.mentalhealthamerica.net/positions/death-penalty. (accessed on 17 June 2017).

12 Amnesty International. *USA: The execution of mentally ill offenders*. Available from https://www. amnesty.org/en/documents/AMR51/003/2006/en. (accessed on 13 June 2016).

segregation, and using a Taser or 37mm gun without considering the mental health needs of the prisoners.[13]

A special problem with its own ethical dilemma occurs in the treatment of mental illnesses in death row prisoners. While prisoners who are mentally incompetent because of, for instance, a psychotic disorder cannot be executed, this no longer applies if these prisoners are successfully treated and regain competence.[14]

Death row prisoners, who suffer mental illnesses, are—particularly in combination with the holding conditions on death row and the risk of insufficient psychiatric treatment—likely to be exposed to ill-treatment.

Intellectually disabled prisoners on death row

There is international consensus that death penalty should not be imposed on persons with intellectual disability.[15] Intellectual disability is a disability characterized by significant limitations in both intellectual functioning and in adaptive behavior, which covers many everyday social and practical skills. This disability originates before the age of 18.[16] Still, many disputes prevail regarding the operational assessment of intellectual disability in the context of eligibility for the death penalty, and there seems to be a need of international standards in this regard.

Since people with intellectual disability are still executed,[17] it should be considered whether sentencing such persons to death and holding them on death row constitutes ill-treatment since they are held under death row conditions without the ability to fully understand why.

---

13 http://www.cdcr.ca.gov/DHCS/SMHP_Coleman.html. (accessed on 13 June 2016).

14 Kastrup M. 1988. "Psychiatry and the death penalty." *Journal of Medical Ethics* 14:179-83.

15 Allison Freedman. 2014. "Mental Retardation and the Death Penalty: The Need for an International Standard Defining Mental Retardation." *Northwestern Journal of International Human Rights* 12(1). Available from http://scholarlycommons.law.northwestern.edu/njihr/vol12/iss1/1. (accessed on 13 June 2016).

16 American Association on Intellectual and Developmental Disabilities. Available from http://aaidd.org/intellectual-disability/definition#.V17o_PNf2Ds. (accessed on 13 June 2016).

17 *See for example* Kim Bellware, "Georgia Just Executed An Intellectually Disabled Man Whose Sentencing Was Tainted By Racism," *The Huffington Post*, April 12, 2016. Available from http://www.huffingtonpost.com/entry/kenneth-fults-execution_us_570d65b5e4b0ffa5937d5a6e. (accessed on 17 June 2016).

Death row holding conditions

The conditions under which prisoners sentenced to death are held while waiting for the execution may in and of itself amount to ill-treatment for mentally healthy prisoners, too. In many countries, prison conditions are very poor and the holding conditions amount to ill-treatment. The United Nations Committee against Torture has expressed concerns about the conditions under which prisoners are held on death row and stated that these conditions in themselves may constitute cruel, inhuman, or degrading treatment.[18]

> "Conditions range widely, from the sterile, solitary confine-ment that pervades death row in many states in the United States, to the unsanitary and overcrowded prisons in some parts of the Caribbean and Sub-Saharan Africa. Solitary con-finement leads many prisoners to develop debilitating mental illnesses, and overcrowding, combined with poor nutrition and hygiene, threatens their health and in some cases can lead to premature death."[19]

The factors that directly constitute ill-treatment are mainly over-crowding, overuse of solitary confinement, poor access to health care, a high risk of health deterioration through contagious disease, and prison violence.

Overcrowding of prisons is often an indicator of underfinancing of the prison system and therefore is closely related to poor resources in other aspects of prison conditions, like food and health services.[20] Similarly, overcrowding promotes spreading of communicable diseases[21] and is associated with higher occurrence of attempted suicide.[22]

---

18 E.g., Concluding observations regarding Morocco (CAT/C/MAR/CO/4).

19 Cornell Law School. *Death Penalty Worldwide: Death row conditions.* Available from http://www.deathpenaltyworldwide.org/death-row-conditions.cfm. (accessed on 14 June 2016).

20 *See for example* James Blitz, "UK prison reform will do little to solve the jail problem," *Financial Times,* May 18, 2016. Available from http://www.ft.com/cms/s/0/9bb13410-1ce2-11e6-b286-cddde55ca122.html#axzz4BqJ3hnUg. (accessed on 17 June 2016).

21 F. Biadglegne, A.C. Rodloff & U. Sack. 2015. "Review of the prevalence and drug resistance of tuberculosis in prisons: a hidden epidemic." *Epidemiol Infect* 143(5):887-900.

22 Hans Wolff, Alejandra Casillas, Thomas Perneger, Patrick Heller, Diane Golay, Elisabeth Mouton, Patrick Bodenmann, Laurent Getaz. 2016. "Self-harm and overcrowding among prisoners in Geneva, Switzerland." *International Journal of Prisoner Health* 12(1):pp. 39-44.

Data on death row holding conditions are not systematically available. For the United States, however, information is available for certain aspects, for instance, regime of isolation. Isolation for 23 hours per day is the standard regime on death row in the US, although one state holds the prisoners in their cell 24/7.[23]

On 17 and 18 November 2015, the UN Committee against Torture considered the periodic report of China. The committee expressed concern about "the lack of specific data on the application of the death penalty" and about reports of people on death row being held in shackles for 24 hours a day. The committee encouraged authorities "to establish a moratorium on executions and commute all existing death sentences, and accede to the Second Optional Protocol to the International Covenant on Civil and Political Rights, aiming at the abolition of the death penalty." The committee further called on China to "ensure that the death row regime does not amount to cruel, inhuman or degrading treatment or punishment" by ending the use of restraints on death row prisoners.[24]

The general scarcity of access to medical treatment may be considered another source of ill-treatment for two reasons: Medical conditions are not identified or treated, leading to ill-health and risk of death in custody. And mental illnesses and disabilities, which might be incompatible with execution and which makes it more difficult to endure the prison conditions (especially overcrowding or isolation) are not identified and treated.

Examples of appalling holding conditions for death-sentenced prisoners, including torture on death row and custodial rape, are abundant.[25]

Death row syndrome

Death row phenomenon describes the harmful exposures of death row conditions, including exposure to extended periods of solitary

---

23 Death Penalty Information Center. *Death row conditions by state*. Available from http://www.death-penaltyinfo.org/death-row. (accessed on 11 June 2016).

24 Concluding observations regarding China (CAT/C/CHN/CO/5).

25 Cornell Law School. *Death Penalty worldwide: Death row conditions*. Available from http://www.deathpenaltyworldwide.org/death-row-conditions.cfm. (accessed on 17 June 2016).

confinement and the waiting for the execution.[26] The death row phenomenon is the combination of circumstances to which a prisoner is exposed when held in solitary confinement on death row. These circumstances can be separated into three categories: (1) the harsh, dehumanizing conditions of imprisonment itself; (2) the sheer length of time spent living under such conditions; and (3) the psychological repercussions associated with a death sentence.[27] The associated phenomenon, death row syndrome, describing the mental consequences directly emerging from exposure to the death row phenomenon, are less well defined.[28]

Over the last decades, a body of jurisprudence has developed in support of the notion that the death row phenomenon constitutes ill-treatment.[29] Most of the case law emphasizes the waiting time between sentence and execution. For the United States, where the waiting times are made public, it has increased from 74 to 190 months during the period 1984–2012. In 2013, the average waiting time was 15 years and 6 months.[30] This time include the time spent on exhausting appeal opportunities.

There are case stories of suicides or self-harm on death row, indicating the tough living conditions and emotional stress imposed on death row prisoners. Only few systematic studies demonstrating how often suicide and self-harm occur. One study finds a suicide rate of 115 per 100,000, which is approximately five times the rate of the male background population.[31]

26   K. Harrison, A. Tamony. 2010. "Death row phenomenon, death row syndrome and their affect on capital cases in the US." *Internet Journal of Criminology.* Available from http://www.internetjournalofcriminology.com/. (accessed on 18 June 2016).

27   Ibid.

28   H.I. Schwartz. 2005. "Death Row Syndrome and Demoralization: Psychiatric Means to Social Policy Ends." *J Am Acad Psychiatry Law* 33:153–5.

29   Cornell Law School. *Death Penalty Worldwide: Death row phenomenon.* Available from http://www.deathpenaltyworldwide.org/death-row-phenomenon.cfm. (accessed on 18 June 2016).

30   Death Penalty Information Center: *Time on death row.* Available from http://www.deathpenaltyinfo.org/time-death-row. (accessed on 18 June 2016).

31   D. Leser, C. Tartaro. 2002. "Suicide on death row." *J Forensic Sci.* 47(5):1108-11.

THE EXECUTION AND ITS CIRCUMSTANCES

The execution and its circumstances may constitute torture or ill-treatment. Before going to the execution methods, it should be highlighted that some countries use public executions, which is considered ill-treatment—degrading treatment—of the executed and may also expose vulnerable persons in the audience, e.g. minors, to ill-treatment.[32]

The execution methods used in 2015 include: beheading (Saudi Arabia), hanging (Afghanistan, Bangladesh, Egypt, India, Iran, Iraq, Japan, Jordan, Malaysia, Pakistan, Singapore, South Sudan, Sudan), lethal injection (China, USA, Viet Nam) and shooting (Chad, China, Indonesia, North Korea, Saudi Arabia, Somalia, Taiwan, United Arab Emirates, Yemen). However, more execution methods are at the disposal of the execution authorities: gas chamber, electrocution, and falling from a height.[33]

The United Nations Special Rapporteur on Torture in his 2012 report resumes the jurisprudence concerning execution methods and their violation of the prohibition of torture and ill-treatment. He concludes that there is no categorical evidence that any method of execution in use today complies with the prohibition of torture and cruel, inhuman or degrading treatment in every case.[34] He further states that "Even if the formation of this customary norm is still under way, the Special Rapporteur considers that most conditions under which capital punishment is actually applied renders the punishment tantamount to torture and that under many other, less severe conditions, it still amounts to cruel, inhuman or degrading treatment."

Execution attempts sometimes fail, with severe painful suffering for the victim as a consequence. A number of botched executions by means of lethal injections have been described in the US media. Some of those have occurred because of failure to comply with the standard procedures, e.g. unsuccessful application of access to the veins of

---

32   Concluding observations of the Human Rights Committee: Nigeria (CCPR/C/79/Add.65); UN Commission on Human Rights Resolution 2005/59 20 April 2005.

33   Cornell Law School. *Death Penalty Worldwide: Methods of execution.* Available from http://www.deathpenaltyworldwide.org/methods-of-execution.cfm. Accessed on 19 June 2016.

34   *Interim report of the Special Rapporteur on torture and other cruel, inhuman or degrading treatment or punishment.* 9 August 2012. (A/67/279).

the victim, resulting in the injection of substances in the soft tissue causing excruciating pain and a prolonged execution. Other cases of botched executions have occurred using experimental pharmaceutical cocktails because pharmaceutical companies have withdrawn access to their pharmaceutical products.

In a recent publication,[35] the overall rate of botched executions in the United States was estimated at 3.15%. The execution method with the highest botched execution rate was lethal injection (7.12%). In some of these cases the prisoner is victimized by the infliction of excruciating pain,[36] let alone the psychological impact of a botched execution. Such cases will definitely constitute ill-treatment, and it may be considered whether continued executions using protocols at high risk of inflicting severe pain or suffering may represent gross neglect.

Conclusion

Many single factors may indicate that prisoners sentenced to death are subjected to torture or ill-treatment: (1) They are subject to general prison conditions which themselves constitute ill-treatment. (2) Their confession was coerced by the use of torture. (3) They are particularly vulnerable because of previous torture or mental illness or intellectual disability. (4) Poor access to health care and medicines deteriorates their condition. (5) They are kept under death row conditions with the prospect of being executed—the death row phenomenon—in itself constituting ill-treatment. (5) They are subjected to execution methods and circumstances (public executions, botched executions, painful execution methods) which inflict severe pain and suffering.

In conclusion, most, if not all, death row prisoners are in practice exposed to ill-treatment or even torture.

---

35 Austin Sarat. 2014. *Gruesome Spectacles: Botched Executions and America's Death Penalty.* Stanford University Press.

36 http://news.nationalpost.com/news/botched-and-excruciating-oklahoma-execution-fell-short-of-humane-standards-white-house-says. (accessed on 25 August 2016).

Final Holding Cell, The Omega Suites
©Lucinda Devlin

"Simply put, there is no 'humane' way to extinguish a human life...The middle-of-the-night bedside visits of those I'd executed were relentless. Visions of these dead men sitting on the edge of my bed wouldn't fade-even with heavy doses of alcohol."

— *Ron Mc Andrew*

CHAPTER 3
THE 'HIDDEN' THIRD PARTIES AS VICTIMS

31
FAMILIES OF THE CONVICTED

3.2
PARTICIPANTS IN DEATH PENALTY
PROCEEDINGS AND EXECUTIONS

3.3
VICTIMS' FAMILIES AND CLOSURE

3.1 Families of Convicted

HIDDEN VICTIMS: THE FAMILIES OF THOSE FACING THE DEATH PENALTY

Susan F. Sharp[1]

As of late 2014, approximately 160 countries had abolished the death penalty or no longer use it.[2] Only 20% of all nation states carried out a judicial execution in the decade between 2003 and 2012, and only seven executed at least 10 per year.[3] However, this still represents more than 1,000 executions each year,[4] affecting thousands of family members. Thus, it remains important that we shed light on how these families are affected.

When a family member or loved one faces the death penalty, the families are often ignored, even removed from the equation. Focus is placed on the victims, the perpetrators, and to a slightly lesser degree, on the families of the victims. However, family members of the accused suffer trauma as well. In the first decade of the twenty-first century, I became concerned about these families. I interviewed 53 family members of individuals who were either facing a death sentence or had been executed. My goal was to shed light on the negative consequences of using the death penalty on those who were related to someone facing legal execution. I quickly discovered that not much work had been done in that area.

---

1   Susan F. Sharp is David Ross Boyd Professor of Sociology at the University of Oklahoma, United States.

2   *Justice that kills – the death penalty in the 21st century*—Speech by Ivan Simonovic, assistant secretary-general for Human Rights of the United Nations, October 2014. Available from http://www.ohchr.org/EN/NewsEvents/Pages/DisplayNews.aspx?NewsID=15645&LangID=E. (accessed 24 August 2016).

3   Carolyn Hoyle and Roger Hood. 2015. "Declining Use of the Death Penalty." In *Moving Away from the Death Penalty: Arguments, Trends and Perspectives*. United Nations. pp. 68–93

4   Because information about executions in China is closely guarded, the actual number of annual executions is suspected of being much higher.

There are signs this is starting to change. In September of 2013, the United Nations Human Rights Council focused in a special panel on the impact of the death penalty on children of those sentenced to death. Flavia Pansieri, then United Nations deputy high commissioner for Human Rights, suggested that having a parent executed might impact a child to such a degree that the child's rights would be violated under international human rights law. Issues raised included the legal obligations of states that are parties to the Convention on the Rights of the Child to examine both positive and negative effects on the children affected at the time of sentencing. Evidence was also offered by professor Sandra Jones of Rowan University about negative impacts on children of death row prisoners, including trauma and isolation, which can lead to mental health and behavioural issues. This was further supported by evidence from Francis Ssuubi, executive director of Wells for Hope. Panellists also pointed out the importance of national human rights institutions protecting these children and the need for more child-friendly systems of criminal justice.[5] However, much work is still needed in this area, as countless children, parents, siblings and other relatives continue to suffer trauma and hardship due to a loved one facing the death penalty.

Effects of the death penalty on families of the accused

There are many ways that the family members of those facing the death penalty are affected. Children may grow up without a parent and with the knowledge that their parent was considered so appalling that he or she was not worthy of life. Parents, spouses, and siblings must deal with not only the loss of a family member but also protracted grief and uncertainty. If the accused was a breadwinner, the family suffers economic loss. They may suffer additional economic hardships due to the necessity of obtaining legal counsel as well as from countless hours of missed work. They must also deal with negative publicity and the resultant rejection by others. However, in

---

5   Human Rights Council holds panel discussion on the human rights of children of parents sentenced to the death penalty. United Nations Office of the High Commissioner for Human Rights, 13 September, 2013. Available from http://www.ohchr.org/EN/NewsEvents/Pages/DisplayNews.aspx?NewsID=13709&LangID=E. (accessed 24 August 2016).

nations that continue the practice of death-sentencing, these victims remain largely hidden.[6]

In the United States, the number of annual executions has been steadily declining since 2009, when there were 52 executions, to a low of 28 in 2015. Similarly, the number of individuals sentenced to death has also declined significantly since the turn of the century. In 2000, more than 200 new death sentences were handed down, while in 2015, there were only 49 death sentences. However, nearly 3,000 individuals remain on death rows around the country.[7]

The number of individuals on who are on death row is important because the effects of the death penalty on family members begin when the state announces its intention to seek a death sentence for a crime. In 1976, the United States reinstated the death penalty with *Gregg v. Georgia* after a four-year moratorium. The Supreme Court had found capital punishment as it was then practised to be uncon-stitutional in 1972 and invalidated all death-penalty statutes in the country. The court was concerned about the arbitrary application of the death penalty, with no guidelines for when a crime would be death eligible. With the *Gregg* decision, jurisdictions that wanted to have the death penalty had to have guidelines on what made a case death-eligible. States then came up with lists of special circumstances or aggravators that would distinguish death- eligible crimes from all other crimes, at least hypothetically. This was supposed to eliminate the arbitrariness in death-sentencing. Those crimes eligible for death were thus seen as being the worst cases, and the offenders were con-sequently seen as worse than other offenders and hence not deserving to live.

Although research suggests that the death penalty is still arbitrarily applied, the general public views a crime "worthy" of the death pen-alty as being somehow more heinous, more terrible, than any other crime. Similarly, the accused is frequently seen as qualitatively differ-ent from all other people, including other murderers and offenders. The crimes are viewed as being more depraved, as are those who

---

6   Sharp, Susan F. 2005. *Hidden Victims: The Effects of the Death penalty on Families of the Accused.* New Brunswick, NJ: Rutgers University Press.

7   http://deathpenaltyinfo.org/documents/FactSheet.pdf. (accessed 24 August 2016).

committed those crimes. This view of those who commit crimes for which the death penalty is being sought is then extended to their family members, who are also tainted with the assessment that they are different and somehow deviant themselves. The family members of those facing a potential death sense become vicarious offenders in the eyes of the public and many of their neighbours and friends. This has the effect of isolating them at a time when they desperately need support.[8] Even if the family member is eventually released, the damage has been done. One mother commented to me that the ordeal had ruined her life. In fact, before her son was released, she suffered a heart attack. She added:

> There is nothing…that can explain the terror of what I felt when I thought the state was going to kill my only child. I had nightmares, asleep or awake, trying to imagine me going into a chamber where my child was strapped down and being injected with poison.[9]

A teenage sister of a man on death row reported being harassed at work immediately after her brother was charged. Another family reported having property destroyed and pets harmed. Some family members reported having to quit their jobs or move due to the harassment. In many cases, when the death penalty is sought, the family of the accused loses not only their support but their livelihoods.

Capital punishment in the United States is primarily reserved for those convicted of first-degree murder, although there are certain exceptions, especially in federal cases. When a murder occurs, two families are normally impacted: those of the victims and those of the offenders. The experiences of these two families, however, are vastly different. The grief of the family members of the victims is seen as valid, and there are often resources made available to them to help them cope with the trauma of sudden and violent loss of a loved one. They may be eligible for some financial assistance. Counselling and support groups are also often available to help them deal with traumatic loss. In contrast, the families of those facing state-sanctioned

---

8   Susan F. Sharp. 2005. *Hidden Victims: The Effects of the Death Penalty on Families of the Accused*. New Brunswick, NJ: Rutgers University Press.

9   Sharp, op. cit., p. 59.

death find that their grief is invalidated.[10] Furthermore, it is not finite. It continues long-term as their loved ones move slowly through the criminal justice system toward execution.[11]

Although their grief may not be socially validated and the family members may feel disenfranchised in many ways, they nonetheless experience significant grief. The nature of that grief is particularly destructive, as it is long-term and cyclical. Unlike the grief experienced by individuals who suddenly lose a family member, those who have a relative on death row experience anticipatory grief. They grieve in advance for a family member who is still alive but in many ways lost to them. In many jurisdictions, they may no longer have any physical contact with their loved one, instead visiting through a Plexiglas window on death row, speaking through a telephone handset. The visitation may be uncomfortable, with inadequate seating. Furthermore, the family may have to travel hours or even days to visit, sometimes to find that visitation has been cancelled for administrative reasons. Additionally, there is often a relatively short time limit on visitation, or it may be available on a first-come, first-served basis.

Imagine, if you will, that your only opportunity to have contact with a family member is dictated by institutional rules that only allow collect telephone calls from that family member and place harsh constraints on any in-person contact. For parents or siblings of the prisoner, contact may create economic hardships. The collect telephone calls are unduly expensive, and in most jurisdictions death row is housed in only one prison in an entire state, often necessitating extensive travel. This may often create expenses beyond the cost of getting to the prison. If visitation hours are early in the day, the family may need to pay for lodging the night before.

For a small child, the limited contact may be even more harmful. It may be difficult for children to understand why they cannot call their mothers or fathers when they need to talk with them, instead having to wait until the parent gets access to call home. Additionally, the

---

10 Rachel King and Katherine Norgard. 1999. "What about Our Families? Using the Impact on Death Row Defendants as a Mitigating Factor." *Florida Law Review* 26:1119-1173, 1999.

11 Sandra J. Jones and Elizabeth Beck. 2006-2007. "Disenfranchised grief and nonfinite loss as experienced by the families of death row inmates," *Omega* 54(4):281-299; Walter C. Long. 2011. "Trauma therapy for death row families." *Journal of Trauma Dissociation* 12(5):482-494.

phone calls may be brief, and the child may not understand why the parent has to hang up in the middle of a conversation. It may be even more difficult for the child to understand why he or she can only see the mother or father from behind a glass window and not be able to touch them or be held by them. Furthermore, this contact occurs after standing in line, often for hours, and enduring a body search. Thus, in addition to the trauma of not having regular contact with his or her mother or father, the child is further traumatized when contact does occur.

Families also undergo substantive economic hardships. Many will try to hire a private attorney due to concerns about the overburdened public defender system. In one case, the accused individual sold his own home and vehicles in order to get a private attorney. However, the money he paid was only sufficient for the attorney to try to get him to plead guilty for a life sentence, so he terminate the relationship with the attorney. His ageing parents then mortgaged their home to hire another attorney. That attorney, however, was intoxicated throughout the trial and presented no defence. The accused was convicted and sentenced to death despite the fact that the limited evidence was very flawed. On direct appeal, now represented by a public defender, the judge handed down a directed verdict of acquittal after the prosecution failed to present an adequate case. This individual was freed from death row, but both he and his family had already experienced considerable loss and trauma. The accused was the father of two small girls, and his wife had been the victim. Those children lost both parents when he was charged with the crime, tried, and sentenced to death. Because his parents felt unable to take on the burden of raising the children, they were adopted. Although he was able to have contact with them after his release, the parent–child bond had been broken. After his release, he suffered from depression and post-traumatic stress disorder, causing further concerns for his parents and siblings. He had no resources left upon his release, and his family's financial resources were also depleted. Sadly, like many exonerees, he died several years after his release, although his was still relatively young. In this case, although the accused was not executed and was actually exonerated, the impact on the family was very harmful. Two children lost their father, a father lost his children, and other family members experienced ongoing stress and trauma from the time of his arrest. Additionally, both the accused and his family lost most of their life savings paying for legal representation.

Children of death row prisoners

As noted above, children may be especially harmed when a parent is sentenced to death. Younger children have little understanding of why the parent is gone and why they can no longer see or talk to him or her regularly. Older children especially teenagers, may be deal with the situation by becoming angry and rebellious. These harmful effects on children extend into their adult lives.

According to research, children with a parent on death row may feel the need to defend their parents. They are at high risk of suffering from depression and anxiety, and they often have behavioural problems or aggressiveness.[12] They are frequently subject to stigma and social isolation. Children may feel they should have somehow prevented their parent from committing the crime.[13] While the children of all prisoners experience some stigma and shame, the experiences of children with a parent sentenced to death are qualitatively different from the children of other prisoners.[14]

The two children of a woman sentenced to death and subsequently executed provide a poignant example. The children's mother was convicted of hiring someone to kill her husband. The actual killer did not receive a death sentence, but the woman and her boyfriend did. After the murder, the family of the victim took the children and raised them, allowing them no contact with the condemned mother. Shortly before the execution, the older child, then a teenager, chose to visit he mother and reach reconciliation. The younger child, a son, refused to see his mother. After the execution, the daughter suffered from depression. The son ended up committing suicide.

---

12 *Hidden' victims: the children of parents on death row*. Available from http://www.ohchr.org/EN/NewsEvents/Pages/HiddenVictims.aspx. (accessed 24 August 2016).

13 Jones and Beck, op. cit.

14 Beck, Elizabeth and Sandra Jones. 2007-2008. "Children of the condemned: Grieving the loss of a father to death row." *Omega* 56:191-215.

Coping strategies used by family members

How well an individual deals with a family member's death sentence depends on part on the coping strategies he or she uses. My interviews with family members uncovered three primary ways of coping: withdrawal, anger and joining.[15] Anger is not uncommon initially. However, anger is often conflicted. Family members may be angry at their loved one for his or her actions that brought about a death sentence. At the same time, they may be angry at a system that they see as unfair. They are often unsure of how to respond. For example, one father was very angry because he saw the trial as unfair. The judge refused to sever the cases of the two youths accused of three murders. This meant that neither defendant could imply that the other was more culpable and tied the hands of the defence attorneys. After the trial was over and his son sentenced to death, this father was so angry at his son that he had very little contact with him and did not visit. To get away from the situation, he and his wife moved to another state for a while.

Other family members initially respond by withdrawing. Many reduced or eliminated any interaction with others, except for one or two family members. Some even quit working. The stigma and condemnation they experienced from others in their community was painful, and they responded by staying away from other people. One woman I interviewed said that she lost faith and quit attending her church, had no time for vacations, and that the most difficult issue was facing other people. Sometimes, withdrawal occurs slowly. Family members who initially reached out for support may find that others, even their own relatives, have little sympathy. Others withdrew to put distance between themselves and the crime, fearing they would also be blamed. Additionally, withdrawal may result when the family member has gone through long-term strain due to the criminal justice process. The father described above withdrew because he felt overwhelmed by all the stress from the trial. He and his wife moved away so that they would not have anyone ask about their son or the case.

The last response was joining support groups or churches to find emotional support. Several individuals told me that they tried joining

---

15   Sharp, op cit.

support groups for the families of prisoners. However, some felt that the issues they faced were very different from those faced by families of prisoners who were not facing a death sentence. Unfortunately, it is difficult to develop a support group specifically for families of death row prisoners. Death sentences are relatively rare, limiting the number of potential participants. Furthermore, most states have only one death row. Thus, families may be spread out across the state making it difficult for them to get together except when visiting their relatives on death row. Other organizations they join are organized religion and abolitionist groups. The former can be a great source of support if the minister and congregation are willing to lend emotional support to the family members. However, a number of individuals that I interviewed reported that their congregations had not been accepting. In some cases, they experienced rejection and condemnation. More than one stated they had been asked to leave the church. Others, however, reported that their churches were strong sources of support for them. Abolitionist groups also provided support to family members. Some became very active in these groups, in part because they sought assistance in getting a conviction overturned or a stay of execution. Others joined because they wanted emotional support from people who were against the death penalty. The majority of those who joined these groups did so for brief periods, usually when their family members case was at a strategic point in the appeals process or execution was getting close.

It is important to understand that individuals often moved between these responses at different stages of the process. The father described above moved from anger to withdrawal to joining. When his son was executed, he remained active in an abolition group for a while. However, he eventually withdrew again because he said it was too painful.

Protracted and cyclical grief

The grief process for those who are sentenced to death is unlike normal grief, where there is a definite loss. It is far more complex. When an individual is sentenced to death, he or she may languish on death row for a decade or more. During that time, there may be alternating hope and despair. Grief is not straightforward, because the loss is ambiguous. The family member on death row is not yet dead, although he or she is lost to the family in many ways. Furthermore, the appeals process may lend itself to renewed hope. There is always the possibility that a sentence or even a conviction may be overturned at some point in the appeals process. Thus, the family members experience hope prior to the decision on each appeal, but those hopes are dashed when the appeal is not upheld. In many ways, their experiences are like those of families of military service personnel missing in action. Initial hope gives way to despair and exhaustion. The family members may find themselves just wanting it all to be over with, followed by guilt for feeling that way. This leads to renewed hope that somehow a miracle will occur and the loved one will be set free. There is no resolution, only a cycle of despair, guilt, and hope, often repeated many times over many years.[16]

This cycle of hope and despair often takes a severe toll on the families of the accused. It is not unusual for family members to experience physical as well as mental health problems. Family members often experience a grief cycle with four distinct stages. First, upon realizing their loved one is facing a death sentence, they may alternate between denial and horror, believing a mistake has been made. In the second stage, the family members get caught in a cycle, of hope, bargaining with a higher power, desperation and disillusionment. The latter occurs when they perceive the justice system as unfair. This may occur when an appeal is denied due to late filing by an attorney or something else beyond the control of the accused. In the third stage, the family members come to terms with what is happening. Finally, the fourth stage involves picking up the pieces of the family's lives once the accused has been executed, exonerated, or had the sentence commuted. Family members, however, do not always progress through these in a linear fashion.

The first stage can be extremely traumatic. One family, whose son and brother was eventually executed, first found out about the charge when the police arrived at their home late at night. The officers broke down the door and entered with drawn weapons. The accused, his mother and his two younger siblings were home. The family did not understand what was happening, and they were taken to the police

16   Sharp, op. cit.

station to be questioned. The impact on the youngest child, age 13, was devastating. After his brother was arrested and charged, he began getting into trouble and was sent away to live with his grandparents. The other sibling, a high school freshman, commented, "I was in shock. It was kind of like a movie because you see 9 million cops…I was on the floor crying. First, I didn't know what was going on and then I just remember crying." The mother, prior to the trial, had a co-worker ask her if she was glad the state had lethal injection. Thinking about lethal injection added to her horror. The sibling of another prisoner expressed her initial denial, noting, "When you've been with somebody from the moment you were born and you've grown up with that person, I don't think anybody wants to think that somebody they love would commit such a crime."

The second phase is highly destructive to family members due to its repetitive cycle of conflicting emotions. Family members may initially bargain with God, only to have their faith shaken when the accused is not released or the sentence not commuted. As the process towards execution progresses, many engage in frantic activity looking for assistance. This can lead to physical health problems. Some suffer from insomnia and turn to alcohol or drugs for relief. Others develop cancer and heart disease. Health problems are made worse by the ongoing stress of trying to obtain help with the case.

One young wife noted that since her husband's trial, she has had to work two jobs and cannot afford to take off even when sick. Families also become very disillusioned with the system. In the United States, it is not uncommon for the prosecutor to have the most culpable defendant testify against others less involved in the crime in exchange for a life sentence. This then allows the prosecutor to obtain a death sentence for the less guilty parties in the crime. In other cases, the prosecutor may imply that the family is lying. The father of a man who was later exonerated talked about the district attorney implying in his closing argument that the family had forged the documents showing the date of purchase on a car supposedly seen at the scene of the crime but purchased nine months later. This father, a retired military man, said he lost faith in the justice system as a result. This family went through almost 20 years of trials, overturned convictions and retrials before the son was finally exonerated. During this process, the mother's health deteriorated, although she was still alive at the time he son was released from death row.

The stress during the second stage can be so great that families disintegrate. Parents of offenders may file for divorce; the repetitive stress takes its toll on their relationships. Children may be sent to live away from home while the family focuses on helping the offender. Heart attacks and other health issues are common. As one might expect, mental health problems are also prevalent. In particular, family members develop anxiety disorders and severe depression.

One family reported that the mother of the offender had to be put on antidepressants and had difficulty sleeping. She attended the trial during the day and then worked the evening shift at a hospital. Although her doctor wanted her to take off, the family needed the income. Her husband had to quit working because he was unable to concentrate. He became angry and violent due to lack of sleep. Their youngest child was sent to live with his grandparents, who also developed health issues because of the additional stress they were experiencing. The other sibling of the offender was a teenage girl who experienced rejection and ostracism from some of her high school classmates. The taunts and rejection exacerbated the anxiety and depression she was already undergoing due to her brother being charged and later convicted of a capital crime. Years after the crime, she was still suffering from depression and anxiety. Ultimately, the parents of the offender divorced, the youngest child ended up in the criminal justice system for a burglary, and the other child experienced chronic depression. Unfortunately, the experiences of this family are fairly typical. The ongoing and repetitive stress, social isolation, and cycles of hope and despair produce many negative consequences for family members. This may go on for decades, robbing them of physical and mental health.

Reaching acceptance and coming to terms with the death sentence occurs in the third stage. However, the timing and nature of surrender is individual. The majority of family members begin to prepare themselves when the execution gets close. If clemency has been denied, many recognize the almost certainty that their loved one will be put to death. However, some family members do not accept that their relative will be executed until right before the actual execution. Often, the family members hold on to hope that something will intervene until the execution itself. There is always the possibility that a stay of execution will be issued at the last minute, although this is fairly rare. If a stay does occur, the family members are pushed back into the second stage cycle of hope, bargaining, activity and despair. In one case, the Pardon and Parole Board of the state unanimously recommended commuting the death sentence, and the family's hopes were high, only to be dashed when the governor denied clemency. This occurred only three hours prior to the execution, giving the family little time to accept that their loved one was going to be put to death.

For some family members, surrender is so difficult that they become physically and emotionally overwrought. The mother of Gerald Bivins, who was executed in 2001, attempted suicide after her last visit with her son. At the time of his death, she was in the intensive care unit of a hospital. Another woman, watching her husband die on the gurney, collapsed and had to be hospitalized for shock and exhaustion.

Some family members reach acceptance by reframing the impending execution in a positive light. This is most likely when the family members are religious. Those who view death as the step toward eternal life report experiencing some relief that their family member is no longer suffering. However, they still grieve. For others, surrender is more resignation than acceptance. Both types of families are negatively affected by the death, but the impact appears to be even more destructive when the family is unable to find something positive to hold on to.

After the execution, or in rare cases the exoneration or commutation, the family members enter the final stage where they must find a way to go on with their lives. This can be difficult when so much of their energy has been invested in trying to get the death sentence commuted or overturned. It is often very difficult for individuals to resume their lives. One mother called me two days after witnessing her son's execution. She told me that she found herself reliving her son's last gasping breaths over and over again. She was haunted by those visual images but had felt that she needed to be there for her son. Months after the execution, she said that she stayed home almost all the time and rarely even answered her telephone. She thought about the execution constantly. Her only close friend, the mother of another man who was executed the same year, died of heart failure shortly after the execution. The sister of a man who had been executed a decade before our interview, reported that her health had been destroyed and she now suffered from high blood pressure and migraine headaches. Her sister, the only other surviving sibling, had become alcoholic. Their mother's health was failing.

Sometimes, family members react with anger after the execution. For example, a sister of a man executed for murder in Oklahoma believed that her brother's execution had been deliberately botched and was vocal about her anger.

Conclusion

It is important to remember, when speaking of the death penalty, that we are not just talking about punishment but instead about the lives of real people. Offenders are more than the crime they were convicted for. They are someone's daughter or son, wife or husband, mother or father, brother or sister. When the state sentences someone to death, the family is punished as well. The death penalty affects far more people than just the offenders. In particular, it has a terrible impact on their families.

Family members sometimes find themselves judged guilty by association, and they may suffer from shame. This can lead to social isolation, sometimes due to rejection by others and at other times self-imposed. Some family members may break off contact with their loved one out of fear of people in their own communities finding out they were related to someone whose behaviour was so terrible that he or she was deemed unfit to continue living.

The ongoing cycle of hope and then despair takes a toll on the families of those facing a death sentence. Years or even decades of stress cause both physical and mental health problems. Children grow up under the pall of having a parent on death row or already executed. Parents of offenders struggle to stay alive long enough to support their child through the process. Even if the accused is exonerated or the sentence is commuted, damage has been done. The damage done by creating a new class of hidden victims must be considered when debating the death penalty.

THE IMPACT OF THE DEATH PENALTY ON THE CHILDREN WITH A PARENT ON DEATH ROW OR EXECUTED

Francis Ssuubi[1]

Children whose parents have been sentenced to death or those who have had one or both parents executed are too often forgotten in the ensuing discussions on the use of the death penalty as a punishment. As the main collateral victims, these young people end up carrying the disastrous effects throughout their lives, whether their parents are already dead or continue to await execution.

If death is alarming to adults, how alarming must it be to children? To the adults it is easy to explain circumstances under which one had to die, but to the children this is very difficult to fathom. So when it comes to death of a parent for a reason of serving a punishment, it is so perplexing to a child and can yield disastrous effects to the child.

The death of a parent on death row is devastating to children, and it can turn their lives upside down.

This death is sanctioned by the state to punish the parent, but actually after they have died, it is the children who are left to bear the consequences of not only dealing with the grief of the death of their parent but also the difficulties that come with not having a parent.

When a parent is executed, it affects the child to such an extent that his or her rights are violated under international human rights laws. And we have seen that the children of those sentenced to death usually end up being discriminated against and facing alienating social conditions that are in contradiction of the Convention on the Rights of the Child:

---

1   Founder Wells of Hope, Uganda and coordinator International Coalition for Children with Incarcerated Parents, California, United States.

What does the Convention on the Rights of the Child say?

- The state has an obligation to ensure that the best interests of the child are taken into account and protected (Article 3).

- Children whose parents have separated have the right to stay in contact with both parents unless this might hurt the child (Article 9).

- The child of a parent sentenced to death has the right to receive essential information on the whereabouts of his or her parents as well as to be informed in good time the date of execution. Information given to children should be appropriate to their age or provided through a legal guardian or a family member (Article 9).

- Governments must do all they can to ensure that children are protected from all forms of violence (specifically mental violence), abuse, neglect, and bad treatment by their parents or anyone else who looks after them (Article 19).

- Children have the right to special protection and assistance when state action causes a child to be deprived of his or her family environment (Article 20).

- Children have the right to a standard of living adequate for their physical, mental, spiritual, moral, and social development (Article 27).

Acknowledging the negative impact of the death penalty on the human rights of children whose parent(s) have been sentenced to death, the United Nations Human Rights Council at its 22nd session adopted Resolution 22/11. The resolution deals specifically with the Human Rights of Children of Parents Sentenced to Death or Executed and the state's obligations in such circumstances.

What does the 22/11 resolution say?

- It expresses concern at the negative impact carrying out the death penalty has on the human rights of children of parents sentenced to the death penalty or executed.

- It urges the state to provide those children with the protection and assistance they may require in accordance with the Convention on the Rights of the Child, especially articles 2, 3, 9 and 20 and the HRC resolution on the Rights of the Child.

- It calls upon states to provide these children with information and access to their parent(s), with due regard for the best interest of the child.

RISKS AND IMPACT OF THE DEATH PENALTY ON CHILDREN

There are similarities between what children with imprisoned parents generally go through and what children with parents sentenced to death or executed go through, but children with parents sentenced to death or executed are affected more intensely. Available research suggests that there are various negative short-term and long-term effects on children whose parents are sentenced to death or executed.

What do these children go through?

These children experience a sadness that someone they love is taken away from them and is going to be killed. They exhibit fear of what is happening to their parents in prison, they have a threat of powerlessness, and they harbor a mixture of anxiety and shock (or trauma).

These children have low self-esteem, they are embarrassed about themselves, and they may blame themselves for what is happening to their parents. They get angry; they may have sleeping problems (nightmares, insomnia and night terrors).

On two occasions we hosted two children with a parent on death row, and they would frequently get nightmares, and in the morning they might not remember what had been happening to them.

Jane, 10 years old, got up in the middle of the night and started sleepwalking out of the house toward the road. When we asked what had happened to her, she said she had been dreaming that her mother was being hanged.

The community responds with hostility towards these children. The children face extreme stigma, and therefore more discrimination: they are ostracized, they are called names. In some countries, children of parents who are on death row or executed are considered to be criminals themselves.

In some communities, the children may be sacrificed in rituals, for example in Uganda.

They may face sexual exploitation and child labor, which is in contravention of Article 19 of the CRC.

Most people on death row are poor and are from racial, ethnic, or religious minorities, so being on death row creates further impacts of poverty and discrimination on the child. A child may feel discrimination on grounds of race, ethnicity, religion, or economic condition, as well as owing to the stigma due to the having a parent with a death sentence or executed.

In some countries, children become household heads, especially in cases where a father killed the mother , where mother killed the father of her children or if both parents are on death row. They may perform poorly in school; in many cases these children will drop out of school due to lack of school fees or encouragement to attend school.

Their growth may be stunted and they may be malnourished due to lack of proper diet, lack of food, and neglect.

Some children turn to the street where they become more exposed to exploitation and risk of trafficking. Girls may be defiled, raped, and become pregnant an early age.

Behavioral issues:

In further response, the children with a parent on death row or executed may exhibit behavioral issues such as aggression and violence, alcoholism, substance abuse, running away from home, disobedience and stubbornness, and they may turn to committing crimes and end up being arrested and imprisoned like their parents.

Mental health issues:

Children of parents who are on death row or executed are at a significantly higher risk of developing complex trauma and post-traumatic stress disorder with long term mental health consequences. Symptoms of neural dysregulation caused by unresolved trauma can impact all aspects of functioning, disrupting the possibility of healthy development, learning, impulse control, pro-social behavior and the capacity for secure attachment. This may be particularly aggravated where the parent is on death row for a long time either due to a pending appeal or where executions dates are not known.

Lack of contact:

I think the worst difficulty these children face is having no direct contact with their parent on death row and a loss of bond. Children sometimes have many years without seeing their parents or even knowing where they are. And yet Article 9 of the CRC calls for state parties to respect the right of the child who is separated from one or both parents to maintain personal relations and direct contact with both parents on a regular basis, except if it is contrary to the child's best interests.

Lack of information:

In some cases, the convicted prisoners are not informed of the date of their forthcoming execution, nor are their families, and bodies of the executed parents may not be given back to the families. This kind of secrecy violates the right of the child to information regarding sentencing of their parents under Article 9(4) of the CRC. UN Human Rights Council resolution 22/11, called upon states to provide children of parents who are on death row or have been executed with access to their mother or father and to all relevant information about their situation.

The negative role of the media:

Children with parents on death row or executed may suffer discrimination, especially where the parent's offence is known publicly.

Although children of parents who have been sentenced to death would likely face judgment simply on the basis of the crimes their parents have been charged with, for example the Ugandan media's sensationalized approach makes the problem even worse. In many cases, the reports are exaggerated and unsubstantiated. An innocent person may be reported to be guilty, and suspects are characterized as so evil that they are already judged and condemned in the public's mind, even before the courts decide the matter. With no established guidelines regarding fairness or accuracy in how crimes are reported, especially those crimes that are eligible for the death penalty, media stories can generate public hostility and desire for revenge against not only the suspected parents but against their children as well.

The way death row and executions are reported by the media especially through TV and films is not only confusing but also traumatizing to the children.

HOW CHILDREN ARE AFFECTED AT EACH STAGE

Children are affected differently at each stage of the process that eventually leads to the execution of a parent and a difficult life after execution. Each stage plays a vital role in how the child will be affected and presents a progression of grief and trauma.

Arrest

The impact of arrests on children, especially when they are carried out violently, is rarely considered in many parts of the world. Though there is no formal research on the impact on children of witnessing their parents' violent arrest, it is not hard to imagine that witnessing their parents being beaten and lynched by police officers would be traumatic for children. Hearing the stories these children tell and seeing how they are affected by such experiences makes it clear that the impact on them should be given greater consideration.

Crimes that may eventually receive a death sentence often follow violent arrests, and this is what children are most likely to witness.

Children may develop a rage with in themselves and a desire for revenge. In the community where they live and the schools they attend, the children may be stigmatized or radicalized after witnessing their parents' arrests. In the schools, the children may be ridiculed and shamed by their teachers and peers who might have witnessed the arrests or seen it via print and electronic media. This causes more panic, shame, and fear to the children, thus leading to poor grades and possible dropout.

People who are close to the victims may also desire revenge, and because the parent has been taken away, they often turn to the children of the suspected parent. Moses, who was 5 years old at the time of his mother's arrest, was rescued from a crowd of people who wanted to throw him into a pit latrine to avenge the death of a baby who had died as a result of being thrown in the same pit toilet by his mother.

Some children are not present during the arrest or are still too young to know what is happening, and they may never have explained to them what happened. This makes children wonder, worry a lot, and develop fear. Sometimes, they live with lies for many years and later when they find out the truth, it creates a conflict in their minds.

Pretrial Period

The pretrial period may increase uncertainty and cause distress to the children especially when the justice process takes too long.

Parents in death-sentence cases often cannot afford bail, or the state may refuse to grant bail, so they will spend the pretrial time in prison.

Visitations are important at this time, and as the parents are not yet sentenced to death, the visits are supposed to be nonrestrictive as required by international standards. But in many cases, prisoners who are most likely to be handed a death sentence are treated the same way as those who are already on death row. This affects the way children may access their parents in prison; they are most likely to see their parents through barriers such as glass or wire nets and will not be allowed to touch their parent.

A little boy under our care said that the first time he was taken to see his father in prison, he saw him through wire mesh and there was much noise because there so many visitors who came to see inmates. He cried and never wished to go back again to visit.

Trial

Children often may not attend court, perhaps because they are at school, or because of customs or decision by parents, or because the courts are far away, or because they have not been informed about court sessions. Yet, we have heard from children that attending court has been useful, and in most cases attending court is the only way they can meet the parent in a nonrestrictive environment. At the same time, there are some parts of the court sessions that may be harmful to children, especially graphic accounts of the case or negative testimonies about the parent.

Some children wonder if it could have been helpful if their voices were added to the trial, or if the judge saw them, he or she would be lenient to their parent. And if their parent is sentenced to death, they may wish they could have done something about it to prevent their parent's predicament. This could lead to the child condemning him or herself.

If the trial is being carried out abroad, it is likely that the children will not be told what is happening or may never attend court.

Sentencing

Sentencing guidelines in most countries fail to take into consideration what a death sentence may mean to the children and therefore will not suggest other sentences in case of a guilty verdict.

In cases where the children input at the sentencing stage may lead to a death sentence, some children grow up with guilt, thinking that they led to the death of their own parents. These children could have been victims of the offence or were witnesses. If one of the parents killed the other, this can cause a feud among the children, as to whether or not to defend the living parent to save him or her from death row.

In some cases, children are coached and may lie in court, an act the children may come to regret, feeling they were used. In other cases, evidence presented at mitigation to help the parent survive the death penalty may be humiliating to the children because such information may be details of traumatic stories concerning the family, and the children will have to deal with consequence of such information when it goes to the public.

Upon sentencing, some children may not know what happens after a death sentence has been given to their parent. Some assume that the parent will be executed immediately, yet this may take many years pending appeals or because an execution order has not been signed or because there is a moratorium on executions.

Following a 2009 Uganda Supreme Court ruling on the Constitutional Court petition by Susan Kigula, it is no longer mandatory for anyone convicted of a capital offence to be sentenced to death. The last time convicts were killed by hanging in Uganda was in 1999. Since that time, the president has not signed for the execution of anyone on death row. Meanwhile in the local communities, the message is different, from what they have always known and what the media reports, it's believed that whoever is handed a death sentence would be hanged the next day. Many people are considered dead by family members although they are still alive, and the impact of this is placed on the children who are now being called "orphans" and given a name like child of the person who died in prison.

As Wells of Hope Uganda, in 2013 we visited 37 families of prisoners in Uganda; of these 21 were families of prisoners of death row. Thirteen families with people on death row thought that the relative on death row had died, and when we visit such families, it's like a resurrection, because we inform them that the parent on death row whom they had already declared dead is alive. For example, we took Brenda, 16, to see her father on death row; she had lived for eight years thinking he was dead. She said that although she was alive, she was a walking dead body and that she was resurrected the day she saw her father in prison.

In some countries for example Libya, Iraq, and Yemen, the family may be able to prevent a death sentence by forgiving the offender, but the forgiveness may require a financial compensation called diyya. It can be devastating if the family cannot afford to pay the required amount of money.

Life on death row

The period before execution is difficult for children because they live in wonder about what is going to happen. They find themselves in a hopeless and stressful situation, which may cause mental and physical health problems.

Prisoners on death row are placed under maximum security conditions in most countries that have the death penalty. And after assessment of the risk of the prisoner on death row, the prisoner may be put in isolation or under other restrictions. This condition may damage the prisoner's psychological well-being, and this would eventually affect how they would perform as a parent.

Visits to prisoners on death row are usually restricted, in terms of frequency and the possibility of direct contact, meaning mean children usually see their parents through glass or netting.

Prisoners on death row, are usually given a different uniform from other prisoners. For instance, in Uganda the death row inmates put on white while other inmates put on yellow uniforms. One child was saddened on seeing her parent putting on white during a visit, for all the other times we had accompanied her to see her father, he was putting on yellow. White uniform to her means someone who is going to be killed in prison. She cried the whole night, was sad and uncontrollable for several weeks.

Prisoners on death row are usually placed in prisons that are very far away from their children, which make visiting very expensive and many times practically impossible.

The distress that accompanies visits to death row inmates will discourage many children from wishing to visit their parents.

Children visiting their parents in prison is helpful in helping the child to maintain a relationship with their parent, however, for children with a parent sentence to death, the situation would vary. When the parent is given a death sentence, the child starts to grieve, and this could go on for countless years and be aggravated by numerous appeals.

Because of the new conditions given that the parent is sentenced to death, the parent-child relationship will be hampered. It is like an umbilical code being twisted and eventually cut when the parent is executed.

Schools have not been involved and are not sensitized on how to help children with a parent on death row or executed, so a place that is supposed to be a haven for the children ends up being a place where children receive more discrimination and stigmatization. This leads to children dropping out of school for fear of being ridiculed.

One teenage girl in Uganda collapsed in class and was taken to hospital after a teacher mentioned that her father on death row was going to be hanged. The teacher had been teaching about capital punishment in Uganda and had given an example of a famous prisoner on death row as one among the others who were going to be hanged. Little did the teacher know that the prisoner she mentioned had a child in her class.

Execution

UN Human Rights Council Resolution 19/37 on the Rights of the Child (69[f]) calls upon states:

To ensure that children whose parents or parental caregivers are on death row, the inmates themselves, their families and their legal representatives are provided, in advance, with adequate information about a pending execution, its date, time and location, to allow a last visit or communication with the convicted person, the return of the body to the family for burial or to inform on where the body is located, unless this is not in the best interests of the child.

However, the domestic laws in a state where the death penalty exists will determine whether the families will be notified in advance of the execution date and also whether the families' may be allowed to pay the last visit.

Informing a child of such a visit is important because it allows the child to say the last goodbye, but it is usually a very hard moment for a child. It is very important that there is adult accompaniment and that the child is listened to properly and explained to, in an age appropriate manner, what is going to happen to his or her parent.

Sometimes executions may be delayed or cancelled, and if the child is not informed this leaves the child to believe that the parent has already been executed. This increases the likelihood of the child to experience ambiguous loss and unresolved and disenfranchised grief.

Pauline Boss, in her book, "Ambiguous Loss: Learning to live", says ambiguous losses can freeze people in place so that they can't move on with their lives and it can traumatize, leading to post-traumatic stress disorder. Boss explains that all too often, those confronted with ambiguous loss fluctuate between hope and hopelessness. Suffered too long, these emotions can deaden feeling and make it impossible for people to move on.

The execution will be the final blow to the child that not only brings fear but also untold sadness arising from a cruel death done by state machinery. It creates an increased fear, loss, anxiety, a sense of helplessness, hopelessness in the child, and this is a pathway to PTSD or traumatic symptoms. The child will exhibit withdrawal behaviors, absent mind-edness, and disenfranchised grief because the society does not socially validate their pain and they feel that no one understands them.

Usually when a loved one dies, people mourn the loss, they find comfort in the rituals to mark the passing, and they have people around them are able to support them. Children of executed parents need a lot of support, but instead they are shunned, aggravating their pain further. They may well suffer a complicated grief whereby they mourn endlessly—chronic mourning.

Either children witness the execution or not depends on the jurisdiction of the country, and also choice of parents or guardian or even the capability of the children to go and witness because such prison are in far to reach areas which would require children to incur transport costs and to be accompanied. If the children don't attend the execution, this can lead to a sense of remoteness from the experience. It should be noted however, that a child witnessing the parent being executed can create distress to him/her as a result of watching and dealing with surrounding circumstances such as a hostile crowd in support of the execution and the presence of the press.

In cases where children are related to both the victim and offender, for example in cases where a mother kills the father or vice versa, the children will be left with no career. In executing the only living parent, the state makes the children total orphans and this places them to numerous threats and untold crisis.

How the press reports the execution escalates the stigma the children may suffer because they will be further exposed and everyone will be pointing fingers at them. Because their parent is already gone, it's the children who are left as remembrance of the deceased and a reference point whenever the deceased is talked about.

The state is supposed to be a defender, but it ends up being a killer. To the children whose parents have been executed, the state is an enemy. Children will develop animosity against the state and its officials, including the police or court officials. They will become unwilling to seek or accept state assistance. Some children may seek revenge against the state. This could explain why they are more likely to commit crimes and end up in prison like their parent.

We asked Ali, 10, what he wanted to do if he grew up. He said he wanted to get a gun to go to the prison and release his father on death row.

There are cases where the parent on death row will die before execution is carried out—from illness, poor conditions in prison, old age, suicide, or maybe violence. Sometimes families are never informed, and they find out years later.

In 2011 we accompanied a young boy to go see his father on death row, when we got there we were told the father had died several weeks back. Since that time, the boy keeps telling us to take him to visit the prison whether the father is there or not.

There are two children who grew up not knowing that their father was in prison. He had been imprisoned when they were toddlers. One day the father's body was brought home, and they were told he had died in prison of natural illness. The only time they saw their father was when he was dead.

After the execution is carried out by the state, the body is supposed to be handed back to the families so they can organize a funeral. But this is not so in many countries where the death penalty still exists.

In Uganda, the body is sprayed with acid and buried in an unmarked grave within the prison cemetery.

If the bodies are not given to the relatives, this complicates the grieving process for the children and creates further hostility the children will have towards the state. The days that follow after the execution are the hardest daysfor the children. its unfair that innocent children end up paying the biggest price of their parents death penalty .. After their parents have been killed by the state the intensity by which these children suffer increases, these Children will face emotional problems, they will be stigmatized, they will lack support to grow and enjoy their rights as children.

The loss children go through after the execution precipitates a lot of suffering for these children because they are often left without support. These children, whose numbers are not known, are often neglected, ostracized, and stigmatized, which further pushes these children to endure great humiliation and untold shame within the society that they live.The consequences are far-reaching, even beyond their own personal growth and well-being.

CHILDREN OF FOREIGN NATIONALS FACING THE DEATH PENALTY

Citizens of one country may find themselves facing the death penalty in another. This is an issue that affects all states, whether they have the death penalty or not. The children of the parent on death row or executed may not be in the country where the parent is. These are children who are not supported because of the distances and hardships that exist in trying to access their parent.

In 2014 two Ugandans were executed in China; the families were not given adequate information and the bodies were never returned to them. There are over 200 Indonesians migrant workers who are facing the death penalty abroad, and the families at home are not supported. The trauma and suffering their children go through cannot be measured.

Conclusion

The best option that should be considered to help children with a parent on death row or executed would be abolishing the death penalty. If the abolition of the death sentence is looked at in the eyes of the children with parents on death row or executed, we could see most states stopping this cruel, inhuman, and degrading form of punishment because, at the end of it all, the death sentence punishes the innocent children. As one child said, "*When they kill my father, it's me they will have killed.*"

States that still maintain the death penalty should undertake quick measures to lessen the harm suffered by the children of parents sentenced to death or executed as stated in the UN Human Rights Council resolution 22/11.

Since a big number of states ratified the UN Convention on the Rights of the Child, which sets out the best interests of the child as the primary consideration, all states should take this into account at each stage of the criminal justice system a parent goes through before he or she is executed and even during the post-execution period.

There is a need of collaboration of all stakeholders—police, courts, prisons, community and social service agencies, schools, and policy-makers—to begin to coordinate their efforts so that there are able to develop and implement programs that will maximally help children with parents on death row or executed.

ENDING SILENCE, ENDING SHAME

Susannah Sheffer[1]

"You want other people to know that you're human and your people were human and you love them, too." — Jonnie Warner, sister of an executed man, in *Creating More Victims: How Executions Hurt the Families Left Behind,* published by Murder Victims' Families for Human Rights in 2006

Founded on International Human Rights Day in 2004, Murder Victims' Families for Human Rights determined from the beginning that the NGO would include family members of executed persons within its membership. The death certificate of an executed person in some US states lists the cause of death as *homicide,* and, like family members of murder victims, surviving family members of executed persons have lost a loved one as a result of the deliberate act of another human being rather than as a result of illness or natural disaster. It made sense for families of the executed to join with families of murder victims in speaking out against the death penalty.

The organization also recognized that in addition to the commonalities between these two groups, there are important differences, and so the goal would be to highlight what was common among all these family members while also drawing attention to the distinct experience of losing a family member to execution. The No Silence, No Shame project was established for that purpose, and the project launched its efforts in 2005 by bringing a group of family members of executed persons in the United States together for a private support gathering and then a public remembrance ceremony and press conference.

A report based on interviews with these and other family members of executed persons was published the following year, titled *Creating More Victims: How Executions Hurt the Families Left Behind.* That report proposed that family members of executed persons should be covered

---

1   Susannah Sheffer, a a US-based writer and clinical mental health counselor, directed the No Silence, No Shame project at Murder Victims' Families for Human Rights.

within the parameters of the Declaration of Principles of Justice for Victims of Crime and Abuse of Power, which defines victims of abuse of power as:

> Persons who, individually or collectively, have suffered harm, including physical or mental injury, emotional suffering, economic loss, or substantial impairment of their fundamental rights, through acts or omissions that do not yet constitute violations of national criminal laws but of internationally recognized norms relating to human rights.

Following the release of the *Creating More Victims report,* the No Silence, No Shame project continued to support family members of executed persons in preparing testimony for a variety of public occasions. Three examples below highlight several of the key issues on which the project has focused, including the particular pain of losing a loved one to execution, the intersection between the death penalty and mental illness, the need for more resources about and recognition of the experience of family members of executed persons, and the understanding that a great range of family members may be affected by a single execution, including children, parents, siblings, cousins, and others.

From Celia McWee's statement at the press conference marking the launch of the No Silence, No Shame project in 2005:

> *I have lost children to two different kinds of killing. In 1979, my daughter Joyce was murdered in Florida. Fifteen years later, my son Jerry was executed by the state of South Carolina for the 1991 murder of John Perry, a clerk in a convenience store.*

> *In both cases, I lost a child, but there is such a big difference between the two kinds of losses. When they call you and say your child has been murdered, you don't know anything about what happened. You don't know if she suffered or if she tried to get help.*

> *That's how it was with my daughter. But with my son, I knew that the day was coming. I knew that he was going to be killed. In the weeks before, I went to visit him every single day, but even though*

we knew what was going to happen, it was so difficult to talk about it. We couldn't even talk about things like, what hymn would you like them to play at the service. When somebody's ill, you can discuss that sort of thing with them, but with Jerry, we just couldn't do it. I had to fight with him because he didn't even want me to be present at the execution. He didn't want to see me cry. He said, "You've cried enough," and I said, "I promise I won't."

When the day of the execution came, I kept my promise to Jerry. In the one instant that he turned to look at me, I wiped my tears away so he didn't see them.

I don't know how to explain to you that when the state executes someone, they are killing someone's child. Jerry was my son, the child of my body, and I sat and watched him strapped to a cross—not a gurney, because what it looks like is a cross, with the arms straight out—and I saw him take his last look at me and then I saw all the blood drain from his face.

I know that this experience has had a big effect on me. A huge effect. Some days I wonder about my ability to go on. But I have seen that many families of death row prisoners withdraw from everyone after the execution takes place. I know that I don't want to live it like that. I know that I want to help others who have gone through this. I know that we are stronger if we join together. I know that ending our silence and moving away from our shame will help us heal ourselves and help us bring about a better world.

From Lois Robison's statement at a press conference in 2008 at which family members of executed persons and family members of murder victims came together to oppose sentencing people with severe mental illness to death:

We're just an average family, except we have a son who was executed by the state of Texas. Larry was the kind of boy that every mother dreams of having. He was a good student, active in his church youth group, played Little League ball, was on the swim team, played drums in the school band, had a paper route, and would have made Eagle Scout if he hadn't become ill.

We realized something was wrong by the time he was a teenager, and we took him to the University of Kansas Medical Center in Kansas City, where we lived at the time. But he wasn't diagnosed with paranoid schizophrenia until after he got out of the Air Force at age 21. Because our insurance no longer covered him, he was discharged quickly. We were told to take him to the county hospital, where he was kept for 30 days and then discharged because he was "not violent " and they "needed the bed". We were told that we should not take him home under any circumstances. I said, "He has no job, no money, no car, and no place to live. You can't put him out on the street." They said, "We do it every day."

We got him into the Veterans Administration Hospital, where they again kept him for 30 days and then discharged him. We were told that he was not well and would get worse without treatment, but they couldn't keep him any longer. If he became violent, we were told, he could get the long-term treatment that everyone agreed he needed. Unfortunately, the VA doctors forgot to have Larry sign a medical release before he left, so we were not able to get medication for him. Larry disappeared and went without medication or other treatment for four years.

Larry's first act of violence was to kill five people, very brutally. We were horrified, and terribly distressed for the victims and their families. We thought that Larry would probably be sent to a mental hospital for life. We were wrong: he was jailed for a year, tried, and sentenced to death. After the sentencing, I collapsed outside the court-room and was taken to the hospital in an ambulance, screaming all the way, "They're going to kill my son."

I was in the hospital for four days. When I came up out of it, I got angry and I said, "This is not right. They told us if he ever got vio-lent they would give him treatment, and instead they gave him the death penalty." I determined that I was going to tell this story. Larry was on death row for 17 years and was executed on January 21, 2000. The day that he died I promised him I would spend the rest of my life working to help people with mental illness and people on death row. How can a modern, civilized society choose to exterminate its mentally ill citizens rather than treat them?

*From Melanie Hebert's testimony on the Murder Victims' Families for Human
Rights panel at the Third International Women's Peace Conference in 2007:*

*My uncle Spencer Corey Goodman was executed in Texas in 2000.
He had been adopted by my paternal grandparents, and he was
much younger than their natural children. He and I had a very
close relationship and he felt much more like a brother to me than
an uncle. We were just seven years apart in age and we spent a lot
of time together during my childhood. He became estranged from the
family when I was in elementary school, and the next thing I heard
about him was after he had committed a murder and my grandfather
was called to testify at the trial.*

*My family wanted us to have nothing to do with him, and they
didn't speak about him much. I kind of just put it out of my mind
and went about my life until shortly before he was executed. My
sister had been visiting him and he requested that I come and visit
before his execution. She asked me if I would, and I agreed. When I
went to visit him, I was really surprised that he wasn't the monster
that I had been led to believe he was. My heart was really changed as
I spent the next couple of days with him before his execution.*

*We didn't have a lot of support from our friends or from our church;
people didn't know what to do or say, so they left us to deal with it
on our own. In any other circumstance when you know someone who
has had a loss, the neighbors and friends and church pull together to
support that person. As well, a surreal aspect of the experience was
that while we were mourning the loss of our loved one, people were
cheering about it and saying that justice had been served. That's
something I don't think people experience with any other death.*

*It would have helped if we had been treated with more compassion
by the judicial system. One of the most difficult parts of dealing
with Spencer's execution was that we had to learn the information
from the television. That's a really difficult way to learn about your
loved one's fate. We learned about the death sentence from the TV
on a night that happened to be my father's birthday. It was very
hard. Later, I asked every single person at the prison to please call
our family to let us know when the execution was complete. No one*

called us. Finally, we turned on the television and learned that he had died. It's a really cruel way for families to be treated.

When my uncle was sentenced to death, I was just entering high school. For a young girl who is not dealing with any kind of issue, the transition to high school is still difficult, so you can imagine how it was compounded by the fact that I was from the same town and shared the last name with my uncle who had just been sentenced to death, and it was a very big news story. I was really taunted at school, and I went into a deep depression for the first two years of high school. I had a very tough time going to school every day. There's so much shame attached to it.

I wish that the adults at my high school had had more knowledge and awareness about how to help a young person in my situation, and I also wish that they had been more proactive in coming to me. I didn't know what resources were available to me, I didn't know to go to the counselor or if this was something it would be appropriate to go to her about. I wish that people in the school system had come to me and offered more support.

IMPACT OF THE IMPOSITION OF THE DEATH PENALTY ON FAMILIES OF THE CONVICTED IN THE CARIBBEAN

Florence Seemungal, Lizzie Seal and Lynsey Black[1]

Introduction

The goal of this article[2] is to draw attention to the negative impact of the imposition of the death penalty on the potentially wide range of persons beyond the individual sentenced to suffer execution. By shedding light on this issue, we respond to calls from within the Caribbean, such as from Jamaican Dr. Lloyd Barnett, for an under-standing of the true nature of the death penalty and its futility,[3] and Stephen Vascianne,[4] who stated that support for the death penalty is driven by emotion in which the need for retribution is a base sentiment, and not justice. The European Union's representative in Barbados, Ambassador Mikael Barfod, made efforts to bring to the attention of Barbadians the negative impact that the death penalty imposes on the families of those sentenced to death. He saw this as a key reason to end capital punishment. However, his comments were wrongly interpreted to mean that those who draw attention to the welfare of the loved ones of the condemned were not concerned about the loved ones of the victims of murder. The editor of *Barbados Today* wrote:

---

1   Florence Seemungal, University of the West Indies, Jamaica, Lizzie Seal, University of Sussex, United Kingdom, and Lynsey Black, Trinity College, Dublin, Ireland.

2   We are grateful to Professor Roger Hood and Gregory Delzin for their comments on the drafts of this chapter.

3   Dr. Lloyd Barnett. 2013. *The Death Penalty in Jamaica.* Available from http://www.worldcoalition.org/media/jm2103-map/video-barnett-en.htm. (accessed 21 June 2016).

4   Stephen Vascianne, "Reflection on the Death Penalty," *Jamaica Observer*, September 6, 2015. Available from http://www.jamaicaobserver.com/news/Reflections-on-the---death-penalty_19227461. (accessed 16 June 2016). Vascianne is professor of international law, University of the West Indies, Mona, Jamaica. He is also a former Jamaican ambassador to the United States of America and the Organization of American States.

Barfod-type advocates present the case for the well-being of the adult guilty, particularly if put on death row, and the welfare of their offspring — no way figuring in their mandate consideration for the solace and security of the victims and their progeny.[5]

The weighting of crime victim and societal rights above concerns for condemned prisoners is also illustrated in a citation from The Republic of Trinidad and Tobago's Second Status Report on the implementation of the mandatory death penalty:

> The right of the convicted prisoner to life must be weighed against the rights of the victims and the right of the community to live in peace and security.[6]

Concern for the hardships of condemned prisoners and their families and concern for the victims of murder are not mutually exclusive or incompatible viewpoints. The impact of the death penalty on parties beyond the condemned prisoner is covered extensively in the international literature,[7] but it remains unaddressed in the Caribbean context. Many of the restrictions that make life on death row difficult for the prisoners also affect their families.[8] Whether or not the person receives a death sentence or is executed, the family undergoes certain types of stress.[9] The last executions in Trinidad and Tobago took place between June 4 and July 28, 1999, when 10 men were hanged in 1999. Since then in the Commonwealth Caribbean there was one execution in the Bahamas in 2000 and one in St. Kitts and Nevis

---

5   "Surely a time for far more reflection...," *Barbados Today*, 17 December 2015. Available from http://www.barbadostoday.bb/2015/12/17/surely-a-time-for-far-more-reflection/. (accessed 16 June 2016).

6   Ministry of the Attorney General and Legal Affairs. 2000. *Republic of Trinidad and Tobago's Second Status Report on the Implementation of the Death Penalty in Trinidad and Tobago.* Trinidad and Tobago, p. 20. We are grateful to Miss Gina Maharaj and Mr. Sheldon Singh for providing this document to us.

7   For a discussion of death row families as hidden victims see, amongst others, Lizzie Seal. 2014. *Capital Punishment in Twentieth-Century Britain: Audience, Justice, Memory.* Abingdon, UK: Routledge; Susan F. Sharp. 2005. *Hidden Victims: The Effects of the Death Penalty on Families of the Accused.* New Brunswick, NJ: Rutgers University Press; http://www.willsworld.com/~mvfhr/MVFHReport%20Creating%20More%20Victims.pdf. (accessed 16 June 2016).

8   Roger Hood and Carolyn Hoyle. 2008. *The Death Penalty: A Worldwide Perspective.* Oxford: Oxford University Press, 4th ed., p. 183.

9   Sharp, 2005, *xii. See also,* Michael L Radelet, Margaret Vandiver, and Felix M Berardo. 1983. "Families, Prisons, and Men with Death Sentences: The Human Impact of Structured Uncertainty." *Journal of Family Issues* 4(4):593-612.

in 2008. Amnesty International reported that Trinidad and Tobago was the only country in the Americas, other than the United States, to impose the death penalty in 2015.[10] Records from Trinidad and Tobago reveal that a death sentence was imposed upon 21 persons —all men— in 2015.[11] There are approximately 40 persons on death row in Trinidad and Tobago as of 7 March 2016, including the 21 men. Appellate Judges identify another way in which condemned prisoners and families are affected; that is, the "undoubted anxiety… endured due to the uncertainty of the success of an appeal."[12]

We report the pain and hardships that families of condemned prisoners in Trinidad and Tobago made known to the public. We argue that the anxiety and depression that a death sentence causes prisoners also burdens their loved ones. We include conversations with Trinidadian death penalty lawyers who shared their recollections of their interactions with families of condemned prisoners and their views on how Trinidad and Tobago as a society was affected by the country's last hangings. The death penalty is not the most humane way to administer justice to convicted defendants and the dehumanization of convicts and their families is acknowledged.[13] The Republic of Trinidad and Tobago's Second Status Report on the implementation of the death penalty stated:

> The Government did not allow these 10 convicted persons to beat the system by using the delays in the judicial processes and delays before international human rights bodies to escape the death penalty. The Government prevented them from making a mockery of the Constitution, the laws and the criminal justice system of Trinidad and Tobago.[14]

The quotation suggests a distancing between the state and those upon whom the mandatory sentence of death is imposed, a failure to

---

10   Amnesty International. *Death Penalty 2015: Fact and Figures.* Available from https://www.amnesty. org/en/press-releases/2016/04/death-penalty-2015-facts-and-figures/. (accessed 22 June 2016).

11   Schedule of Prisoners on Death Row in Trinidad and Tobago, Quarterly Update to 7.03.16, provided by Gregory Delzin, 13 April, 2016. Amnesty International cites a lower figure of nine death sentences imposed in 2015, Amnesty International. *Death Sentences and Executions in 2015.* London: Amnesty International. Available from https://www.amnesty.org/en/latest/research/2016/04/death-sentences-executions-2015/. (accessed 24 August 2016).

12   *Lester Pitman v The State* Cr. App. No. 44 (2004), para. 79.

13   Craig Haney. 2005. *Death by Design: Capital Punishment as a Social Psychological System.* New York: Oxford University Press, p. xiv.

14   Ministry of the Attorney General and Legal Affairs, 2000, p. 2.

take into account the circumstances of the offence and the offender, as well as the offender's home life. In the Caribbean context this means that the hardships that condemned prisoners and their families experience daily remain largely hidden. Making the home life of condemned prisoners visible restores humanity and dignity to these capital convicts.

Hidden Victims: Home Life, Impact of a Death Sentence on Relatives and Family Support

In this section, we focus our attention on the families of those sentenced to death. Families of condemned prisoners are described as "hidden" for the following reasons: They are viewed as an unintended, unavoidable outcome of capital punishment and not considered in the sentencing exercise. A mandatory sentence of death eliminates a mitigation plea in which the home life of the defendant would usually be presented to the court along with the impact of the sentence on the dependents of the convicted. Relatives of condemned prisoners may maintain a low profile and shun publicity because of a feeling of shame or guilt that the murder occurred. They possibly face public condemnation for their relative's criminal actions. They might be tainted by association with a feared criminal. For example, Shiva Boodram, son of Trinidadian Dole Chadee, who was executed for murder in 1999 along with eight members of his drug gang, appeared to be reluctant to recall the past but maintained the innocence of his father when interviewed by a newspaper reporter.[15] The reporter who interviewed Shiva Boodram and members of his community concluded that the community in which Dole Chadee resided was still gripped in fear and reluctant to discuss the case even 15 years after Chadee's execution. Relatives of condemned prisoners might be concerned about their safety because of reprisal attacks or revenge killings. Caribbean communities are geographically small; murder victims and their killers often live in the same village, and these villages or small towns are socially networked so that victim and murderer know each other. Hood and Seemungal reported that in

---

15   Rhondor Dowlat, "Piparo 15 years after: Living in Dole's shadow," *Trinidad and Tobago Guardian*, July 28, 2014. Available from http://www.guardian.co.tt/news/2014-07-28/piparo-15-years-after-living-dole%E2%80%99s-shadow. (accessed 16 June 2016).

two-thirds of all incidents which led to a person being prosecuted for murder, it has been established that the defendant was known to the victim. A somewhat higher proportion of those convicted of murder were known to the victim.[16] In light of this finding, it is likely that family members of a convicted murderer also know the victim and the victim's family.

Home Life

When one discusses the impact of the imposition of a mandatory death sentence on the families of condemned prisoners, it is difficult to estimate how many dependents are affected. Some indication of the home life of defendants sentenced to death can be gleaned from the study by Hood and Seemungal (2006).[17] In this study, all the murder committals to the High Court of Trinidad and Tobago for the period 1998–2002 (297 defendants) were examined and case outcomes followed to December 2005. By the end of 2005, there were 279 completed prosecutions with 58 defendants convicted for murder and 97 defendants convicted for manslaughter, either by jury verdict or a guilty plea. Examination of the committal files for the 58 Trinidadian defendants convicted for murder—and the available evidence for these convicts—suggests that for each prisoner sentenced to death, there are at least four dependents, including children and spouse.[18]

Of the 58 murder convicts, four were female. With respect to the employment status, information was available for 47 defendants. The four females were unemployed with two of them being listed as housewives while 23% of the males were unemployed. Of the 43 employed males, 68% were employed full time and the remainder part time. Most of the employed were manual unskilled workers (49%) comprising jobs such as bottle or snow cone vendor, working in the family's parlour, fisherman, gardener, or labourer; 30% were manual skilled workers (bus conductor, construction worker, welder

---

16 Roger Hood and Florence Seemungal. 2006. *A Rare and Arbitrary Fate: Conviction for Murder, the Mandatory Death Penalty and the Reality of Homicide in Trinidad and Tobago, report prepared for the Death Penalty Project*. London, The Death Penalty Project and University of the West Indies Faculty of Law, co-funded by the Foreign and Commonwealth Office, p. 36.

17 Ibid., p. 26.

18 Ibid., 2006.

electrical installer, electrician, security guard), and the remainder were clerical workers. One can extrapolate from the employment data that the dependents of these employed men would suffer economically from the imposition of a death sentence. The background data shown in Table 1 suggest that condemned prisoners are primarily from a working class background, thus offering some support for Radelet's view that the family members of those under death sentences are among the most powerless in the community because of their under-privileged background.[19] Records to 7 March 2016 revealed that of these 58 persons, none of them was executed, none of them was released, and only one remains on death row (Daniel Agard). One can conclude that the conviction and sentence of the other 57 persons were either not affirmed when appealed against, or that some of these received a commutation from their death sentence in 2008.[20]

Table 1: Where known, background of the 58 murder convicts in Trinidad and Tobago

Sex (n=58)	Female (4)	Male (54)	
Employment data (n=47) convicts	All 4 females unemployed; 2 housewives	23% of 43 males employed and 68% of the 43 males employed full time	49% of employed males (manual unskilled)
Parental role data (n=23)	3 of 4 females married with children	14 of the 19 males had 30 children between them	
Living Arrangements data (n=29)			Lived alone (3) Partner (11) Parents (6) Relatives (5) Friends (4)
Highest Education (n=14)	No education (1) Primary school only (1) Secondary school (2)	Primary school only (7) Secondary school (2) Post-secondary (1)	

Reported Impact of the Imposition of a Death Sentence on Families of the Convicted

---

19   Michael L. Radelet cited in the foreword to Sharp, 2005.

20   Justice Nolan Bereaux ruled on 15 August 2008 in favour of a Constitutional motion brought by the prisoners that they be removed from death row following the judgments of *Roodal v The State of Trinidad and Tobago* 1 AC 328 (2005) and *Matthew v The State of Trinidad and Tobago* 1 AC 433 (2005). Local prisoners sentenced to death before 7 July 2004 would have their sentences commuted to life imprisonment, while the others would remain on death row.

As illustrated in Table 1, a condemned prisoner is almost always a member or participant in a social network. This network includes the immediate and extended family, friends, neighbours, and, in some cases, associates in committing crime, including a "gang." Persons are affected, albeit indirectly, by the imposition of a death sentence upon their relative or friend, but they are affected more dramatically when their relative or friend is executed. According to the prisoner's role in their social network, there are attendant responsibilities. These social connections and responsibilities do not cease suddenly at the point of arrest, or while being on remand for years awaiting trial, or upon being convicted and sentenced to death. Families of the condemned prisoners feel tension while waiting for the hangman; there are socio-economic hardships; the breakdown of family life occurs when a parent is sentenced to death, particularly a mother who is also a housewife; the impact of a death sentence on the children while a parent or close relative remains on death row, and especially when the defendant is executed, is likely to be greater than on the adult relatives and friends of condemned prisoners. According to the international nongovernmental organization *Child Rights Connect:*

> The children's mental health and well-being, living situation, and relationships with others can all be affected, usually in a devastating manner. The inherent trauma of knowing that a loved one is going to be executed can be exacerbated by public indifference or hostility, and by authorities who either fail to recognise or deliberately refuse to consider the situation of these children.[21]

Lehrfreund[22] discussed the Trinidad case of Ann Marie Boodram[23] who was convicted of killing her husband. She had three children aged 17, 11 and 6 years and spent years on death row. Convictions for domestic murder warrant special mention with respect to the impact of a death sentence on the family of the convicted. Having one parent

---

21 Child Rights Connect. 2013. *Children of Parents Sentenced to Death or Executed.* Switzerland: Federal Department of Foreign Affairs, p. 17. Available from http://www.quno.org/sites/default/files/resources/English_Children%20of%20parents%20sentenced%20to%20death%20or%20executed.pdf. (accessed 15 June 2016).

22 Saul Lehrfreund. 2014. "Wrongful Convictions and Miscarriages of Justice in Death Penalty Trials in the Caribbean, Africa and Asia." In *Moving Away from the Death Penalty: Arguments, Trends and Perspectives.* New York: United Nations Human Rights, Office of the High Commissioner.

23 *Boodram v. The State* UKPC 20 (2001) (PC Trinidad and Tobago).

deceased and another languishing on death row or executed must surely have a devastating impact on children and further disrupt their development. If the surviving parent is executed, the children become orphans. There are intergenerational family victims and in these cases there is the failure of the condemned parent to fulfil the role as mother or father. Andrew (Andy) Paul Douglas who spent four years on death row explained that he was 22 years old at the time of his murder charge and had a 2-year-old son, his only child. He felt that his son was negatively affected by his time on death row.[24] Julian Neaves reported the sentiments of prisoner Natasha De Leon:

> She told her daughter and grandson that she loved them and that she appreciated that they never rejected her though she has not been able to fulfil her duties as a mother.[25]

There are instances in which relatives are capital co-defendants, as in the case of the Vincent family, in which the father and one son was acquitted of murder but another son was sentenced to hang.[26] According to the newspaper article, Emmanuel Vincent, 66, and his son Sylvester, 45, broke down in tears when a San Fernando judge freed them of a 2005 murder but sentenced Sterlin Vincent to hang. Emmanuel Vincent said:

> As the father, I just feel halfway out and I feel halfway inside because of my son (Sterlin).[27]

The emotional impact of having a relative executed as opposed to being on death row is different. The trauma is evident in the memories of the close relatives of executed convicts. US data show that

---

24 Recorded interview conducted by Sr. Gwenolyn Ruth Greaves on 16 January 2016 with Andrew Andy Paul Douglas for her Trinidad and Tobago television program, *Your Family Matters*. Sr. Greaves provided a copy of the CD recording to Florence Seemungal on 2 May 2016 and agreed to its use for this publication. Sr. Ruth's contribution to this chapter is gratefully acknowledged. The interview is also available from YouTube, https://www.youtube.com/watch?v=dKmX1fL-meT8. (accessed 15 June 2016).

25 Julian Neaves, "Prison moms delighted by Mother's Day visit," *Trinidad and Tobago Newsday*, May 8, 2016. Available from http://www.newsday.co.tt/news/0,227488.html. (accessed 15 June 2016).

26 Sascha Wilson, "Second son sentenced to hang," *Trinidad and Tobago Guardian*, July 28, 2012. Available from http://www.guardian.co.tt/news/2012-07-28/second-son-sentenced-hang. (accessed 16 June 2016).

27 Miranda La Rose, "Convicted killer laments son's murder," *Trinidad and Tobago Newsday*, February 28, 2016. Available from http://newsday.co.tt/crime_and_court/0,224635.html. (accessed 16 June 2016).

executions hurt the families left behind, creating more victims.[28] The Trinidad citations below support the US evidence:

> At first when they hanged my dad I was very angry. Then confused and sad. However, after years I have now gotten over it and moved on. At that time, there was no one to counsel you... that's why I needed my family around and moved back here to live from London. (Shiva Boodram, son of Dole Chadee)[29]

The case of Mooniah Ramiah is unusual in that her sons were part of the Dole Chadee gang. One son Joey Ramiah was hanged in 1999 and three other sons are on death row after also being convicted for murder in the same case. Their death sentence was later commuted to life imprisonment. In a newspaper interview in 2008. She stated: "'I feel dead inside' and indicated that her heart is still full of pain, anguish and hurt and her agony is compounded by having three other sons languishing on death row."[30] The newspaper reporter said that Mooniah Ramiah is the only known mother who has three sons serving life terms in Trinidad and Tobago. She maintains the innocence of her three sons and told the reporter that she visits her sons every two months. Recounting the day her son Joey was taken to the gallows, Ramiah said she was sitting in her living room when she heard the news:

> I started to scream and then burst into uncontrollable tears. I couldn't believe my son was gone... There was no way to be consoled. Everything started to fall apart because I had so much anger and hatred in my heart for the world. I felt as though everyone was against me.[31]

Seal commented upon the emotional state of the families of the condemned on the day of the execution; emotions could be added to by the presence of relatives of the condemned at the execution

---

28 Susannah Sheffer and Renny Cushing. 2006. *Creating More Victims: How Executions Hurt the Families Left Behind*. Cambridge, MA: Murder Victims' Families for Human Rights. Available from http://www.willsworld.com/~mvfhr/MVFHReport%20Creating%20More%20Victims.pdf. (accessed 16 June 2016).

29 Rhondor Dowlat, "Piparo 15 years after: Living in Dole's shadow," *Trinidad and Tobago Guardian*, July 28, 2014. Available from http://www.guardian.co.tt/news/2014-07-28/piparo-15-years-after-living-dole%E2%80%99s-shadow. (accessed 16 June 2016).

30 Shaliza Hassanali, "I feel dead inside," *Trinidad and Tobago Guardian*, May 11, 2008. Available from http://legacy.guardian.co.tt/archives/2008-05-11/news10.html. (accessed 16 June 2016).

31 Ibid.

scene.[32] A similar account is given during the last hangings in Trinidad and Tobago. A BBC report stated: "Graves have already been dug for the gang in the prison grounds and their families were allowed to see them for the last time on Wednesday."[33] According to the timelines published in the media, Dole Chadee was the first convict to be hanged on Friday, 4 June 1999, and the final two, Anthony Briggs and Wenceslaus James, were hanged on 28 July 1999.[34] Relatives of the condemned were allowed to see the prisoners for the last time on Wednesday, 2 June 1999. The intervening period between the visit of the families and an unknown date of execution would have caused the relatives and the convicted emotional anguish.

Family Support

Radelet, Vandiver, and Bernardo drew upon their observations and interviews with men sentenced to death in Florida—as well as their families—and concluded that the stresses of death row have major consequences for family and friends, with some withdrawing and others reacting with renewed support.[35] Counsel are well poised to offer first-hand accounts of the level of support that relatives provide to condemned prisoners and the high expectation that they have that lawyers can help their relative to escape the hangman's noose. Gregory Delzin an eminent Trinidadian lawyer and former temporary judge, defended approximately 150 death-penalty clients or represented those on death row between 1990 and 2003. He was involved in 15 to 20 stays of execution proceedings, including a client who was executed (Glen Ashby, 14 July 1994). Delzin stated:

> I interact with the families. I can see their desperation and the hope of preventing their father's execution or their husband's [execution]. I try to distance myself from them but you cannot do it. They are still hopeful.[36]

---

32 Lizzie Seal, 2014, p. 41.

33 "Americas: More Hangings in Trinidad," *BBC News*, June 5, 1999. Available from http://news.bbc.co.uk/2/hi/americas/359835.stm. (accessed 16 June 2016).

34 "The debate on hanging," *Trinidad and Tobago Newsday*, September 6, 2010. Available from http://www.newsday.co.tt/features/0,127119.html. (accessed 16 June 2016).

35 Michael L Radelet, Margaret Vandiver and Felix M Berardo. 1983. "Families, Prisons, and Men with Death Sentences: The Human Impact of Structured Uncertainty." *Journal of Family Issues* 4(4):593-612, p. 593.

36 Conversation with Lizzie Seal and Florence Seemungal, 14 April 2016.

Delzin's comments are consistent with the view of Larry Cox, executive director of Amnesty International USA, that families of the condemned are also ensnared in the cycle of hope and despair.[37]

Roberta Clarke, UN Women Regional Director for Asia and the Pacific, an experienced lawyer with years of representation in Caribbean capital trials and death row appeals, also agreed that family members are very supportive of their relative. She estimates that 80% of families of capital offenders are supportive of them and said that family members would inform her if the inmate needed food. Families also advocate in public for the welfare of their relative.[38] Clarke's comments highlight the multiplicity of roles that the families of condemned prisoners assume. The role of family members is not always a powerless, passive, silent or hidden one. Families may form informal support groups, give media interviews, and bring to the attention of the public, the politicians, and criminal justice agents their dissatisfaction with the system and the need to improve the situation of their relative who faces the possibility of execution at any time. They contribute financially to the cost of legal appeals.

When families of condemned prisoners choose to be visible and vocal about their condemned relative's plight, it illustrates how these primarily lay persons, untrained in law, acquire legalese and construct legal knowledge about the process of conviction and appeals that are part of the death-penalty process. The level of dissatisfaction that relatives of the convicted and their families express with the sentencing exercise and delays in the appellate process is shaped by their interactions with many agents in the death-penalty process over a lengthy period of time. Some of these points are illustrated in the action taken by the mother of Lester Pitman, who was sentenced to death for murder on 14 July 2004 and had his first appeal rejected and the mandatory sentence of death affirmed on 15 April 2005. The judgment on his second appeal was delivered on 18 December

---

37   Larry Cox, Foreword, in Susannah Sheffer and Renny Cushing. 2006. *Creating More Victims: How Executions Hurt the Families Left Behind.* Cambridge, MA: Murder Victims' Families for Human Rights. Available from http://www.willsworld.com/~mvfhr/MVFHReport%20Creating%20More%20Victims.pdf. (accessed 16 June 2016).

38   Conversation with Lizzie Seal and Florence Seemungal, 27 April 2016.

2013.[39] Pitman had his death sentence commuted by the Trinidad and Tobago Court of Appeal to a life term with a minimum of 40 years. Shortly before the judgment date his mother—a hairdresser with six children—was interviewed by the media. She is reported to have said: "I just want the Chief Justice to have a little mercy," and that her son was "suffering due to the delay". She said it was the frustration over the delay which had driven him to escape from death row at the Frederick Street prison on 9 December 2012. She explained that her son has been behind bars for 12 years awaiting justice and that her son, who turned 34 in August 2013[40] had the intelligence of a child.[41] Her comments suggest knowledge gained over the nine-year period of her son's incarceration of what constituted "delay" and the relevance of her son's low level of intelligence as a possible mitigating factor in the commission of the murder and as part of the legal arguments his counsel submitted to the Appeal Court in Trinidad.

Impact of a Death Sentence on Society

Society can be collectively affected by the enforcement of the death penalty. Considering the social impact helps to identify the cultural meanings that underpin support for or against capital punishment. How this support is affected by context and time[42] is useful to know and has been examined with respect to public opinion and the mandatory death penalty in Trinidad and Tobago.[43] Prominent Trinidadian constitutional and death penalty lawyer, Douglas Mendes S.C.,[44] said the Trinidad and Tobago public did not appear to have the appetite for hangings when 10 men were executed in 1999. Delzin stated:

---

39   *Lester Pitman v The State*, Cr. App No. 44 (2004). Available from http://www.deathpenaltyproj-ect.org/wp-content/uploads/2014/11/14.08.11-Annex-B-Court-of-Appeal-Judgment-18-Dec-2013.pdf. (accessed 24 August 2016).

40   Ibid, p. 22, para. 72.

41   Darren Bahaw, "Pitman's mom denies CJ conspiracy," *Trinidad and Tobago Guardian*, December 11, 2013. Available from http://www.guardian.co.tt/news/2013-12-11/have-mercy-my-son. (accessed 16 June 2016).

42   Seal, 2014, p. 1.

43   Roger Hood and Florence Seemungal. 2011. *Public Opinion on the Mandatory Death Penalty in Trinidad*, London, The Death Penalty Project and University of the West Indies Faculty of Law, co-funded by the Foreign and Commonwealth Office.

44   Conversation with Lizzie Seal and Florence Seemungal, 14 April 2016.

> Three men hanged on one day; six in one weekend. It [the Dole Chadee execution] was traumatic for society as a whole. They [the hangings] took place on a Friday, a Saturday and a Monday. The country was silent, sullen, people left Port of Spain.[45]

Is public support for the death penalty subject to change when a state conducts executions? Delzin's comments suggested that citizens in Trinidad and Tobago were prepared to accept it despite their ambivalence because of their fear of crime:

> When you get what you asked for, it did not make them abolitionist; they were prepared to accept how they felt. People feel that on its own is wrong, but they are fearful [of crime].[46]

Anecdotal evidence of the Barbadian public's ambivalence towards the imposition of the death penalty is captured in the comment by the Attorney General of Barbados:

> Barbadians generally feel that once you commit murder you should forfeit your life, but that is until one of their family members is involved.[47]

These examples support Haney's view there is deep-seated moral and psychological ambivalence about capital punishment.[48]

Conclusion

Three key points emerge from our discussions. First, there is shared emotional trauma, anxiety, stress, and depression by condemned prisoners and their families. Second, retentionist states need to recognise this fact and to support academic research to uncover the "hidden victimization" caused by the imposition of the death

---

45   Ibid.
46   Gregory Delzin, ibid.
47   "Barbados to scrap mandatory death sentence for murder," *BBC News*, March 26, 2014. Available from http://www.bbc.com/news/world-latin-america-26743629. (accessed 15 May 2016).
48   Haney, 2005, p. 3.

penalty. Third, families of condemned and executed prisoners are innocent victims of a death sentence who require counselling and support. Shiva Boodram, son of Dole Chadee, referred to emotions of anger, confusion and sadness after his father was hanged in 1999 and the fact that counselling was not available at that time in Trinidad and Tobago to assist him to cope with his life-changing events. Currently, there are support groups for victims of crime such as the Victim and Witness Support Unit of the Trinidad and Tobago Police Service (TTPS), but this group may not cater for families of condemned prisoners. The plight of prisoners and their families is brought to the attention of the public by other groups. Greater Caribbean for Life aims to improve human rights and works towards the abolition of the death penalty.[49] Sister Gwendolyn Ruth Greaves offers support via her organization Apart House Ministries and her television program "Your Family Matters."

Capital punishment is not a neat and tidy issue to discuss. There are many paradoxes; for instance, the ambivalence that the public showed towards hangings in Trinidad and Tobago. A collaborative effort is required from Caribbean academics, counsel, state agencies, and nongovernmental organizations to implement alternatives to capital punishment. In a functional social and legal system, punishment should be combined with rehabilitation. A death sentence falls intentionally on the prisoner but unintentionally on his or her family. What lessons can we learn? When we consider the visible primary parties (e.g. the prisoner, executed prisoner, murder victim, murder victim's family), we are skimming the surface of the issue of capital punishment. There is a need to consider the hidden parties, including the families of condemned prisoners, how these persons are affected and how they can be supported. The citations in this chapter suggest that capital trials and appeals are fraught with delays which impose a cycle of hope and despair, of uncertainty of case outcome and strong beliefs in the miscarriages of justice. The loss of confidence in, and frustration with, the legal process is likely to be shared by the condemned prisoners and their relatives. These parties may also share Delzin's sentiments:

---

49   Greater Caribbean for Life Newsletter 2015. Available from https://gcforlife.org/2015-speaking-tour/. (accessed 15 June 2016).

I developed a cynicism of the legal process as a just system. I am cynical in relation to the integrity of the process in relation to the death penalty litigation.[50]

We conclude by asking, is it not time to kill capital punishment? Contemporary abolition debates revolve around the unfairness of imposing a death sentence on the families of condemned prisoners when a non-death sentence can serve the same deterrence that is expected from punishment. Imprisonment also serves to protect the society from further harm of the convict while allowing him or her to retain family connections during prison visits and exchange of letters.

---

50   Conversation with Lizzie Seal and Florence Seemungal, 14 April 2016.

SOCIO-PSYCHOLOGICAL CHALLENGES OF 'DEATH ROW FAMILIES'

Sandra Joy[1]

The pain that death row families endure in their daily lives is not validated by the larger society. Any attention they receive is typically negative, as they are made to feel guilty for their association with a murderer. Indeed, the public scrutiny given to their family dysfunction by the courts and the media may even leave them feeling as though they are to blame for their loved one's murderous behaviour. Given the invisibility of their pain in the best-case scenario and the coded if not outright blame assigned to them for murder in the worst, it is not surprising that death row families tend not to seek mental health treatment. The stigma that these families typically internalize promotes such a deep sense of shame that they find it difficult to reach out for help from anyone, professional or otherwise.

Getting death row family members into therapy to address the range of mental, emotional, and behavioral problems that have resulted from, or made worse by, their loved one's incarceration and subsequent death sentence does not necessarily ensure that they will receive the best possible treatment. Therapists who work with these families must also be properly equipped with clinical tools that will enable them to provide coping skills that families will need to survive the nightmare of having a loved one on death row.

The complex set of issues that family members deal with when a loved one is incarcerated negatively impacts them on many levels. The economic dimension of their plight is closely tied to threats these families face with regard to the social capital, educational opportunities, housing concerns, and the emotional and mental welfare of its members

---

1   Sandra Joy is associate professor in the sociology department at Rowan University, New Jersey, United States.

across generations.[2] The clinician who strives to address the myriad problems arising from incarceration frequently fails to recognize that the symptoms manifesting within the family serve as evidence of a grieving process initiated by the loss of their loved one to prison. This grief process is further complicated for death row families because they have not simply lost their loved one to prison, rather they have lost him or her to the part of the prison that is easily viewed as the harshest, both in terms of its impact on the family and with its fatal outcome.

It might be argued, however, that there is little need for the mental health community to become more aware of the issues confronting this relatively small population. As I have noted, it is certainly the case that these families typically do not seek therapy for the grief that they suffer from losing a loved one to death row. At the same time that these families tend not to reach out for therapeutic intervention to help them cope with the distress they are experiencing from having a loved one on death row, they are nonetheless very likely to find their way into a therapist's office due to other reasons. The potential reasons for family members seeking treatment are many. The mother of the child who has a father on death row may seek counseling for her disruptive, depressed, or anxious child. It may be couples counseling that is sought by the former significant other of the death row inmate and her new partner. Individual counseling may be the treatment sought by a chronically depressed mother. Perhaps it is substance-abuse treatment that a sibling receives, whether voluntarily or through court order.

Regardless of the particular avenue that leads death row family members into some form of mental health or substance abuse treatment, it remains that many of them eventually find their way into a therapist's office at some point during their loved one's journey from arrest to execution. A family member may be reluctant to reveal to the therapist that she has a loved one facing the possibility of execution due to the shame that the family has internalized from the larger community. A thorough psychosocial assessment conducted by a warm, empathic therapist, however, is likely to uncover the horror that a client is living with a loved one on death row. This knowledge can then allow for

---

2   Clear, Todd A. 2009. *Imprisoning Communities: How Mass Incarceration Makes Disadvantaged Neighborhoods Worse*. New York: Oxford University Press; Eddy & Poehlmann. 2010. *Children of Incarcerated Parents: A Handbook of Researchers and Practitioners*. Urban Institute Press.

a greater understanding of the complicated grieving process that is largely responsible for, or at least further fuels, the mental health and substance abuse disorders that tend to surface within death row families.

The nightmare shared by the families in my study unfolds in the United States within the state of Delaware. These families know all too well the pain felt by the rest of the families across the nation who suffer the daily anguish that comes with having a loved one on death row. They live in constant fear that one day much too soon, they are likely to receive a call from their incarcerated loved one bearing the news that he has been served a death warrant containing an execution date. While a majority of the family members who spoke with me have not yet met with this fate, there are some who have already survived the horror of an execution. Accordingly, the family members in my study either have a loved one who is currently sitting on Delaware's death row or they have already lost their loved one to an execution carried out by this state.

This chapter offers suggestions for clinical interventions that can be utilized by professionals when they are presented with opportunities to work with the loved ones of death row inmates. While the specific treatment indications will differ from client to client, depending on the symptoms displayed, there are general treatment approaches and strategies that may prove to be extremely valuable to therapists as they aim to provide the most effective care for these clients.

Theoretical Background

It is essential for therapists who seek both to understand all that these families endure and to implement the clinical interventions suggested at various points throughout their journey to have a grasp of particular theoretical perspectives drawn from the field of grief and bereavement studies that apply to the experience of having a loved one on death row. There are two concepts found in the literature on grief that are particularly helpful to gaining an understanding of the nature and intensity of death row families' bereavement. These concepts are *nonfinite loss* and *disenfranchised grief*. Nonfinite loss refers to those situations in which losses are slowly manifested over time, and often do not have an impending ending. Therefore, the loss includes family members of the developmentally disabled or children who are born with a life-shortening condition, such as cystic fibrosis. It is the loss that is continuous and exacerbated by such things as milestones not met by the affected individual. The continuous nature of the loss eludes the family member's ability to go through the stages of grief to a point of recovery.[3] Authors Bruce and Schultz, who coined the term, state that the grieving person is lost between two worlds, one that is known and one that is dreaded.

There are three conditions for nonfinite loss. The first is that the loss must be continuous and often follows a major event. The second involves developmental expectations that cannot be met. This is well illustrated by examining the experiences of parents of developmentally or physically disabled individuals. These parents grieve when their children reach an age that carries significant milestones that cannot be obtained. The last condition described by Bruce and Shultz is the loss of one's own hopes and ideals. Those who experience a nonfinite loss question who they could/should/might have been.[4]

When the grief experienced by those families directly affected by the death penalty is examined, it becomes apparent that many aspects of their mourning are indicative of a "nonfinite loss." In all cases, the pain started after a specific event: the crime and subsequent arrest. The sudden event then spawns what might be considered the most overarching experience for family members, which is the continuous nature of the loss. With each new phase of their loss, including the arrest, conviction, sentencing, death warrants, numerous failed appeals, and, in some cases, eventual execution of their loved one, family members feel as if they are experiencing the loss for the first time. In terms of sheer years, the length is fairly long. The time between arrest and execution is often more than 10 years, and throughout the years, the process of hearings and appeals occur frequently.

3   Bruce, E. J. & Schultz, C.L. 2001. *Nonfinite loss and grief: A psychoeducational approach*. Baltimore: Paul H. Brooks.
4   Ibid.

The second condition for nonfinite loss is the inability to meet developmental expectations. As soon as the loved one is incarcerated, it is as if he or she has been frozen in time, at least with regard to the usual milestones that he or she would have most likely been able to reach in the free world. Many of the young men who are charged with murder and sent to await their fate in the state prison are young adults who have not yet fathered any children. They may not have completed their high school or college education that they once began before their arrest. These men often have not yet married. While all of these unmet milestones are losses deeply felt by those who await their trials, they are also felt by their families. Prior to the incarceration, the families had fully expected to share in the joy of their loved ones they met significant milestones.

In addition to the continuous nature of a nonfinite loss, Bruce and Shultz note that a common characteristic of such mourning is the loss of one's own hopes and ideals. This aspect of nonfinite loss is readily apparent in the remarks of the family members interviewed. The most overarching loss of ideal is the families' loss of what their state government meant to them. This loss of ideal is specifically targeted to the criminal justice system. Prior to their loved one's conviction, many of these individuals saw the state as their protector. After the conviction, their interaction with the state left them feeling quite jaded and betrayed, and they were forced to reconcile their earlier notion with their current view of the state as being no less than a premeditated murderer.[5] Over the years that follow their loved one's death sentence, the families' disillusionment with the state and criminal justice system only grows, as their encounters with representatives of the system are typically negative. Many family members spoke of the harsh treatment that they received by the guards at the prison during visits. Others shared their disgust with the court system, as they recalled their poor interactions with attorneys, including the defense attorney, and judges assigned to the case. Perhaps the greatest sense of violation came from incompetent defense lawyers. Defense attorneys run the gamut from exceptional to appalling, and the literature carries such examples as defense lawyers during a capital trial

---

5   Jones, Sandra & Beck, Elizabeth. 2007. "Disenfranchised Grief and Nonfinite Loss as Experienced by the Families of Death Row Inmates." *Omega* 54(4):281-99.

sleeping in court, coming to court inebriated, and calling their client by a racial slur.[6]

Family members additionally grieve changes within their own identity. With their loved ones' lives truncated, many family members grieve that they would never become a grandmother, aunt, or other relative to the children that their loved ones would never bear. They often grieve that they would not be the family member of the groom or the proud parent of the college graduate. The more challenging task before the families is reaching a level of acceptance that many of their hopes and dreams for their loved one's life would most likely never be realized.

The concept of "disenfranchised grief" sheds light on another dimension of the unique grieving process experienced by the families of death row inmates. The stigma associated with having a loved one on death row is so enormous that the families who were interviewed for this research frequently indicated that they do not feel comfortable acknowledging their loss with anyone outside of their family. Of course, it is not so easy to keep this information from people within the community due to the high level of publicity that typically surrounds the case of their loved one. When people within the community note the associations that family members have with death row inmates, the reaction is typically negative. As a result, the families of these men on death row are essentially disenfranchised from their grief.

Kenneth Doka developed the theory of disenfranchised grief to refer to instances when the bereaved are denied the "right to grieve" by the larger society.[7] Disenfranchised grief occurs when a loss cannot be openly acknowledged, publicly mourned, or socially supported. Doka and others have found that when disenfranchised grief occurs, the emotions of the bereaved are intensified and healing becomes more difficult. In addition, the bereaved often experience high levels of distress, disorganization, and prolonged grieving. The concept of disenfranchised grief becomes more profound when it is considered

---

6   Beck, E., Blackwell, B. S., Leonard, P. B., & Mears, M. 2003. "Seeking sanctuary: interviews with family members of capital defendants." *Cornell Law Review* 88(2):382–418.

7   Doka, K. J., ed. 1989. *Disenfranchised Grief: Recognizing Hidden Sorrows.* Lexington, MA: Lexington Books.

alongside Romanoff's finding that grief is most effectively addressed when there is community support for the bereaved, and the relationship between the dead and his or her mourners is acknowledged.[8]

Doka distinguished between several categories of "disenfranchised grief." He found disenfranchised grief to occur in several cases: (1) when the relationship is not recognized, (2) the loss is not acknowledged, or (3) when the griever is excluded.[9] Perhaps no better illustration of disenfranchised grief exists than the grief of death row families, given that their experiences bear a relationship to each of the categories of this concept as identified by Doka.

The relationships that exist between family members and loved ones on death row are rarely recognized. Kin relationships that would ordinarily be recognized with the grieving are not so easily acknowledged when the loss involves death row inmates. Doka asserts, "Disenfranchised relationships include associations that are well accepted in theory but whose full implications are not appreciated."[10] Often the offender is made to look like such a monster or villain that it is difficult to imagine the existence of loved ones, and if loved ones are acknowledged then they are also viewed as questionable individuals by extension. Rare is the individual who considers the anguish felt by a mother who will lose a son or daughter to execution. Fewer still imagine the private hell that the children of death row inmates enter as the state prepares to execute their father, forcing them to say goodbye to this man who may have become more of a father to them during his incarceration than ever before.

The families of death row inmates are further disenfranchised from their grief in that their loss is never acknowledged. Even if their relationship with an inmate were to be recognized as a legitimate and significant one, many people would not consider the unfortunate experience of having a loved one on death row to be a real "loss."[11]

---

8   Romanoff B. D.; Terenzio M. 1998. "Rituals and the Grieving Process." *Death Studies* 22(8):697–711(15).

9   Doka, K. J., ed. 1989. *Disenfranchised Grief: Recognizing Hidden Sorrows.* Lexington, MA: Lexington Books.

10   Doka, K. J., ed. 2002. *Disenfranchised Grief: New Directions, Challenges, and Strategies for Practice.* Illinois: Research Press.

11   Jones, Sandra & Beck, Elizabeth. 2007. "Disenfranchised Grief and Nonfinite Loss as Experienced by the Families of Death Row Inmates." *Omega* 54(4):281-99.

Research of the relationship between disenfranchised grief and non-finite loss is further highlighted when we consider Rando's discussion of "anticipatory mourning."[12] One reason that the experience of having a loved one on death row is typically not recognized as a loss in the larger community is because it serves as an example of anticipatory mourning. This concept was initially used by Rando to refer to the grieving process that individuals go through when their loved one is expected to die as a result of a terminal illness.[13] When individuals anticipate the death of someone who is terminally ill, the nature of their loss exacerbates the actual death of their loved one. There are many secondary losses along the way that family members mourn as well. It is crucial to note that the community's failure to recognize the secondary losses occurring with the anticipatory mourning further serves to leave them feeling disenfranchised from their grief.

As he describes the various forms of disenfranchised grief, Doka contends that another reason why individuals fail to receive social recognition for their loss is because the characteristics of the bereaved lead those within society to view them as incapable of grief. The groups that Doka recognizes as most often being subject to this form of disenfranchised grief include children, the elderly, and the mentally disabled. When individuals within any of these groups experience a loss, the need that they have to mourn is frequently neglected.[14] If grieving adults are even recognized by others in the community at all, they are typically presumed to be highly dysfunctional, therefore blamed for the murderous behavior of their loved one.

Two other concepts that have received increasingly more attention in contemporary bereavement studies include *complicated mourning* and *traumatic bereavement*. As is certainly the case with the concepts and theories elaborated upon above, there is often overlap between these various forms of grief. Therese Rando has taken the lead in the examination of both the theoretical and clinical aspects of complicated

---

12 Rando, Therese, ed. 2000. *Clinical Dimensions of Anticipatory Mourning: Theory and Practice in Working with the Dying, Their Loved Ones, and Their Caregivers.* Illinois: Research Press.

13 Ibid.

14 Doka, K. J., ed. 1989. *Disenfranchised Grief: Recognizing Hidden Sorrows.* Lexington, MA: Lexington Books.

mourning.[15] Having noted in the early 1990s the dearth of literature dedicated to this type of grief, Rando published extensively on
the contributing factors, assessment, and treatment of complicated
mourning. She asserts that complicated mourning occurs "whenever,
taking into consideration the amount of time since the death, there
is some compromise, distortion, or failure of one or more of the six
'R' processes of mourning." The six "R" processes of uncomplicated
mourning are identified as follows: (1) *Recognize* the loss, (2) *React* to
the separation, (3) *Recollect* and re-experience the deceased and the
relationship, (4) *Relinquish* the old attachments to the deceased and
the old assumptive world, and (5) *Readjust* to move adaptively into
the new world without forgetting the old, and (6) *Reinvest*.[16]

While Rando's theory of complicated mourning concerns those who
survive the death of a loved one, her theory can easily be applied to
those who lose loved ones to incarceration, even when execution
has not yet occurred. Many of the high-risk factors that Rando has
identified as complicating the mourning process are frequently found
among the families who are grieving the loss of their loved one to
death row. For instance, she identifies specific types of deaths that
complicate mourning, such as deaths that are sudden, unexpected,
traumatic, violent, death that results from lengthy illness, death of a
child, and death that is viewed as preventable.[17] When a loved one
is sent to death row, the family often feels like the death sentence
that is handed down is sudden and unexpected. The grief they feel
upon losing their loved one to prison can be traumatic for the family,
particularly as they anticipate the violent nature of the death should
the state succeed in the execution. The execution would follow a
lengthy appeals process, evoking grief in the family much like that
experienced by those who lose a loved one to a lengthy illness. While
those on death row are all adults, most of them have at least one
parent involved in their life. Finally, death row families view the constant threat of execution that their loved one is facing as entirely
preventable, further complicating the sorrow they feel from their loss.

15 Rando, T.A. 1993. *Treatment of Complicated Mourning*. Champaign, Il: Research Press; Rando, T.A.
    2012. *Coping with the Sudden Death of your Loved One: Self-Help for Traumatic Bereavement*. Dog Ear
    Publishing.
16 Rando, T.A. 1993. *Treatment of Complicated Mourning*. Champaign, Il: Research Press.
17 Ibid.

Rando also identifies antecedent and subsequent variables that predispose survivors to complicated mourning as they deal with the death of their loved one. These variables include "a premorbid relationship with the deceased that was markedly angry or ambivalent, or markedly dependent; prior or concurrent mourner liabilities—specifically, unaccommodated losses and/or stresses and mental health problems; and the mourner's perceived lack of social support."[18] Each of the variables that Rando has noted as complicating the grief process when they enter or follow a death are easily found upon examination of grieving death row families.

In addition to the concept of complicated mourning, Rando has most recently developed the concept of traumatic bereavement.[19] Certainly, there have been others before Rando to acknowledge that the death of a loved one can be very traumatic for the surviving loved ones. At the same time that studies of bereavement slowly emerged over the decades that followed World War II, clinicians were starting to conduct their own studies about the trauma experienced by those who suffered from abuse, war, or disasters.[20] For the most part, these studies were carried out in parallel fashion. Several researchers eventually began to examine cases in which both bereavement and trauma were clearly present among those who had survived the death of a loved one.[21] These researchers were among the first who "conceptualized loss as not only associated with responses of bereavement, but with responses of trauma."[22] By the 1990s, Edward Rynearson had narrowed the attention that was being given to "traumatic bereavement" to those who had survived the violent death of a loved one. While his research considered the trauma of those grieving the suicide or the accidental death of a loved one, he found that "homicide appears to be the most distressing form of violent death for the surviving family member."[23]

Rando has published most recently and most extensively about the bereavement process experienced by those who survive a traumatic

---

18   Ibid.
19   Rando, T.A. 2012. *Coping with the Sudden Death of your Loved One: Self-Help for Traumatic Bereavement*. Dog Ear Publishing.
20   Rynearson, Edward K. 2001. *Retelling Violent Death*. Philadelphia, PA.: Brunner-Routledge.
21   Figley, et al., 1997; Rando, 1993; Horowitz, 1976.
22   Rynearson, Edward K. 2001. *Retelling Violent Death*. Philadelphia, PA.: Brunner-Routledge.
23   Ibid.

death. She defines traumatic bereavement as "the state of having suffered the loss of a loved one when grief and mourning over the death is overpowered by the traumatic stress brought about by its circumstances."[24] When the grief process of death row families is examined from the perspective of traumatic bereavement, it becomes apparent that these families are experiencing this type of unique loss. Given the fact that homicides often occur within the same family, it is not uncommon for the families to lose at once a loved one to murder and the accused family member to prison. For those death row families who did not know the murder victim prior to their loved one being charged with the murder, they nonetheless remain tormented by fear that they will soon be made homicide survivors by the state that plans to execute their loved one. In the meantime, the graphic details of the murder their loved one has been accused of killing are enough alone to cause extreme traumatic stress in the family member of the accused. Clearly, the trauma they have endured and continue to suffer as they await the execution of their loved one, or deal with its aftermath, serves as a major complication in their grief process.

Clinical Interventions

While is not necessary for therapists who work with death row families to be experts in the field of grief therapy, it is extremely helpful for them to have an understanding of the concept of disenfranchised grief.[25] With such an understanding, the therapist is able to describe to a client how and why certain individuals are disenfranchised from their own grief by the larger community. From the process of simply naming the dragon called "disenfranchised grief", the families are able to gain an understanding of the cultural context that intensifies the already painful loss they are experiencing with the incarceration of their loved one. Particularly at such an early point of their loss, it is helpful for the family to understand why their support system is likely to dwindle as their nightmare unfolds in the years ahead. The lack of support that they encounter will still be difficult to bear, yet if the family members come to understand that they are being

---

24   Rando, T.A. 2012. *Coping with the Sudden Death of your Loved One: Self-Help for Traumatic Bereavement*. Dog Ear Publishing.

25   Doka, K. J., ed. 1989. *Disenfranchised Grief: Recognizing Hidden Sorrows*. Lexington, MA: Lexington Books.

disenfranchised from their grief, they may be able to cope more easily with the shame that they tend to feel from their association with an accused murderer. Once they realize that those within the community are failing to recognize their loss because it falls outside of the "grieving rules" determined by society, they may come to view the lack of support they receive as the failing of society rather than due to any fault of their own. Placing the onus for the treatment they receive in society upon others may, in turn, allow these families to reject the shame they previously internalized.

Perhaps the time when the families of death row inmates are most often left feeling as though their loss is not recognized occurs soon after their loved one is arrested and convicted, when the community's memory of the horrific crime that has been committed is still fresh. Several family members who were interviewed recalled exchanges that they had early on with the family members of the murder victim or others who were intimately familiar with the case against their loved one. These exchanges often left the death row families feeling not only as though their loss had gone unrecognized, but also that they were being scoffed at for the mere suggestion that they might be in pain. Particularly when the loss suffered by the family of the murder victim was contrasted to their loss, the families of death row inmates were made to feel as though they did not have a right to their grief. They received remarks like "at least *you* can still see your son; *mine* is dead."

It is certainly safe for the therapist to assume that the family member of someone who stands accused of murder is feeling disenfranchised by the larger community from grieving this significant loss. The source of their disenfranchisement needs to be closely assessed, however, as it may not originate solely from the community. Many of the families who spoke with me shared that they felt as though members of their own family were denying them their right to grieve the incarceration of their loved one. This was particularly the case for those families whose loved one was accused of killing a member of their family. When family members are made to be "double losers",[26] at once surviving the loss of a loved one to murder and another to

---

26   Sharp, S. F. 2005. *Hidden Victims: The Effects of the Death Penalty on Families of the Accused*. New Brunswick, NJ: Rutgers University Press.

incarceration, they are frequently made to feel bad for grieving the loss of their loved one to incarceration. Such grief is assumed to be evidence of disloyalty to the loved one who was murdered. It is not uncommon to find that some of the immediate or extended family members related to both the murder victim and the accused become so angry with their incarcerated loved one that they disenfranchise their family members who dare to openly grieve the loss they feel from the incarceration.

The clinical importance of validating the disenfranchised grief felt by those death row family members who seek treatment cannot be underestimated. Indeed, the grief they feel from the original loss of their loved one to incarceration is so complicated by the additional grief they feel from being disenfranchised that it is argued that they are unable to fully address their original loss until after they grieve the feelings of loss that are attributed to their disenfranchisement. Psychotherapist and thanatologist Jeffrey Kauffman has engaged extensively in both the study and treatment of disenfranchised grief. Kauffman (2002) has emphasized the importance of providing disenfranchised clients with treatment that places priority on their grief from being disenfranchised over their grief from the original loss.

Psychotherapy for the complications of disenfranchised grief gives consideration to (a) complications inherent in the loss and in grief that has been disenfranchised and (b) the grief inflicted by disenfranchisement. Therapy for disenfranchised grief concerns itself with both the grief of the original loss and the grief of the disenfranchisement. The grief of disenfranchisement may have priority in treatment, both in clinical triage and in persistence, over the grief that has been disenfranchised. The meaning of the original loss may come to be determined by the loss inflicted in the act of disenfranchisement. Grief over what is lost and the grief of disenfranchisement may merge into an insistent grief, a wound caused by the failure of others to recognize it, so that what is most disturbing and injurious is the way that being disenfranchised in one's grief signifies to the self its own disenfranchisement.[27] When grief is self-disenfranchising, "*oneself* is the agent carrying out the sanctions against the self and operating psychologically on behalf of societal grief expectations…oneself is not only disenfranchis*ed* (the object of

---

27   Kauffman, 2002: 66–67.

disenfranchisement), but also disenfranchising."[28] In order for the perpetuation of disenfranchisement by the self to occur, the role of shame to this process cannot be underestimated. For those who experience disenfranchised grief, "shame is the psychological force that prevents the experience of grief from occurring and that may outright foreclose the experience of grief.... Shame is the psychological regulator allowing and disallowing recognition of grief."[29]

Among the death row families that I interviewed, many family members presented as currently battling self-disenfranchisement, or having dealt with this form of disenfranchised grief earlier in their grieving process. As they described their initial reaction to their loved one's murder charge, the word "shame" was often used, providing evidence of their self-disenfranchisement.

Surviving their loved one's indictment for homicide can be traumatic for all family members, yet the amount of traumatic stress that family members endure varies from one homicide to another. For instance, when the surviving family members are deemed "double losers,"[30] having lost family both to homicide and through incarceration, their losses are almost always complicated with severe symptoms of trauma. Furthermore, if members of the offender's family were present at the time of the murder to witness either the actual homicide or its aftermath, the severity of their traumatic stress will be especially high. Yet even those family members of the accused who are not physically present to witness the traumatic events surrounding the murder are prone to be traumatized by news that their loved one has been accused of and incarcerated for a horrific murder within their community.

There are a number of possible reactions to traumatic stress that can be found among those who have experienced a sudden loss. It is important to note that post-traumatic reactions of someone who is confronted with a loss need not develop into full-blown post-traumatic stress disorder (PTSD), as it is specified in the Diagnostic and Statistical Manual of Mental Disorders, Fifth Edition, in order for

28 Kauffman, 2002: 61.
29 Kauffman, 2002: 63.
30 Sharp, S. F. 2005. *Hidden Victims: The Effects of the Death Penalty on Families of the Accused*. New Brunswick, NJ: Rutgers University Press.

these reactions nonetheless to confirm that the person has indeed been traumatized by loss. Regardless of the severity of the symptoms of traumatic stress, however, a number of common reactions appear among those who experience a traumatic loss. Most people who survive a traumatic event tend to undergo extreme frustration, anger, and heightened arousal, yet it is their feelings of helplessness that "may be not only the most distressing and threatening aspect of the trauma, but also the most difficult to integrate and the most traumatic to the individual's stimulus barrier."[31]

Nearly all of the death row family members who spoke with me about their initial reaction to their loved one's indictment for the crime of murder and subsequent incarceration shared the extreme frustration and anger that they were flooded with at that time. Their heightened arousal combined with intense feelings of helplessness frequently manifest through various symptoms of anxiety. Therese Rando (1993) lists over a dozen forms of anxiety commonly exhibited by people who have experienced complicated, traumatic losses. As the death row families shared their pain with me, many of these forms of anxiety emerged or the families indicated that they have experienced such anxiety at various points since their loved one's indictment. The manifestations of anxiety from Rando's list that are most dominant among death row families include:

• Anxiety arising from the unknown, unfamiliar, and uncertain
• Anxiety arising from the helplessness, vulnerability, and insecurity during and after the trauma
• Anxiety arising from unexpressed and/or unacceptable feelings, thoughts, behaviors, and impulses during and/or after the trauma or from internal conflicts the mourner sustains concerning them
• Anxiety caused by heightened emotional and physiological arousal
• Separation anxiety
• Anxiety arising from the violation of the assumptive world caused by the trauma and victimization of the mourner, as well as by the fact that the mourner is now so different than before the trauma
• Anxiety stimulated by defenses used to cope with the trauma
• Anxiety stemming from survivor guilt[32]

---

31   Rando, 1993: 575.
32   Rando, 1993: 574–75.

While there are various therapeutic approaches that therapists utilize in their treatment of the client who suffers from traumatic loss, the general goals of all interventions are "to empower the individual and to liberate him from the traumatic effects of victimization. Issues of grief and mourning are consistently mentioned as inherent aspects of healthy adaptation to traumatic stress."[33] In order to move the traumatized client toward healthy grieving, there are many different strategies that are available to therapists. After the therapist has estab-lished a therapeutic relationship with a client, thereby providing with a safe environment where the client can most comfortably release pain, one of the first interventions typically taken is to "bring into consciousness the traumatic experience, repeatedly reviewing, recon-structing, re-experiencing, and abreacting the experience until it is robbed of its potency."[34]

In the vast majority of cases, if the newly traumatized family member even seeks counseling, by the time that they meet a therapist they have already had contact with the legal team who is assigned to represent the incarcerated loved one. One of the first messages that family members receive loud and clear from the defense attorney and the rest of the legal team is that if anyone in the family has witnessed the homicide or has any information, they are *not* to speak about what they saw or what they know regarding the crime to *anyone*. In rare instances, this legal advice posed a temporary barrier that I had to overcome as I sought to gather data for my study. For the most part, it did not pose problems for my research, however, since I had come to know many of the defense attorneys through my activism over the years prior to my study. The attorneys who did not know me prior to my research soon learned that the information gathered by my study does not focus on the details of the crime. As a result, the families were typically not discouraged by the attorneys from speaking with me. Defense attorneys may inadvertently discourage the decision of family members to speak to a therapist, however, due to the nature of the information typically discussed with the therapist. This could cause concern among the team of legal professionals at any point throughout the years leading up to execution, since a case is typically under appeal long after a death sen-tence and family members may be asked to testify at appeal hearings. It

---

33   Rando, 1993: 588.
34   Rando, 1993: 588.

is most likely to pose an issue during the pre-trial period, however, as the attorneys take every precaution possible to ensure that their client is not given a death sentence.

While the therapist is bound to treat the revelations of clients confidentially, it is possible that any documentation that the therapist has entered into a client's chart can be subpoenaed by the court. While the possibility of these records being subpoenaed by the state is unlikely, if it were to occur it would certainly concern the defense team, as the traumatic memories shared by a family member with a therapist may contain details that could harm the legal defense of a loved one. The therapist must be sensitive to the possibility that any reluctance from a death row family member to discuss the circumstances surrounding a loved one's incarceration may be due less to avoidance on the part of the family member to deal with pain than it is an attempt to honor the wishes of the defense team. While defense attorneys are certainly not inclined to interfere with family members seeking mental health treatment, they may give off a vibe that discourages the families from speaking to a therapist about their traumatic experience. This outcome is particularly likely for those family members who are already reticent to share their pain with mental health professionals, due either to cultural norms against such treatment or the stigma that they have internalized from the community.

An awareness of the potential barrier to treatment posed by the instruction that families receive from defense attorneys can help therapists as they strive to identify possible reasons for their client's reluctance to share their traumatic experiences surrounding their loved one's incarceration. Recall that many family members who find themselves in the office of a mental health professional are there because they have been encouraged to seek treatment for what, at least initially, appears to be an unrelated issue, such as a disruptive child, drug addiction, or some other family concern. With these cases, it may only be discovered through a gathering of a psychosocial history that the client has an incarcerated loved one. What might appear to be resistance from the client to share more detail around a loved one's incarceration and its impact on the family may instead stem from legal instruction from a legal team.

The member of the defense team who is likely to interact most closely with the family members of the accused is the mitigation specialist assigned to the case. Many mitigation specialists are social workers, yet it is not at all uncommon to find a variety of professionals among those who work in the area of mitigation, including journalists, educators, anthropologists, psychologists, and attorneys.[35] The role of the mitigation specialist is to "conduct a comprehensive life history investigation of the client and identify all relevant mitigation issues, including facts and circumstances to rebut the prosecution's case in aggravation."[36] The mitigation specialist gathers the information needed to construct a life history, interviewing the defendant numerous times. In addition, the mitigation specialist meets with family members, friends, and even past acquaintances who are able to speak to the circumstances of the defendant's life that play a role in shaping his or her actions, particularly the alleged murder for which the defendant is accused. These life circumstances might include those that have contributed to diminished mental capacity, a history of child abuse, an impoverished family background, or alcohol and drug addiction. Such circumstances of the defendant's background fall within the three broad categories of mitigating evidence, which are "reduced culpability, general good character, and lack of future dangerousness."[37] It has been argued by those within the National Association of Criminal Defense Lawyers that "the capital mitigation specialist is arguably the most important member of the capital defense team, especially when the client is facing a sentencing hearing in a death penalty case. This person, in effect, enables the capital defense team to develop and 'tell the story' of the client—the key to saving the client's life."[38]

While the mitigation specialist clearly plays an important role in building a defense for the capital defendant, the approach of the mitigation specialist is likely to be at odds with that of the therapist who is working with the family. The mitigation specialist has a fixed time frame to work within, as she or he must gather all of the appropriate information required from the family members of the client in time

---

35   Bruno, Paul J, "The Mitigation Specialist," *The Champion*, June, 2010. Available at http://www.nacdl.org/Champion.aspx?id=14626. (accessed 24 August 2016).

36   Dudley & Leonard, 2008.

37   Garvey, 1998.

38   Bruno, 2010.

to build the best possible defense for the court hearing. The course of treatment proposed by the therapist, on the other hand, is dictated by the mental and emotional welfare of the family member engaged in therapy rather than to any other outside forces or timelines beyond the control of the family. The urgency with which the mitigation specialist must dig deep alongside the family members to uncover all of the sordid details of abuse, addiction, or any other latent family secrets (i.e., mitigating factors for defense of the accused) is likely to undermine efforts made by the therapist to establish a sense of safety for family members who are seeking therapeutic intervention.

Typically, family members have already been so significantly trau-matized by the events surrounding their loved one being accused of murder that they find it tough to withstand the additional emotional and mental anguish that comes with having to relive traumatic family memories that had long remained buried. Indeed, as the mitigation specialist uncovers mitigating evidence, it is not that uncommon for family members to learn the details of such a painful family history for the first time, either from their incarcerated loved one or from another family member who had previously maintained the family secret. When these distant traumatic memories are brought up and discussed with the mitigation specialist, they may overwhelm the family member who is already attempting to deal with the present traumatic event sparked by the murder their loved one is alleged to have committed. The therapist may find the already daunting task of helping a client heal made even more challenging by the reopening of old wounds caused by the mitigation specialist's need to delve into the family's dysfunctional background.

This potential conflict posed by the agendas of the mitigation special-ist and the therapist is likely to emerge more than once throughout the family nightmare. The frequent appeals filed on the behalf of death row inmates typically contain repeated attempts at mitigation evidence collection, often by new mitigation specialists assigned to a given case. As a result, family members may find themselves having to revisit trauma from their past over and over again. This may prove to cause occasional setbacks in the therapeutic process for the family member who has engaged in therapy. Just as she or he starts to heal from the trauma of the alleged criminal behavior and subsequent incarceration of a loved one, the traumatic memories from the past that resurface after a meeting with the mitigation specialist may sabotage any progress made.

An awareness of the role that the defense team plays in the lives of the family members of the accused is essential for any therapist who is working with these families. It is particularly crucial for the therapist to be aware of any involvement of mitigation specialists. As the therapist goes over the rules regarding confidentiality with a new client, it may prove helpful for to approach the topic of the defense team. The client may need encouragement to share what he or she has been told by the defense team regarding the need to remain silent about the facts surrounding the case. If it is determined that the client has indeed been advised by the defense team not to talk about a loved one's case, the therapist can then assure the client that any information shared during their therapy sessions is protected by the privileged relationship between client and therapist. The therapist may go one step further to communicate to the still skeptical client that in preparation for the rare case when the records of their therapy sessions are subpoenaed, any documentation of the details surrounding the case will be kept to a bare minimum.

Another basis for the therapist broaching the subject of the mitigation collection process with a new client is to prepare this client for the emotional distress of being interviewed by the mitigation specialist. The therapist might even go so far as to suggest that a client schedule a therapy session to take place within the day or two immediately after a meeting with a mitigation specialist. Certainly, the death row family member is unable to completely avoid the pain of recalling family history, often traumatic in its content. At the same time, a plan to meet with a therapist soon after summoning up such painful memories may allow the client to curtail possible setbacks to the therapeutic process caused by these memories.

As the family nightmare unfolds, one of the primary tasks facing its members is to build upon their support system. Toward that end, the therapist can assist them in their search to find others within the community who may be able to serve as a support. As numerous death row family members have shared with me, there are few people who they feel support them as they go through the crisis of losing their loved one to incarceration. Indeed, the comments they shared that I have quoted reveal that they cannot necessarily even count on getting the support that they need from within their own family.

Given the vast assortment of support groups that exist for people who have suffered a loss, the therapist may be inclined to refer a client to one of these support groups. The groups that have been organized to offer support to the bereaved, however, are not typically used to thinking of the families of the incarcerated as suffering a loss. Equally important to the way that other bereaved populations view the loss of death row families is the way that these families *perceive their own loss* relative to other bereaved groups, such as those who have survived the loss of a loved one to terminal illness or accidental death. Since the families of the accused are not used to thinking of their own loss as legitimate in comparison to other types of losses, they are not willing to risk rejection by these other groups that are traditionally viewed as bereaved.

While death row parents may not feel comfortable sitting alongside other grieving parents in such support groups as Compassionate Friends,[39] death row parents and other family members of those charged with murder may find it helpful to join support groups that have been created for families of the incarcerated, or those more specifically organized on behalf of death row families. The problem with death row families joining such support groups is that they are exceedingly rare and difficult to form and sustain.

Therapists who are able to get a death row family engaged in therapy during this early stage of their nightmare should have an awareness of the abolitionist organizations in their client's state and community. The least that can be gained by the client's new awareness of the death penalty abolition movement is comfort knowing that there are people, strangers even, who want to save the life of a loved one. Prior to this knowledge, the death row family member may have felt as though the whole world was trying to kill their loved one. Beyond simply gaining awareness of the anti-death penalty movement, the family member may wish to seek support from these activists. At

---

39   http://www.compassionatefriends.org. (accessed 24 August 2016).

times, the activists may seek out the family as well, after hearing about the alleged crime of their loved one through the local news, to let them know that there are people within their organization who wish to help them get through this incredibly stressful time when many others have ostracized them.

Many family members of death row inmates face the harsh reality of an execution looming. The numerous challenges that confront them throughout this ordeal and various concepts within the study of grief and loss have been described and utilized to clarify the experiences of death row families. It is my hope that these families soon find their way to the office of a therapist in order to receive the support and mental health treatment that they need to endure the pain that comes with loving someone who is faced with the threat of execution.

It is certainly true that these families are largely forgotten by the rest of us within society. When we count the victims of a murder and the harm that it brings, we do not usually consider the family of the accused murderer. The families of death row inmates are indeed victims, however, on many levels. They are victimized in that they are stigmatized and criminalized by criminal justice and media representatives, as well as within the larger society. They have been victimized by their loss of a loved one to incarceration, if not also victimized by the "double loss" of loved one(s) to murder. They may be further victimized if they eventually lose their loved one to an execution. It is crucial for the treatment of these families' needs that we consider the ways that they are victims so that they are no longer forgotten. Mental health professionals will further be able to gain an appreciation of the ways in which the families' unique loss of a loved one to death row shapes their grieving process at various points throughout their nightmare. In order for these families to awaken from their nightmare and begin the healing process from their grief, they must be forgotten no more.

3.2 Participants in death penalty proceedings and executions

DEATH PENALTY AND ITS IMPACT ON THE PROFESSIONALS INVOLVED IN THE EXECUTION PROCESS

Lizzie Seal, Florence Seemungal and Lynsey Black [1]

In debates about the death penalty, there is frequently little consideration given to the people who are involved in the execution process as part of their jobs. This includes a wide range of individuals, from those who oversee and administer the execution itself, to those who offer emotional and spiritual support to the person sentenced to death such as prison ministers, to those who try to prevent the execution, such as death row lawyers. All of these people face the risk of being traumatized by their experiences[2]—what Robert M. Bohm refers to as the "human element, the impact of capital punishment on the lives of those who are involved."[3] To be responsible for trying to preserve someone's life is a heavy burden. To be responsible for killing them is arguably a heavier one.

This chapter examines the "secondary trauma" that affects professionals involved in the execution process. It begins by outlining what is meant by secondary trauma and then draws on personal testimonies from prison wardens, executioners, death-penalty witnesses and death-penalty lawyers to explore the traumatic effects of execution. It considers both contemporary and historical examples from the United States, Britain and Trinidad and Tobago, and finishes by

---

1   Lizzie Seal, University of Sussex, United Kingdom, Florence Seemungal, University of the West Indies, Jamaica, and Lynsey Black, Trinity College Dublin, Ireland.

2   The number of individuals traumatized by execution potentially runs into the tens of thousands when legal personnel and court staff are also included. Cynthia F. Adcock. 2010. "The Collateral Anti-Therapeutic Effects of the Death Penalty." *Florida Coastal Law Review* 11(2):289–320, p. 293.

3   Robert M. Bohn. 2012. *Capital Punishment's Collateral Damage.* Durham, NC: Carolina Academic Press. p. 3.

briefly considering how the issue of professionals' secondary trauma has been adopted in abolitionist campaigns.

Secondary Trauma

Post-traumatic stress disorder (PTSD) refers to psychiatric impairment resulting from direct personal exposure to death, serious injury, or threat to physical integrity, but it can also be caused by witnessing such an event.[4] Individuals closely involved in executions, such as executioners and prison wardens, have experienced effects consistent with PTSD, such as problems with physical health, depression, addictions, suicidal thoughts, or even suicide. Feeling numbness, insomnia, and recurrent nightmares are other commonly reported elements of "executioner stress."[5] This "secondary trauma" is one of the "relatively unknown social psychological consequences" of capital punishment.[6] Exposure to death is potentially traumatizing in itself, but participation in botched executions, where procedural failure means that the prisoner visibly suffers, are especially likely to traumatize members of the execution team.[7] Despite changes in the technology of execution and attempts to introduce methods that are "humane," such as lethal injection, botched executions continue to happen[8]—and in many countries hanging, which is easily botched, remains the method of choice. Even if individuals involved in the execution process are not traumatized to the point of psychiatric impairment, they may still experience stresses and negative effects that illustrate the death penalty's wider negative impacts.

4   Amanda Gil, Matthew B. Johnson and Ingrid Johnson. 2006. "Secondary Trauma Associated with State Executions." *The Journal of Psychiatry and Law* 34(1):25-36, p. 27.
5   Robert Jay Lifton and Greg Mitchell. 2000. *Who Owns Death? Capital Punishment, the American Conscience, and the End of Executions.* New York: HarperCollins. p. 78.
6   Lauren M. De Lilly. 2014. "'Antithetical to Human Dignity': Secondary Trauma, Evolving Standards of Decency, and the Constitutional Consequences of State-Sanctioned Executions." *South California Interdisciplinary Law Journal* 23(1):107-46, p. 120.
7   Adcock, 2010, p. 315.
8   Austin Sarat. 2014. *Gruesome Spectacles: Botched Executions and America's Death Penalty.* Stanford, CA: Stanford University Press.

PERSONAL TESTIMONIES

Prison Wardens

Our knowledge of the traumatic impact of execution on professionals involved in the process comes from individuals' accounts of their experiences. Clinton T. Duffy, warden of San Quentin Prison in California 1940–1952, asserted "Each of the 150 executions I watched was a separate and distinct ordeal, unsavoury, nauseating, and infuriating. I faced all of them with dread and I look back on them with revulsion."[9] Although a "lifelong death-penalty opponent," Wayne Patterson had to oversee gas chamber executions as part of his role as warden of Colorado State Penitentiary from 1965-1972, and in 1967 initiated the gassing of Luis Jose Monge, the last person to be executed in the United States for a decade until 1977.[10]

As warden at Parchman Penitentiary in Mississippi in the 1980s, Donald Cabana oversaw three executions in the gas chamber. He stated that execution left him "feeling dirty" and asserted "Every time the warden executes a prisoner, a piece of him dies too."[11] The first execution over which he presided was that of Edward Earl Johnson, who was widely believed to have been innocent. Cabana's friendship with another condemned man, Connie Ray Evans, led him to leave the prison service and enter academia. Cabana became a vocal abolitionist until his death in 2013. He argued that although the public might support the death penalty, the public does not bear the consequences of execution—executioners do,[12] and cautioned "You don't have the right to ask me, or people like me, to kill for you."[13] He articulated the emotional burden of worrying "what my wife and children and my friends would think of me" and, crucially for a man of faith, "wondered if my God would forgive me."[14]

---

9   Quoted in Bohm, 2012, p. 204.
10   Ibid., p. 219.
11   Terry McCaffrey and Amnesty International, "Interview with an Executioner," Midpen Media Center, 2003.
12   Cabana was not an executioner in the sense of directly carrying out the execution but, as he put it, "my hand was on the lever as well." Donald Cabana. 1996. *Death at Midnight: The Confession of an Executioner*. Hanover MA: Northeastern University Press. p. 17.
13   *Interview with an Executioner*. 2003.
14   Cabana, 1996, p. 18.

Ron McAndrew, warden of Florida State Prison, 1996–2002, is a self-confessed former "staunch supporter" of the death penalty turned abolitionist campaigner. He has provided extensive testimony of the traumatic effects of execution on those involved in carrying it out. He states "I myself have been haunted by the men I was asked to execute in the name of the state of Florida"[15] and had nightmares in which he saw "the faces of the men that I executed. I woke up and saw them literally sitting on the edge of my bed."[16] These nightmares prompted him to see a therapist. At this point, he could not sleep without drinking alcohol and taking sleeping pills. A particularly terrible experience was the botched execution of Pedro Medina in 1997, whose mask burst into flames when he was executed in the electric chair. McAndrew says "we burned him to death."[17] However, witnessing six lethal injections in Texas was no less traumatic. He has also elucidated the 'suffering and trauma' experienced by other prison staff.[18] He explains that some of his past colleagues became drug addicts and alcoholics and that the majority of death team members he has worked with share "horrible, down deep feelings."[19]

The former commissioner of the Georgia Department of Corrections, 1992–95, Allen Ault, has recounted similar experiences of ongoing trauma to Ron McAndrew. He describes the effects of supervising the execution process as "something very much like post-traumatic stress", which for him entailed either insomnia or being "plagued by nightmares."[20] Unlike McAndrew, who initially thought that he would not be troubled by overseeing executions, Ault unwittingly assumed responsibility for capital punishment. A trained psychologist, he was hired to develop a prison-based diagnostic programme in the 1970s at a time when the death penalty was suspended. Ault was never pro-death penalty but ended up presiding over five executions. He felt that giving the order for prisoners to be killed in the electric

15 Ron McAndrew's Testimony the New Hampshire Death Penalty Study Commission, New Hampshire Coalition to Abolish the Death Penalty, 2010.

16 Jason Silverstein, "Ron McAndrew is Done Killing People," *Esquire*, 14 January 2014. Available from http://www.esquire.com/news-politics/news/a26833/ron-mcandrew-is-done-killing-people/. (accessed 4 April 2016).

17 Ibid.

18 Testimony to the New Hampshire Death Penalty Study Commission, 2010.

19 Ibid.

20 Allen Ault, "Ordering Death in Georgia Prisons," *Newsweek*, September 25, 2011. Available from http://europe.newsweek.com/ordering-death-georgia-prisons-67483?rm=eu. (accessed 5 April 2016).

chair was "giving the order for [them] to be murdered."[21] He experienced "personal damage", which led him to seek treatment.[22] He has been left with a "large sense of guilt"[23] and is sure that he will have "re-occurring problems" for the rest of his life.[24] Ault argues that "The men and women who assist in executions are not psychopaths or sadists. They do their best to perform the impossible and inhumane job with which the state has charged them."[25]

Executioners

Jerry Givens differs from Cabana, McAndrew, and Ault in that he was a corrections officer who acted as an executioner, rather than a warden in a supervisory role. As such, his identity as an executioner was secret and is only known because he now speaks publicly about his experiences. At the time, he kept his role secret from his wife and children.[26] Givens was involved in executing 62 people in Virginia during his 17 years working in corrections. He describes seeing smoke rise from those executed in the electric chair and smelling their burning flesh. However, he regards lethal injection as worse than the chair as it takes longer, requiring the prisoner to wait for the drugs to take effect. The issue of executing the innocent helped to transform Givens into an abolitionist. Earl Washington Jr., wrongfully convicted of rape and murder, was exonerated three weeks before Givens would have executed him.[27] Givens explains "If I had known what I would have to go through as an executioner, I wouldn't have done it. It took a lot out of me to do it. You can't tell me you can take the life of people and go home and be normal."[28] The enduring nature of the executioner's secondary trauma is articulated by Givens: "The person that carries out the execution itself is stuck with it the

21 "Allen Ault—Former Commissioner of Corrections, Georgia, USA," *HARDtalk*, BBC News Channel, February 14, 2014. Available from http://www.bbc.co.uk/programmes/b03v13qd. (accessed 4 April 2016).

22 Ibid.

23 Ibid.

24 Interview with Allen Ault, *The Ed Show*, MSNBC, September 21, 2011.

25 Ault, 2011.

26 *Jerry*, [Documentary] dir. Jeff Reynolds, USA, 2011.

27 Selene Nelson, "'I Executed 62 People. I'm Sorry': An Executioner Turned Death-Penalty Opponent Tells All," *Salon*, October 8, 2015. Available from http://www.salon.com/2015/10/08/i_executed_62_people_im_sorry_an_executioner_turned_death_penalty_opponent_tells_all/. (accessed 5 April 2016).

28 Ibid.

rest of his life. He has to wear that burden. Who would want that on them?"[29] Like Ault, Givens describes the death penalty as committing "murder."[30]

Concern about the impact that the execution process has on those who must administer it is not only a recent phenomenon. Work on the history of capital punishment in Britain, I found that there is a strong tradition of executioners relating the death penalty's negative effects.[31] These portrayals and accounts do not use the modern language of "trauma," but do articulate similar experiences to the ones discussed above. James Berry, a late-Victorian hangman, became an evangelical preacher following his resignation from the list of executioners. In his sermons, he explained that "So loathsome was the task that he could do no other than get drunk to dull his feelings." Before finding religion, he had intended to kill himself, "so wretched, wicked and debauched had he become."[32]

Hangman, John Ellis, attempted suicide by shooting in 1924 and in 1932 committed suicide by cutting his own throat. In 1923, Ellis hanged Edith Thompson in what was widely believed to have been a botched execution. A news story about his suicide recorded that after Thompson's execution Ellis was "a bundle of nerves and, in 1924, he retired and told me it was on account of not being able to sleep as a result of hanging Mrs. Thompson."[33] Ellis's son commented "He was haunted. We all knew what prevented him from sleeping."[34] John Ellis had an American counterpart in John Hulbert, a former state executioner of New York, who killed himself in 1929, three years after retiring from his role.[35] There is necessarily an element of speculation involved in relation to how far these men's careers as executioners influenced their suicides. However, contemporary news stories that

---

29 Michael Daly, "I Committed Murder," *Newsweek*, September 25, 2011. Available from http://europe.newsweek.com/i-committed-murder-67463. (accessed 5 April 2016).

30 Ibid.

31 Lizzie Seal. 2014. *Capital Punishment in Twentieth-Century Britain: Audience, Justice, Memory*. London: Routledge, and 2016. "Albert Pierrepoint and the Cultural Persona of the Twentieth-Century Hangman," *Crime, Media, Culture* 12(1):83-100.

32 "An Ex-Hangman's Story," *Gloucester Citizen*, February 18, 1907.

33 "Ellis the Hangman Commits Suicide: Haunted by the Memory of Mrs. Thompson's Suicide," *Daily Express*, September 21, 1932.

34 Ibid.

35 Seal, 2016, p. 94. Hulbert originally worked at Auburn Prison as an electrician and took over operating the electric chair in 1913.

emphasized how executioners felt "haunted" by the executions they had carried out demonstrate that concern about capital punishment's long lasting negative effects is not confined to the present.

Death-Penalty Witnesses

Some jobs involve witnessing, rather than helping to carry out, executions. In jurisdictions such as Texas, where high numbers of people have been executed, this can mean having been present at many state orchestrated deaths. Larry Fitzgerald retired from his position as Public Information director of the Texas Department of Criminal Justice in 2003, a role which made him the "face" of the death penalty in a state that was notorious for its use in the 1990s and early 2000s.[36] Fitzgerald witnessed 219 executions and announced their completion to the public. He explains that "there are a number of people who were executed who I truly liked that as you see them on the table, on the gurney, you think about conversations you've had with them"— as they die.[37] A particularly hard case was that of Napoleon Beazley, executed in 2002 at age 25 for a murder committed when he was just 17. Fitzgerald came to know Beazley and was disturbed that he had to be put to death for a crime that he committed as a minor, especially as he showed deep remorse. Beazley was one of the last people to be executed for a murder committed as a juvenile before the Supreme Court ruled this practice to be unconstitutional in 2005.[38]

Fitzgerald recounts that doubts about the death penalty in certain cases gave him a "helpless feeling."[39] He is not opposed to capital punishment but acknowledges "the system has flaws and it bothers me."[40] He understands racial bias to be one of these flaws. Fitzgerald now assists death-penalty attorneys when they try to secure life

---

36 Between 1992 and 1996, an average of 40 death sentences per year was handed down in Texas. The most enthusiastic practitioner of the American death penalty, since 1977 Texas has accounted for more executions than the next six highest executing states combined. Since 2005, there has been a decline in death sentencing. *See* David McCord. 2011. "What's Messing with Texas Death Sentences?," *Texas Tech Law Review* 43:601-13: pp. 601-2.

37 *The Man Who Witnessed 219 Executions*, [documentary] BBC3, United Kingdom, 2016.

38 Alexis J. Miller and Richard Tewksbury. 2015. "Sentenced to Die: Controversy and Change in the Ultimate Sanction for Juvenile Offenders." In Peter J. Benekos and Alida V. Merlo, eds, *Controversies in Juvenile and Justice and Delinquency* (2nd ed.). London: Routledge. p. 284.

39 Ibid.

40 Ibid.

imprisonment, rather than execution, during the sentencing phase of capital trials.[41] He explains that "there is something besides the death penalty in Texas" and that life imprisonment offers a sufficient penalty in many cases.[42]

While working for the Texas Department of Criminal Justice, Fitzgerald in 2001 recruited Michelle Lyons, a young journalist, as a public information officer. This entailed her witnessing every execution carried out at the Walls Unit in Huntsville, Texas. Lyons had previous experience of witnessing the death penalty as a journalist for local newspaper, the Huntsville *Item*. Altogether, she attended 278 executions, all by lethal injection.[43] Lyons prided herself on the objectivity and neutrality that she brought to her role. She found maintaining this emotional distance harder after she became a mother and could empathize with the mothers of both the murder victims and the condemned. After leaving the Department of Criminal Justice in 2012, Lyons found that she constantly relived memories, such as conversations with inmates who were soon to die and the reactions of their mothers as they were executed. She was surprised to discover that Larry Fitzgerald, her mentor, former boss, and friend, was plagued by dreams about condemned prisoners. She reflects "there is a difference between supporting the death penalty as a concept and being the person who actually watches its application. Being human, I knew there were bound to be cracks in the veneer. I just thought somehow it wouldn't happen to me."[44]

Death-Penalty Lawyers

Death-penalty lawyers sit on the other side of the fence from those who carry out or assist in the execution process in that they actively try to prevent the death penalty from happening. They also experience adverse effects from trying to save their clients' lives. Cynthia Adcock represented women and men on North Carolina's death row for 13

41 Steve Mills, "Voice of Death Testifies for Life," *Chicago Tribune*, June 12, 2008. Available from http://articles.chicagotribune.com/2008-06-12/news/0806120010_1_death-penalty-execution-prison-system (accessed 3 May 2016).

42 *The Man Who Witnessed 219 Executions*.

43 Pamela Coloff, "The Witness," *Texas Monthly*, September 2014. Available from http://www.texasmonthly.com/articles/the-witness/. (accessed 3 May 2016).

44 Ibid.

years—directly representing five executed individuals and attending four executions. She explains that "the death row lawyer uniquely experiences the vicarious trauma within a system that is bent on killing her client,"[45] which induces a cycle of hope and despair and feelings of guilt. Michael Mello wrote of how in 1985, when he had a mere two years' experience of practising law, he worked as a capital defender in Florida with responsibility for 35 condemned prisoners. In 1995, Mello concluded that he must become a "conscientious objector" to capital punishment—to stop participating at all in a system that was so flawed. In his memoir, he related his "exhausted sadness [...] for the manifold ways capital punishment has deformed our law and the people who practice it."[46]

Gregory Delzin and Douglas Mendes are both attorneys who have worked on capital appeals in Trinidad and Tobago. In conversation with two of the authors of this article,[47] Delzin explained that the execution of Glen Ashby in 1994 was the one instance where he felt traumatized by a case. Ashby's case was still under appeal and a stay of execution had been granted by the Judicial Committee of the Privy Council.[48] The attorney general had confirmed that Ashby would not be hanged until applications for a stay had been exhausted.[49] However, at 6.40 a.m. on 14 July, only a day after this assurance was made, Ashby was executed.[50] Delzin described how he felt tricked by the authorities and also shocked, as he expected that Ashby would still be alive that morning. He felt deeply affected emotionally. Mendes related how Delzin told him that Ashby had already been executed despite the fact that they were still arguing his case before the courts. This was "unbelievable" and the cause of "fits of anger" at the state's unreasonable behaviour.

45   Adcock, 2010, p. 297.
46   Michael Mello. 1997. *Dead Wrong: A Death Row Lawyer Speaks Out Against Capital Punishment*, Madison, WI: University of Wisconsin Press. p. 12.
47   Conversation with Lizzie Seal and Florence Seemungal, April 14, 2016.
48   This is based in the UK and is the highest court of appeal for Commonwealth Caribbean countries, *see* Dennis Morrison. 2006. "Judicial Committee of the Privy Council and the Death Penalty in the Commonwealth Caribbean: Studies in Judicial Activism." *Nova Law Review* 30(3):403-24.
49   Geoffrey Robertson. 2006. *Crimes Against Humanity* (3rd ed.). London: Penguin. p. 187.
50   Amnesty International. "Trinidad and Tobago: Man Executed While Appeals Still in Progress," *Death Penalty News International*, September 1994, p. 1. Available from https://www.amnesty.org/download/Documents/184000/act530031994en.pdf. (accessed 19 April 2016).

Delzin acknowledged that another difficult aspect of death-penalty lawyering is losing a client after interaction with them over several weeks. In particular, the desperation of their families and their hope that hanging could be averted weighed heavily. The need to protect his own family was another consideration. After Glen Ashby, there were no further executions in Trinidad and Tobago until June 1999, when nine men were executed over just four days.[51] Delzin, who was involved in these cases, recalled how he took his family to stay at the beach that weekend with no television or radio. He wanted to create a "cocoon" around them to shield them from the awfulness of these hangings.

Delzin also discussed experiencing people's opprobrium for trying to save the lives of convicted murderers. He endured verbal abuse and also received phone calls from individuals threatening to kill his children to show him what it was like to lose someone. Delzin interpreted these as attempts to intimidate him rather than as serious threats. For him, the abiding effect of experience of the capital punishment process was a sense of mistrust and cynicism, and a lack of faith that legal and political elites will "do the right thing." He estimated that he was involved in 15–20 attempts to get stays of execution (covering many more individuals) and became accustomed to the tactics employed by the state, such as scheduling hearings at two or three different courts on the same day. Ultimately, the arbitrariness with which lives were taken through capital punishment underlined the moral bankruptcy of the system.

Douglas Mendes referred to elevated stress levels as one of the main effects of death-penalty lawyering.[52] Before the Privy Council introduced a mandatory five-day notice period of the intention to execute, there was only a short, urgent period in which to try to get a stay. The state could read the warrant for the execution to take place the next morning so all papers had to be filed that night. This entailed working into the early hours of the morning under the stress of knowing that the state would resist—and failure would mean that the client could be executed. Work took place in an atmosphere of frayed tempers.

---

51   Mark Fineman, "Triple Hanging Returns Death Penalty to Trinidad," *Los Angeles Times*, June 5, 1999. Available from http://articles.latimes.com/1999/jun/05/news/mn-44346. (accessed 19 April 2016).

52   Conversation with Lizzie Seal, April 14, 2016.

Mendes cited the Glen Ashby case as one which for him illustrated the reality that public officials would do whatever they could to carry out an execution. In one case, Mendes and Delzin were threatened with contempt of court because they had managed to get an order for a stay of execution from the Privy Council after it had been denied by the Court of Appeal—and were only saved from the charge by senior lawyers who sat in the court until it was eventually adjourned.

Like Delzin, Mendes was also subject to threats, and although he agreed that he did not believe they would be carried out, he stated that there was a cost to the death-penalty lawyer in Trinidad and Tobago in terms of dealing with the hostility of both the public and politicians. He recalled that on one occasion, the minister of National Security called on the population to stop lawyers who were attempting to avert execution from going into the court. Businessmen asked that Mendes' firm be boycotted and a trade union no longer wanted his representation due to his anti-death penalty work.

Some of the more emotionally affecting aspects of such work were having to say goodbye to clients who were to be executed and, simply, as a member of a relatively small community, seeing the effects of cases on the relatives of those involved. Mendes has never sought counselling in relation to his death-penalty lawyering but reflected that an individual does not always know the effect that experiences have had on them.

Secondary Trauma and Abolitionist Campaigns

In the United States, abolitionist groups now highlight how "executions create more victims" by traumatizing corrections officers, wardens, clergy, jurors and journalists.[53] The National Coalition to Abolish the Death Penalty's website states "those involved in executions have reported suffering PTSD-like symptoms such as flashbacks, nightmares and other forms of distress."[54] Ex-executioner Jerry Givens serves on the board of Virginians for Alternatives to the

---

53   Equal Justice USA. *Executions Create More Victims.* Available from http://ejusa.org/learn/secondary-trauma/. (accessed 14 June 2016).

54   National Coalition to Abolish the Death Penalty. *Harm to Prison Workers.* Available from http://www.ncadp.org/pages/harm-to-prison-workers. (accessed 14 June 2016).

Death Penalty. This recognition of the extension of the death penalty's victimization beyond the condemned prisoner is an important part of making the case for the wide reach of the adverse personal costs of capital punishment, but also the social costs associated with this. Further, more rigorous academic research could greatly add to our understanding of secondary trauma and the death penalty. If a large number of people are left traumatized by the death penalty then its damage is not only a personal matter—it also negatively impacts on the communities and societies in which it takes place. The specific example of the effects of capital punishment on professionals raises the issue of what it is reasonable to ask someone to experience as part of their job and whether, as Donald Cabana questioned, governments or the public should have the right to demand that others become killers on their behalf.

EXECUTIONERS AT WORK:

Collateral Consequences of Executions for Officers Working on Death Row and in the Death House

Robert Johnson[1]

Overview

This chapter is about the experiences of prison officers cast in the role of executioner—indirectly by manning death rows or directly by serving on execution teams—and the way these officers cope and fail to cope with the pressures of what I have called "death work."[2] The dehumanizing legacy of executions for officers, inmates, and the larger society is considered.

Prisoners who are condemned to die are generally confined in a setting called death row, under the control of prison officers.[3] The specifics of death row regimes vary, but all death rows are ultimately human warehouses in which condemned prisoners are stored for execution like objects rather than persons.[4] The great majority of death rows in America, as well as in several other countries around

---

1   Professor of Justice, Law and Criminology, American University, Washington, DC, United States.

2   *See, generally*, Robert Johnson. 2005. *Death Work: A Study of the Modern Execution Process* (2nd ed.). Boston: Wadsworth.

3   Portions of this paper are drawn, with modifications, from Robert Johnson. 2005. *Death Work: A Study of the Modern Execution Process* (2nd ed). Boston: Wadsworth. *See also* Robert Johnson. 1981. *Condemned to Die: Life Under Sentence of Death*. New York: Elsevier, and Robert Johnson & Harmony Davies. 2014. "Life Under Sentence of Death: Historical and Contemporary Perspectives." In J. R. Acker, R. M. Bohm, & C. S. Lanier, eds. *America's Experiment with Capital Punishment: Reflections on the Past, Present, and Future of the Ultimate Penal Sanction* (3rd ed). Durham, NC: Carolina Academic Press. pp. 661-686; Robert Johnson. 1989. *Condemned to Die: Life Under Sentence of Death* (revised ed.). Long Grove, Ill: Waveland Press.

4   In America, "The vast majority of death rows—90% by a recent count—store condemned prisoners in their solitary cells for up to 23 hours a day as they await execution. Other death rows offer what amounts to congregate solitary confinement: condemned prisoners are allowed out of their cells, sometimes for many hours during the day, but are contained in small groups in dayrooms on the pod or tier in which they are housed, in complete isolation from the larger prison." *See* Robert Johnson. 2016. "Solitary confinement until death by state-sponsored homicide: An Eighth Amendment assessment of the modern execution process." *Washington & Lee Law Review* 73 (forthcoming).

the world, impose a regime of solitary confinement.[5] Those prisoners about to be executed are moved to a setting called the death house or death chamber, where they are put to death by an execution team made up of selected prison officers. All death houses enforce a regime of solitary confinement leading up to executions.[6] Prison officers who manage death rows and participate in executions, then, are working in the context of solitary confinement as a punishment in itself and as a prelude to the ultimate punishment: state-sponsored homicide.[7]

Living and Working on Death Row

Death row is an extremely stressful environment for prisoners, which makes it a difficult setting for prison officers to manage. Death row prisoners commonly report depression and varying degrees of emotional and mental deterioration as reactions to their solitary confinement under sentence of death.[8] One condemned prisoner I interviewed offered a telling description of the pressures of life in a solitary cell on death row, an experience that threatened his emotional and mental health on a daily basis:

> I sit in that cell, you know, and it seems like I'm just ready to scream or go crazy or something. And you know, the pressure, it builds up, and it feels like everything is—you're sitting there and things start, you know, not hearing things, things start to coming in your mind. You start to remember certain events that happened, bad things. It just gets to a person. I sit up at night, you know. You just sit there, and it seems like you're going to go crazy. You've got three walls around you and bars in front of you, and you start looking around, you know, and it seems like things are closing in on you. Like last

---

5 *See* Johnson and Davies, 2014.

6 *See*, generally, Johnson, 2005.

7 *See* Robert Johnson. 2016. "Solitary confinement until death by state-sponsored homicide: An Eighth Amendment assessment of the modern execution process." *Washington & Lee Law Review* 73 (forthcoming).

8 "Solitary confinement in particular degrades prisoners' mental health on death rows; it is common practice in countries including Japan, Jordan, South Korea, USA and elsewhere. In Japan, in the latter stages before execution, all communication between prisoners or between guards and prisoners is forbidden." Walter C. Long and Oliver Robertson. 2015. *Prison Guards and the Death Penalty*. Briefing Paper, Penal Reform International. pp. 1 and 4.

night, when I sit in there and everything's real quiet, things, just a buzzing noise gets to going in my ears. And I sit there, and I consciously think, "Am I going to go crazy?" And the buzzing gets louder; and you sit there and you want to scream and tell somebody to stop it. And most of the time you get up—if I start making some noise in my cell, it will slack off. And it sounds stupid, I know, but it happens…. Sometimes I wonder if I don't get it stopped, I'm going crazy or something. And you know, maybe tonight when I lay down it's not going to break when I get up and try to make some noise.[9]

Adding to the stresses of solitary confinement, death row prisoners typically report feeling helpless and vulnerable at the hands of staff, who exert great control over the prisoners' highly circumscribed daily lives. Alone and essentially defenseless when in their cells, living at all times in harsh and deprived conditions as convenient objects of contempt, condemned prisoners feel vulnerable to abuse by their keepers. Moreover, death rows are housed in highly secluded quarters of the prison. Thus, the isolation of death row, in concert with the isolation of the condemned within death row, is seen by prisoners to invite abuse. From the point of view of condemned prisoners, death row is a world of its own and a law unto itself. "They can do anything they want to you," noted one prisoner. "Who's going to stop them?"[10]

It is troubling to realize that many—perhaps most—condemned prisoners believe that their guards—with or without provocation—would resort to violence. In extreme cases, fear of officer violence may merge with fear of execution. One death row prisoner, visibly afraid when speaking with me, had this to say:

When you're on death row and you're laying down in your cell and you hear a door cracking, you'll think of where it comes from. When you hear it crack. And when you hear the keys and everything, when something like this happens, the keys come through here: I'm up. I'm up because you don't know when it's going to take place. The courts give you an execution date, that's true. But you don't know what's

---

9   Johnson, 1981, p. 49.
10   Johnson, 2005, p. 101.

going to take place between then and your execution date. You don't know when you're going to be moved around to the silent cell over here. That's right down the hall, what they call a waiting cell. You don't know when you're going to be moved down there. And this keeps you jumpy, and it keeps you nervous, and it keeps you scared.[11]

Such fear, which borders at times on raw panic, is a reflection of the vulnerability many of these prisoners feel, as well as the distrust they have for their keepers.

In my experience, condemned prisoners describe death row as a human pressure cooker.[12] The world they are forced to endure is marked by tension so palpable that it can be disabling. "The main thing", one condemned prisoner informed me, describing his emotional deterioration, "is the mental pressure: you're always depressed. But I think another main thing is the physical deterioration of the body. You sit up there and you just feel yourself getting weaker, you know? Your back hurts, you know? You're sick a lot—cold and low blood. You lose your energy."[13] The risk of deterioration on death row is real, affecting most death row prisoners to some degree.[14] Fear of deterioration can be a source of considerable anxiety, leading prisoners to question their capacity to survive psychologically. "I'm already walking on a hairline of being sane and insane," one prisoner informed me. "I could fall either way at any time."[15]

---

11 Johnson, 2005, p. 104.

12 *See*, generally, Johnson, 1989.

13 Johnson, 2005, p. 104.

14 Professor Stanley Brodsky and I independently found that 70% of Alabama's condemned prisoners exhibited signs of deterioration. My finding, based on content analysis of interviews, was that "7 of every 10 prisoners diagnosed themselves as suffering physical, mental or emotional deterioration in what was typically portrayed as the interpersonal vacuum constituting the human environment of death row." *See* Robert Johnson. 1988. "Life under Sentence of Death." In R. Johnson and H. Toch, eds. *The Pains of Imprisonment.* Prospect Heights, Ill: Waveland Press. pp. 132. Brodsky found a 70% deterioration rate for this same population using objective personality tests. Brodsky's results are reported in depositions pertaining to *Jacobs v. Britton*, No. 78–309H et al. (S.D. Ala., 1979). *See* Johnson, 2005, p. 116. Anecdotal evidence from interviews on Texas' death row suggests that deterioration is widespread. *See* Dave Mann, "Solitary Men," *Texas Observer*, 10 November 2010. Available from http://www.texasobserver.org/solitary-men (accessed 24 August 2016). For a general discussion of the threats to mental health posed by solitary confinement in general, *see* Craig W. Haney. 2003. "Mental health issues in long-term solitary and 'supermax' prison confinement." *Crime & Delinquency* 49(1):pp. 124-156.

15 Johnson, 2005, p. 104.

Working on death row has been described as not merely difficult, as one can imagine, but dangerous and degrading as well.[16] Death row officers in Texas, the most active American death-penalty state, recently appealed "for better death row prisoner conditions because the guards faced daily danger from prisoners made mentally ill by solitary confinement and who had 'nothing to lose.'"[17] They contended that during their solitary confinement on death row, "routine safety practices were imposed that dehumanized prisoners and guards alike, such as every exit of a cell requiring a strip search."[18] It is telling that the officers "protested that their own dignity was undermined by the obligation to look at 'one naked inmate after another' all day."[19]

It is not clear if the concerns of the Texas death row officers are shared by officers in other jurisdictions or what reforms could be instituted to allay their concerns and still maintain adequate security. (Texas had a more relaxed regime years ago, but it was replaced with the current extremely strict solitary regime after several prisoners escaped from death row.[20]) It is clear, however, that most death row officers, much like the inmates they guard, report being suspicious, vigilant, and fearful; in their view, danger encroaches on their daily work lives, potentially compromising their safety and, in fact, the overall security of death row. These officers typically cite the dangers posed by the prisoners as justification for custodial repression, including long stints for prisoners in their cells and elaborate security procedures that are called into play whenever prisoners are removed from their cells (with or without the recurring strip searches that troubled the officers in Texas). In my experience, death row officers—rightly or wrongly—are quick to point out that condemned prisoners are men of proven violence with little to lose in trying to escape. Because condemned prisoners face execution and often live in the most depriving environment the prison has to offer, it is widely believed by staff that they feel free to attack or even kill guards. "What more can we do to them?" worried officers ask. The guards thus come to fear the potential violence of their captives just as the prisoners fear the potential

---

16 Ibid., p. 109, quoting Donald Cabana. Even the best death row, in Cabana's view, takes away some of the humanity of "both the keepers and the kept".
17 Long and Robertson, 2015, p. 1.
18 Ibid.
19 Ibid.
20 *See, generally,* Johnson and Davies, 2014.

violence of their keepers. Too often, shared fears give way to mutual hate, making life on death row a trial for officer and inmate alike.[21]

For some death row officers, my interviews revealed, an insidious fear lurks in the background of their daily work lives. Said one officer, "You know in the back of your mind who you're dealing with, *what* they are, but still you don't bring it to the surface." Other officers spoke of conscious fears very much in the forefront of their thinking. The prisoners, they believe, are violent men bent on escape. These officers work under constant pressure. As one said, "They will hurt you to get away. You've got to watch them all the time. You know if these guys get a chance, you're gone. They'll kill you. They've all killed before." In the words of another officer, "There was always that thought in my mind, 'If they ever get out of here, I'm as good as dead.' I feel they don't have anything to lose. If we get in their way, they just get rid of us quick." Security procedures are in place to restrain the prisoners and protect the officers, but they fail to reassure many officers. Assessed against a backdrop of fear, regulations appear flawed. "If they want to escape, they can," said one officer with an air of futility. "Somebody's going to slip up somewhere along the line."[22]

A troubling and pervasive sign of fear, revealed in my interviews, is that some officers see themselves as potential hostages. This is particularly true on the few death rows that operate as congregate solitary confinement death rows—those with prisoners out of their individual cells in small groups much of the day, but strictly isolated from the rest of the prison within the confines of death row. "The inmates constantly threaten to take hostages," said one officer.[23] That fearful eventuality preoccupies a number of officers, who envision scenarios that would result in their being taken hostage. A common fear is that a harried, and thus distracted, control officer will open the wrong door at the wrong time, unleashing one or more inmates on a defenseless fellow officer. The officers respond to such intimidating contingencies with a grim fatalism, taking the attitude that they should do what they can to control their own lives and let other matters sort themselves out. "Anybody can get attacked or taken hostage at any time. But I just have a job to do, and I just go ahead and do it

---

21   Johnson, 2005, p. 110.
22   All quotations in this paragraph are drawn from Johnson, 2005, p. 110.
23   Ibid., p. 110.

and hope that nothing will happen. I just try to do my job, be alert and observant, and nothing should go wrong. If it does, I'll just have to deal with it."[24] As another officer put it, "You have to deal with it as it comes. You do what you have to do in the line of your duties, your job. You focus on what you're doing."[25]

Given these fears, officers may be tempted to be distant and harsh as a sort of preemptive strategy to maintain control or, instead, to placate death row prisoners, trying to appease them to gain their cooperation. Officers note that the job requires strict scrutiny and control of the prisoners, so what outsiders would consider harsh and impersonal treatment is simply the norm for officers. Appeasement, in contrast, is a more troubling response. One officer stated the premise underlying appeasement quite baldly: "Anybody facing death, they gotta be dangerous. If he calls and he needs something, you got to try to get it for him." The problem for the staff—and for the weaker inmates they must protect—is that appeasement corrodes the officers' authority and undermines control, ultimately lowering the general level of security and making everyone unsafe. "We're supposed to be a team," complained one officer, "and what happens to [fellow officers] happens to me." If colleagues are visibly fearful, they are a liability: their presence emboldens the more predatory prisoners, which in the long run spells trouble for officers and inmates alike.[26]

The officers' fears are sufficiently widespread that they are visible to at least some death row prisoners, who see the fears of officers generating both abuse and neglect, with consequences that are troubling for officers as well as inmates:

> There seems to be too much security. There seems to be an abnormal amount of fear in the guards simply because we have a death sentence and that makes it hard for us to have the same courtesies that we should—that other inmates have. For example, the guards are so afraid of us where they won't get close to us or they won't come up and talk to us when we need something done seriously. It could be a medical problem or something. And because of this fear in the guards,

---

24 Ibid., p. 111.
25 Ibid.
26 All quotations in this paragraph drawn from Johnson, 2005, p. 111.

we don't get the assistance we need like other inmates do.... You can easily tell it's fear in the officers and other employees of the institution. Just because we have this death sentence, people are so afraid of us that they don't want to get close to us and because of this very thing we just don't get what I would say [is] the compassion that we need or the assistance that we need. Sometimes it's hard to find the right word, but I know that it is something that we don't get that every man, regardless of his condition, should have.[27]

The main casualty of fear, then, is simple human compassion. The limited compassion found on death row contributes to the distinctively cold interpersonal climate found in these settings, leaving officers and inmates alike feeling isolated, vulnerable, and alone.

Compassion is not a salient feature of daily life on death row, due in part to mutual fears, but human connections do form among at least some of the officers and inmates and sometimes can be seen when executions are imminent. [28] Even prisoners who have been disruptive on death row—presumably the same prisoners who represent an explicit and specific source of fear for officers—can be seen as vulnerable fellow human beings when they are transferred to the death house. One officer said:

They have that look—like they know what's coming.... Man, it's hard to look at them in the eyes.... You get to know them. You wouldn't call them friends, but you understand them a bit. You get that human contact. So when you're getting them ready for that last day and they have that lost look in their eyes, you can't help feeling a little for them.[29]

When prisoners are executed, it can be a loss to the officers who have

---

27   Johnson, 1989, p. 73.

28   For example, "Managing visits from family members can be emotionally tough for guards, especially when prisoners are banned from touching their visitors and visits take place through glass partitions or nets. The 'most difficult thing' as an attending guard is 'to see on the other side of the glass … the families. Children. Never be able to touch. Never be able to hug.' Final visits by families prior to execution can be even harder, as can the time when guards see the prisoner for the last time." Long and Robertson, 2015, p. 2.

29   Alex Hannaford, "Inmates aren't the only victims of the prison-industrial complex," *The Nation*, September 16 2014. Available from http://www.thenation.com/article/inmates-arent-only-victims-prison-industrial-complex/. (accessed 24 August 2016).

come to feel a sense of community with them. Parting with prisoners one has come to know can be at once touching and depressing. One officer, supervising a prisoner's last visit with his family before he was transferred to the death house, reacted in a revealingly human way.

> The reality of that last family visit really made me feel bad. His daughter didn't even know him. It was depressing to be there. It's supposed to be part of the job, like being a doctor or something. You lose a patient and that's just it, but it's not that easy. You never forget this type of thing, but you can put it behind you.[30]

For this officer, one "loses" a prisoner to execution. Like any genuine loss, it doesn't come easily.[31]

Be that as it may, human connections between death row officers and prisoners are not common or deep, and certainly are not the norm. No officer mourns the loss of condemned prisoners. When bonds form between officers and inmates they are likely to be tenuous, stress-producing, and directly in conflict with the distance and impersonality sought in death row regimes, where something approaching a combat duty mentality is meant to prevail.[32] The jobs of officers on execution teams are arranged in ways that minimize contact and virtually eliminate any human connections between the prisoners and the officers. It is assumed that execution is a job for which it is better, if not essential, to have no personal knowledge of, or relationship with, the condemned prisoner. Since death row officers have had extensive contact with condemned prisoners, these officers are typically excluded from execution teams.[33]

---

30 Johnson, 2005, p. 115.

31 Ibid.

32 *See, generally,* Johnson, 1989.

33 McGunigall-Smith, reporting on her study of Utah's execution team, indicated that some death row officers "expressed feelings of kinship" with some condemned prisoners and "volunteered to be part of the execution team" for them to ensure that the prisoner was not alone and friendless at the end. (Personal Communication, email dated June 24, 2016.) This is by no means the norm, but does fit with the unusual characteristics of death row in Utah, at least at the time of McGunigall-Smith's study—a small solitary confinement death row run by a stable cohort of professional officers led by a charismatic and humane captain, since retired, carrying out executions with prisoners some of them have guarded on death row for years, even a decade or more. *See* McGunigall-Smith, Sandra, *Men of a Thousand Days: Death-sentenced inmates at Utah state prison* (Unpublished doctoral thesis). Bangor: University of Wales.

EXECUTIONERS AT WORK

Executions are seen by prison officials and officers as a job that has to be done, and done right. In this context, "done right" means that an execution should be proper, professional, and dignified. In the words of a prison official,

> It was something, of course, that had to be done. We had to be sure that we did it properly, professionally, and [that] we gave as much dignity to the person as we possibly could in the process.... You gotta do it, and if you've gotta do it, it might just as well be done the way it's supposed to be done—without any sensation.[34]

Here, the word "proper" refers to procedures that are carried out smoothly, and "professional" means without personal feelings that intrude on the procedures in any way. The phrase "without any sensation" almost certainly expresses a desire to avoid media sensationalism, particularly if there should be an embarrassing and undignified hitch in the procedures—for example, a prisoner who breaks down or becomes violent and must be forcibly placed in the electric chair or gurney as witnesses, some from the media, look on in horror. Still, the phrase may also be a revealing slip of the tongue. For executions are indeed meant to occur without any human feelings, without any sensation. A profound absence of emotion would seem to embody the bureaucratic ideal for the modern execution.[35]

In my experience, execution team officers see themselves as doing a job, as professionals who approach their work without passion or prejudice. One executioner described himself as "a normal John Doe that walks the streets every day. I work and live a normal social life." How ironic that this person would characterize himself as a John Doe—an anonymous man, often a corpse—as if in subconscious recognition that it takes a nameless, dehumanized entity—dead to others—to kill other men in cold blood for a living.[36]

---

34 Johnson, 2005, p. 128.
35 Ibid., pp. 128-9.
36 Ibid., p. 126.

It is well established that the job of executions—whatever the specific execution method[37]—is made easier and less stressful by breaking the process down into simple, discrete tasks that are practiced repeatedly until they become routine and unremarkable. The leader of an execution team I studied described the division of labor in these words:

> The execution team is a nine-officer team and each one has certain things to do. When I would train you, maybe you'd buckle a belt; that might be all you'd have to do.... And you'd be expected to do one thing, and that's all you'd be expected to do. And if everybody do what they were taught, or what they were trained to do, at the end the man would be put in the chair and everything would be complete. It's all come together now.[38]

When asked, what is the purpose of breaking it down into such small steps, the officer replied:

> So people won't get confused. I've learned it's kind of a tense time. When you're executing a person, killing a person—you call it killing, executing, whatever you want, the man dies anyway—I find the less you got on your mind, why, the better you'll carry it out. So it's just very simple.[39]

With this precise and simple division of labor, each member of the execution team becomes a specialist in one specific task, an expert technician who takes pride in his work. Here's how two officers saw their specialized roles:

> My assignment is the leg piece. Right leg. I roll his pants leg up, place a piece [an electrode] on his leg, strap his leg in.... I've got all the moves down pat. We train from different posts;

---

37 "The dynamics of Missouri's execution team, using lethal injection, offer an exact parallel to those of the execution team I studied using the electric chair. There is a detailed protocol in which every step in the execution process is laid out clearly, broken down into small steps, and rehearsed so that things go off like clockwork.... The focus is on teamwork and on the maintenance of morale; all members take responsibility for the execution and all members stress humaneness, defined as the 'desire to ensure that the inmate's suffering is reduced to a minimum.' The shared view is that 'The constant practice, the breaking down of the process into specific roles, the clear understanding on the part of staff precisely what their role is,' yields an execution procedure that is 'competent, professional, and stress-free'." Johnson, 2005, p. 139.

38 Ibid., p. 132.

39 Ibid.

I can do any of them. But that's my main post.[40]

I strap the left side. I strap his arms and another man straps his legs and another one puts his head in the cap. But my job is strapping his left arm in. ... I was trained with those straps. The way those straps is on.[41]

This division of labor also distributes responsibility across the group, making the execution a shared obligation rather than an individual burden for team members.

We're all as a team, together. We all take a part of the killing, the execution. So, this guy that pulled the switch shouldn't have more responsibility than the guy that cut his hair or the guy that fed him or the guy that watched him. We all take a part in it; we all play 100% in it, too. That take the load off this one individual [who pulls the switch].[42]

Individually and as a team, the officers maintain emotional distance from the condemned prisoner, which means that officers must actively suppress any natural feelings of kinship they may feel for the fellow human being they are about to put to death. This they are trained to do, both as prison officers and as members of the execution team. In the words of a warden responsible for a series of executions, "from the cradle to the grave, correctional officers are told, 'Don't get personally involved', and that's what they try to do."[43] Officers become expert at denial of the humanity of prisoners—especially condemned prison-ers—a process of dehumanization[44] that, in this warden's view, amounts to "tucking things in the recesses of their minds, where they don't have to deal with it." One effective technique execution team officers use to dehumanize the prisoner is to remind themselves of the gruesomeness of the crime that brought the man to death row and the justice of his punishment. As one execution team officer explained to me:

---

40   Ibid., pp. 132-3.
41   Ibid., p. 133.
42   Ibid., p. 126-7.
43   Ibid., p. 147.
44   "The executioners," compared with regular prison staff with less-direct roles in the execution process, "exhibited the highest level of disavowal of personal responsibility, and dehumanization." Michael J. Osofsky, Albert Bandura, and Philip Zimbardo. 2005. "The role of moral disengagement in the execution process." *Law and Human Behavior* 29(4):pp. 371.

We don't see him all that much or talk to them, but, I mean, a human being is a human being. But you, the way you get around getting to like them, you read the papers and things, and you brush up on the case and just see what this man has done, you know. And when you find out that he drove nails through a woman's, an old woman's hand and nailed her to a chair and set the house on fire with her in it, then you kind of get to saying, "Well, this man here, he can't be no good.... So, so you say, "Well, OK, it's OK. It's all right, all right to put him to death."[45]

The notion that "We don't see him all that much or talk to them", does not apply to all officers on an execution team. In my experience, which is borne out in other research,[46] one or two officers are assigned to sit outside the prisoner's cell during the final hours preceding an execution. These officers observe and engage with the prisoner, the better to understand his frame of mind and allow them to anticipate any problems that might arise. These officers become more involved with the condemned prisoners than do their colleagues. Indeed, they *seek* relationships with the condemned. But these relationships are calculated and superficial, and are sought for the control they offer. In effect, the *job* of these officers, in addition to the narrow tasks they are assigned in the execution proper, is to establish relations with the condemned prisoners, and they do so solely to achieve control over the prisoner. They seek what I have termed a "calculated camaraderie" leading to a "fatal collusion" of officer and inmate that culminates in the prisoner's last walk to the execution chamber. In the end—and until the end, when the execution is completed—these officers use their relationship with the prisoner to manipulate his behavior, often admonishing him to "go out like a man," so that he will comply with the etiquette of a dignified execution.[47]

An execution is an act of violence—it is a homicide in which lives are forcibly taken—but the dynamics of modern executions hinge on social control: The condemned prisoner must be under the social,

---

45 Johnson, 2005, p. 147.
46 See note 31 pertaining to the Missouri execution team.
47 Johnson, 2005, pp. 148–151.

not physical, control of his keepers at the end. He must submit to the execution routine. The officials' goal—and in the end perhaps the prisoner's as well—is a smooth, orderly, and ostensibly voluntary execution, one that looks humane and dignified and is not sullied in any way by obvious violence by officers or displays of weakness by the prisoner.

The execution team—working under the authority of the law, in full awareness of the horror of the crime for which the offender is to be put to death, in strict compliance with execution protocols and while maintaining social control—seeks a smooth execution drill that unfolds rapidly and conforms to proper institutional operating procedures. As a practical matter, doing an execution "right" means, perhaps above all else, doing it fast.

> We've got a time schedule for everything that we do. The head man has got to see that everything is going according to the clock. The clock—we're timed on everything. There's a certain time—you gotta go by the IOPs [Institutional Operating Procedures] on the thing, and each thing has got to be done at a certain time....You know everything you've got to do. You just got to, you just got to do it in a certain time, a certain time you got to do this. The schedule is boss. You've got to break it down to the schedule, every last minute.[48]

The result, in the view of execution team members, is a killing that is as humane and dignified as is reasonably possible under existing conditions:I've seen it. I know what it is. I've smelled it. I've tasted it. I've felt it.... I'm not sure the death penalty is the right way. I don't know if there is a right answer. So I look at it like this: If it's gotta be done, at least it can be done in a humane way, if there is such a word for it. 'Cause I know it can be a nasty situation. Executions have been here for a long time. And for a long time it's been done, you know, unprofessionally and for primitive reasons. The only way it should be done, I feel, is the way we do it. It's done professionally; it's not no horseplaying. Everything is done by documentation. On time. By the book.[49]

---

48   Johnson, 2005, p. 134.
49   Johnson, 2005, pp. 130-1.

Tragically, some executions do not go by the book and in fact are badly botched. Though I know of no research bearing directly on this point, botched executions, which occur infrequently but with regularity,[50] are no doubt an enormous emotional burden for officers, who pride themselves on treating prisoners with dignity and respect.[51] Indeed, even executions that go off without a hitch can prove traumatic for some officers. The experiences of some execution team officers "are consistent with acute stress disorder or post-traumatic stress disorder".[52] One officer, without warning, "began crying and shaking uncontrollably when the eyes of all the inmates he had executed began flashing before him".[53] Another, who transported inmates to the execution chamber, developed nightmares, cold sweats, and sleeplessness that led to a change in his whole persona.[54] Others appear to have developed "obsessive compulsive behavior, nightmares and other emotional disturbances" as a consequence of their involvement in executions.[55]

Evidence of such trauma among execution team officers is real and powerful and has been reported for executioners in a range of countries.[56] Nevertheless, this evidence is anecdotal and is not supported by more systematic studies of officers who play direct or support roles in the carrying out of executions. Most execution team officers appear to cope reasonably well with the job of carrying out executions—compartmentalizing their work and home lives, falling back on religious beliefs, taking refuge in their group identity as execution team officers and in the administrative support they receive from correctional officials, as well as their "capacity to dissociate and rely on diffusion of responsibility to suppress painful emotions."[57]

Rather than experiencing overt trauma, my research suggests that officers experience a subtle and potentially insidious deadening of feelings for themselves and others, arguably not unlike the deadening

---

50   Austin Sarat. 2014. *Gruesome Spectacles: Botched Executions and America's Death Penalty*. Stanford, CA: Stanford University Press.

51   *See, generally*, Johnson, 2005; Michael J. Osofsky and Howard J. Osofsky. 2002. "The psychological experience of security officers who work with executions." *Psychiatry* 65(4):pp. 358-370; Osofsky, Bandura, and Zimbardo, 2005, pp. 371-393.

52   Long and Robertson, 2015, p. 3.

53   Ibid.

54   Ibid.

55   Ibid.

56   Ibid.

57   Osofsky and Osofsky, 2002. See also Osofsky, Bandura, and Zimbardo, 2005.

of feelings experienced by many prisoners on the threshold of execution. Deadening of feelings among executioners likely operates as an extension of the dissociation produced by the detailed and fragmented execution drill described earlier, which is reinforced by the way officers compartmentalize their individual roles in the execution process and, more generally, their work and home lives. One officer on the execution team I studied reported suffering a deadening of feelings that, over time, came to affect his entire life.

From the interview:

> I just cannot feel anything. And that was what bothered me. I thought that I would feel something, but I didn't feel anything. … The actual participation of killing a person—I hadn't experienced that [before]. And I didn't feel anything. That was the thing that bothered me.
>
> *You know you should feel more but you*
> *don't, and that's what troubles you?*
>
> Yeah, 'cause you're supposed to feel something
>
> *So somewhere along the line, you've shut*
> *down some faculties to get through this?*
>
> You better believe it.
>
> *Do you find this in other parts of your life? Less feeling than*
> *you would normally expect? Or is it just in this one area?*
>
> It's laying over my whole life.
>
> *So it seems to have started here and spread elsewhere?*
>
> Ever since I joined the team. Very seldom do I get upset or get upset to a point where I would feel my voice rise. I just shut everything down.

This officer feared that emotional numbness, disquieting in itself, may portend even deeper problems.

From the interview:

I don't want to wake up tomorrow and recognize that my mind is gone, because I figure the stress will come later. ... There's nothing to protect you from that. If it do come, like it's something that I'll have to deal with for the rest of my life. You never know when you might wake in the middle of the night in a cold sweat and you lost your mind.

Do you have any hints that something is going on inside you that would get worse if you kept going?

The hint is that I haven't felt anything.[58]

This deadening of feeling is a real and painful cost of carrying out executions. Paradoxically, a corollary of this difficult adaptation is that executions get easier over time. Osofsky and colleagues report that carrying out "multiple executions" did not enhance stress but instead "reduced the level of distress over performing them" as a result, primarily, of "desensitization through routinization." In the words of one officer they studied:

No matter what it is, it gets easier over time. The job just gets easier. The process has become very routine and the next day is easy. The job is something that must be taken care of. It is a duty of my job that has to be done.[59]

I saw this effect in my research as well. As a result of the practicing and performing of them, executions take place with increasing efficiency and, eventually, with precision. "The first one was grisly," a team member confided to me. At that time, the team in question used electrocution as the method of execution. The officer explained that a certain amount of fumbling made the execution seem interminable. There were technical problems as well: The generator was set so high that the body was mutilated. The execution chamber stank of burnt flesh, described as having a greasy odor reminiscent of fatty pork. (Air fresheners were subsequently installed throughout the death house.) But that is the past, the officer assured me. "The ones now, we know what we're doing. It's just like clockwork."[60]

---

58 Johnson, 2005, pp. 181–2.
59 Osofsky, Bandura, and Zimbardo, 2005, p. 388–9.
60 Johnson, 2005, pp. 134.

Dead Men Walking: Abolishing the death penalty

Death work is a moral and psychological burden that must be borne by prison staff who shoulder the role of executioner, but the real horror is not that executions are hard on staff, though they are, but rather that executions get easier for them over time. In the prescient words of G. K. Chesterton, we are reminded that "It is a terrible business to mark out a man for the vengeance of men. But it is a thing to which a man can grow accustomed.... And the horrible thing about public officials, even the best ... is not that they are wicked ... not that they are stupid ... it is simply that they have got used to it."[61]

Executioners get inured to death work because they become dead to the prisoners they kill just as those prisoners become dead to themselves as the execution process unfolds. Executions get easier for many of us in society as well: for most of us, executions are increasingly unremarkable and indeed only newsworthy when they go badly wrong or involve inherently gruesome methods such as beheading. We, too, are dead to the condemned in the sense that they become lifeless statistics, before and after their deaths. We should abolish the death penalty, then, not so much to save executioners from stress, even disabling and dehumanizing stress. We should abolish the death penalty to put an end to an institution that kills empathy and compassion, and ultimately corrupts us all.

---

61   Quoted in Johnson, 2005, p. 121.

PAINFUL THEN, PAINFUL NOW

Ron McAndrew[1]

Death as punishment for any crime makes horrible murderers of us all. Simply put, there is no "humane" way to extinguish a human life.

What could be more "heinous, atrocious, and cruel" than a death described by US Supreme Court Justice William Brennan (in his dissent in *Glass v. Louisiana*, 1985) as follows:

> The evidence suggests that death by electrical current is extremely violent and inflicts pain and indignities far beyond the "mere extinguishment of life". Witnesses routinely report that, when the switch is thrown, the condemned prisoner "cringes", "leaps", and "fights the straps with amazing strength". "The hands turn red, then white, and the cords of the neck stand out like steel bands." The prisoner's limbs, fingers, toes, and face are severely contorted. The force of the electrical current is so powerful that the prisoner's eyeballs sometimes pop out and "rest on [his] cheeks". The prisoner often defecates, urinates, and vomits blood and drool.

Brennan concluded by stating that electrocution is "nothing less than the contemporary technological equivalent of burning people at the stake."

> What could be more "cold, calculated, and premeditated" than informing a man of the date and time that he will die? And after the death warrant is read aloud, the inmate is removed to isolation for 20 to 35 days, so that he can contemplate for *days* the shortness of his hours, the hopelessness of his situation, and the futility of his remaining time.

What is more "substantially planned" (*premeditation*) than the actual execution? On the pronounced day, with great ceremony, the inmate's head and right leg are shaved. He is dressed in *new* black slacks and a *new* white shirt. He is escorted to a small chamber and strapped into a

---

1   Retired Florida Prison Warden, United States.

chair, where his final words will be spoken. His face is concealed with a heavy mask that breaks his nose in order to smother his screams and prevents the eyeballs from popping out of his head.

What could be more akin to "torture" than administering 1,900 volts at 13 amps of electricity to a human being at 30-second intervals, turning off the current long enough for the body to cool so that a doctor is able to check to see if he is dead, and repeating the procedure until his heart stops beating?

And that is only the abhorrence of a normal execution. What about the revolting horror of unspeakable hundreds whose deaths have gone awry?

Even now, I remember the sound of the *pop* as the current was turned on for the execution of Pedro Medina. A plume of smoke arose from beneath the helmet, and I am plagued by the memory of flames consuming the man's head when the electric chair malfunctioned and set him on fire. The stinging smoke and the putrid odour of this death by inferno filled the chamber. A flame shot out from beneath the helmet. I was almost three feet from the chair and it almost hit me in my face. I'll never forget the twisting muscles of his body, the clenching of his fists, the spreading out of his toes as if they were being pried apart by a wrench. My telling the executioner to continue, even knowing that we were at a point of no-return, haunts me still.

Eleven minutes later, when Medina was finally pronounced dead, I retrieved the phone from the captain who was to remain on the line with Governor Lawton Chiles, giving blow-by-blow details. I advised the governor only of the time of death, assuming the sordid details had been conveyed to him as they had occurred. Little did I know that the governor, totally ignorant of this horrid mishap, had left his office immediately upon the termination of our conversation, and was heading to the airport to catch a flight to Washington, DC, for a "garden party luncheon" with President Clinton. Only later, when I was hotly accused of hiding the malfunction from him did I discover that he had learned the exaggerated, fiery details of the botched execution from a television monitor in the back of his limousine.

The governor's assumption that he had been "kept in the dark" about such a tragic event was totally erroneous, but understandable under the circumstances. His anger was extreme.

I was fired and rehired twice that day. Was it clemency or punishment to remain at Florida State Prison for another year? During that time, I shadowed a number of lethal injection executions in Huntsville, Texas, gathering training and material for a new way of ceremonial killing for Florida.

I had taken the position of warden at Florida State Prison with an unwavering support for the death penalty. And even though I was still *professing* this belief, my soul and my mind were both conflicted. The questions of why we were killing people and why our politicians pounded their chests in support of these ghastly spectacles confronted me daily.

At this point, one of our inmates told me that Kirk Bloodsworth, whom he had known on death row, had been exonerated. As I searched for details of that exoneration, I began to slow down just a bit and examine, not only *what* I was doing, but *why*. After all, if one man was found to be innocent, how many others were sitting in their solitary cells, awaiting an unjust death?

Thankfully, before I was tested again, I was transferred. Leaving Florida State Prison was both bitter and elating. But death row and the ceremonial killing of my fellow man were not simply going to leave me to my peace. There was no ceasefire! My mental health was affected by troubling nightmares. The middle-of-the-night bedside visits of those I'd executed were relentless. Visions of these dead men sitting on the edge of my bed wouldn't fade—even with heavy doses of alcohol.

The pressure of carrying out the death penalty was no longer an issue. But searching my soul led me inexorably to a new reality: (1) that the death penalty was wrong; and (2) I wanted to do something about it.

I had become an abolitionist.

Some years later, I was invited by the National Coalition to Abolish the Death Penalty as one of the speakers at their annual conference in Harrisburg, Pennsylvania. As I strode down the hallway and into the foyer of the hotel, I glimpsed a man and we locked eyes for a moment. I'd seen him before. As we approached one another, our eyes met again and again. When we came within arms' reach, he grabbed me and hugged me tightly. I realized that this wonderful person was none other than Juan Melendez, a death row exoneree from Florida State Prison's death row! We wept and shared.

Later that afternoon, following my speech, I experienced a cold-sweat chill when I realized the possibility that I could have taken this fine man to that dirty little chamber and burned him to death. Minutes before an execution, it's the warden's responsibility to sit with the prisoner and read the black-bordered death warrant aloud. During such moments, I would always ask the condemned if there was anything that could be done for them or if there was anyone I could call or if they had something very personal or confidential they'd like me to pass on after their imminent death. While I never shared any of the words or requests I'd heard during those quiet moments, the whispers were sincere and promises were kept. But no word, no request, no promise, would ever bring back to life an innocent man. Being an abolitionist took on a whole new motivating purpose.

Now, not only am I an abolitionist—I'm an activist, as well.

Former Illinois Governor George Ryan spared the lives of 167 condemned inmates, stating that because the "Illinois death penalty system is arbitrary and capricious—and therefore immoral—I no longer shall tinker with the machinery of death." Ryan called the issue of the death penalty "one of the great civil rights struggles of our time." May I live to see American sanctioned ceremonial killings follow slavery securely into the annals of history.

FIGHTING FOR CLIENTS' LIVES: THE IMPACT OF DEATH-PENALTY WORK ON POST-CONVICTION CAPITAL DEFENCE ATTORNEYS

Susannah Sheffer[1]

Introduction

Defence attorneys would be the first to declare that they do not stand at the centre of the death–penalty story and cannot claim the greatest suffering. Working as advocates for individuals who will lose their lives if they lose their cases, capital defenders' focus is, quite rightly, on their clients and not on themselves. If you see a capital defender quoted in a news story about the death penalty, the comment will not be about the stress inherent in doing such a job or the particular helplessness and grief that a client's execution engenders in his or her attorney.

The experience of capital defenders is, nevertheless, part of the story of the impact of the death penalty. Defence attorneys' distinct role has distinct emotional consequences, and perhaps especially so for those who work at the post-conviction stage. Representing clients who are already sentenced to death, post-conviction capital defence attorneys enter the story charged with the task of trying to stop an execution – in other words, to save an individual's life.

Taking on that task when the odds are so great that they frequently don't succeed puts post-conviction capital defence attorneys in a

---

1   Susannah Sheffer, a US based–writer and clinical mental health counselor, directed the No Si-
    lence, No Shame project at Murder Victims' Families for Human Rights. She is the author of the
    book *Fighting for Their Lives: Inside the Experience of Capital Defense Attorneys*. Vanderbilt Univer-
    sity Press, 2013. All quotations from attorneys from the United States are from *Fighting for Their
    Lives: Inside the Experience of Capital Defense Attorneys*. Vanderbilt University Press, 2013, and these
    interviews were conducted in 2010. Quotations from attorneys outside the United States are from
    interviews conducted in 2014 for a briefing paper published by Penal Reform International, as
    follows: attorney from Iran: interview with Hossein Raeesi; attorney from India: interview with
    Yug Mohit Chaudhry; attorney from Japan: interview with Maiko Tagusari; attorney from Nige-
    ria: Interview with Ja'afaru Adamu.

unique relationship to each pending execution; they feel that their clients' lives are in their hands. Realistically, the attorneys may understand that many factors influence the outcome of a capital case, but when they do speak about what it is like for them to do what they do, they reveal the weight of the responsibility they carry and how personal the losses feel. No understanding of the death penalty can be complete without taking the impact on defence attorneys into account.

So much need

The looming threat of execution makes death row prisoners' need for representation extremely urgent, and the enormity of that need when relatively few attorneys are sufficiently knowledgeable in this area can place great demand on those who do have the necessary expertise. "I'm already juggling too many things, and yet there is so much need," an attorney from the United States explains. "There's so many people saying *help, help, help*. … That is the thing I'm haunted by: the people I cannot help."

In the US, the American Bar Association estimates that there are hundreds of prisoners on death row without any representation at all. At one time, federally funded Capital Resource Centers enabled attorneys who specialized in capital defence to represent clients on death row and to provide extensive guidance to other attorneys who agreed to take a capital case. The US Congress eliminated funding for these resource centres in 1995, however, and today's capital post-conviction offices, often operating as struggling nonprofits, are typically deluged with more requests than they can fulfil.

The situation is comparably urgent in other retentionist countries, where the challenge may be a scarcity of lawyers who view the death penalty as a human rights violation and are willing to defend those who are facing execution. An Iranian attorney with two decades of experience, for example, estimates that of 50,000 lawyers in the country, less than 50 were his colleagues in this sense, and he eventually had to leave the country because of the risk he faced working as a lawyer for people on death row.

As well, attorneys at the post-conviction stage are often working under great time pressure. As one from the US explains, a court can set a deadline such that a defence attorney has to do "five years of work in three months." Having more essential work to do than it seems possible to complete in the required time frame can cause an acute stress that one attorney describes as "paralyzing, feeling like you're going to come out of your skin, feeling like you're losing it, or screaming." The combination of urgency and time pressure can feel almost intolerable.

Sometimes prisoners are unaware of their right to seek relief at such a late stage and do not contact an attorney until the execution is imminent. An attorney from India explains:

> Most death row prisoners are illiterate and extremely poor. They have no access to knowledge about rights, remedies, etc., and no real access to lawyers. Their families, already impoverished and defeated, have long given up hope or abandoned the prisoner to his fate. ... They usually only manage to reach me just a few days or hours before the execution. It is in this very small window of time that I have to devise some way of getting an interim stay on the execution on the grounds of breach of rights or due procedure.

Attorneys at this stage seek an interim stay with the hope that doing so will buy them time to do the more extensive investigative and legal work that could overturn the death sentence and thus halt the execution entirely. In some cases, attorneys may be trying to show that a client is innocent of the crime and was wrongfully convicted, but it is important to note that belief in a client's innocence is not the only reason defence attorneys will choose to represent a client at the post-conviction stage and to work under such immense pressure to save that client from execution. Whether out of general opposition to the death penalty as a human rights violation or out of a commitment to ensuring that the death sentence was issued fairly and in accordance with the country's constitution or other laws, defence attorneys can believe that both the guilty and the innocent deserve representation at the post-conviction stage.

Even if the "breach of rights or due procedure" was egregious, overturning a death sentence is generally understood to be harder than preventing that sentence from being issued in the first place. Post-conviction capital defence work is about stopping a train that is already barrelling towards a client, rather than blocking that train from leaving the station.

An attorney from Nigeria explains some of the challenges he faces as a capital defence attorney in that country:

> There are several challenges to being a death-penalty lawyer here: a judicial and justice system that stacks the deck against you and your client, especially, God save you, if they are poor/indigent, and the fact that over 90% of convictions in all criminal matters are substantially based on confessions, mostly secured under torture. Also other legal and constitutional rights are ignored or abused without remedy.

Attorneys at this stage know that the odds are not in their favour. As one from the United States puts it, "It's the norm to lose", and this is true even for the most experienced and skilful defenders. Managing their clients' and their clients' families' hope and disappointment—and their own as well—is a core part of the challenge. They don't want to make false promises but don't want to leave their clients in total despair, either. They need to have enough hope, themselves, to get up and do the work each day, and they want to be able to offer hope to their clients who are otherwise left to anticipate their fate without even that buffer. But attorneys also feel the need to help their clients prepare for the (all too likely) possibility that the legal efforts will not be successful. One attorney from the US explains that he tries to maintain this delicate balance by saying to clients, "I'm going to file a petition on your behalf. There's a minimal chance that it might work, but the chance is so slim that you should be doing all you need to do to prepare for dying, including meeting with everyone you need to see and saying everything you need to say."

These defence attorneys are managing hope and disappointment within the context of a broader society that is typically indifferent or even hostile to the need the attorneys perceive. Working without much cultural approbation and sometimes under outright threat from their government puts further pressure on attorneys who specialize in capital defence.

The weight of responsibility

Scarcity of available attorneys, time constraints, and long odds all exacerbate the challenge, but the primary burden that post-conviction capital defence attorneys bear is inherent in the task itself: trying to save each client's life. The attorneys describe this ever-present weight in similar terms, regardless of where they practice:

> Taking a death-penalty case is a huge responsibility of course and the realization that a life hangs in the balance can motivate you at some times and scare you at others. — attorney from Nigeria

> When a client gets an execution date, it's like the big dark cloud for many weeks or months. It's a really hard thing to live with, the rising panic. … It's always present. — attorney from the United States

> I specialize in end-stage death cases. … I dread these cases and shudder every time a new one comes my way. Having taken it on, I feel I am living with a coffin tied to my back. It takes over my life, dominates my thoughts during the day, corrupts all pleasure and invades my dreams at night. — attorney from India

With this sense of responsibility permeating their lives, it is difficult for attorneys whose clients are imminently facing execution to maintain any kind of reasonable balance between their work lives and their personal lives; capital defence is not an endeavour that can easily be put out of mind at the end of the day. "It is really difficult to separate between your job and your private life," an attorney from Iran observes. "I am involved in the case all the time." Attorneys talk about having to miss family events, or being distracted and preoccupied, or fearing that they are bringing their worry, outrage, and grief into their family lives even if they do not discuss their work directly.

Even if they know that the responsibility for preventing the execution does not rest entirely on their shoulders, the weight nevertheless feels very personal, and thus the loss does as well. "You know, intellectually, that the execution is not your fault. But your job is to save this person's life!" an attorney from the US observes. "No matter how much you tell yourself that you've done everything you could do, your job was to save his life and you didn't." Another attorney from the US echoes this thought with the comment, "Every time someone's executed, you feel like you've failed. Even if you know going into it that the deck is stacked against you."

"It's just so deeply personal," a third attorney from the United States explains. "It's the notion that you put yourself between your client and the execution. And so when you fail, what that means is that they've walked *over you and gotten your client in the [execution] chamber.*"

The impact of clients' executions

When they lose in the biggest possible way and are unable to save their clients' lives, attorneys describe a devastation that, once again, is common across national borders:

> I felt incapacitated for a while, after each execution. I couldn't move. My body felt very heavy. — attorney from the United States

> I think when executions have gone through, what I've felt is a devastating numbness. A complete sapping of energy. — attorney from the United States

> After my client was executed, I was always thinking of what else I could have done or what I could have done differently. For a few months, I could not sleep well, and I sometimes dreamed of my client. I could not eat much and lost weight. I was depressed for a long time. — attorney from Japan

> It stayed with me for months. It would come on you unbidden, in the same way that all kinds of really bad trauma do, in

that you wouldn't even be thinking about it, and suddenly it would intrude on your thoughts, and you couldn't get it out of your thoughts. — attorney from the United States

When I am not successful and a client is executed, it is very sad and upsetting, especially when I know the details about the person and how he or she got involved in this situation. I never forget the face of the person who was executed. — attorney from Iran

Though all the defence attorneys interviewed here describe client executions as devastating, the nature of the experience is affected by whether the attorney is working in a country that announces execution dates in advance or not. Knowing exactly when an execution is scheduled to occur creates one kind of burden; being taken by surprise is difficult in its own way. "The lack of information, lack of transparency about the death penalty and execution process, is a big challenge," explains an attorney from Japan. "When a client of mine was executed, I only learned about it after it happened, when I heard the Ministry of Justice announce it at a press conference that morning. That was very hard."

It is difficult to learn about a client's execution from a news story or to arrive at the prison for a visit only to be told that the individual has already been executed. Even in the United States where attorneys know when an execution date is set, they (and their clients) may not know until the final hours that the execution will actually take place, as the attorney is often litigating until the last possible moment, hoping to stay the execution at least for that day.

Attorneys who do have an opportunity for a last visit or phone call with a client describe those conversations as extremely wrenching. After working so hard and trying to maintain some hope, they are now forced to explain that there is nothing else that can be done. One attorney from the United States remembers a client with intellectual disabilities who "was too impaired, too distraught and angry and confused" to comprehend fully what his attorney was telling him. "I did everything I could," his lawyer explains. "We were litigating in every possible realm. ... He came to trust me at a certain point, but then I think he felt like I had betrayed him because I couldn't keep him from being executed."

Even when clients are more accepting, that too can be emotionally wrenching, as it was for the attorney from the United States whose client assured him, "It's OK, son, you did your best" just before he was taken to be executed. Moreover, in addition to having to explain that they have run out of litigation options, attorneys are faced with the challenge of trying to console or at least simply be present with an individual who is about to be put to death. As one attorney wryly notes, "There's no course in law school in bedside manner at an execution." Another, also from the United States, observes that last visits with clients before execution are the hardest part of the whole experience:

> That's the most emotional stuff for me, the most loaded, the stuff that puts me over the edge, the stuff that's the hardest to talk about. ... You're trying to offer solace to somebody who's about to die. It's unbelievable. No one can be adequate in that situation. How could you possibly?

It frequently falls to defence attorneys to explain to clients' family members that an execution date has been set or that all possible legal remedies have been exhausted. Helplessness in the face of the anguish of clients' families is another wrenching aspect of the experience, as this attorney from the United States describes:

> [I was outside the prison with my client's mother], who's hunched over, and she is just—broken down. Sobbing, delirious, you know, she's just said goodbye to her son for the last time. That was one of the hardest moments. And, you know, that's the thing about the death penalty that people don't see. It was just brutal. I remember that scene so vividly. What can you do? You can't leave, and you can't change anything. You can't do anything for her.

In some countries, attorneys are prohibited from witnessing a client's execution. Even when witnessing is allowed, as in the United States, some attorneys opt not to do so, either because witnessing would make them feel complicit with the process or because they worry that it would make it harder for them to carry on as a capital defence attorney. Attorneys who choose to witness the execution generally do so out of a personal commitment to the client and a desire to stick with him or her through to the end.

Long-term impact

Capital defence attorneys who have lost clients to execution describe feelings of numbness, sadness, and anger; they recall having panic reactions at films or lectures that depict execution scenes; they recount feelings of alienation and depression that can last for days, weeks, or even longer. Are these symptoms of what is known as secondary traumatic stress—the result of hearing about traumatic events indirectly—or are the attorneys themselves directly traumatized?

The newest edition of the Diagnostic and Statistical Manual of Mental Disorders, the DSM-5, includes among its criteria for post-traumatic stress disorder "exposure to actual or threatened death", with the possible circumstance, "learning that the traumatic event(s) occurred to a close family member or close friend." Notably, the DSM-5 also includes the following criterion not for secondary traumatic stress but for post-traumatic stress disorder itself: "Experiencing repeated or extreme exposure to aversive details of the traumatic event(s) (e.g., first responders collecting human remains; police officers repeatedly exposed to details of child abuse)."[2] Apparently, this criterion was added to the newest edition of the manual in order to take into account the experiences of "professionals who have never been in direct danger, but who learn about the consequences of a traumatic event day-in and day-out as part of their professional responsibilities."[3]

The expansion of PTSD criteria in this way may reflect an expanded understanding of the kinds of experiences and encounters that leave individuals vulnerable to developing symptoms of trauma, and it highlights the particular vulnerability of those in the front lines of helping

2   American Psychiatric Association. 2013. *The Diagnostic and Statistical Manual of Mental Disorders: DSM-5.* Washington, DC: American Psychiatric Association Publishing.
3   Friedman, M. J. 2013. "Finalizing PTSD in the DSM-5: Getting from here to there and where to go next." *Journal of Traumatic Stress, 26(5):*548–556.

professions. We can reasonably count capital defence attorneys among the professionals whose work contains this inherent risk, with the added dimension that defence attorneys are not only exposed to the traumatic event of the execution but must bear the knowledge that it had been their specific job to try to avert it.

The inclusion of capital defenders in this group may not be obvious to all, however. Societal support for the death penalty and a lack of sympathy for those who suffer as a result of trying to defend "monsters" suggest that recognition of capital defenders' traumatic experience will be less readily forthcoming than will similar recognition for others who are in the business of working to save lives. Nevertheless, any inventory of the impact of the death penalty as a societal practice must take capital defence attorneys' experience into account. It is clear that they are deeply affected by the challenges and losses inherent in this high-stakes work.

3.3 Society as the victim?

THE DEATH PENALTY: KILLING WHAT WE INSTEAD COULD BE

James R. Acker[1]

The death penalty makes victims of us all: the society that supports it, the legal system that sustains it, and the citizens who endure its existence. It works subtly, like a virus, to sap the strength and undermine the well-being of its host institutions and beings. While the time, energy, and resources consumed in fueling systems of capital punishment are considerable, the less immediately apparent costs—the lost potential to use precious commodities for purposes more hopeful and salutary than extinguishing life—are all the more extravagant. Preoccupied with affirming sovereign authority and responding to crime, the death penalty not only taxes what it purports to serve, it robs the future by killing what we instead could be. It makes victims of us all.

Societal Costs

As practiced in the United States, capital punishment entails substantial fiscal costs. Trials in which the death penalty is sought routinely involve more investigators, expert witnesses, pretrial motions, and attorneys than comparable noncapital trials. Jury selection is prolonged by the questioning required to screen out individuals who are not "death qualified" or "life qualified," i.e. who are unwilling to consider imposing a sentence of death or life imprisonment, respectively, as required by law. If the defendant is convicted of a capital crime, a separate sentencing hearing is required, where additional lay and expert witnesses will testify. The resulting hefty up-front expenditures are incurred in all capital trials, whether or not they result in a

---

1   James Acker is a Distinguished Teaching Professor at the School of Criminal Justice, University at Albany, New York, United States.

death sentence. Offenders sentenced to death are incarcerated under conditions of heightened security, which are expensive to maintain.[2] Years of appeals will follow, and many prisoners will have their convictions or death sentences overturned.[3] Only 16% (1,359) of the 8,466 prisoners sentenced to death nationwide since 1973 had been executed by year's end 2013, although nearly 3,000 remained under active death sentences.[4]

Studies in multiple jurisdictions have concluded that trials are much more expensive when a death sentence is pursued—with estimates ranging from $100,000 to $1.7 million more per case—than trials for death-penalty eligible crimes when a capital sentence is not sought.[5] The cumulative costs of supporting death penalty systems far exceed what is required to finance individual trials and greatly surpass what would be needed to incarcerate offenders for life if capital punishment were not an option. In California, which has carried out 13 executions during the modern (post-*Furman v. Georgia, 1972*) *death-penalty era while currently housing nearly 750 death row prisoners,*[6] it has been estimated that $184 million was needed to sustain capital punishment in 2009 and that total death penalty–related expenditures between 1978 and 2010 topped $4 billion.[7]

The money spent enabling state-sponsored systems of death, of course, becomes unavailable to deploy elsewhere. The millions of

---

2   Bohm, Robert M. 2003. "The Economic Costs of Capital Punishment: Past, Present, and Future." In James R. Acker, Robert M. Bohm & Charles S. Lanier, eds., *America's Experiment With Capital Punishment: Reflections on the Past, Present, and Future of the Ultimate Penal Sanction* (2nd ed.). Durham, NC: Carolina Academic Press. p. 573. *See* also, Garey, Margot. 1985. "The Cost of Taking a Life: Dollars and Sense of the Death Penalty." *U.C. Davis Law Review* 18:1221.

3   Liebman, James S., Fagan, Jeffrey & West, Valerie. 2000. *A Broken System: Error Rates in Capital Cases, 1973-1995.* Available from http://www2.law.columbia.edu/instructionalservices/liebman/ (accessed 22 March, 2006).

4   U.S. Department of Justice, Bureau of Justice Statistics. 2014. *Capital Punishment, 2013—Statistical Tables.* Available from http://www.bjs.gov/content/pub/pdf/cp13st.pdf. (accessed 19 March, 2016).

5   Roman, John K., Chalfin, Aaron J. & Knight, Carly L. 2009. "Reassessing the Costs of the Death Penalty Using Quasi-Experimental Methods: Evidence from Maryland." *American Law and Economics Review* 11:530. *See* also, Dieter, Richard C. 2009. *Smart on Crime: Reconsidering the Death Penalty in a Time of Economic Crisis.* Available from http://www.deathpenaltyinfo.org/documents/ CostsRptFinal.pdf. (accessed 19 March, 2016).

6   *Furman v. Georgia* (1972). 408 U.S. 238. *See* also, Death Penalty Information Center. 2016. "Executions by State." Available from http://www.deathpenaltyinfo.org/number-executions-state-and-region-1976. (accessed 19 March, 2016).

7   Alarcon, Arthur L. & Mitchell, Paula M. 2011. "Executing the Will of the Voters? A Roadmap to Mend or End the California Legislature's Multi-Billion Dollar Death Penalty Debacle." *Loyola of Los Angeles Law Review* 44:S41.

dollars invested to fund the executioner are lost to help support such other, distinctly more benign purposes as diverse as bolstering law enforcement, assisting crime victims and their survivors, developing effective crime prevention programs, shoring up education systems, providing services for the infirm and elderly, subsidizing housing and health care, and countless others. Government funds, whether dispersed for death penalty-related purposes at the federal, state, or local level, are finite. "There are not two spigots from which appropriations can flow forth, one for capital punishment and one for other services. Choices must be made."[8] Alternatively put, opportunity costs are an inevitable and irredeemable, even if less-directly visible, consequence of using public monies to finance the death penalty.[9]

Making real the potential trade-offs between investing in capital punishment and alternative causes is not purely hypothetical or simple wishful thinking. For example, leading up to the state's repeal of its capital punishment law in 2007, the New Jersey Death Penalty Study Commission recommended that "any cost savings resulting from the abolition of the death penalty be used for benefits and services for survivors of victims of homicide."[10] When Illinois abolished its death penalty in 2011, the repeal legislation provided that funds previously allocated to support capital litigation be transferred to a Death Penalty Abolition Fund and expended "for services for families of victims of homicide or murder and for training of law enforcement personnel."[11] A narrowly defeated 2012 referendum in California asked voters to substitute life imprisonment without parole for capital punishment and thus "save the state $1 billion in five years ... that could be invested in law enforcement ..., in our children's schools, and in

---

8   Gradess, Jonathan E. & Davies, Andrew L. B. 2009. "The Cost of the Death Penalty in America: Directions for Future Research." In Charles S. Lanier, William J. Bowers & James R. Acker, eds, *The Future of America's Death Penalty: An Agenda for the Next Generation of Capital Punishment Research*. Durham, NC: Carolina Academic Press. p. 397.

9   Dieter, Richard C. 2014. "The Issue of Costs in the Death Penalty Debate." In James R. Acker, Robert M. Bohm & Charles S. Lanier, eds, *America's Experiment With Capital Punishment: Reflections on the Past, Present, and Future of the Ultimate Penal Sanction* (3rd ed.). Durham, NC: Carolina Academic Press. p. 598.

10   *New Jersey Death Penalty Study Commission Report. 2007. Available from* http://www.njleg.state.nj.us/committees/dpsc_final.pdf (accessed 23 March 2016). *See* also, Martin, Robert J. 2010. "Killing Capital Punishment in New Jersey: The First State in Modern History to Repeal Its Death Penalty Statute." *University of Toledo Law Review* 41:485.

11   Illinois Compiled Statutes Annotated. 2011. Chap. 725, Article 119-1(b). *See* also, Warden, Rob. 2012. "How and Why Illinois Abolished the Death Penalty." *Law & Inequality* 30:245.

services for the elderly and disabled."[12] Similar choices have figured explicitly in death-penalty policy debates in other jurisdictions.[13]

In short, every dollar spent in pursuit of an execution represents a dollar not spent elsewhere. As hundreds of millions and even billions of dollars are invested over time in supporting capital punishment, legions of future, largely invisible victims of the death-penalty enterprise inevitably are created. They are created through the criminal violence enabled by ill-equipped and understaffed police departments, through the denial of mental health and other essential services for the immediate victims of crime, and through the diversion of scarce resources that are desperately needed to shore up substandard schools, health care, housing, and other urgent social programs. Society at large is victimized in a real sense by the glaring imbalance between the death penalty's illusory benefits and its considerable costs.[14]

The Legal System Suffers

The legal system is burdened by the death penalty in different ways. Most fundamentally, the law's legitimacy is undermined by the substantial gulf between the rules constructed in fulfillment of the constitutional mandates that govern the death penalty's administration and how those same rules operate in practice. An additional cost is the politicization of the administration of justice, with particular relevance to the judicial function and the corresponding mandate for impartiality.

---

12   California Proposition 34, §2(5), 2012. See also, Acker, James R. 2013. "Your Money and Your Life: How Cost Nearly Killed California's Death Penalty." Correctional Law Reporter 24:69.

13   Dieter, Richard C. 2014. "The Issue of Costs in the Death Penalty Debate." In James R. Acker, Robert M. Bohm & Charles S. Lanier, eds, America's Experiment With Capital Punishment: Reflections on the Past, Present, and Future of the Ultimate Penal Sanction (3rd ed.). Durham, NC: Carolina Academic Press. p. 595. See also, Johnson, Kirk, "Death Penalty Repeal Fails in Colorado," New York Times, May 4, 2009. Available from http://www.nytimes.com/2009/05/05/us/05colorado.html?_r=0. (accessed 24 March 2016); McLaughlin, Julie. 2014. "The Price of Justice: Interest-Convergence, Cost, and the Anti-Death Penalty Movement." Northwestern University Law Review 108:675, and Urbina, Ian, "Citing Cost, States Consider End to Death Penalty," New York Times, February 24, 2009. Available from http://www.nytimes.com/2009/02/25/us/25death.html?_r=0. (accessed 24 March 2016).

14   Gradess, Jonathan E. & Davies, Andrew L. B. 2009. "The Cost of the Death Penalty in America: Directions for Future Research." In Charles S. Lanier, William J. Bowers & James R. Acker, eds, The Future of America's Death Penalty: An Agenda for the Next Generation of Capital Punishment Research. Durham, NC: Carolina Academic Press. p. 397. See also, Tabak, Ronald J. & Lane, J. Mark. 1989. "The Execution of Injustice: A Cost and Lack-of-Benefit Analysis of the Death Penalty." Loyola of Los Angeles Law Review 23:59.

Capital punishment laws in the United States were enforced almost exclusively by the states, with scant federal oversight, well into the 1960s. Only then, when the Eighth Amendment's prohibition against cruel and unusual punishments and other Bill of Rights safeguards were recognized as binding on the states, did death-penalty laws begin to receive serious scrutiny by the federal courts. A new era of capital punishment began when the Supreme Court invalidated death-penalty laws nationwide in Furman v. Georgia (1972). The justices subsequently affirmed the constitutionality of replacement legislation in *Gregg v. Georgia* (1976) and companion cases.[15] The newly approved laws incorporated procedural safeguards designed to minimize the risk of arbitrariness in the death penalty's administration. They shared common features including narrowing the class of crimes punishable by death, bifurcating capital trials so information critical to the sentencing decision—including evidence offered by the defendant in mitigation of punishment—could be introduced at a separate penalty phase after guilt was determined, incorporating legislative standards to guide the exercise of sentencing discretion, and providing for appellate review of capital convictions and sentences.[16]

A basic doctrinal tension was embedded in the new constitutional mandates. On the one hand, the reforms were implemented in an attempt to harness discretion and purge arbitrariness from the capital sentencing process. Simultaneously, however, the sentencing authority was required to give consideration to the specific offense circumstances and idiosyncratic characteristics of the offender before deciding between punishment by death or life imprisonment. The twin constitutional sentencing imperatives of "nonarbitrariness" and "individualization" thus worked in fundamental opposition to each other. Various members of the Supreme Court came to the conclusion that the same rules they had manufactured and demanded compliance with were impossible to reconcile. Some of the justices renounced allegiance to the previously endorsed sentencing procedures while

---

15 Banner, Stuart. 2002. *The Death Penalty: An American History.* Cambridge, MA: Harvard University Press. *See* also, Steiker, Carol S. & Steiker, Jordan M. 2014. "Judicial Developments in Capital Punishment Law." In James R. Acker, Robert M. Bohm & Charles S. Lanier, eds, *America's Experiment With Capital Punishment: Reflections on the Past, Present, and Future of the Ultimate Penal Sanction* (3rd ed.). Durham, NC: Carolina Academic Press. p. 77.

16 Acker, James R. & Lanier, Charles S. 2014. "Beyond Human Ability? The Rise and Fall of Death Penalty Legislation." In James R. Acker, Robert M. Bohm & Charles S. Lanier, eds, *America's Experiment With Capital Punishment: Reflections on the Past, Present, and Future of the Ultimate Penal Sanction* (3rd ed.). Durham, NC: Carolina Academic Press. p. 101.

others gave up entirely, concluding that the death penalty defied constitutional regulation and hence should no longer be condoned.[17]

The Supreme Court's elaborate constitutional jurisprudence,
grounded in the requirements of the Eighth Amendment and considered essential to eliminate unconscionable arbitrariness in capital
punishment's administration, in actuality amounted to little more
than a façade. The justices unwittingly created and then perpetuated
a crisis in death penalty laws' perceived legitimacy. One commen-
tator wryly observed that the court had "reduced the law of the
death penalty trial to almost a bare aesthetic exhortation that the
states just do something—anything—to give the penalty trial a legal
appearance."[18] Equally condemning criticisms were voiced even by
justices who continued to affirm the death penalty's constitutionality. Justice Rehnquist charged that "the new constitutional doctrine
will not eliminate arbitrariness or freakishness in the imposition of
[capital] sentences, but will codify and institutionalize it."[19] Justice
Scalia complained:

> To acknowledge that "there perhaps is an inherent tension"
> between [the objectives of achieving rational, consistent cap-
> ital sentencing and requiring unconstrained consideration of
> individualized mitigating circumstances] is rather like saying
> that there was perhaps an inherent tension between the Allies
> and the Axis Powers in World War II. And to refer to the
> two lines [of cases] as pursuing "twin objectives" is rather
> like referring to the twin objectives of good and evil. They
> cannot be reconciled.[20]

Essentially agreeing with those sentiments, the prestigious American
Law Institute, which in the 1960s had supplied the basic framework for the post-*Furman* guided-discretion capital punishment
laws through its Model Penal Code, withdrew the death-penalty sections of the Model Penal Code in 2009. It did so because

---

17   Acker, James R. 2003. "The Death Penalty: An American History." *Contemporary Justice Review*
      6:169. *See* also, *Baze v. Rees, 553 U.S. 35. (2008) (Stevens, J., concurring in the judgment); Callins v.
      Collins, 510 U.S. 1141. (1994) (Blackmun, J., dissenting from denial of certiorari),* and *Glossip v. Gross,*
      135 S.Ct. 2726. (2015) (Breyer, J., dissenting).
18   Weisberg, Robert. 1983. "Deregulating Death." *Supreme Court Review 1983:305.*
19   *Lockett v. Ohio. 438 U.S. 586. 632, (1978) (dissenting opinion).*
20   *Walton v. Arizona. 497 U.S. 639 (1990) (concurring opinion).*

notwithstanding the conceptual elegance of the model statutory framework, experience revealed "current intractable institutional and structural obstacles to ensuring a minimally adequate system for administering capital punishment."[21] The vast chasm between death-penalty laws as written and their operation in practice—a practice that remains rife with inequities the laws were designed to cure, including systemic arbitrariness, racial discrimination, putting innocent persons at risk, and more—cannot help but cast a dark shadow on the laws' legitimacy.

Capital punishment further tarnishes the law through its politicization of justice systems. It perhaps is understandable why some governors, legislators, and prosecutors boast about their enthusiasm for the death penalty as they attempt to bolster their tough-on-crime credentials with the public. There is something seriously amiss, however, when judges—whose duty to be impartial encompasses scrupulous protection of citizens' rights—engage in similar rhetoric. And some do. The trial judges in most states within the U.S. are elected by voters from the county or district served by the court. Where capital punishment flourishes, some elections have been distinguished by candidates for judgeships acclaiming their support for the death penalty with a fervor equal to that of other elected politicians.[22] Voters and their death-penalty attitudes not only can influence the election of trial judges, but also the retention of state appellate court judges who have made unpopular rulings in capital cases.[23] The result is the risk that judicial independence is compromised.

Alabama's capital-punishment system has come under special scrutiny because elected trial judges have unconstrained authority to impose

21 Steiker, Carol S. & Steiker, Jordan M. 2010. "No More Tinkering: The American Law Institute and the Death Penalty Provisions of the Model Penal Code." *Texas Law Review* 89:353.

22 Brace, Paul & Boyea, Brent D. 2008. "State Public Opinion, the Death Penalty, and the Practice of Electing Judges." *American Journal of Political Science* 52:360. See also, Bright, Stephen B. & Keenan, Patrick J. 1995. "Judges and the Politics of Death: Deciding Between the Bill of Rights and the Next Election in Capital Cases." *Boston University Law Review* 75:759, and Weiss, Joanna Cohn. 2006. "Tough on Crime: How Campaigns for State Judiciary Violate Criminal Defendants' Due Process Rights." *New York University Law Review* 81:1101.

23 Bills, Bronson D. 2008. "A Penny for the Court's Thoughts? The High Price of Judicial Elections." *Northwestern Journal of Law and Social Policy* 3:29. See also, Blume & Eisenberg, 1999; Bright, Stephen B. 1997. "Political Attacks on the Judiciary: Can Justice Be Done Amid Efforts to Intimidate and Remove Judges from Office for Unpopular Decisions?" *New York University Law Review* 72:308, and Uelmen, Gerald F. 1997. "Crocodiles in the Bathtub: Maintaining the Independence of State Supreme Courts in an Era of Judicial Politicization." *Notre Dame Law Review* 72:1133.

sentence in capital cases after considering a jury's advisory sentencing recommendation. In most states and under federal law, juries make the final sentencing decisions in capital cases. Alabama is one of just three states where judges have the power to override a jury's sentencing recommendation. Only in Alabama can a trial judge ignore a jury's recommended sentence of life imprisonment and impose a death sentence unfettered by pre-established criteria or standards. Between 2000 and 2013, Alabama judges made such life-to-death overrides in 26 cases.[24] "What," asked U.S. Supreme Court Justice Sonia Sotomayor, "could explain Alabama judges' distinctive proclivity for imposing death sentences in cases where a jury has already rejected that penalty?"[25] The answer she supplied was not reassuring. "Alabama judges, who are elected in partisan proceedings, appear to have succumbed to electoral pressures".[26] Such capitulation, Justice Sotomayor concluded, "casts a cloud of illegitimacy over the criminal justice system."[27] That assessment is hard to dispute.

Divisiveness and Distraction

Most subtly and invidiously, the death penalty is a powerfully polarizing issue. It not only impedes discourse about effective crime control and ameliorative social programs and policies, but it also obscures the important commonalities that virtually all citizens value irrespective of their views about capital punishment. Without the formidable wedge that divides the death penalty's proponents and opponents, adherents of both positions are unburdened to discover and affirm their shared commitment to a substantial body of compelling social causes. And with these new understandings in place, prospects are considerably enhanced for accomplishing objectives that are of far greater moment and social value than maintaining the death penalty.

Such an air-clearing dynamic has recently been exhibited in New York. New York's death-penalty law was declared unconstitutional

---

24   *Woodward v. Alabama. 134 S.Ct. 405. (2013).*
25   Ibid.
26   *Woodward v. Alabama. 134 S.Ct. 405. (2013). See* also, Burnside, Fred B. 1999. "Dying to Get Elected: A Challenge to the Jury Override." *Wisconsin Law Review* 1999:1017, and *Harris v. Alabama,* 513 U.S. 504 (1995) (Stevens, J., dissenting).
27   *Woodward v. Alabama, 134 S.Ct. 405 (2013) (dissenting from denial of certiorari).*

in the mid-1970s. Relentless, acrimonious disagreement about its reinstatement ensued over the next two decades.[28] Replacement capital punishment legislation finally was enacted in 1995, only to be invalidated on constitutional grounds by the state's highest court in 2004.[29] A new era dawned thereafter when it became clear that the state legislature was through debating the death penalty and would not try to resurrect the voided statute. New Yorkers for Alternatives to the Death Penalty, an organization that previously had focused almost exclusively on abolishing capital punishment, embarked on a new agenda. Said its executive director:

We came to the conclusion that true abolition is more than the absence of the death penalty. Abolition means that responses to violence are constructive, just, and work toward the betterment of all members of society.

Thus, we will be working with five important groups. The mission is to unite victims, law enforcement, advocates for the mentally ill, restorative justice practitioners and families of the incarcerated around policies that address their real and immediate needs and reduce the likelihood of violent crime.[30]

Marked by invigorating collaborations among stakeholders who had previously defined themselves as antagonists, the post-capital punishment discussions among representatives of those groups were distinctive and productive.

The end of the death penalty created space for genuine collaboration among previously entrenched adversaries within the criminal justice system. In the words of one prosecutor, the death penalty sucked all the air out of the room. With its demise came opportunities to replace this failed policy with better ones.

---

28 Acker, James R. 1990. "New York's Proposed Death Penalty Legislation: Constitutional and Policy Perspectives." *Albany Law Review* 54:515. *See* also, Acker, James R. 1996. "When the Cheering Stopped: An Overview and Analysis of New York's Death Penalty Legislation." *Pace Law Review* 17:41.

29 *People v. LaValle, 817 N.E.2d 341 (2004) (N.Y.)*. *See* also, *People v. Taylor, 878 N.E.2d 969 (2007) (N.Y.)*.

30 Kaczynski, David. 2008. "Life After Death." *NYAPD News 2008 (Fall):1.*

A set of shared values emerged among all affected parties for preventing crime, helping victims of crime to heal and rebuild, and restoring communities afflicted by violence to peace and health.[31]

It is telling that the common values that emerged unexceptionally found expression in plans laid for constructive, life-affirming actions. This positive, hopeful orientation stands in marked contrast to promoting the designedly destructive, life-ending eventuality of carrying out executions in punishment for crime. In the place of time-consuming and distracting disputation about capital punishment—an expensive, inequitable, and error-prone "failed policy" lacking demonstrable impact on crime—surfaced a shared commitment to ward off violent crime by combatting the social conditions which fuel it and to mend, as much as possible, the resulting harm instead of compounding the hurt and suffering by resorting to more lethal violence.

The death penalty is a powerful symbol. Throughout history, executions have served to demonstrate the might of the sovereign and the inviolability of government authority.[32] While still employed to those ends, it is increasingly difficult to credit the power to execute as an essential aspect of state sovereignty. To some in post-Furman America, maintaining capital punishment signifies the prominence of states' rights in defiance of unwanted federal oversight. For others, it effectively masks racial and social class biases.[33] Yet current support for capital punishment is linked most closely with fidelity to law and order and to waging an aggressive war on crime. This symbolism is both ironic and perverse. Opposition to capital punishment in no way suggests a disrespect for the law. And in reality, the rhetoric and resources devoted to supporting the death penalty are tragically counterproductive in preventing or responding to violent crime.

---

31 Gradess, Jonathan E. & Silberstein, Shari. 2014. "Pumping Oxygen into the Room." *New York State Bar Association Government, Law and Policy Journal* 16(2):10.

32 Foucault, Michel. 1979. *Discipline and Punish: The Birth of the Prison*. New York: Vintage Books. *See* also, Gatrell, V.A.C. 1994. *The Hanging Tree: The Execution and the English People 1770-1868*. New York: Oxford University Press, and Masur, Louis P. 1989. *Rites of Execution: Capital Punishment and the Transformation of American Culture, 1776-1865*. New York: Oxford University Press.

33 Garland, David. 2010. *Peculiar Institution: America's Death Penalty in an Age of Abolition*. Cambridge, MA: The Belknap Press of Harvard University Press. *See* also, Kirchmeier, Jeffrey L. 2015. *Imprisoned by the Past: Warren McCleskey and the American Death Penalty*. New York: Oxford University Press, and Zimring, Franklin E. & Hawkins, Gordon. 1986. *Capital Punishment and the American Agenda*. New York: Cambridge University Press.

Conclusion

Death penalty systems are expensive. They consume scarce resources that could be used for causes far more compelling and worthwhile than extinguishing human life. The life and death sentencing decisions made in criminal trials are incapable of being harnessed by law. Capital punishment makes a mockery of legal rules and their underlying constitutional principles, and hence breeds disrespect for the very institution that authorizes it. And the death penalty cleaves public opinion and hardens attitudes pertaining to crime and justice. In so doing, it blinds citizens who share a deep commitment to the same incontrovertibly worthwhile ends—ends such as reducing criminal violence, eradicating the conditions that spawn it, and investing in strong communities and their future—from recognizing their crucial commonalities and preempts their working collaboratively to accomplish them. In these many ways, capital punishment kills what we instead could be, and makes victims of us all.

THE DEATH PENALTY AS A PUBLIC HEALTH PROBLEM

Walter C. Long[1]

Introduction

Capital punishment is intentional homicide. Yet the World Health Organization's 2002 World Report on Violence and Health and the 2014 follow-up report on state implementation of its recommendations do not mention capital punishment.[2] This is a major oversight, as the efficacy of United Nations violence prevention policies cannot accurately be evaluated without inclusion of data regarding the impact of the state's own employment of violence[3] on its citizenry. Abolition of the death penalty should be robustly joined to all public health efforts at stemming violence because the death penalty's anti-therapeutic effects on individuals and systems will not be ameliorated by ignoring that it is a traumatogenic force.[4]

Qualitative studies and narrative accounts show compelling evidence of the anti-therapeutic effects of the death penalty on all classes of

---

1   Walter Long is a criminal defence attorney and the founder of the Texas After Violence Project, www.texasafterviolence.org.

2   World Health Organization. 2002. *World Report on Violence and Health*. Geneva; World Health Organization. 2014. *Global Status Report on Violence Prevention 2014*. Geneva.

3   The World Health Organization defines "violence" as "the intentional use of physical force or power, threatened or actual, against oneself, another person, or against a group or community, that either results in or has a high likelihood of resulting in injury, death, psychological harm, maldevelopment or deprivation." WHO Global Consultation on Violence and Health. 1996. *Violence: a public health priority*. Geneva: World Health Organization. (document WHO/EHA/SPI.POA.2).

4   Sandra L. Bloom and Michael Reichert. 1998. *Bearing Witness: Violence and Collective Responsibility*. New York: Haworth Press. pp.18 ("Traumatogenic forces are those social practices and trends that cause, encourage, or contribute to the generation of traumatic acts."); Alfred L. McAlister. 2006. "Acceptance of killing and homicide rates in nineteen nations." *European Journal of Public Health* 16:pp. 259, 264 (finding that differences in national homicide rates correlate with differences in the "social acceptability of killing" reflected in the presence or absence of the death penalty).

persons involved in capital cases.[5] It is an understatement to say that the "human mind is not well suited to killing [and that] killing tends to make the mind sick."[6]

The death penalty has a profoundly negative effect on the individuals who are the direct and indirect objects of the punishment as well as the persons charged with carrying it out. The direct objects of the punishment, of course, are the persons sentenced to death, those the penalty was designed to deter—through the threat of homicide—from committing acts unacceptable to the state. The emotionally dysregulating effect of the death penalty on the condemned themselves is a staple of the experience of their visiting family members, advocates, fellow inmates, and jailers. However, researchers seem to have written little about the effects on the inmates of the sentence itself. One reason, probably, is restrictions imposed by legal appeals. The few studies on the impact of the sentence are drawn from exonerated or released inmates.[7] The paucity of research on inmates also may reflect resistance to viewing death-sentenced inmates as victims, although the vast majority are. For example, a 2000 study of sample of United States death row inmates found prior

5   Cynthia F. Adcock. 2010. "The collateral anti-therapeutic effects of the death penalty." *Florida Coastal Law Review* 11:289-320; Marilyn Armour and Mark Umbreit. 2007. "The ultimate penal sanction and 'closure' for survivors of homicide victims." *Marquette Law Review* 91:381; Elizabeth Beck, Sarah Britto, & Arlene Andrews. 2007. *In the Shadow of Death: Restorative Justice and Death Row Families*. Oxford: Oxford University Press; Robert Bohm. 2012. *Capital Punishment's Collateral Damage*. Durham: Carolina Academic Press; Robert Bohm. 2010. *Ultimate Sanction: Understanding the Death Penalty Through Its Many Voices and Many Sides*. New York: Kaplan Publishing; Lauren M. De Lilly. 2014. "'Antithetical to human dignity': Secondary trauma, evolving standards of decency, and the unconstitutional consequences of state-sanctioned executions." *Southern California Interdisciplinary Law Journal* 23:107-145; Sandra Joy. 2014. *Grief, Loss, and Treatment for Death Row Families* Plymouth, UK: Lexington Books; Rachel King. 2005. *Don't Kill in Our Name: Family Members of Murder Victims Speak Out Against the Death Penalty*. Piscataway, NJ: Rutgers University Press; Penal Reform International, Briefing Paper. 2015. "Prison Guards and the Death Penalty," available from: http://www.penalreform.org/wp-content/uploads/2015/04/PRI-Prison-guards-briefing-paper.pdf. (accessed 24 August 2016); Michael L. Radelet. 2016. "The incremental retributive impact of a death sentence over life without parole." *University of Michigan Journal of Law Reform* 49:4:795-815; Susan Sharp. 2005. *Hidden Victims: The Effects of the Death Penalty on Families of the Accused*. Piscataway, NJ: Rutgers University Press; Susannah Sheffer. 2013. *Fighting For Their Lives: Inside the Experience of Capital Defense Attorneys*. Nashville, TN: Vanderbilt University Press; Saundra D. Westervelt and Kimberly J. Cook. 2012. *Life after Death Row: Exonerees' Search for Community and Identity*. Piscataway, NJ: Rutgers University Press.
6   Rachel M. McNair. 2007. "Killing as trauma." In Elizabeth K. Carll, ed. *Trauma Psychology: Issues in Violence, Disaster, Health, and Illness*. London: Praeger. vol. 1, 147, 147.
7   *See* Westervelt and Cook, *supra* note 4, and Lloyd Vogelman, Sharon Lewis, and Lauren Segal. 1994. "Life after death row: post-traumatic stress and the story of Philip Takedi." *South African Journal of Psychology* 24:91-99.

victimization by family violence in all 16 cases studied and 14 of 16 with post-traumatic stress disorder.[8]

The death penalty also works emotional dysregulation in its indirect objects: the families, friends, legal advocates, other defenders or sympathizers of the condemned, and many survivors of homicide victims. It similarly negatively affects those charged with levying and carrying out the sentence, including the police, courts, prosecutors, jurors, wardens, guards, chaplains, and executive officers. Finally, serious concern should be raised about the death penalty's transmission of trans-generational trauma, especially within marginalized groups that often are its disproportionate targets[9]—not merely social or racial minorities, but impoverished families that experience criminal history cycles. In nations such as the United States, where the death penalty has been disproportionately applied to racial minorities and has arisen out of a historical context of widespread extrajudicial execution used to marginalize them, it should be examined as a residual tool of that marginalization.[10]

The Death Penalty is a Trauma-Organized System

The purpose of the death penalty is to inspire dread through the threat and performance of state homicide[11] and it is effective at instilling long-term dread in the persons within its realm of immediate influence. In many jurisdictions, once an arrest is made and the state has made its decision to pursue death, the state's prospective

---

8   David Freedman and David Hemenway. 2000. "Precursors of lethal violence: a death row sample." *Social Science and Medicine* 50:1757-1770: *see also* David Lisak and Sara Beszterczey. 2007. "The cycle of violence: the life histories of 43 death row inmates." *Psychology of Men and Masculinity* 8(2):pp. 118, 125 (finding a "vast majority" had suffered "multiple forms of abuse and neglect" and "strong majorities experienced extreme levels of terror" in their lives prior to the crime that sent them to death row).

9   William E. Cross, Jr. 1998. "Black psychological functioning and the legacy of slavery." In Yael Danieli, ed., *International Handbook of Multigenerational Legacies of Trauma*. New York: Plenum Press; Joy DeGruy. 2005. *Post Traumatic Slave Syndrome*. Uptone Press. (coining "Post Traumatic Slave Syndrome" as "multigenerational trauma [resulting from centuries of slavery] together with continued oppression and absence of opportunity to access the benefits available in the society").

10   Equal Justice Initiative. *Report, Lynching in America: Confronting the legacy of racial terror*. Available from http://www.eji.org/lynchinginamerica. (accessed 24 August 2016); Jennifer Schweizer. 2013. "Racial disparity in capital punishment and its impact on family members of capital defendants." *Journal of Evidence-Based Social Work* 10:91-99.

11   *Gregg v. Georgia*, 428 U.S. 153, 183 (1976) ("The death penalty is said to serve two principal social purposes: retribution and deterrence of capital crimes by prospective offenders.").

act of violence becomes the overriding issue and all persons within that realm of influence become fixated on the penalty. In the present administration of capital punishment, lives are taken over by the drama surrounding the prospective execution of the defendant—not infrequently for decades in those states that otherwise are concerned with fair judicial process. The death penalty, thus, has been described as a "sustained catastrophe during which the danger and threats to life and self extend over a period of time . . . [continuing] day after day, year after year with no discernible end."[12]

Social science has preoccupied itself with the question whether the death penalty is a better general deterrent to murder than other sentences.[13] This statistical inquiry into the effect of the lethal threat on unknown, potential, individual criminals tends to overshadow the actual stories of harm resulting from state homicide on the aforementioned groups of persons within the direct influence of the punishment system. Fundamentally, this analysis that prioritizes and isolates cause and effect on individuals' behaviour fails to comprehend the breadth and profundity of human interconnectedness. It is at least as myopic as studies that also isolate rates of violent crime or suicide without looking at systemic interactions and asking how "our collective actions contribute to human violence."[14]A punishment carried out against an individual always will have a communal and intergenerational impact, not merely an impact on isolated prospective criminals. The more violent the punishment, the more wide, deep, and deleterious the impact on the given system of human relations.

Humans are neurobiologically communal creatures, not isolated sets of individuals. Trauma studies are opening new understandings of what it is to be human, helping us to be mindful that the Cartesian individualism that underlies our theories of retributive punishment is

---

12 *Westervelt and Cook, supra* note 4, at 131.

13 National Research Council of the National Academies, Committee on Deterrence and the Death Penalty. 2012. *Deterrence and the Death Penalty.* Washington, D.C.: The National Academies Press, 2 (concluding that "research to date on the effect of capital punishment on homicide is not informative about whether capital punishment decreases, increases, or has no effect on homicide rates"); *see also* Keith Humphreys and Peter Piot. 2012. "Scientific evidence alone is not sufficient basis for health policy." *British Medical Journal* (online) at *BMJ*2012;344:e1316 doi: 10.1136/bmj. e1316 (proof that the death penalty has a deterrent effect "can never tell us whether the taking of a helpless individual's life by the state is morally acceptable").

14 Bandy X. Lee, Phillip L. Marotta, Morkeh Blay-Tofey, Winnie Wang, and Shalila de Bourmont. 2014. "Economic correlates of violent death rates in forty countries, 1962-2008: a cross-typological analysis." *Aggression and Violent Behavior* 19: pp. 729, 736.

a "socially constructed illusion"[15] that theorizes and, thus, to an extent manufactures the person as an autonomous entity who chooses to initiate relationships with others in moral or immoral ways.[16] Neuroscience suggests the opposite, that "from relationships, the very possibility of independent persons emerges."[17] Our individual neural systems are intertwined with those of others.[18] In fact, we are dependent on the inner lives of others for our construction of our identities and very survival. If, for example, a human baby is fed and clothed but deprived of emotional contact, he or she will start to fail and can die.[19] We share with other mammals a limbic region in our brains that not only evolved to give us a better means to process experiences that appear threatening, but also to provide us with attachment to caring others through "limbic resonance." "The mammalian nervous system depends for its neurophysiologic stability on a system of interactive coordination, wherein steadiness comes from synchronization with nearby attachment figures."[20]

Limbic states leap between human minds without restriction and, thus, we constantly engage in "emotional contagion," the "tendency to automatically mimic and synchronize facial expressions, vocalizations, postures, and movements with those of another person and consequentially to converge emotionally."[21] We are not unmoved observers of others' emotional states. Prior to our engagement of our higher cortical processes, evaluating our experience, we already have participated in those states. Between individuals, verbal arguments may accelerate, for example, when we imitate and ingest on the nonverbal, sub-cognitive level, another's agitated (or emotionally dysregulated) inner state and then react. Whole communities may become emotionally dysregulated almost in an instant by experiences of violence and the quick spread of emotional contagion. On a large scale, the coordinated assault

---

15   Sandra L. Bloom. 1995. "When good people do bad things: meditations on the 'backlash.'" *Journal of Psychohistory* 22(2):273-304.

16   Thomas Szasz. May 2000. "Mind, brain, and the problem of responsibility." *Society* 37:pp. 34, 35 ("When we use the word 'mind' in law or psychiatry, it stands for a reified-hypothesized 'organ' that we treat as if it were the seat of responsibility.").

17   Kenneth Gergen. 2009. *Relational Being*. Oxford: Oxford University Press. pp. 38.

18   Thomas Lewis, Fari Amini, Richard Lannon. 2000. *A General Theory of Love*. New York: Vintage. pp. 85.

19   Ibid.

20   Ibid. at 84.

21   Elaine Hatfield, John T. Cacioppo, and Richard L. Rapson. 1993. *Emotional Contagion*. Cambridge: Cambridge University Press. pp. 5.

on America on 11 September, 2001, dysregulated a nation through emotional contagion.[22] Gang violence dysregulates communities.[23] Individual homicides dysregulate families and communities. With regard to the dysregulating effect on persons under the sway of a homicide, there is little basis to distinguish the death penalty from murder.[24]

The ways in which we utilize our higher brains to make meaning of our experience after dysregulating acts of violence contribute to our individual and communal emotional regulation.[25] On individual and communal levels, constructive stories responding to perceived or accomplished threats generally cool our individual and social systems. There may be no better example of that than the South African Truth and Reconciliation Commission process for the cooling of a society through constructive stories.[26] Destructive stories — in contrast — perpetuate or enhance a sense of threat, spreading emotional contagion, at times triggering "traumatic re-enactment" (repetition of the triggering event) between individuals and within social systems.[27] Neuropsychiatrists refer to individuals or communities in the thrall of destructive stories as "trauma-organized systems."[28]

There are two elements in a trauma-organized system. First, a victimizer-victim relationship. The essential actors in the system include a victimizer who "traumatizes" and a victim who is "traumatized." In

22   Sandra L. Bloom. 2006. "Neither liberty nor safety: the impact of fear on individuals, institutions, and societies, part IV." *Psychotherapy and Politics International* 4(1):4–23.

23   John A. Rich. 2009. *Wrong Place, Wrong Time: Trauma and Violence in the Lives of Young Black Men.* Baltimore: Johns Hopkins University Press.

24   Kate King. 2004. "It hurts so bad: comparing grieving patterns of the families of murder victims with those of families of death row inmates." *Criminal Justice Policy Review* 15(2):pp.193, 209 (finding the distorted grieving patterns so similar between murder victim and defendant family members as to describe them as "mirror images on either side of the homicide, both being thrown into a situation of horror and hopelessness").

25   Marilyn Armour. 2003. "Meaning making in the aftermath of homicide." *Death Studies* 27(6):519–40; Lawrence Miller. 2009. "Family survivors of homicide: II. Practical therapeutic strategies." *The American Journal of Family Therapy* 37:85–98.

26   Antjie Krog. 1998. *Country of My Skull: Guilt, Sorrow, and the Limits of Forgiveness in the New South Africa.* New York: Times Books.

27   Sandra L. Bloom. 2008. "By the crowd they have been broken, by the crowd they shall be healed: the social transformation of trauma." In Richard G. Tedeschi, Chrystal L. Park, and Lawrence G. Calhoun, eds., *Posttraumatic Growth: Positive Changes in the Aftermath of Crisis.* New York: Psychology Press. pp.179, 208 (In re-enactment, the traumatized individual "adapts to a hostile environment and then proceeds to recreate a similar environment in order to make the best use of these adaptations. If groups — communities and even nations — respond in a similar way, then we're dealing with a dangerous and volatile situation".).

28   Bloom and Reichert, *supra* note 3, at 14; Sandra L. Bloom. 2001. "Conclusion: a public health approach to violence." In Sandra L. Bloom, ed., *Violence: A Public Health Menace and a Public Health Approach.* London: Karnac Books. p.84.

this context, "there is an absence of a protector, or the potential protectors are neutralized."[29] Second, the system is not self-aware, is amnesiac, and re-enacts toxic, traumatic events. Within the system, individuals and communities "create 'stories' by which they live their lives, make relationships, initiate actions, and respond to actions, and maintain and develop them."[30] In the words of Arnon Bentovim, a British psychiatrist, "abusive traumatic events have an exceptionally powerful effect in creating self-perpetuating 'stories' which in turn create 'trauma-organized systems' where 'abusive' events are re-enacted and re-enforced."[31]

The death penalty appears to be one such trauma-organized system. Through its own act of traumatic re-enactment, the state becomes an overwhelmingly powerful, almost irresistible victimizer. The state's judicial system spins self-perpetuating stories justifying its violence against an individual on the basis of that person's mental state at the time of an offence, which is itself constructed by the state from testamentary and circumstantial evidence.[32] In the process, the state creates a "solitarist identity"[33] for the criminal ignoring that (1) individuals are composed of multiple identities formed in multiple relationships and cannot authentically be reduced to an entity to be punished in an absolute way[34] and (2) that every individual is a product of that web of interrelationships and forces that make personal responsibility relative, not absolute. In doing this, the state, perhaps most importantly, ignores its own failures in relation to the co-creation of the person who committed the offence.[35]

---

29 Arnon Bentovim. 1992. *Trauma Organized Systems.* London: Karnac Books, at xx-xxi, quoted in Bloom, "Conclusion: a public health approach to violence." In *Violence: A Public Health Menace and Public Health Approach, supra* note 27, at 83-84.

30 Ibid.

31 Ibid.

32 Robert Cover. 1985-1986. "Violence and the word." *Yale Law Journal* 95:pp. 1601, 1608 ("Beginning with broad interpretative categories such as 'blame' or 'punishment,' meaning is created for the event which justifies the judge to herself and to others with respect to her role in the acts of violence.").

33 Amartya Sen. 2008. "Violence, identity and poverty." *Journal of Peace Research* 45(1):pp. 5, 14 (referring to the "violence of solitarist identity").

34 Ibid. at 10 ("In the recognition of plural human identities, the increased concentration on class and other sources of economic disparity has made it very hard to excite communal passions and violence in Kolkata along the lines of a religious divide—a previously cultivated device that has increasingly looked strangely primitive and raw.").

35 The vast majority of death row inmates in the United States have addiction and mental health issues that also reflect prior institutional failures. In 15 of 16 cases in the study of California death row inmates, institutions including schools, juvenile detention facilities, prisons, foster homes, medical and psychiatric facilities had failed to recognize and remediate needs prior to commission of their violent offence. Freedman and Hemenway, *supra* note 7, at 1763.

The Death Penalty is Extreme Violence

The death penalty is an abusive social construction and poses a serious threat to public health in at least three ways distinct from other criminal punishments: (1) the death penalty is state-regulated extreme violence; (2) in most states, the death penalty is future-oriented—a dogged pursuit of future state violence; and (3) the death penalty emphasizes shaming.

1. The death penalty is uniquely state-regulated extreme violence.

The first way the death penalty differs from other punishments and is detrimental to health is that, rather than erecting a bar to violence, it regulates violence. In most (arguably in all) other contexts, law's function is to find peaceful means to transform potential or actual physical disputes into words and to help parties find repose, aided by nonlethal government coercion. That includes even the law of war, which by nature is designed to mitigate, not channel, physical conflict. In criminal law, punishments other than the death penalty certainly are maintained through coercive state power, but they are motivated by concerns about accountability, incapacitation, safety, and rehabilitation. In contrast to all other areas of law, death penalty law, if it is to be considered "law,"[36] is designed to effectuate fair killing without excuse. It is uniquely a legal "application that prescribes the killing of another person" and requires judges to "set in motion the acts of others which will in the normal course of events end with someone else killing the convicted defendant."[37] As it is constituted of the state's threat of homicide, absent the exception that swallows the rule ("pain and suffering arising only from . . . lawful sanctions"),

---

36 Finn Kjaerulf and Rodrigo Barahona. 2010. "Preventing violence and reinforcing human security: a rights-based framework for top-down and bottom-up action." *Revista Panamericana de Salud Publica* 27(5):382, 382 (observing that violence discourages the rule of law and is a threat to essential liberties and human rights, "in particular, the right to life without fear").

37 Robert Cover. "Violence and the word," *supra* note 31, at 1622.

the death penalty meets the United Nations definition of torture,[38] and "is arguably the most extreme form of torture."[39]

The extreme violence of the death penalty (in other words, the threat of homicide and homicide itself carried out by government) places it squarely in the category of events described by the Diagnostic and Statistical Manual[40] and International Classification of Diseases[41] as precipitating psychological trauma and post-traumatic stress disorder.

2. The death penalty is uniquely future-oriented extreme punishment.

Second, in most places the death penalty is future oriented—the government only secures at trial a conditional right to pursue execution of the defendant at an often much later date. In states that allow substantial appeals of the death sentence—lasting for many years in democracies like the United States and Japan—repeated exposure to the facts of the crime occurs. For a "long duration", actors within the capital punishment system, including the defendant and prison personnel, advocates on both sides, and the survivors of the victim and defendant's family, are trapped in a seemingly endlessly present, claustrophobic moment between the past terrible murder and the government's future killing. This requires the government to remain in an emotionally up-regulated fight mode against the defendant for years until it eliminates

---

38 United Nations Convention Against Torture and Other Cruel, Inhuman or Degrading Treatment or Punishment, art. 1, Dec. 10, 1984, S. Treaty Doc. No. 100-20 (1988), 1465 U.N.T.S. 113 (defining torture as "any act by which severe pain or suffering, whether physical or *mental*, is intentionally inflicted on a person for such purposes as . . . punishing him for an act he . . . has committed . . . when such pain or suffering is inflicted by or at the instigation of . . . a public official") (emphasis added).

39 Christina M. Cerna. 1997. "Universality of human rights: The case of the death penalty." *ILSA Journal of International and Comparative Law* 3:465, 468, 475 ("The imposition of the death penalty itself is the most extreme form of torture imaginable, but is excluded from the definition of torture by means of a legal fiction."); *see also Soering v. United Kingdom*, 161 Eur. Ct. H.R. (ser. A) (1989) (finding the "very long period of time spent on death row . . . with the ever present and mounting anguish of awaiting execution" likely to violate Article 3 of the European Convention on Human Rights, which prohibits "inhuman or degrading treatment or punishment"); *Glossip v. Gross*, 135 S. Ct. 2726 (2015) (Stephen Breyer & Ruth Ginsberg, dissenting) (comprehensive list of jurisdictions recognizing "death row phenomenon", that lengthy delay in execution is cruel).

40 DSM-5, Section 309.81 (Post-traumatic Stress Disorder) ("Exposure to actual or threatened death . . . in one (or more) of the following ways: 1. Directly experiencing the traumatic event(s); 2. Witnessing, in person, the event(s) as it occurred to others; 3. Learning that the traumatic event(s) occurred to a close family member or close friend. In cases of actual or threatened death of a family member or friend, the event(s) must have been violent or accidental; 4. Experiencing repeated or extreme exposure to aversive details of the traumatic event(s)."). The DSM refers to first responders' and police officers' experiences as examples of No. 4.

41 ICD, Section F43.1 (Post-traumatic Stress Disorder) ("Arises as a delayed or protracted response to a stressful event or situation (of either brief or long duration) of an exceptionally threatening or catastrophic nature, which is likely to cause pervasive distress in almost anyone.").

him. For prosecutors, repeatedly reiterating the death threat might be as emotionally dysregulating as it is for defence counsel on the other side, anticipating and fighting against the eventual execution.[42]

The future orientation leaves family members and other survivors of the murder victim in limbo, often unable to properly go through the steps of grieving as they are stirred throughout appellate events to recall the sharp grief and trauma of their loss. Survivors describe being brought back to "square one" every time something happens in a case over the years, sometimes decades, that appeals last.[43] As they may find themselves unable to process grief, being repeatedly interrupted and thrown back to square one, their anger tends to be re-aroused at the defendant, at the defendant's advocates, at the prosecutors, and at the system.[44]

The future-orientation also uniquely damages the defendant's family and friends and, sometimes, the defendant's advocates,[45] who all undergo a "chronic dread" related to anticipatory grief, a constant threat of loss intimately tied to serially traumatizing events (appellate losses, stayed execution dates).[46] Anyone who cares about the defendant may be affected by this, including prison personnel. Recognizing this, the state of Texas has utilized execution-day chaplains to work with the condemned during the execution process who are otherwise employed in places other than death row in the prison system. This shields the chaplains actually working on death row from the likely detrimental emotional and psychological consequences that would attend to their participation in the killing of persons they had come to know and care about.[47]

3. *The death penalty is uniquely shaming.*

Lastly, precisely because the death penalty is intentional homicide, it is profoundly shaming in a way that no other punishment (or action short

---

42 *See* Sheffer, *supra* note 4.

43 Armour and Umbreit, *supra* note 4, at 408–409.

44 Jennifer Connolly and Ronit Gordon. 2015. "Co-victims of homicide: a systematic review of the literature." *Trauma, Violence, and Abuse* 16(4):494–505.

45 Sheffer, *supra* note 4.

46 Joy, *supra* note 4, at 9.

47 Walter C. Long. 2015. "The constitutionality and ethics of execution-day prison chaplaincy." *Texas Journal on Civil Liberties and Civil Rights* 21(1):1,3.

of murder) is. United States Supreme Court Justice William Brennan described as the death penalty's "fatal constitutional infirmity" its direct assault on "human dignity", treating "members of the human race as nonhumans, as objects to be toyed with and discarded."[48] In 1993, three Canadian Supreme Court justices assessed the assault on dignity more colourfully: "[The death penalty] is the supreme indignity to the individual, the ultimate corporal punishment, the final and complete lobotomy and the absolute and irrevocable castration. [It is] the ultimate desecration of human dignity."[49] The death penalty is an exercise of extraordinarily extreme shaming. If in some abstract sense it is about "incapacitating an offender", in real operation it is about decapitating the offender. It is overkill. It mirrors the action taken by an individual who has suffered a "narcissistic wound."[50] In this instance, a government or society reacts—in a trauma-organized way—perceiving its own cohesion to be under threat.

Survivors of murder victims often experience stigmatization.[51] Some survivors, particularly those of already marginalized groups, undergo "disenfranchised grief,"[52] which "occurs when a loss cannot be openly acknowledged, publicly mourned, or socially supported."[53] Even in cultures disposed to assist victims of violent crime, survivors nevertheless feel isolated because they experience other people as avoiding contact with them.[54] The death penalty may exacerbate problems survivors face. Perhaps already feeling misunderstood and isolated, survivors find themselves obligated—usually within their own family systems as they respond to the state—to take positions on the death penalty. Discord over the death penalty creates rifts within survivor family systems, further isolating some family members who may be shamed for favouring or opposing the sentence, depleting the best available resources for recovering from trauma within family systems.[55]

48   *Gregg v. Georgia*, 428 U.S. 153, 230 (1976) (Brennan, J., dissenting).
49   *Kindler v. Canada*, 6 CRR (2d) 193, 241 (SC) (Cory, J.).
50   James Gilligan. 2000. "Violence in public health and preventative medicine." *The Lancet* 355:1802 (referring to "narcissistic wound" as one of "40 synonyms" for "shame").
51   King, *supra* note 23, at 195-196.
52   Lawrence Miller. 2009. "Family survivors of homicide: I. Symptoms, syndromes, and reaction patterns." *The American Journal of Family Therapy* 37:pp. 67, 68.
53   Joy, *supra* note 4, at 11.
54   King, *supra* note 23, at 196.
55   Gabriela Lopez-Zeron and Adrian J. Blow. 2015. "The role of relationships and families in healing from trauma." *Journal of Family Therapy*, DOI: 10.1111/1467-6427.12089. (early version online before inclusion in print publication) (reviewing relational evidence-based trauma treatment protocols).

Family members of the defendant also undergo disenfranchised grief, at times feeling stigmatized as though they themselves are blamed for the defendant's behaviour.[56] In the United States, the role of trial and habeas attorneys to develop mitigation evidence enhances their shame, as it tends to validate their self-condemning feelings. US prosecutors also make disparaging comments about them in court. Referred to sometimes as the death penalty's "other victims", they sense that they are the objects of pity and ostracization within their communities and even their own extended families. Meanwhile, they go through what has been described as a BADD cycle—Bargaining, Activity, Disillusionment, and Desperation—akin to the experience of family members of someone with a terminal illness, in which they bargain with God or the criminal justice system, hoping for a positive outcome, engage in frantic activity on behalf of their family member, experience disillusionment with the system, and become desperate when an execution date is set.[57] In some lengthy appeals processes, this sequence may repeat itself. It becomes exhausting, as reflected in shame felt by the brother of a Texas inmate subjected to multiple dates when the thoughts ran through his head—what was his brother being saved for? more maltreatment?—and he concluded to his shock, "Go ahead and kill him."[58]

Inmates' family members perceive the annihilating theme of "nobodiness"[59] being projected upon the defendant as also being about them. This is particularly dangerous, as a matter of public health, when the defendant's family already is marginalized (as it actually is in most cases). There is a virtual public health consensus that the "experience of overwhelming shame and humiliation" is the "pathogen that seems to be a necessary but not sufficient cause of violent behaviour."[60] Through emotional contagion, the message of nobodiness not only can spread its damage horizontally through the trauma-organized system, shaming family, friends, and

---

56   King, *supra* note 23, 197.

57   Sharp, *supra* note 4, at 64–79.

58   Walter C. Long. 2011. "Trauma therapy for death row families." *Journal of Trauma and Dissociation* 12:pp. 482, 489.

59   Martin Luther King, Jr. 1986. "Letter from Birmingham Jail." In James M. Washington, ed., *The Essential Writings and Speeches of Martin Luther King, Jr.* New York: Harper Collins. p. 293 (describing the "degenerating sense of 'nobodiness'" projected on African Americans by racial discrimination arising from slavery).

60   Gilligan, *supra* note 49, at 1802.

advocates of the defendant, but also vertically, dangerously affecting the next generation and setting the stage for traumatic repetition—victimization or perpetration (or both) in next generations through transgenerational transmission of trauma.[61]

Finally, the executioners (and associated wardens, chaplains, and guards) not infrequently suffer trauma symptoms resulting from their mere participation in the act of killing or from having a caring prior relationship with the inmate, and they experience a similar distancing from others that may be an institutional consequence (they are prohibited from speaking to others about their experience) or a personal choice (they withdraw feeling shame associated with homicide, believing that others judge them or cannot comprehend their experience).[62] PTSD symptoms not only result from their acts of killing but "may be more severe under that circumstance."[63]

Trauma experienced by actors carrying out violence for the state has been dubbed "perpetration-induced traumatic stress."[64] Recognizing that executions are traumatic, corrections authorities take prophylactic measures to reduce the emotional damage on personnel: they promote "professionalism" in the task while having execution teams focus not on "the meaning of their activity, but on performing the sub-functions proficiently;"[65] they set up execution teams that do not include guards who have known the condemned inmates; they disperse the sense of moral responsibility by distributing execution tasks among a sizeable number of guards; and they obfuscate for all of the actors who the executioner is (e.g. by loading some guns in a firing squad with blanks). Sometimes the prophylaxes fail. Among a growing number of personal accounts of trauma by executioners made public, one American execution-team

61 Kaethe Weingarten. 2004. "Witnessing the effects of political violence in families: mechanisms of intergenerational transmission and clinical interventions." *Journal of Marital and Family Therapy* 30(1):45-59.

62 Penal Reform International, Briefing Paper. 2015. "Prison Guards and the Death Penalty." Available from: http://www.penalreform.org/wp-content/uploads/2015/04/PRI-Prison-guards-briefing-paper.pdf. (accessed 24 August 2016).

63 Rachel M. McNair. 2007. "Killing as trauma." In Elizabeth K. Carll, ed., *Trauma Psychology: Issues in Violence, Disaster, Health, and Illness*. London: Praeger, vol. 1, 147, 160.

64 Rachel M. McNair. 2002. *Perpetration-Induced Traumatic Stress: The Psychological Consequences of Killing*. London: Praeger/Greenwood.

65 Michael J. Osofsky, Albert Bandera, and Philip G. Zimbardo. 2005. "The role of moral disengagement in the execution process." *Law and Human Behavior* 29(4):pp. 386.

guard described reaching a threshold that broke when he began shaking uncontrollably while seeing the eyes of all the inmates he had executed flashing before him.[66]

Conclusion and Recommendations

As a trauma-organized system, the death penalty reinforces multiple solitudes and enmities rather than promoting cooperative efforts at justice. Where the death penalty is imposed for murder, it obscures who the "victim" is by creating a new "victim" or set of victims. This creates cognitive dissonance and conflict throughout the system. The state's lethal targeting of the defendant, leading to a vigorous defence of the defendant, is experienced as a new offence by many survivors of murder victims who perceive the defendant as getting unmerited notoriety and attention, and their deceased innocent family member unfairly besmirched by unsupportable comparison with the defendant, as the defendant gets sympathy in light of the state's violent action. Within both victims' and defendants' families, formidable, painful divisions arise over the death sentence itself, disrupting or blocking potential, positive, intra-familial, inter-personal, reciprocal resources for post-violence (murder) and pre-violence (execution) emotional resiliency. Defendants' families sometimes experience alienation from every other actor in the system, even from the defendant's attorneys who, when building arguments to mitigate the sentence, often blame the defendant's family members for things having a bearing on his behaviour. Prosecutors and defence attorneys shame each other for their positions on the death penalty and appellate defence attorneys shame prior defence counsel for errors alleged to have led to the death sentence. The system is one of constant aggression, blame displacement, and avoidance, frustrating by design restorative processes and meaning making in the aftermath of violence.

From a public health perspective, the death penalty is inherently anti-therapeutic on a systemic level and, thus, must be abandoned where society can successfully incapacitate violent persons with non-violent means. Sustainable abolition of capital punishment, however, cannot be accomplished if it is approached as a problem in isolation.

---

66   Werner Herzog, *Into the Abyss* [documentary film], 2011.

In medicine, the excising of a malignant mole cannot be divorced from exploration and treatment of underlying disease processes without great risk of recurrence or worse. In the same way, the death penalty is as much a symptom as a cause of societal dysregulation and cannot be sustainably eliminated without addressing and treating those systemic processes for which it is only a sign or a correlate. Bearing in mind the placement of the death penalty within larger systems, the following recommendations are made:

1. The U.N. should recognize the death penalty as violence.

Public health requires that the death penalty be redressed as a component of—not merely a governmental response to—societal violence.[67] Violence as traumatic re-enactment is contagious. So, when the government commits intentional homicide, it is difficult to see how that does not breed contempt for life and invite anarchy.[68]On the other hand, within a context that recognizes the death penalty as violence, public discussions over the goals of violence restraint or elimination should be consensus building in direct contrast to the present way in which arguments over capital punishment are not. Thus, simple recognition by the U.N. World Health Organization that the death penalty falls within its own definition of violence would constitute a large step towards fostering and supporting that consensus seeking serious violence reduction in retentionist nations.

2. The U.N. should encourage cultural and legal pursuit of human dignity as an antidote to violence.

A public health perspective understands that the prioritizing of human dignity means the advancement of negative rights (protecting the individual from government tyranny) and positive rights (requiring government to perform its duty "to protect individuals from violence and abuse"[69]). Dignity intrinsically is hard to define across cultures, but assuming that, at minimum, it includes a right held by

---

67   James Welsh. 2000. "The death penalty as a public health issue." *European Journal of Public Health* 10(1):2, 2 ("Modern thinking on penology rejects the view of society as being a battleground between the state and criminals, each drawing on the tools of violence to assert their will.").

68   James Gilligan. 2000. "Punishment and violence: is the criminal law based on one huge mistake?" *Social Research* 67(3): pp.745, 754.

69   Michael Ignatieff. 2001. *Human Rights as Politics and Idolatry*. Princeton: Princeton University Press. p. 83.

every individual not to be the object of homicide (an intrinsically shaming event in every culture), then it requires states to abstain from homicide that is not excused (as necessary defence of self or third parties) and to engage in primary prevention through provision of the positive rights indisputably proven to reduce homicide: "ensuring that people have access to the means by which they can achieve a feeling of self-worth, such as education and employment, and a level of income, wealth, and power that is equal to that which other people enjoy, by universalizing social and political democracy."[70] "Nations with the lowest murder rates . . . have the highest degrees of social and economic equity."[71]

Considering human rights to be culturally particular social constructions—and not of natural, divine, or metaphysical origins—enhances rather than diminishes them. From a public health perspective, the transcultural discussion on the nature of human dignity, even as it exposes cultural and ideological disagreements, is a very good development, as it is a manifestation of our natural interdependence and mutual regulation focused on a positive outcome through dialogue.[72] Such discussion stresses a search for, reverence for, and co-discovery and co-creation of a quality that, notably, is the antidote to violence. Whatever additional causes, contexts, and conditions there are, besmirched dignity is at the heart of human violence. The cultivation of dignity, thus, is violence's cure and should be highly prized. It has been argued that progress in understanding "bodily integrity and empathetic selfhood" was integral to the creation of the law of human rights in the Eighteenth Century and led to the rejection of torture in the judicial process.[73] In the same way, neurobiological insights into trauma and aggression may be incorporated now into the construction of rights defining and supporting dignity in local communities, expanding into "ever-wider circles", ultimately into "universal validity, freely embraced."[74] Qualitative studies and narrative accounts

---

70   Gilligan, *supra* note 49, at 1802.
71   Ibid.; *see also* Bandy X. Lee, Bruce E. Wexler, and James Gilligan. 2014. "Political correlates of violent death rates in the U.S., 1900-2010." *Aggression and Violent Behavior* 19:721-728 (finding violent deaths to rise during Republican administrations and with rising unemployment and a falling GDP).
72   *See* Benjamin Gregg,. 2012. *Human Rights as Social Construction.* Cambridge: Cambridge University Press. (recommending a neurobiologically informed social constructionist approach to rights).
73   Lynn Hunt. 2008. *Inventing Human Rights: A History.* New York: Norton. p. 30.
74   Gregg, *supra* note 71, at 235.

provide the best windows into the human needs articulated in contexts of rights provision or lack thereof, calling for systemic changes that reduce violence and enhance human well-being.[75]

3. The U.N. should encourage cultural and legal reduction of shame-inducing punishment.

From a public health perspective, retributive punishment "increases feelings of shame and decreases feelings of guilt"[76] and, thus, increases the potential for "traumatic re-enactment" in violent acts by those punished. "Increasing punitiveness toward criminals is the most powerful stimulus to violent crime . . . just as increasing rates of violent crime can reinforce the punitiveness of society."[77] Punishing violent people by restraining them beyond what is necessary to prevent them from actively physically harming others is likely to engender more violence in them. Additionally, the use of prisons for nonviolent crimes—e.g. for drug offences or property crimes—is the most effective way to turn nonviolent persons into violent ones.[78]

Science tells us that we are neurobiologically interdependent. That does not mean that we are not also individual actors who should be respected and treated as free agents, but we are not "autonomous" in the sense that we are fundamentally separate from others and beholden only to abstract universal religious, natural, or moral rules. As individuals, we vary in our "genetic susceptibilities to arousal, temperament, and reactivity."[79] Aggression and arousal are on a continuum and we need some aggression for our "motivated functioning," which we regulate within interpersonal boundary rules.[80] We socially construct those rules and violence occurs when those rules are broken. In this sense, violence is "a breach of duty not to

75   E.g., the Texas After Violence Project collects digital video oral history accounts of persons directly affected by death penalty cases in Texas. These are stored online, available for viewing anywhere, at the University of Texas' Human Rights Documentation Initiative. https://www.lib.utexas.edu/hrdi; www.texasafterviolence.org. The stories provide the kind of bottom-up information needed to define human needs, rights, and co-create less violent structures that support human security.

76   James Gilligan, *supra* note 49, at 1803.

77   James Gilligan. 2001. "The last mental hospital." *Psychiatric Quarterly* 72(1): pp. 45, 57.

78   James Gilligan. 2001. *Preventing Violence.* New York: Thames and Hudson. p. 117.

79   Gwen Adshead. 2001. "A kind of necessity? Violence as a public health problem." In Sandra L. Bloom, ed., *Violence: A Public Health Menace and a Public Health Approach.* London: Karnac Books. pp. 1, 4.

80   Ibid. at 5.

harm others and also a breach of a connection between the victim and the offender."[81]

When a "solitarist" framework of human being is replaced with a communitarian social framework focused on the mutual pursuit of dignity, our demonstrable biological "interdependencies" can be given "symbolic significance as attachments which invoke personal obligation to others in a community of concern."[82] In this context, shaming can be transformed into a more benign influence. Relieved from the context of "purely deterrent punishment," less-intense shaming may constructively assist communities or courts to "moralize with the offender to communicate reasons for the evil of her actions."[83] Re-integrative shaming labels the boundary violation morally wrong while it nevertheless refuses to stigmatize an offender as permanently deviant and subsequently makes efforts to fully restore the offender after a finite time into the community of rule-abiding persons. Pursuit of restorative processes within a context of understanding of the neurobiological network of human interdependencies has promise for stopping enemy-aggressor and survivor-victim cycles otherwise generated within trauma-organized systems like that maintained by the death penalty.[84]

4. The UN should encourage cultural and legal support of victims.

A victim-centered culture emphasizes primary prevention of violence first: stopping the causes—"namely, shaming and humiliating people by subjecting them to hierarchical social and economic systems characterized by class and caste stratification, relative poverty, and dictatorship."[85] Of course, elimination of all violent crime is impossible, even in societies that have achieved a significant diminution of wealth and power disparities in addition to other causes of violence. So there will be victims.

One of criminal law's "crucial issues" is finding a balance "between the security of the citizen and the rights of the suspect, between

---

81   Ibid. at 25.
82   John Braithwaite. 1989. *Crime, Shame, and Reintegration*. Cambridge: Cambridge University Press. pp. 100-101.
83   Ibid.
84   Carolyn Yoder. 2005. *The Little Book of Trauma Healing*. Pennsylvania: Good Books.
85   James Gilligan, *supra* note 49, at 1802.

the victim and the offender."[86] A strong position for the victim in a criminal prosecution is therapeutically better for the rehabilitation of both victim and offender. "If the trial is going to be a platform for renewal and a new start, is it essential that the victim feels that he or she is a protagonist, not merely a piece of evidence."[87] That applies to survivors of murder victims in the case of a homicide. However, in the United States, because of the presence of the potential death sentence, the rights of victim survivors to trial participation have been considered to be at great tension with the concern for fairness.[88]

Where the death penalty does not exist an opportunity is presented for the survivors to be greatly empowered at trial without diminution of the defendant's rights. In Sweden, for example, every victim of a serious offence gets an attorney, gets to be a party next to the prosecutor in court, can present "charges, claims, evidence and arguments." Every convicted defendant has to pay a significant contribution to victimology research, and every victim can get damages from the state if the defendant cannot pay and the victim has no insurance that will pay.[89] The rights of the defendant are not diminished, because the state still bears the burden of proof. But the real parties to an offence are brought into virtual equipoise, giving victims or survivors restored self-esteem and empowerment to move on, at the same time giving defendants an opportunity not to see themselves merely victimized by the state but to directly encounter the victims or survivors and, when guilty, truly contemplate their responsibility and the effects of the act—all of this favouring "regret, remorse and rehabilitation" of the defendant.[90]

A legal system like that of Sweden's which incorporates all of the provisions in the United Nations' declaration on victims' rights[91]

86   Christian Diesen. 2012. "Therapeutic jurisprudence and the victim of crime." In T.I. Oei and Marc Groenhuijsen eds., *Progression in Forensic Psychiatry*. Dordrecht: Kluwer Academic Press. pp. 580, 594.

87   Ibid. at 595.

88   *Booth v. Maryland*, 482 U.S. 496 (1987) (holding testimony by survivors about their trauma created an impermissible risk of unfairness); *Payne v. Tennessee*, 501 U.S. 808 (1991) (overruling *Booth* and holding victim impact evidence of survivors admissible because a jury should have all evidence before it of the specific harm caused by the defendant).

89   Diesen, *supra* note 85, at 579.

90   Ibid. at 595.

91   United Nations Declaration of Basic Principles of Justice for Victims of Crime and Abuse of Power, adopted by the U.N. General Assembly Nov. 29, 1985, A/RES/40/34.

replaces the kind of shame that accompanies a trauma-organized legal system containing the death penalty—annihilating shame—with the more benign shame intrinsic to human interpersonal relations. It allows the state the power it needs for fair, equitable administration of justice while preventing the state from disempowering victims. Such a system supports remorse in the defendant and solutions that victims need, such as an accounting by the defendant of what happened and why the crime occurred. In contrast, victim-offender encounters in a trauma-organized system are seldom, fraught, and distorted. The post-conviction appeals process, during which defendants fight for their lives sometimes for decades, blocks (except in some extraordinary cases[92]) the possibility of communication between victim and offender. Most death penalty appeals are about the punishment only. Without a death sentence, many cases would open to the possibility of dialogue and, probably, more survivors would seek it when they did not feel that, by trying to talk to the defendant, they were going against the cultural current supporting the institutionally legitimated homicide.[93]

Broadly speaking, the United Nations declaration on victims' rights also theoretically legitimizes the family members of death row inmates as potential victims of state abuse. Article 18 defines a "victim of abuse of power" as a person who has suffered harm as the result of "acts or omissions that do not yet constitute violations of national criminal laws but of internationally recognized norms relating to human rights". Article 19 provides that states should provide such victims "restitution and/or compensation, and necessary material, medical, psychological and social assistance and support". In a world in which the declaration were an enforceable treaty binding on the United States, for example, the family of Napoleon Beazley, executed in the United States in 2002, would be remunerated because his execution violated a decision by the Inter-American Commission on Human Rights that he was ineligible for the death penalty as he was a juvenile at the time of his offence. Every year since Beazley's execution, the Commission has asked the United States to provide

---

92   Leo G. Barrile. 2015. "I forgive you, but you must die: murder victim family members, the death penalty, and restorative justice." *Victims and Offenders* 10:239-269.

93   Ibid. at 265.

his surviving family restitution.[94] Some suggestions have been made under U.S. domestic law to hold the state accountable to death row family members' rights to family unity and association.[95] But appreciation by the trauma-organized system of the status of such persons as victims is categorically blocked by the state's right to legal homicide.

5. *The U.N. should interrogate the death penalty on its relationship to human security or insecurity.*

The United Nations has committed itself to foster conditions that lead to human security.[96] That model may be more amenable than other developmental models to the goals of violence prevention and elimination because it emphasizes sustainability ("in terms of peace, physical health, mental health, ecology"), prioritizes rights in the face of challenges, differs significantly from the "human development approach" in viewing persons first as group members rather than individuals, considers persons to have multiple identities that "can be sources of conflict and sources of solace in the face of conflicts, with scope for evolution," and brings forth a "philosophy of inter-connectedness" that takes a bottom-up approach to the discovery of sources of threats to security and values threatened by them.[97] The death penalty should be interrogated by this framework about its contribution to security, or the contrary, and, perhaps more fundamentally, about its relationship to human sustainability. Trauma-organized systems (such as the death penalty, war, slavery, systemic discrimination on the basis of immutable characteristics, and economies built on great disparities in wealth and resources) and the abusive cultural stories that support those systems probably give humanity itself a shortening shelf-life, because of the violent individual and social conflict they generate.

---

94 Inter-American Commission on Human Rights, Case 12.412, *Napoleon Beazley*, Report No. 101/03 (December 29, 2003), para. 60 (1) (recommending that the U.S. "provide the next-of-kin of Napoleon Beazley with an effective remedy, which includes compensation"). The author was one of Beazley's attorneys.

95 Rachel King. 2007. "No due process: how the death penalty violates the constitutional rights of the family members of death row prisoners." *Public Interest Law Journal* 16:195-253.

96 U.N. Commission on Human Security. 2003. *Human Security Now*, 4 (defining "human security" as the protection of "the vital core of all human lives in ways that enhance human freedoms and human fulfillment").

97 Des Gasper. 2011. "The human and the social: a comparison of the discourses of human development, human security and social quality." *International Journal of Social Quality* 1(1):pp. 91, 103-104.

View from Witness Room, The Omega Suites
© Lucinda Devlin

"I wish that this publication will help
States and other stakeholders to move
forward the discussion of ending permanently
the use of the death penalty."

—*Zeid Ra'ad Al Hussein*

AFTERWORD

In 1931, George Orwell famously described a hanging. As the condemned man was marched, in handcuffs, to the gallows, he stepped slightly aside to avoid a puddle—an ordinary, tender, very human gesture. Orwell wrote: "*Till that moment I had never realised what it means to destroy a healthy, conscious man…the unspeakable wrongness.*" What Orwell understood so well was how human reason, tugged by the presence of one puddle placed inconveniently in the path of a man about to die, demanded a more complex human response. What he saw was fundamentally a form of revenge. And revenge, however dressed up it was by a judicial process, still remained a crude act of state vengeance. And with 8,000 years of practice behind it, drawn from the belief that life, even though not created by society, can nevertheless be withdrawn by it, the urge for vengeance had separated humanity from its own, very necessary, sense of decency. This notion of justice in the form of revenge is, however, changing.

The 70 years since the establishment of the United Nations have witnessed a remarkable shift in the death penalty. At that time, only 14 countries had abolished the practice. Currently, more than two-thirds of member states have either abolished it or introduced moratoria by law or in practice. In the period from the General Assembly's adoption of the last moratorium resolution (69/186), seven states abolished the death penalty for all crimes. However, serious challenges still remain. It is a matter of a grave concern that the overall number of executions worldwide increased in the last year. Furthermore, despite having maintained long-term moratoria, some states resumed executions. Frequently, the rights of victims of crimes, and of their families, are invoked as justification for these policies. This publication addresses many aspects of the use of the death penalty and victims' rights. As discussed in this publication, states must examine all aspects of victimhood relating to the death penalty regime—not only the rights of victims of crimes, but also others who may be victimized by the death penalty regime itself, directly and indirectly.

There is a widespread assumption that victims' families believe only execution of the perpetrator can provide justice. In reality, research shows that not all families of victims of heinous crimes, or victims themselves, believe that responding to one violence with another honors the victim. Often, victims and their families conclude that the death penalty is profoundly harmful to their hopes of recovering from loss, partly because of the long delays and repeated appeals that are involved. One survivor of the Rwanda Genocide famously said: "We are happy with the life sentence because they are going to be there for the whole of their life, they have the entire time to think about what they did. For us, it is a real punishment." In Algeria, Argentina, Bosnia and Herzegovina, Cambodia, Central African Republic, Chile, Croatia—and I have only reached the letter C—many victims of appalling crimes, including genocide, crimes against humanity, war crimes and terrorism, have raised their voices to campaign for an end to the practice of legal killings. Indeed, the statutes of the International Criminal Court, which tries the most severe crimes, do not permit the death penalty; 124 states have accepted the jurisdiction of this court.

There is no question that victims and their families do have rights that must be respected. Among these rights is the right to justice and effective remedy for the crimes they have endured. But punishment alone is not justice. Victims and their families also have a right to demand redress for the harm that they have suffered, through judicial and administrative mechanisms that are expeditious, responsive, fair, and accessible. For justice to be served to the wrongdoer or served up to the wronged party—the victim—requires not just retribution, but a genuine recognition by the wrongdoers of their wrongdoing. It requires genuine remorse, and reckoning. The dignity of victims and their families must be acknowledged by all law enforcement and judicial personnel, with compassion and respect maintained at all times. And the safety of victims, their families, and witnesses from intimidation and reprisal should be a paramount concern. The UN Declaration of Basic Principles of Justice for Victims of Crime and Abuse of Power clearly states these and other rights of victims of crime, and it outlines the measures that should be taken to secure them. Many states could do far more to realize these principles in practice and thus truly honour the victims of crime and their families.

We also must acknowledge consequences arising at various stages of the imposition and application of the death penalty on the enjoyment of the human rights of other affected persons, including the negative impact on the human rights of children whose parents are subject to the imposition and execution of the death penalty. In its omnibus resolution 68/147 on the rights of the child, adopted in 2013, the United Nations General Assembly acknowledged that "a parent's deprivation of liberty, sentencing to death or life imprisonment, has a serious impact on children's development, and urges states, in the framework of their national child protection efforts, to provide the assistance and support these children may require."

The welfare and mental health of lawyers and court and prison officials can be negatively affected by participation in a case involving the death penalty, in particular when a client is executed. Many legal practitioners do this work only for a brief period of time. It is a very brutal practice that may have a serious impact in their lives. Furthermore, in accordance with the Basic Principles on the Role of Lawyers, access to lawyers and confidentiality between lawyers and their clients are essential rights of the accused. In some cases, these rights are restricted in practice in cases involving the death penalty.

And, indeed, we all know of the risk of executing innocent people. Hundreds of innocent individuals have been executed throughout the world. No judiciary anywhere in the world is so robust that it can guarantee that innocent life will not be taken, and there is an alarming body of evidence showing that even well-functioning legal systems have sentenced to death men and women who were innocent. This is unacceptable. When an innocent person is wrongly executed, hope for justice also dies. The whole justice system loses the trust and confidence of the people and itself becomes a victim of injustice.

Furthermore, in practice, the use of the death penalty is often discriminatory in respect of the condemned. The poor, the mentally ill, the powerless and people from minorities are disproportionately among those executed. Many societies apply a presumption of dangerousness and guilt to persons with different racial, religious, or ethnic background or those economically or socially marginalized.

Such prejudices lead to wrongful arrests, wrongful convictions, and wrongful executions. There is no question that many societies have a long history of seeing people through the lens of racial, ethnic, and other differences. Whether a direct line from slavery to the treatment of black suspects in one country or whether a direct line from extreme poverty to the treatment of the poor in another country, we must acknowledge that these shameful, heinous social ills have resulted in the execution of many innocent people—victims of rotten justice systems.

States that persist in use of the death penalty must examine all these concerns. Pending full and complete abolition, they should consider developing measures to minimize the harm suffered by all individuals affected by the death penalty, including family members of both victims of crimes and convicts. In this effort, states must first establish a moratorium on the use of the death penalty. Moratoria are useful "transition tools". States with a moratorium should maintain and strengthen their policy against the death penalty, examine all aspects of the use of the death penalty and facilitate national debates on securing full abolition. Pending abolition, national prosecutors may consider refraining from seeking the death penalty. Judges may consider not imposing it.

States that have abolished the death penalty should not reintroduce it. In this 25th anniversary year of the entry into force of the Second Optional Protocol to the International Covenant on Civil and Political Rights aiming at the abolition of the death penalty, states that have not yet done so should ratify this protocol and end the use of this practice. When a state ratifies the protocol, it accepts that nobody can be executed in its jurisdiction. Importantly, international law does not permit a state which has ratified or acceded or succeeded to the covenant and its Second Optional Protocol to denounce it or withdraw from it. In its General Comment 26, the Human Rights Committee stated that the drafters of the Covenant deliberately intended to exclude the possibility of denunciation. The same conclusion applies to the Second Optional Protocol, in the drafting of which a denunciation clause was also deliberately omitted. Thus it guarantees the permanent non-reintroduction of the death penalty in states that have ratified the protocol.

Today, we face the challenge of ensuring that international commitments to end the use of the death penalty are implemented. For international organizations, such as the United Nations, the essential focus must be on working with national stakeholders, including victims of crimes and other individuals involved with the justice process. I wish that this publication will help states and other stakeholders to move forward the discussion of ending permanently the use of the death penalty. My office, together with the Special Procedures of the Human Rights Council and the human rights treaty bodies, will continue to offer detailed guidance and technical assistance. This publication is a humble effort in this endeavour.

Zeid Ra'ad Al Hussein
United Nations High Commissioner for Human Rights

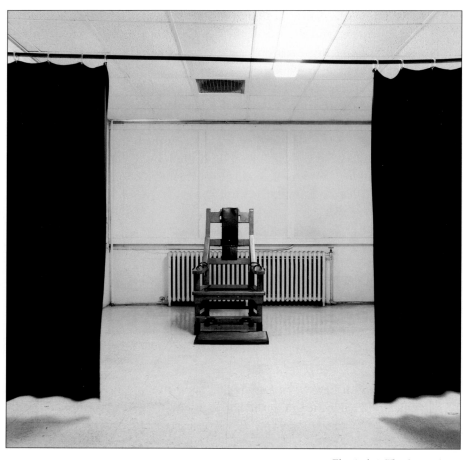

Electric chair, The Omega Suites
© Lucinda Devlin

ACKNOWLEDGEMENTS

I would like to thank the many people who contributed each one in his or her way to this new death penalty publication.

I am extremely grateful to the United Nations Secretary-General Ban Ki-moon for providing the preface for this book and for his contribution to the 2015 event on *Moving Away from the Death Penalty - The Voices of Victims' Families*, an event which drew a large number of Member States as well as members of the civil society and academia. I am also grateful for the support of the governments of Argentina, Benin, Fiji, France, Italy and Rwanda that co-sponsored the panel event. In addition, my gratitude to Amnesty International who helped us to establish contact with many panellists and contributors to this book. This publication would not have been possible but for the financial contribution of the Swiss Government and the Government of Chile, for which I am very thankful.

Colleagues from the UN Office of the High Commissioner for Human Rights in Geneva, led by High Commissioner Zeid Ra'ad Al-Hussein have been extremely supportive of our panel events on death penalty, including the last focused on victims' families, as well as this publication. So were colleagues from the Department of Public Information, who supported the launch of our previous death penalty publication -*Moving Away from the Death Penalty: arguments, trends and perspectives*- and its sale and dissemination through the various United Nations bookshops worldwide. I hope that we shall have equally successful cooperation with this publication.

Daily challenges and last minutes changes and surprises would have not allowed me to edit this book on time without the immense help and support from the whole team of the New York Human Rights Office.

Thank you all.

Ivan Šimonović

Editor